OBSESSIVE IMAGES

Library of Congress Cataloging in Publication Data

Beach, Joseph Warren, 1880-1957.
  Obsessive images.

  Reprint of the ed. published by University of
Minnesota Press, Minneapolis.
  Bibliography: p.
  1. American poetry--20th century--History and
criticism. 2. Symbolism in literature. 3. Figures
of speech. I. Title.
[PS310.S9B4 1973]   811'.5'20915   73-11620
ISBN 0-8371-7079-6

Originally published in 1960 by University of Minnesota Press, Minneapolis

The second Greenwood reprinting is from an original copy in the collections
of Friedsam Memorial Library and Resource Center, St. Bonaventure
University

Reprinted in 1973 by Greenwood Press, a division of Congressional
Information Service, 88 Post Road, Westport, Conn. 06881

Library of Congress catalog card number 73-11620

ISBN 0-8371-7079-6

Printed in the United States of America

10 9 8 7 6 5 4 3 2

Obsessive Images

◄§ SYMBOLISM IN POETRY OF THE 1930's AND 1940's

by Joseph Warren Beach

EDITED BY WILLIAM VAN O'CONNOR

GREENWOOD PRESS, PUBLISHERS
WESTPORT, CONNECTICUT

◄§ FOREWORD

BY WILLIAM VAN O'CONNOR

Obsessive Images is clearly an unfinished book. Joseph Warren Beach was a scrupulous and exacting scholar and writer. He was capable of devoting weeks to tracking down a sentence or a line of poetry that would illuminate a given paragraph. I have seen manuscript pages with fifteen or twenty question marks in the margin, referring to points he would reconsider or phrases and sentences he would rewrite. At his death, he left a good many pages of notes to himself, with this heading: "Very Important Notes – to be used in the rewriting." Apparently he was satisfied with the general organization of *Obsessive Images*. If the process of writing and reworking can be so measured, I should guess he felt he was about nine-tenths finished. The manuscript had been set aside for a number of years, but a few days before his death he had reread it and expressed general satisfaction with what he had done.

The interruption was a characteristic one, I think. During the several years preceding his retirement from the University of Minnesota, in 1948, he had read very widely in twentieth-century poetry. After his retirement he worked at the manuscript fairly regularly, although he also wrote a large number of poems and did teaching stints at Harvard, Johns Hopkins, the University of Illinois, the Sorbonne, Strasbourg, and the University of Vienna. He and his wife, Dagmar Doneghy Beach, returned to Minneapolis from Vienna about January 1955. I believe he began to work at it rather systematically at this time, with two periods lost because of illness. In working on it, however, he became interested in Auden's revisions — Auden looms large in *Obsessive Images*. He became so interested in fact that he stopped work on *Obsessive Images* and wrote *The Making of the Auden Canon*. Frequently in the process of writing that book he showed sections to Leonard Unger and to me. I can recall many afternoons in our offices in Folwell Hall or at the Beach house on University Avenue when he talked about the manuscript. Often he held a cigarette in his left hand and used his right hand and arm for gestures, usually a rounded movement that seemed to have something to do with making a graceful formulation of what he was trying to say. Or one would run into him on his way to or from the library, with a half-dozen books under his arm. *The Making of the Auden Canon* came from the printers a few days before his death, August 13, 1957.

No one can know the precise changes Joseph Beach would have made in the manuscript of *Obsessive Images*. I have made only minor changes. The reader who advised the University Press to publish *Obsessive Images* said, "I think you should candidly present the book for what it is — the last, unfinished work of a distinguished, well-loved critic, poet, and professor." We have followed his advice.

The tone of *Obsessive Images* is much more personal than that of Joseph Beach's other books. Many sentences use the first person pronoun, and sometimes he seems to be arguing with himself, trying to arrive at a conclusion. He ends the discussion of one poem with "I give it up!" Sometimes he is exasperated, as when he says, "I do not see how poetry could descend to lower depths of pretentious balderdash. . . ." Joseph Beach might have decided to edit out some of these sentences. But they are a part of the book's charm, and I have not tampered with them. There is another sense in which the book is personal. It is a work of love. During his career at the University of Minnesota, Joseph Beach had written many books, and one might expect that in his retirement he would have given his time to less onerous tasks. But for him the writing of a long book about poetry was not onerous. One can see him as a kind of latter-day Sir Thomas Browne giving himself to study and speculation and to writing because doing so delighted him. The sense of his delight comes through.

Joseph Beach wrote in many fields, but because he did such distinguished work on the techniques of fiction he is usually labeled a student of the novel. But he was also a fine poet, especially in his later years. And he was an excellent critic of poetry. For example, there are three uncollected articles on Edith Sitwell (*New Mexico Quarterly*), Robert Frost (*Yale Review*), and W. H. Auden (*Virginia Quarterly*) that catch the special quality as well as the strengths and the limitations of these poets in a way rarely achieved in criticism. "As a critic," he once wrote, "I do not aim so much to render final judgments and deliver certificates of greatness, which is something manifestly impossible and a trifle ridiculous, as to analyze and interpret stories and poems as expressions of our humanity and as effective works of art."

Obsessive Images is further evidence of his critical powers. I do not believe there is another book of modern criticism quite like it. At the beginning there are a few speculations about why certain words and images recur in the poetry of the 1930's and 1940's; there are analyses of a great many phrases and a few whole poems; and there are little essays or even digressions along the way. But let us get on to the subject of the book, the rhetoric, for it is largely that, of two decades of modern poetry.

In *Essay on Rime* (1945) Karl Shapiro wrote:

> The man whose impress on our rhetoric
> Has for a decade dominated verse
> In London, Sydney and New York is Auden.
> One cannot estimate the consequences
> Both good and bad of his success. To open
> A current magazine of rime is but
> To turn to Auden; and this is not a fad
> But some kind of distemper in the practice
> Of modern poetry.

Shapiro singles out the words *history* and *luck* as Audenesque abstractions that achieved great currency with other poets. Joseph Beach's study does not include an examination of these terms. But

Foreword

his study of other words substantiates Shapiro's claim that Auden's influence on rhetoric has been a dominant one. Auden terms that he did study are *assassin, mountains, islands, exile, frontier,* and *the city*. In reading through *Obsessive Images* one sometimes feels that many of the poets contemporary with Auden and younger speak not only with their own voices but with Auden's too, as though he taught them their intonation, and even gave them a vocabulary. I shall not list the poets, or comment on the success of their poems — Joseph Beach does that. But I should observe that many, certainly not all, recognizably Audenesque phrases, his own and those of his imitators, already seem outmoded, part of a period style. *Obsessive Images*, however, is not solely concerned with the influences of Auden on his fellow poets. To stay with the question of influences — there are Eliot, Yeats, Crane, Stevens, and others to be considered. In *Essay on Rime* Shapiro also said that Eliot's influence "on our rhetoric is as small / As his influence on our belief is great." He added,

> One would be rash to imitate a style
> Which signs its name at every even pause.

Only Conrad Aiken and Richard Hayes were rash enough to imitate Eliot openly. But the spiritual malaise, the preoccupation with terror in dreams, and the spring of a beast, all found in Eliot's poems, are developed in various ways by almost all modern poets. Yeats gave the word *ceremony* to younger poets — it has had a notable history. A good many poets have been concerned with the *hero*, modern style, and with the term *definition*, but there appears not to be a common poetic source for either word. And of course certain of these words have been used by poets in all periods, and a given poet, a Hart Crane or a Wallace Stevens, will use one or another of them, say *voyage* or *quest*, with no sense of its having been used by Eliot or Auden or anyone else. Sometimes Joseph Beach studies a poet, for example, St.-John Perse, because the concepts and sometimes key words to be found in his poetry are to be found elsewhere, as though the tentacular roots of all modern poetry touch or intertwine underground. Studying the obsessive images

x

and key words of a period is of course a way of getting at the characteristic attitudes of a generation of poets.

Beginning with section 26 (entitled "The Age of . . .") Joseph Beach becomes less concerned with "obsessive images" or key words; here he deals with the themes and attitudes of a variety of poets, their criticism of middle-class values, of a materialistic world, of science, of the doctrine of progress, and other matters. It is in these pages that Mr. Beach's own "secular humanism," as he liked to call it, comes out most clearly. In a sense, Mr. Beach belonged to the nineteenth century, to the scientific-utilitarian line of John Stuart Mill and Thomas Henry Huxley. He is very critical, for instance, of E. E. Cummings' anti-science stance. But he was capable of truly disinterested study, and, following that, of giving his admiration to imaginative creations quite different from those he himself might have created. For example, he rehearses the history of his attitudes toward the poetry of Robert Penn Warren. At first he viewed it rather critically but later he gave it his rapt admiration.

In the final or summing-up section of *Obsessive Images*, Joseph Beach explains why Robinson, Ezra Pound, Robert Frost, Carl Sandburg, the Imagists, and other poets do not enter his study in any significant way. The reason is simple enough. He has concerned himself with the poets of the 1930's and 1940's, most of whom were young during the Great Depression and were still young during World War II and after. These poets were drawn toward Auden, Eliot, and Yeats, or were preoccupied with themes and images found in these poets.

Joseph Beach makes some interesting observations about the achievements of these younger poets. He sees the period as one of great earnestness, ingenuity, and sophistication, but he does not see it as one that produced poets of the stature of Robinson, Pound, Stevens, Crane, Frost, Sandburg, Masters, and Jeffers. For these younger poets the revolt against the Victorians was an accomplished fact and belonged to history. Thus they had to discover their own place in the rhythms of history. He sees them as having given up any hope of reaching a wide audience of the sort that Robinson, or Frost, or Millay had found. They settled for appear-

Foreword

ing in "little magazines" and being read by their fellow poets and a handful of critics. He sees them as being in revolt against a "corrosive science" and sympathetic with religion. But, and Joseph Beach is very interesting on this point, he says their "religion" is neither liberal Protestantism, the sort of teaching that is short on theology but strong on utilitarian and humanitarian messages, nor Fundamentalist. He says these poets insist that myth is the "life-breath of poetry," and he is inclined to agree with them. But he wonders whether there is much that is valid, or solid, or credible back of their symbols or evoked by their mythologies. It is an observation worth pondering. In the last few pages, he offers them an alternative to their preoccupation with guilt and agony and anti-philistinism — but this is for the reader to discover for himself.

◄§ TABLE OF CONTENTS

OBSESSIVE IMAGES

◆§ SINCEREST FLATTERY

I. CEREMONY THROUGH THREE DECADES

In this discussion I shall be concerned with certain words that turn up with unusual frequency in modern American poetry, especially during the 1930's and 1940's. They are words often used in unusual senses, or senses unusual in prose, or carrying a special symbolism or implying a peculiar philosophical attitude. As an example of what I have in mind I will begin with the word *ceremony* as it has been used since a special stamp was given to it by Yeats in two poems of his 1920 volume, *Michael Robartes and the Dancer*.

In "A Prayer for My Daughter," Yeats wishes that his daughter's bridegroom may

> bring her to a house
> Where all's accustomed, *ceremonious*; *
> For arrogance and hatred are the wares
> Peddled in the thoroughfares.
> How but in custom and in *ceremony*
> Are *innocence* and beauty born?
> *Ceremony's* a name for the rich horn,
> And custom for the spreading laurel tree.

Next to this poem in the *Collected Poems* of Yeats is the more famous "The Second Coming," in which the word *ceremony* appears again in connection with *innocence*. Both poems seem to have been partly suggested by the troubled political situation in Yeats's world which made him think of the Biblical association between "wars and rumours of wars" and the last day. In "The Second Coming" we read:

* EDITOR'S NOTE: Throughout in the poetry excerpts, the italics were added by Mr. Beach unless otherwise noted.

3

> Mere anarchy is loosed upon the world,
> The blood-dimmed tide is loosed, and everywhere
> *The ceremony of innocence is drowned.*

In Auden's 1930 volume of *Poems* there is found a fascinating and somewhat riddling poem beginning:

> The strings' excitement, the applauding drum
> Are but the *initiating ceremony*
> That out of cloud the ancestral face may come.

The word *ceremony* is here used in a somewhat different sense from that of Yeats. Auden has in mind the necromantic ceremonial employed by savage people for calling up the ghost of a dead ancestor. But there are several circumstances suggesting that Auden had been deeply impressed by Yeats's "Prayer for My Daughter," and that in using the word *ceremony* as well as in other points he was "inspired" by that poem and perhaps also by "The Second Coming." While Yeats is calling upon supernatural power in behalf of his daughter, Auden (or his imagined speaker) is calling upon his father (the ancestral face) for spiritual direction in a time of stress. He describes a state of war. Some natural features found in Yeats's poem are matched by Auden: in Yeats, "the murderous innocence of the sea," in Auden "the lunatic agitation of the sea." And again, where Yeats is

> Imagining in *excited* reverie
> That the future years had come,
> Dancing to a *frenzied drum*,

Auden gives us

> The strings' *excitement*, the *applauding drum*.

No poet of the earlier twentieth century except Eliot, and possibly Yeats, has been more sedulously read than Auden by the later "highbrow" American poets. And it is Auden who, beginning with 1930, has taken second place to Eliot alone as an influence on younger poets (and a subject for imitation).

Auden's use of the word in such an intriguing context doubtless bore its part in making it a pet word in later poets. Still, it is Yeats's use that mostly prevails, and it is Yeats who is best remembered as

4

its originator. Thus Jean Garrigue in "The Park" (*The Ego and the Centaur*, 1947; italics in original) expressly quotes:

> *The ceremony of innocence is drowned,*
> Yeats says, and I who cannot understand
> Go to the public park to weigh
> That elusive and prehensile datum.

And John Malcolm Brinnin, in "New Year's Eve" (*The Garden Is Political*, 1942), pays Yeats the compliment of incorporating some of the accompanying images:

> And whose small death is next?
> Who names the untranslatable and good,
> *Drowned innocence in blood?*

As for the word *ceremony* itself, in "The World Is a Wedding" (*No Arch, No Triumph*, 1945) Brinnin uses it in a way suggesting a combination of Yeats and Auden:

> Not in the softness of white *ritual*,
> Is our appointment, nor in the *ceremony*,
> Of wheatfields and the fruition of houses
> Blessed for a boy . . .

As early as 1933, we find John Peale Bishop using the word *ceremony* in connections suggestive of both Yeats and Auden. In "Speaking of Poetry" (*Now with His Love*), Bishop is using Desdemona and Othello as symbols of elements that must be combined to make good poetry (perhaps refinement of form and strong substance). And his image is this:

> The *ceremony* must be found
> That will *wed* Desdemona to the huge Moor.
> · · · · · · · · · · · · ·
> The *ceremony* must be found
>
> *Traditional*, with *all its symbols*
> ancient as the metaphors in dreams;
> strange, with never before heard music; continuous
> until the torches deaden at the bedroom door.

Here the wedding and the emphasis on tradition suggest both Yeats and Auden; while the symbols and metaphors are straight out of Auden —

5

> And all emotions to expression came
> Recovering the *archaic imagery*,

where the archaic imagery is itemized through the two final stanzas.

It is now time to consider more carefully the senses in which the word *ceremony* is used by Yeats and by Auden — to distinguish between them and to ask what they have in common. And first we note that in Auden the word is used in its concrete first dictionary sense of "an act, or series of acts, often of a symbolical character, prescribed by law, custom or authority, in the conduct of important matters, as in the performance of religious duties, the transaction of affairs of state," etc. (Webster). And in Auden and several of his followers, the image is ceremony in magic, necromancy, and other primitive "archaic" rites. In Yeats the word is used in a less concrete, more generalized sense, as ritual observance, or the formal quality appropriate to religious, or merely to traditional or formal, conduct of life. It is notable that it is definitely associated in him with *innocence*, "radical innocence," which is characterized by courtesy, modesty, and freedom from arrogance and hatred. Innocence is thus almost a synonym for virtue. But it is favored by a traditional ("customary") and ceremonious manner of life. And thus, in "The Second Coming," when "the ceremony of innocence is drowned" (in blood, in violence and anarchy), what Yeats is saying is that the anarchy which threatens to destroy the old order is not simply a political phenomenon, but follows upon a disintegration of men's souls. "Things fall apart; the centre cannot hold." There is a want of the faith that went with the old "ceremony":

> The best lack all conviction, while the worst
> Are full of passionate intensity.

"The ceremony of innocence" is not a natural prose way of speaking, but a highly compact and indirect "poetic" locution, whereas Auden's "initiating ceremony," in spite of the metaphorical daring in its reference to necromancy, is in itself a plain and natural rendering of the act referred to. The poets who follow show a curious mingling of the two different uses of the word, and a considerable range of poetic indirection, or "obliquity," as Professor

Tillyard calls it. Sometimes it is simple and unnecessary obscurity that results from an elliptical use of the word in its context. Thus in the passage cited above from Brinnin, where he speaks of "the ceremony / Of wheatfields and the fruition of houses / Blessed for a boy," "the fruition of houses / Blessed for a boy" reminds us of Yeats's theme of a wedding for his daughter. As for "the ceremony of wheatfields" we are at a loss to make out a meaning until we realize that *ceremony* is here used in Auden's sense of a magical ritual, in this case a fertility rite, performed for the success of the crops, as similar rites are depended on for "the fruition of houses." Even more obscure is the context in which the word appears in "Munich Elegy No. 1" (*Selected Poems*, 1941) by the British poet George Barker. Barker is speaking, like Yeats, of some kind of last day, when "I shall hear the *ceremony of heaven* and God's roar." Here one is not much impressed with "God's roar" for the voice of God at the Last Judgment, and the "ceremony of heaven" makes one think more of pipe organs and church processions than of the rich core of ethical meanings that Yeats has crowded into his "ceremony of innocence."

Howard Nemerov makes interesting use of Yeats's and of Auden's *ceremony* in a poem having to do, like Bishop's, with the art of poetry. His theme in "Praising the Poets of That Country" (*Guide to the Ruins*, 1950) is what the poet owes to the traditions and received techniques of his art.

> The poet then is seen as bearing *a priestly part*
> In the *ritual*, confirming the continuance
> Of this that and the other thing, humbly
> Refreshing the hearer with his *ceremony*.

The priestly part in the ritual is reminiscent of Auden's necromantic "initiating ceremony." As for the ceremony with which the poet refreshes his hearer, the word probably echoes both Yeats and Auden with a telescoping "ambiguity." Nemerov is referring to the traditional niceties of poetic art, and his ceremony may be thought of as a concrete prescribed ritual for conjuring the spirits of the dead, bringing us face to face with the wise "ancestral face" by the marshaling of archaic symbols, or it may suggest mere gen-

7

eralized *ceremoniousness* in the employment of the usual formal techniques, rhyme, symbolism, etc.

John Berryman is perhaps the most interesting of the younger poets in his employment of this word significantly in connections suggesting both Auden and Yeats. In "Canto Amor" (*The Dispossessed*, 1948) he is speaking of a marriage. Marriage, he says, is a kind of music. But then there is another music (seemingly that of life itself), in which we perceive "a gladness,"

> but we are drawn
> less for that joy than utterly to take
> our trial, *naked in the music's vision*,
> the *flowing ceremony* of trouble and light . . .

Here we are reminded of "the strings' excitement, the applauding drum" as the ceremony evoking "the music's vision." But this poem is unduly crabbed, strained and obscure. It is in "Boston Common: A Meditation upon the Hero" (also *The Dispossessed*) that we have Berryman's most meaningful and felicitous use of our word – this time in a sense more akin to Yeats's. Here Berryman is reflecting on the plight of our military heroes caught in the debasing trade of war. It is not to our heroes, he argues, that we must look for a way out of this impasse, but to the ordinary unheroic individual man, "superb of civil soul." He is taking his imagery from Saint-Gaudens' bronze statue of Colonel Shaw, which has an angel spreading his wings above and the unheroic common man lying under the belly of Shaw's horse. Our hope is that in the end the common man and the angel may meet. But

> Where shall they meet? *what ceremony* find,
> Loose in the brothel of another war . . .

How can a "citizen enact his timid will" among all these tanks and guns, "where will is mounted and gregarious and bronze?" The word *ceremony* recurs in the following stanza, in the same sense, and in what is essentially Yeats's sense. This poem too is crabbed and strained and obscure in somewhat the manner of Barker's. The connection of the thought is hard to dig out, and quotation would not serve to clear it up for the reader who is not prepared for long and hard work. For our present purpose it is sufficient to indicate that Berryman is the poet who comes nearest to rendering the deep and subtle meaning the word had for Yeats. Berryman is evidently taking up the word of a great literary predecessor in Eliot's manner of literary allusion, and paying his reader the compliment of assuming that he is familiar with the context in which it appears in the earlier work. In Berryman there is no reference to innocence; but by ceremony he understands much the same thing as Yeats — an ordered and traditional society in which the civil virtues may flourish, or rather, we might say, the civil virtues that flourish best in an ordered traditional (or ideal) society. And of course it is taken for granted in both writers that a state of war is incompatible with that kind of society and that set of virtues.

Berryman was perhaps the very first of our American poets (after Bishop) to exploit the poetic possibilities of this word *ceremony* in the interesting new slant given to it by Yeats and Auden and before it threatened to turn into a cliché. In his "Ceremony and Vision," published in *Five Young American Poets* in 1940, it is featured in the title, along with the characteristic Yeatsian "Vision." Unfortunately this poem is peculiarly esoteric in its symbolism, and peculiarly dark and irritating in the sequence and collocation of its symbolic images. There is nothing in the text of the poem to give a clue to the application of either of the nouns in the title. It can only serve to remind us how "all the rage" was this slanted use of the word *ceremony* among the more sophisticated poets of the 1940's and even on into the fifties. Each of the poets gives it his individual slant. John Ciardi in his "Ode for School Convocation" (*Other Skies*, 1947) uses it in a more normal dictionary sense, describing the parents as "starched and honorable with *ceremony*," that is, with the *ceremoniousness* appropriate to a solemn academic occasion. In 1950 Richard Wilbur published a volume entitled *Ceremony and Other Poems*. In the title poem, "Ceremony," he gives his own graceful and charming version of the classical aesthetic problem of Art and Nature, which he resolves with essentially the same formula as Bishop's in "Speaking of Poetry" and Nemerov's in "Praising the Poets of That Country." In Wilbur ceremony (art) is represented by a lady in a striped blouse in a painting by Bazille;

nature is represented by the striped blouse by which she simulates the effect of the shadow of leafy boughs falling on a sunlit clearing in the woods. He admires the "wit" displayed by this "feigning lady":

> What's lightly hid is deepest understood,
> And when with social smile and formal dress
> She teaches leaves to curtsey and quadrille,
> I think there are most tigers in the wood.

Here again we have the wedding of Desdemona with the swarthy Moor.

It is somewhat too early to determine whether the word *ceremony* in the Yeatsian sense has entered permanently into our poetic and our dictionary use, or whether it has run its course and is likely to be avoided by our poets in future out of a sense that it has become a cliché. It is still turning up in gifted poets who represent a generation later than most of those considered here.

Thus in Howard Moss's *A Swimmer in Air* (1957), in a poem in memory, at a guess, of Einstein ("The Gift to Be Simple"), reference is made to "one who *hated violence and ceremony / equally.*" Here the word is used in its most familiar dictionary sense, and one would not think of citing it at all except for the Yeatsian (and Berryman) collocation of ceremony with its opposite violence. In W. S. Merwin's *The Dancing Bears* (1954), however, the word is more strongly tinged with the Yeatsian idiosyncrasy. In his "Canso," Merwin twice uses the precious word. In both places he is playing with the concept of eternity as it is associated with lovers in time. In one place he describes the slow deliberation of their loving, as befits persons conscious that there will be (at least in time) an end to their affection. And

> we perform
> All of affections with *a ceremony*
> *Of more than patience*, as though there were to be
> Presently an end . . .

In the second place the lover-poet is reflecting on the magic power of the word, in this case for giving perpetuity to the person loved:

There must be found, then, the imagination
Before the names of things, the dicta for
The only poem, and among all dictions
That ceremony whereby you may be named.
Perpetual out of the anonymity
Of death.

In the first of these passages the word *ceremony* is practically
equivalent to *ceremoniousness*. It refers to the *manner* of cere-
monies, the ritualistic deliberation, gravity, and solemnity appropriate to the occasions they serve, and especially, here, to occasions
which remind us of the ineluctable presence in the background of
the fact of death. In the second passage there is a whole cluster
of associations round the word. We are reminded that in magic as
in religion the naming of sacred persons demands the utmost cor-
rectness as well as ceremoniousness in the use of words. We may
be reminded once again that in Platonic and other mystical-ideal-
istic systems, the idea of Auden's "initiating ceremony" for calling
up the father's spelling (with the designating word) is ontologically
antecedent to the thing — is in some sense essential to the existence
of the thing, and more real than the thing. "In the beginning was
the word." That, or something like it, is the guarantee of the immortality, or at least the eternity, of the spirit. It is what, in this
poem, is relied upon to "name" the poet's mistress "perpetual out
of the anonymity of death." But while this metaphysical background is present for the poet, the more immediate connection is
literary. Or rather, we should say, the metaphysical and the aesthetic views are almost inextinguishably blended. In another poem
of the same volume ("East of the Sun and West of the Moon"),
Merwin has his Psyche character say, "All metaphor is magic."
That is the poetic line. But it is closely associated throughout with
the metaphysical-religious Yeats line, in a Yeatsian manner. In another of his cansos, the poet-lover declares:

Believing is
Conception, is without artifice the making
Perpetually new, is that first holy
Aura and ordinance of creation.

11

I don't know why he says "without artifice," since he is so obviously echoing Yeats's "artifice of eternity," which is surely conceptual. In the ceremony passage, he underlines the creative power of the imagination, which, as he says, comes even "before the names of things." It is the imagination that determines "the dicta for the only poem"; and since he is here celebrating his holy Beatrice, it must determine, "among all dictions," that particular ceremony whereby she is to be named "perpetual." All metaphor is magic, and imagination is the faculty of metaphorical finding. On the whole it is the Auden incantatory magic that is dominant here, but given a Platonic turn not congenial to Auden's ideology in 1930, and faintly colored with reflections from Yeats's "ceremony of innocence."

Our final citation in evidence of the continuing popularity of the word in the fifties is from another very recent poet, Mona Van Duyn. In her "Death by Aesthetics" (published in *Poetry*, January 1954), she gives it a more recherché but witty turn, characterizing a doctor's physical examination of his patient as a "sterile ceremony." By giving an ironic tone of denigration to the prestigious word, she may have opened up new channels for the poetic imagination, and given *ceremony* a new lease on life.

2. WEB OF THOUGHT AND IMAGE

These illustrations of the use of the word *ceremony* through several decades will give an idea of the range of interest that may be found in tracing novel and modish fashions in poetic vocabulary. First in order of time, and last in order of critical significance, is the mere pleasure taken by the scholarly reader in noting how unexpectedly fruitful is his "research" in turning up ever new instances of the special word in a particular period. This is accompanied by a certain amusement taken in observing how large a part mere literary fashion has to play in the picking up of the new word by poet after poet — how, as with the "irony and pity" that Hemingway's newspapermen make so much fun of in *The Sun Also Rises*, writers like to pick up the modish new word and "use it for everything." Then comes the interest in classifying particular instances under significant headings, such as (1) conscious allusion to the use of the word in an admired predecessor, (2) deliberate quotation, (3) conscious or unconscious imitation, (4) unconscious echoing of a striking phrase or locution, or (5) mere following of a prevailing fashion in the use of a locution, with or without knowledge of where it originated.

In the time when Poe attacked Longfellow for the literary crime of plagiarism, several of these cases would have been confounded under the simple notion of dishonesty or appropriation of another's rightful possessions. Since *The Waste Land* conscious allusion and deliberate quotation have become estimable means of enhancing or "thickening" one's effect and deepening one's meaning by reference to classical passages in earlier literature, such as (in Eliot) "To Carthage then I came" (*Confessions of St. Augustine*), "*Quando fiam uti chelidon*" (*Pervigilium Veneris*).

But even in Eliot distinctions must be made. The italicized Latin at once advertises itself as quotation, openly made, and one has only to look up the original to be in a position to make out a connection with the modern context (probably with the help of better informed commentators). "To Carthage then I came" does not have the benefit of italics, but the apparent want of connection with the context suggests that it is quotation, and learned commentators or readers who have read the *Confessions* will put this with the following line, "burning burning burning burning," and see how it gives added moral significance to the episodes of Elizabeth and Leicester (and Cleopatra) in a barge, and the three Rhine Maidens, drearily seduced in a canoe. Even when it comes to Eliot's echoing Laforgue in "La Figlia che Piange," "Simple and faithless as a smile and shake of the hand" (from Laforgue's "Hamlet": "Simple et sans foi comme un bonjour"), while it is hardly to be expected that any English reader will trace this to its source and be conscious of a heightening of the effect from its reference to the French poet, and while Eliot has not here, as in *The Waste Land*, given us a clue to most of his allusions and quotations, the presumption is that Eliot was not consciously or unconsciously borrowing his striking phrase with intent to deceive. He does not expect the full effect and bearing of his allusion or quotation to become clear on first reading, but relies, presumably, on considerable study and research in time to reveal his intention, trusting that the impact of such passages on the reader's mind and imagination will be so much the stronger as it comes to him with the attention-arresting effect of discovery and surprise.

Whether Eliot is justified in making these assumptions is, as Thomas Browne would say, a "wide question." And he has, without this, so brilliant a talent for imagery and evocative statement that one is not certain whether his imaginative effects may not be secured in spite of rather than with the help of these allusions to earlier writers. Eliot is here carrying to its furthest extreme Professor Tillyard's formula for "oblique poetry." The learned reader may feel a certain exhilaration in poetry that challenges him to so much congenial labor. The ordinary though intelligent and well-read reader may resent having to pay so high a tax for appreciation. The "man in the street," even when he likes poetry, is inclined simply to "decline the gambit" and "show fatigue." And many readers in all categories have been inclined to accuse this distinguished poet of pride of learning or literary exhibitionism.

The same questions declare themselves in the case of Auden, not often in his case because of specific reference to literary monuments, but rather because of the extreme "obliquity" of his symbolism in allusion to things in general. And with him and many of his followers, the question becomes more pressing than in the case of Eliot, since Eliot sticks so resolutely in his earlier and more influential poetry to the indirect or oblique mode, and his symbolism is so almost exclusively objectified in scene, character, and dramatic situation, as well as in rhythm and so on, whereas it becomes fashionable in the thirties and forties to employ what is essentially the discursive mode of direct statement, somewhat disguised or "embroidered," to use Tillyard's term, and the statement itself is mainly unfavorably affected by the rage for obliquity. Tillyard is very sympathetic toward the oblique mode in poetry, which, he believes, goes deeper into the essential province of poetry as the rendering of our unformulated, unconscious feeling. But he has also an admiration for the less elevated poetry of statement when it is done with classical art, and he prefers a frankly embroidered statement to one that wears the *disguise* of obliquity.

I am not here concerned primarily with poets of the caliber of Eliot, but am suggesting what critical profit can be had in noting the appearance in later American poets of certain peculiar locutions taken over from early twentieth-century classics. Something can perhaps be learned from comparing the use by individual poets of certain modish words and images. How do they compare in the felicitousness with which the word is made to serve imaginatively in their contexts? How much of moral or intellectual significance do they draw out of the word or image, or put into it? Is their use of the word notable for originality or merely for ingenuity? Or is it notable for neither the one nor the other, but merely for its conformity to the poetic conventions of the time?

In this latter case we are justified in applying the label of cliché. To hear that their pet expressions are clichés would be bad news for American poets of the period under consideration. For avoidance of the cliché is with them a chief title to distinction, and in their view, falling into it a main point in which nineteenth-century poetry is dreary and "old hat." The employment of cliché terms, like the entertainment of *idées reçues*, is tiresome and "bourgeois" — to apply one of the most notorious clichés of the period in which critical vocabulary was dictated by the standards of "proletarian" literature. To anyone whose tastes were formed during the afterglow of Victorianism, and who has enough acquaintance with (say) eighteenth- and fourteenth-century literature to have developed a certain catholicity, it is a source of amused gratification to find that even our present age is capable of the cliché, and that contemporary practitioners, like those of earlier times, are likely to be quite unconscious of the fact when they have themselves fallen into the cliché and even to plume themselves on the use of the very terms which may come to be suspect by a younger generation.

This is, of course, no new phenomenon and nothing for us to be ashamed of. It is a main point urged by Wordsworth against so fine a poet as Gray. The type of cliché that Wordsworth was down on was what he called "poetic diction." And Wordsworth wisely pointed out that what was poetic diction in his time was simply imaginative language, shopworn, fallen into decay by long use, and not accompanied by a steady look at the poet's subject. He wanted in his own writing to avoid personifications of abstract ideas, which had been run into the ground by both the neo-Classic and the Romantic poets of the eighteenth century, and in general to abstain from "a large portion of phrases and figures of speech which from father to son have long been regarded as the common inheritance of poets. I have also thought it expedient to restrict myself still further, having abstained from the use of many expressions, in themselves proper and beautiful, but which have been foolishly repeated by bad poets, till such feelings of disgust are connected with them as it is scarcely possible by any art of association to overpower."

Wordsworth is using rather strong language here, but such as is natural to one devoted passionately and professionally to his creative art, and he carries over into criticism the fervor of the creator, as you will find it in the critical writing of Ezra Pound. For most readers the feeling experienced is not disgust but simple indifference toward a style so conventional and bookish, so far from "life," that it simply cannot hold his attention. And this is fundamentally Wordsworth's objection to writing of this kind — that it is drawn more from literature than life.

In the case of several of the expressions under discussion here there is a special element not noted by Wordsworth and not as a fact observable in the earlier poetry against which he was reacting. It is the use of language in a way not quite natural, or not at any rate in prose. If any of these expressions might seem to be on the way to becoming clichés, this will be in spite of the fact that, to any but the reader deeply immersed in recent poetry, they still retain the challenge of the unnatural or strained. How far, in Elizabethan and seventeenth-century poetry, any particular expression or collocation of words was natural and familiar, we cannot judge unless some expert tells us. We feel more confident in regard to linguistic usage in the eighteenth and nineteenth centuries; and our impression is that, however oblique or fanciful a poem is, however it makes use of symbolism in the modern sense, the use of unexpected, or sometimes forced juxtaposition (such as "ceremony of innocence" or "ceremony of wheatfields") is very infrequent. (There is, by the way, very little of this in Yeats, who is almost a model of fastidiously plain English style.)

I do not have in mind such a natural type of association as is found in synesthesia, where two senses are run together, as in John Gould Fletcher's "color symphonies." Irving Babbitt may have condemned this as not classical; but psychology has long recognized that it is not merely natural but scientifically correct to associate, for example, taste and smell. In individual cases expressions involving synesthesia may be objectionable on other grounds, and much nonsense has been indulged in in the arbitrary association of, say, letters of the alphabet with particular sounds or colors; but this is not because it is unnatural for one to make this association.

In recent American poetry, with its rage for obliquity, the straining of English prose idiom has become for many literary connoisseurs almost a touchstone of good poetry, and in many cases expressions tend to become clichés almost by reason of this straining which draws attention to itself, rather than by reason of an agelong familiarity that makes it pass unnoticed. It is perhaps a whole style of writing that tends to become a cliché.

But the poetic language abjured by Wordsworth and the type of things here under discussion do have this in common, that they tend to be guilty of or open to the same vice or imputation of bookishness, of being begotten by earlier writing.

Thus, the present study, while it is primarily confined to a very special and limited subject — we might call it an abbreviated glossary of favorite expressions among a small group of recent poets — does tend to broaden out here and there into a tentative characterization of the style and tone of poetry in the period covered. And beyond that, it tends to generalization in regard to the dominant spiritual concerns and philosophy of the same period, which includes the great financial depression of the thirties, World War II, and the succeeding years in which our poets were so feverishly busy digesting those cataclysmic world events and attempting to

17

reappraise their values. It will be observed how largely they have been absorbed in a limited number of topics that have special relevance to this task of digestion and reappraisal.

Again, one is surprised by the curious interrelationships of these poems from the 1930's and 1940's. It does not matter at what point one starts; whatever thread one begins to disengage, it brings another with it that is followed by another until the entire web is unwoven. Or to put it better, whatever thread one begins to wind in with another, the texture of the web begins to establish itself, and it goes on growing in complexity, size, and firmness until in the end one comes out with a finished and patterned web.

THE SECRET TERROR IN THE HEART

3. THE TIGER'S SPRING

We will begin, somewhat arbitrarily, with the poetic image of the tiger, as in the line quoted from Richard Wilbur. And here we start with Blake's haunting lines on "The Tyger," in *Songs of Innocence.* Everyone has read this poem, and no one ever forgets the more striking images.

> Tyger! Tyger! burning bright
> In the forests of the night,
> What immortal hand or eye
> Could frame thy fearful symmetry?

It will not be necessary to attempt an explication of the metaphysical or theological meaning of this poem, which has been interpreted in a variety of ways. It seems clear that Blake is here somehow concerned with the problem of evil, and of what mysterious purposes God may have had in creating what is, or seems, evil, or dangerous forces, and introducing them into the same world as innocence (the lamb). What we are mainly concerned with is the unforgettable picture of the magnificent and terrible creature with eyes of fire encountered in the forests of the night. I suppose this fascinating and fearful figure has made his appearance in many poems and stories since Blake's poem was first published. I am considering some of these appearances in American poetry since 1920. But there are some characterizing features of this image that are not present in Blake and not readily to be accounted for by anything in Blake's poem. Blake's tiger was not shown us in action as an immediate menace to anyone destined to be his victim, and there is

nothing specifically to anticipate Eliot's terrifying line in "Gerontion" (*Poems*, 1920):

> The tiger springs in the new year. Us he devours.

But between Blake and Eliot there intervened a closely related set
of images in a prose tale only a little less well known than Blake's
poem and in its way quite as impressive and memorable as that —
Henry James's "The Beast in the Jungle."

In James's story the protagonist is a man haunted by a secret fear.
"Something or other lay in wait for him, amid the twists and turns
of the months and the years, like *a crouching beast in the jungle*."
John Marcher is a lonely man, and he has never confided his secret
to anyone. But when he has at last formed an intimate friendship
with a woman, May Bartram, he hesitates long before sharing his
secret obsession with her. "It signified little whether the crouching
beast were destined to slay him or to be slain. The definite point was
the inevitable spring of the creature; and the definite lesson from
that was that a man of feeling didn't cause himself to be accompanied by a lady on a *tiger-hunt*." So now it is established in James's
figure of speech that the beast in the jungle is identified as a tiger,
like Blake's fearful creature "burning bright in the forests of the
night." As the story proceeds, other features of Blake's poem are
suggested; but there are added further suggestions of an image not
anywhere evoked in Blake's poem, the crouching and the springing
of the beast: "It has always had its incalculable moments of *glaring
out*, quite as with *the very eyes of the very Beast*." (Blake: "In what
distant deeps of skies *burnt the fire* of thine eyes?") Now, May
Bartram had fallen in love with John Marcher, had for years sac-
rificially lavished her love on him, with inadequate return of love
on his part. And it was only after her death that he realized that,
in his blind egotism, he had failed to meet the challenge of love and
life, and it was this inadequacy on his part that had all along hung
over him like a cloud, or better, had lain in wait like a beast in the
jungle: "She had lived — who could say now with what passion? —
since she had loved him for himself; whereas he had never thought
of her (ah, how it hugely *glared at him*!) but in the chill of his
egotism and in the light of her use. Her spoken words came back

to him, and the chain stretched and stretched. The *beast had lurked* indeed, and the *beast, at its hour, had sprung . . .* and it was as if, horribly, he saw in the truth, in the cruelty of his image, what had been appointed and done. He saw *the Jungle of his life* and saw *the lurking Beast*; then, while he looked, perceived it, as by a stir of the air, rise, huge and hideous, for *the leap* that was to settle him. His eyes darkened — it was close; and, instinctively turning, in his hallucination, to avoid it, he flung himself, face down, on the tomb.''

That Henry James was well acquainted with Blake's most famous poem is one of those things that we may well take for granted; perhaps from childhood, he had carried in his conscious or unconscious memory, as we all do, that image of the beast with fiery eyes in the forests of the night. And it may be this that identified his beast in the jungle as a tiger rather than a jaguar or a lion or some other crouching and leaping animal that hunters have to deal with in the tropics. But for the dramatic situation that brings in the crouching and the springing, there is perhaps another literary source almost as well known to connoisseurs in terror in James's day as Blake's poem, or as James's tale was known to connoisseurs in Eliot's day. I refer to a passage in "The English Mail-Coach" by the author of "Murder Considered as One of the Fine Arts" and *Confessions of an English Opium Eater*. Readers who still have some acquaintance with prose writing in the age of Lamb and Hazlitt will remember the place in De Quincey's "English Mail-Coach" when the author, "going down" with great speed (thirteen miles an hour) in the mail-coach at about midnight on a country road, suddenly discovers not far ahead of them "a frail reedy jig, in which were seated a young man, and by his side a young lady," going at about one mile an hour. The coach was on the wrong side of the road, and the coachman was asleep. They were almost certain to run into the gig and be the death of its occupants. DeQuincey tried to shout so as to wake the coach driver and warn the young people in the gig. But he was overcome by a paralyzing fear, which De Quincey spends many pages in analyzing psychologically. The key passage is as follows: "The situation here contemplated exposes a *dreadful ulcer, lurking far down in the depths of human nature.* It is not that

men generally are summoned to face such awful trials. But poten-
tially, and in shadowy outline, *such a trial is moving subterrane-
ously in perhaps all men's natures. Upon the secret mirror of our
dreams* such a trial is darkly projected, perhaps, to every one of us.
That dream, so familiar to childhood, of *meeting a lion*, and,
through languishing prostration in hope and the energies of hope,
that constant sequel of *lying down before the lion*, publishes *the
secret frailty of human nature* — reveals its *deep-seated falsehood
to itself* — records its *abysmal treachery*. Perhaps not one of us
escapes that dream; perhaps, as by some sorrowful doom of man,
that dream repeats for every one of us, through every generation,
the original temptation in Eden."

In quoting this passage, I have italicized not merely the words
referring to the dream of meeting the lion and lying down before
it, but also many in De Quincey's psychological interpretation of
this dream. One is immediately impressed with their startling anticipation, considering the date (1849), of many concepts of the
psychoanalytic school — the subconscious registering of this state
of mind, the recalling of it in dreams, the association of it with
feelings of guilt and moral frailty, and even Jung's notion of the
collective unconscious in which a certain symbolism is passed on
from generation to generation. All that remains to betray the age
in which it was written is the theological cast given by De Quincey's reference to "the original temptation in Eden." It will be seen
as we go along that this type of interpretation has an important
bearing on later poetic invocations of the tiger image. It is at once
obvious that there is much in De Quincey's account of the dream
of meeting the lion and lying down before it that might have contributed to James's final picture of Marcher threatened by the leap
of the lurking beast and flinging himself face down on the tomb in
an instinctive effort to avoid it. But beyond that, there is a distinct
suggestion in James of De Quincey's psychological interpretation.
Throughout the tale there are frequent reminders of the moral
weakness or inadequacy that is the chief feature of Marcher's character, the paralysis of the will that possesses him in anticipation of
the undefined disaster that lies in wait for him. And in the end he

comes to realize that it was his own failure to meet the challenge of May's love in which that anticipated disaster takes form. His obsession with this threatened disaster is in effect a sort of guilt by anticipation.

That Eliot was well acquainted with "The Beast in the Jungle" is again a thing as much to be taken for granted as that James was well acquainted with Blake's poem. There are many evidences, some of them "objective," that Eliot was well-read in Henry James. Eliot's "Portrait of a Lady" takes its title from James's novel. John Marcher in some ways strikingly resembles Prufrock — especially in his shallowness and emptiness of character, his ineffectualness. But there is perhaps a closer resemblance between Marcher and the protagonist in Eliot's "Portrait of a Lady." Indeed, as one of my colleagues has pointed out to me, there is a close parallelism between "Portrait of a Lady" and "The Beast in the Jungle." The man in "Portrait of a Lady" is a man without any marked character except as he is apparently a writer and is restive and uneasy in the arty, sentimental, and humorless atmosphere of his hostess's interior — "an atmosphere," as he says, "of Juliet's tomb," where people talk in a silly way of the intimacy of Chopin's music, and where, we suppose, as in "Prufrock," "the women come and go / Talking of Michelangelo." (In my own young manhood, it was Browning mouthed by candlelight that drove me away.) He grows restive, too, under the personal intimacy forced upon him by a (perhaps older) woman who had hoped to be close friends with him, or, we suspect, to trap him into marriage.

> "For every body said so, all our friends,
> They were all sure our feeling would relate
> So closely! . . .

This pressure of preciosity and sentimentality drives him out to
> take the air, in a tobacco trance,
> Admire the monuments,
> Discuss the late events,
> Correct our watches by the public clocks,
> Then sit for half an hour and drink our bocks.

Unlike our reaction to James's characters, our sympathies are more with the man than with the woman, who, in James, is a model of sincere love and devotion, whereas in Eliot we so fervently share the man's need to get away from all that— affected culture and spurious feeling — that we may be blinded, like him, to his own superficiality and to something genuine in her feeling. But in the end, when he considers the possibility that she may die some afternoon, leaving him

> Doubtful, for a while
> Not knowing what to feel or if I understand
> Or whether wise or foolish, tardy or too soon . . .
> Would she not have the advantage, after all?

We are faced with an alternative reading — with the tables turned and positions reversed. And so, allowing for a characteristic irony and ambiguity in the poet, we arrive at a complete parallelism with James's story in outline.

At any rate, in Eliot's "Gerontion," we have him taking up James's image of the tiger springing or leaping upon his victim to devour or "settle" him; he takes this up from James or some other writer or invents it for himself; in any case, he produces a new link in our chain of related images. In the line quoted earlier, "The tiger springs in the new year. Us he devours," Eliot is having his spiritually corrupt old man refer back to an earlier passage in his monologue.

> In the juvescence of the year
> Came Christ the tiger
> In depraved May, dogwood and chestnut, flowering
> judas,
> To be eaten, to be divided, to be drunk . . .

I believe that experts in theology explain that Eliot here refers to the spiritually mortal effect on communicants of taking the sacrament in an unregenerate state of mind. The placing of this sin in the spring anticipates the opening lines of *The Waste Land*:

> April is the cruelest month, breeding
> Lilacs out of the dead land, mixing
> Memory and desire . . .

The significant point for our present discussion is that, in Eliot as in James and in De Quincey, the springing of the tiger or the lion is associated with moral weakness on the part of the victim, and it is an inner state of mind, a weakness in character that gives rise to the victim's sense of guilt or uncertainty or spiritual error. And so, in later uses of the tiger symbol, it is likely to be associated with some inner corruption. And of this association we shall become steadily more aware as we pass on from the tiger symbolism itself to the innumerable explicit references to fear, and its synonyms, horror, terror, desperation, anxiety, etc., where the poets have more or less given up the effort to keep the oblique method of symbolism from yielding to the literalism of plain statement.

Naturally enough there will be instances of both the tiger image-ry and the unsymbolized terror in which there is no association with the spiritual or ethical interpretation. Thus in Wilbur's poem already discussed in regard to the meanings of the word *ceremony*, where the "tigers in the wood" make so appealing an aesthetic pat-tern along with the lady in the blouse, it is presumably the sheer undifferentiated menace of savage nature that is set off against the sheer undifferentiated charm of civilization. It is true that savagery and civilization are concepts crowded with peripheral associations, and the words are connotative as well as denotative. And so the pattern of contrast here is "thick" enough to satisfy our poetic ideal. But I think I do Mr. Wilbur no injustice in suggesting that the imagery here does not lead us into the ethical or theological depths where it has mostly operated since Blake took it there, but that it stays more on the purely aesthetic level which it would have for the child. The most unsophisticated child is delighted by the shiver that he experiences at the thought of tigers in the wood. I am in-clined to think that the "primitivism" of Rousseau's picture of a highly conventionalized jungle with a tiger peering out from the bushes is more akin to Wilbur's highly sophisticated evocation of "tigers in the wood" than to Eliot's reference, in *The Dry Salvages* (1941) to

> The backward look behind the assurance
> Of recorded history, the backward half-look
> Over the shoulder, towards *the primitive terror.*

Rousseau's and Wilbur's primitive terror, whatever its psychological background, is more like that of a delighted child than De Quincey's or Eliot's backward look to the Garden of Eden. This is one reminder that Wilbur is more "modern" than those poets of the forties who took so many leaves out of Auden's book.

Coming back to Auden, the particular "thickness" of his symbolism often makes it difficult to be sure just what interpretation to give to his imagery. In his early volume of *Poems* we have a piece as haunting as "The Strings' Excitement," the one beginning "Doom is dark and deeper than any sea-dingle." (This was simply called II in the 1930 *Poems*; it appeared in *Collected Poetry* under the wholly misleading and frivolous title "Something Is Bound to Happen." It is ás if Audén in 1945 in his sophisticated maturity were deliberately making light of what he regards as a juvenile work, but which, when the accounts are all in, will certainly stand among his two or three dozen finest poems.) The poem is on the surface a picture, perhaps inspired by the Old English lyric "The Sea-Farer," of a man who feels compelled to go on a long voyage across the ocean to strange places and a strange way of life. It ends with a sort of prayer for his well-being and return home. Here appear the lines:

> Save him from hostile capture,
> From *sudden tiger's spring* at corner . . .

In Auden's very early work, he almost entirely abjures the poetry of statement in favor of the obliquity of symbolism, and in a given case one often finds it difficult to interpret the symbolism with perfect assurance. But there is a marked consistency, over a long course of years, in his use of symbolic motives, and frequently in his later poetry of mixed statement and obliquity one comes upon the clue to his earlier symbolism. The "Doom is dark" poem represents a motive, frequently recurring in him, of a journey; and his journeys all have the character of a spiritual quest or mental exploration. We can be pretty sure that the "tiger's spring at corner" represents something close akin to De Quincey's dream of the lion, to James's final encounter with the beast in the jungle, and to Eliot's spring of Christ the tiger. A few years later we have the figure of a springing tiger in Auden's ode "To My Pupils" (*The Orators*, 1932). Only here the roles are reversed; it is the traditional victim who is himself the tiger: "At five *you sprang, already a tiger in the garden.*" This whole rather long poem is an account of young soldiers preparing themselves for encounter with some unspecified enemy. But it is all clearly symbolic of the process of moral discipline, building up of character sufficient to ensure victory with life's moral challenge. So that here again, though from quite a different angle, the springing tiger is given an ethical significance.

There are at least two more appearances of the tiger imagery in Auden's poetry. The first is in the play on which he collaborated with Christopher Isherwood, *The Ascent of F6* (1937). The figure of the tiger appears in the speech of a Mrs. A, who with her Mr. A seems to represent the ordinary timid, mediocre citizenry, who like to hear of heroic adventure but not to be involved in anything so ambitious and dangerous. They are referring to a difficult mountain climb, undertaken in order to reach a certain peak before citizens of a rival state and thus ensure the imperial interests of the home state. So far as the individual climbers are concerned, their heroic feat is undertaken under some psychological compulsion, perhaps compensating for a sense of inferiority, and essentially by fearless action facing down some moral fear. But the homebodies find enough of fearsomeness in the circumstances of their everyday life.

> For the skidding car and the neighbours' gossip
> Are more terrifying to us than the *snarling leap*
>   *of the tiger.*

To the implications of this we shall return later in discussing the fear motive in itself.

By 1940 Auden had definitely entered into his second stage, in which his poetry consists of philosophical essays, for the most part frankly didactic, with occasional figurative "embroidery." His "New Year Letter" (dated January 1, 1940, published in *The Double Man*, 1941) is a long expository poem dealing with "the situation of our time," meaning not the political and military situation but the ideological situation, taking *ideological* broadly for the spiritual and psychological. It is a devilish clever piece of writing — good talk, it would be, on the responsibilities of the poet, with many allusions to the philosophical attitudes of writers and philosophers from Aristotle, Descartes, and Berkeley, through Wordsworth and Blake, down to Flaubert, Baudelaire, and Rilke. It is ingeniously metered and rhymed in four-accent couplets, and sparkles with intellectual wit. It is larded with terms and proverbs in French, Greek, and Latin, and loaded with psychological references. It is extremely hard reading and calls for great learning and alertness on the reader's part. So far as I can figure out, its central theme is the unhappy divorce between Head and Heart that has prevailed since the age of enlightenment (or reason). That divorce is the villain in the piece; it is

> the Prince of Lies
> If not the Spirit-that-denies
> The *shadow just behind the shoulder* . . .

It is the root cause of the prevalent sense of guilt and the Greater Fears, and "a recurrent state / Of fear and faithlessness and hate." It is, we might say, for our times, the beast in the jungle or the tiger in the wood. In the passage in which the tiger makes his personal appearance, Auden is contrasting Blake and Voltaire. It was Blake who

> Broke off relations with a curse
> With the Newtonian Universe,
> But even as a child would pet
> *The tigers Voltaire never met* . . .

What Auden presumably had in mind was something like this: Voltaire, as a pure disciple of reason, could not conceive of original sin, could not take "sin" or evil seriously, and could not accordingly conceive of the terrors of tigers in the wood; whereas Blake, as a Christian and visionary, not only could believe devoutly in metaphysical evil, but with religious awe could welcome the thought of evil and of the mysterious dispensations of divine power which could make evil so beautiful that it might be made a pet of.

Before going on with this theme in Auden, I will note appearances of the tiger imagery in Stephen Spender, who more than once invokes this imagery in his poem *Vienna* (1935). This has been one of the most widely read of single poems in this century judged by its influence on later poets in the United States, and this not, I should think, by virtue of any great poetic distinction, but because of a combination of topical interest in the period leading to World War II and of philosophical interest in the twin subjects of heroism and fear. In *Vienna* the tiger figure twice makes its appearance, or three times if we count the lines from Wilfred Owen which are quoted by Spender as an epigram to his poem. But in no one of the three passages do I feel at all sure of the meaning, either of the passage as a whole or of the tiger figure. In Owen's "Strange Meeting" (*Poems by Wilfred Owen*, 1921), he describes an imaginary encounter with an enemy soldier he killed, who was himself a poet, but who had not lived to tell the truth about the pity of war. If the latter had been spared he would have washed the blood of defeated soldiers with water from sweet wells, "Even with truths that lie too deep for taint." Meantime, Owen says of the fighting men, continuing the war,

> They will be swift with *swiftness of the tigress*,
> None will break ranks, though nations trek from
> progress . . .

So far as I can make out, the figure of the tigress is wholly conventional for the swift and terrible movement of a destructive force, and cannot be associated with the special meanings ascribed to the tiger in the earlier and later symbology here under discussion. It therefore has little light to throw on Spender's use of this imagery in the poem to which his lines are attached as an epigraph, except that they all refer to men dying in war.

In Spender's poem, too, it is hard to make out the special application of the symbols, and I offer my own interpretations with extreme diffidence, trusting that someone else will come forward with a more satisfactory explication of these texts. In the first passage, Spender, faced with the deaths of workmen in the bloody putting down of the proletarian (socialist) rebellion, is asking himself (as I understand it) how we can be reconciled to these desolating deaths. Unless, he says,

> Unless indeed we stand upon a word,
> Forgiveness, the brink of a renewing river . . .

Then he develops this suggestion:

> A word, a brink, like the first uttered love.
> *Upon the pulsing throat springs the hot tiger.*
> Instantly released, in joy and sorrow they fall,
> Escaping the whole world, two separate worlds of one,
> Writing a new world with their figure 2.
> Accepting the dreaded, the whispered happy postures
> They dive into their dream with dreamed of gestures.

As nearly as I can make out, Spender is saying here: These soldiers, at the moment of receiving their death wounds, having found the word *forgiveness*, fall in a sorrow not unmixed with joy. For in this word they find their escape from a world in which every man is alone and announce a new ideal world of communion — one and one together, and thus, accepting the whispered and happy postures of love, realize their dream of a world filled with the gestures of love. If this is the right interpretation, the postures and gestures of erotic love symbolize the loving togetherness of human beings in a communal world, or ideal society. What then is the pulsing throat and what is the hot tiger that springs upon it? Is it a throat pulsing with the word *forgiveness*, like the first uttered love? And is the springing tiger something suggestive of Christ the tiger (when he does not devour us, but saves us), or is it simply a deathly beast that deals us our death wound?

In the second passage, he is asking why the unemployed in the streets of Vienna stare at us strangers with indifference. We need not ask them why they are indifferent to us, nor need we ask that woman

> With dark eyes neglected, a demanding turn of the head
> And hair of black sulky beasts, because our life is
> A cage of lightest aluminium bars
> *Beyond the strength of tigers, conquering what's most feared*
> *With moral weakness.*

In Spender the greatest source of difficulty is not, as in Eliot, the immediate juxtaposition of disparate symbols, without connective nonsymbolical matter to give us a clue as to how the discrete symbols belong together in some process of association. It is rather the use of connective words or sentences intended to indicate the relation between the discrete symbols which, in many cases, are so elliptical or blind in their reference as to leave the reader more confused than ever; or it is the simple combination of the oblique and direct modes (the symbolical and the explicit prose statement) in such a manner as to be doubly confusing. Thus we have here these symbols: the woman "with dark eyes neglected," the "cage of lightest aluminium bars," and "the strength of tigers." And we have the confusing logical connective "because our life is" and the prose statement "conquering what's most feared with moral weakness." But we cannot make out how the dark-eyed woman, perhaps symbolizing the temptation to sensual love, is connected with what follows by any relation in which the conjunction *because* is relevant; and in the concluding prose statement, "conquering what's most feared with moral weakness," we are at a loss to know whether the conquering is done by the strength of tigers or the "aluminium-barred cage," or "our life," or possibly by us. In view of key passages to be discussed later (with regard to tigers or simply to fear) it seems most probable that our barred cage defends us against our greatest fears (or tigers), but only at the price of our succumbing to moral weakness, which is, paradoxically, the very essence of tigerdom. And even if this is the correct answer to this riddle, it is yet to be discovered how this moral truth constitutes an answer to the question Why do the unemployed in Viennese streets show themselves indifferent to us onlookers? It is perhaps that, being unemployed and occupied only with living on the primitive level (which is mostly making love in an irresponsible and even venal way) these proletarian crowds are perfectly indifferent to the pomp and circumstance of a government that promises no improvement in their condition. It would seem that these starved butterflies in the sun illustrate the way in which aluminium-protected men manage to conquer the tiger (what is most feared) with moral weakness.

It may well be that there is more here than meets the eye, and that I with all my earnest efforts missed the very heart of the matter. I

would not have taken such pains to get at Spender's intention if his
"springs the hot tiger" were not so obviously a link in this literary
chain, and if the passage about the barred cage and the conquered
or conquering tiger did not so strongly suggest an ethical and
psychological interpretation of fear in general and the tiger in particular.

4. THE BEAST IN THE JUNGLE

Thus far we have been following in our poetry the trail of the
springing or leaping tiger. But we have noted that in Blake's famous
poem there is no reference to the beast's leap, which makes its appearance in James's story and in Eliot's "Gerontion"; what most
impresses one in Blake is the tiger's eyes burning bright in the forests of the night. In James what impresses one is not merely the
springing but also the crouching of the beast in the jungle. It is this
image of the crouching beast that has impressed the imagination of
some of our poets, and some of them identify the crouching beast
not as a tiger but as a leopard, a jaguar, or other fearsome denizen
of the jungle, or leave it without identification as a shadow or a
Thing lurking or crouching. In a well-known passage in *The Waste
Land*, it was the jungle that "crouched, humped in silence," and
then "spoke the thunder."

In Frederic Prokosch's three volumes of poetry published between 1936 and 1940, there are half a dozen passages involving
tigers, leopards, and apes, in most cases in the posture preceding the
leap, in others running with proverbial swiftness or roaming with
terrifying eyes. In *The Carnival* (1938), apropos of Machiavelli,
Zaharoff, and Hitler, we read (the poem is titled "The Conquer-
ors") that still "*Gorilla*, plague and tempest / Darken old Europe's
sky" —

> *Through history's savage wood*
> *Still roam the burning eyes,*
> The mind which swells on blood,
> The love which fills with lies.

In *Death at Sea* (1940), death (the craving for death) has cast its
shadow over the faces on the boulevard, "*swift as the tiger*, warm

as the Indies, mathematically exact and delicate as *the deer at evening poised, nostrils trembling*, above the brook" ("The Boulevard").* Thinking of the surface peacefulness and security of rural England, the poet asks, in "The Country House,"

> Who knows what ears are listening to you now?
> Who knows *what apelike arm is ready to strike*
> *Out of the Elizabethan wilderness*, tearing
> Open that awful flaw in the armor: imagination?

And in the same connection, he imagines elsewhere (in "Elegy")

> the electric form
> Of *the leopard poised above the waterfall*;
> Inaccessible lakes ruffled by the flamingo's call.

Again, in "Epilogue," the tiger appears in a moment of repose:

> Even the tiger, in that Euclidian moment
> Between repose and vigilance, as the gathering
> hordes of shadow among the tamarisks
> Are held suspended . . .

Before Prokosch comes Auden, and after Prokosch comes Auden again. We shall later note many evidences of the influence of Auden on Prokosch's imagination, and it is fair to note the probability of an influence running in the other direction. Prokosch may well have been impressed with springing tigers in Auden's earlier poems, and Auden may well have been affected by tigers and poised leopards in Prokosch's poetry.

In the passage last cited from Auden, it is Blake's tiger that is evoked. In another passage of the same poem, we may be reminded again of "The Beast in the Jungle." But here the beast and the jungle are brilliantly transformed into another entity and another setting that have much the tone of James in another area of his imagining as well known as that of the jungle beast — the area of ghosts and haunted houses. Auden starts his "New Year Letter" with a reference to an experience of his own in Brussels on the night of January 1, 1939. He is listening to the "wishful-thinking sigh" of hotel guests

* It is, however, not clear from the context whether this figure applies to the shadow of death or to the last look of passionate desire which each one craves before the shadow of death closes in.

in their beds in the "haunted house." The haunted house is Europe dreading the outbreak of the war, or whatever dreadful things they had to anticipate.

> And the low mutter of their vows
> Went echoing through her haunted house,
> As on the verge of happening
> *There crouched the presence of The Thing.*
> All formulas were tried to still
> The scratching on the window-sill,
> All bolts of custom made secure
> Against the pressure on the door,
> But up the staircase of events
> Carrying his special instruments
> To every bedside all the same
> The dreadful figure swiftly came.

Everyone is acquainted with the several stories of James in which people are waiting in haunted houses for the appearance of some dreadful figure, and everyone who has fallen under the spell of James's peculiar imagination will recognize the words *presence* and *thing* as characteristic of him. And indeed it so happens that this very word *thing* has its part to play in "The Beast in the Jungle" in the final identification by Marcher of what it is precisely that makes his doom — what was, in the last analysis, his jungle beast, his tragic flaw. Before this he had naively supposed that the death of May Bartram was the dreadful thing that fate had been holding in store for him. "Her dying, her death, his consequent solitude — *that* was what he had figured as the Beast in the Jungle, that was what had been in the lap of the gods." But it was much later, after his year's absence in the depths of Asia and his return to England that he came to realize that his real doom was something much more within his own character. He had visited her grave in the cemetery, and there he had encountered a stranger whose terrible grief over his loss suddenly made him realize that he himself had never really loved. "What had the [other] man *had* to make him, by the loss of it, so bleed and yet live? Something — and this reached him with a pang — that *he*, John Marcher, hadn't; the proof of which was precisely John Marcher's arid end. No passion had ever touched him,

34

for this was what passion meant; he had survived and maundered and pined, but where had been *his* deep ravage? The extraordinary thing we speak of was the sudden rush of the result of his question." This was, of course, Marcher's realization that he had never loved May Bartram, and had accordingly quite missed the boat spiritually speaking. And this was the lurking beast that finally leaped upon him as he threw himself face down on the woman's tomb.

I will not labor the point of parallelism, nor will I insist that Auden had in mind James's story. I will not go through the "New Year Letter" and show how for Auden the thing that Europe had most to fear was not totalitarianism or the war but its own spiritual bankruptcy from which these things flowed. I am merely reminding myself how certain favorite words and symbols haunt the imaginations of our poets. My final exhibit from Auden will again illustrate the persistence of the image in question; and here certainly it is on the psychological or spiritual level that the wild beast makes it unexpected leap. In *The Age of Anxiety* (1947) there is a discussion between Emble and Quant about the battle that is forever going on in men between the mere yielding to appetite and custom (the "impermanent appetitive flux") and the dream we have of some way of life in conformity with an ideal or absolute. That is, at least, the way I understand what is at issue. The whole discussion is carried on in that ambiguous sophisticated style of burlesque, in which even the most serious thoughts and attitudes appear in the fancy costume of mocking parody so common in this period of Auden's writing, and these disillusioned fellows in the poems are characterizing that fourth age of men in transition from youth to prime manhood when they are peculiarly subject to confusion and self-deception. So the most earnest interpreter is apt to mistake the author's meaning. Emble seems at any rate to be speaking of the way that men and women, victims of their appetites, yet yearn for some conversion — some critical occurrence that will give their life a more significant direction,

> and a wish gestates
> For explosive pain, a punishing
> Demanded moment of mortal change,

> The Night of the Knock when none shall sleep,
> The Absolute Instant.

To which Quant replies,

> It is here now.
> For *the huge wild beast of the Unexpected*
> *Leaps on the lax recollecting back* . . .

What follows would only confuse our reader. I can do no more than let this stand as further witness to the persistence in the poet's fancy of the image of the leaping beast.

As for the tiger symbolism itself, the last instance of this that I shall bring forward is in Alfred Hayes's poem "Epistle to the Gentiles" (*Welcome to the Castle*, 1950). And this instance will serve to make the transition from the tiger image to the general topic of fear and its synonyms. For Hayes's poem brings in the tiger, along with other beasts that spring and kill, as a symbol of fear; he interprets fear, as I understand him, in an ethical sense, and identifies it with that diffused state of apprehension that psychologists call anxiety, anguish, *Angst*. In this poem the speaker says he manages to survive even though not enjoying the luxuries of the rich. For him the birds sing and there are other pleasant appeals of movement, sound, life. But all these agreeable things are spoiled for him by "this *nausea* at one's center, this sick constriction of the heart." One is here reminded that nausea (*la nausée*) is Sartre's figure for the anguish (*l'angoisse*) which a man feels in facing the senselessness of the universe, until he makes the conscious choice which gives it and him existence.

> There is a *perfect island*, of course, some vacuum of
>   flowers and art, simplest of communities,
> but it exists nowhere for a common poison poisons all.

This perfect island we shall take up later under a special heading, where I shall suggest that this symbolism of the island has its origin for more recent poetry in Auden's famous sestina, to which in his *Collected Poetry* he gives the title "Paysage Moralisé." Here, let us say, Hayes's island symbolizes an imagined earthly paradise where one lives happily with one's fellows in a primitive communal state.

But this is not destined to be realized, for "a common poison poisons all."

> Movement, sound, life: but the bird sings in a tree
>   that could hold an ape, *the bush flowers that could*
>   *release a tiger*,
> for all *horrors* seem possible now, nothing is preventable,
>   all crimes
> have become imaginable.

The speaker then thinks of the snake charmer, the animal trainer. But

> Nothing seems able to keep *the beasts* upon their barrels;
>   *they'll spring* thinking I'm the cause
> of their captivity, their hunger, their iron bars . . .

Then he goes on to say "it all *comes down to fear.*"

> I am separate; the separation grows; the thrush
>   sings a while.
> but eventually they kill.
> Of course they kill. Why did I ever delude myself
>   they do not kill?

Here the beasts which threaten to spring upon the animal trainer and kill him symbolize, if I am not mistaken, the moral weakness and inadequacy, the unregulated passions of a man without any spiritual center. Writing with a vivid awareness, as he does throughout the poems in this volume, of the abhorrent circumstances of war, Hayes is constantly thinking of a spiritual state that is responsible for these catastrophic events in public life — the decay of all moral values which follows on the loss of faith and innocence, and the diffused state of apprehension in which men live, lacking any defense against the fears in which this undifferentiated state of mind is objectified.

In his earlier volume, *The Big Time* (1944), Hayes is constantly haunted by the cheap viciousness, the mediocrity and emptiness of ordinary life in a world where "conscience is a museum relic," love "an explosion . . . limited to dreams," honesty an indulgence, and wit a menace ("My Cousin Herman"). The title poem is a canto of echoes from Eliot; the physical atmosphere and the stage set a fusion of "Portrait of a Lady" and "Prufrock."

37

ELIOT: The yellow fog that rubs its back upon the
          window-panes,
          The yellow smoke that rubs its muzzle on the
          window-panes.

HAYES: Through the slow brown smoke,
          The smoke that bends in a blue gesture to the
          lamp.

ELIOT: Among the *smoke and fog* of a December afternoon,
          You have the scene arrange itself — as it will
          seem to do —

HAYES: *Fog. Drifting smoke.* The unchanged view
          I stared out dully at a day of rain. . . .
          The scene now shifts to a cheap downtown hotel. . . .
          These are the actors selected for the piece . . .
          As Elsie now appears at the prearranged hour
          On the prearranged scene.

The larger scene is that of *The Waste Land*, the third section:

ELIOT: The river bears no empty bottles, sandwich papers,
          Silk handkerchiefs, cardboard boxes, cigarette ends
          Or other testimony of summer nights.

        . . . .

          A rat crept softly through the vegetation
          Dragging its slimy belly on the bank
          While I was fishing in the dull canal
          On a winter evening round behind the gashouse.

HAYES: This is an ordinary day.
          Powerhouses feed the city light,
          Sewers float the garbage to the bay,
          Chicken wings, beer bottles, condoms, codfish heads.

Meantime, in the bar where the protagonist is imagining his sordid drama at Elsie's, there is conversation that somewhat parallels the talk in "Portrait of a Lady."

ELIOT: And so *the conversation slips*
          Among velleities and carefully caught regrets
          Through attenuated *tones of violins*
          Mingled with *remote cornets*
          And begins.

HAYES: The *conversation drifted*

Into a recital of insurance and death.
There was *music coming in from a city station.*

The principal drama (at Elsie's) is straight out of *The Waste Land*,
with occasional echoes from "Prufrock." It is a story of seduction
without passion and without resistance. In Eliot the aggressor is a

young man carbuncular . . .
A small house agent's clerk, with [a] bold stare

and the passive victim is a "typist home at teatime." In Hayes the
woman is Hannigan's wife after the maid has departed and the lover
is "her tanned tennis instructor, her ex-all-American end." In Eliot,
the typist is unresisting; in Hayes, Mrs. Hannigan has momentary
scruples that suggest Prufrock's hesitation to put the overwhelming
question: "Would it be worth the scandal and the shame?" In Eliot
the carbuncular young man indulges in few preliminaries:

Flushed and decided, he assaults at once;
Exploring hands encounter no defence.

The tennis instructor's assault is more explicitly itemized.

His hand,
Exercised on waitresses, slips
With expert pressures down her things and hips,
Invades the lower negligee . . .

Hayes doubles the *Waste Land* situation; for while Hannigan's
wife is performing her dreary adultery with the tennis instructor,
Hannigan is doing the same thing with a pick-up girl in an unap-
petizing hotel room, and failing to find in it the satisfaction he expected:

Hannigan shrinks from the dust, the recollection
Of the deskclerk's casual inspection.
This was not what he had expected
And not the scene that he had guessed.

(Is there perhaps here, along with so many echoes from Eliot, still
another echo, this time from "Prufrock"?

And would it have been worth it, after all,
Would it have been worth while
After the sunsets

. . . .

39

> If one, settling a pillow or throwing off a shawl,
> And turning toward the window, should say:
> "That is not it at all,
> That is not what I meant, at all.")

Hayes's second innovation is the scenes in the bar simultaneous with the "love" scenes, in which the narrator of these events works them out in his imagination and finds himself inexplicably obsessed by them.

> The plot now hastens to its end.
> I, meanwhile, my father ill, myself without a trade,
> Listen to the recital of airshaft sins,
> And watch a woman's hand reach up and draw a shade,
> Her hair in curling pins. . . .

And he wonders,

> Why should these people and their lives
> Obsess me as I lean above the scene.

But then we realize that this narrator is Hayes's substitute for Tiresias in *The Waste Land*, the blind prophet, who with visionary eye "perceived the scene and foretold the rest," who has indeed "foresuffered all / Enacted on this same divan or bed." Hayes's narrator has himself something of the prophetic character, and can say at the end,

> These characters, though fictional, are true,
> And every incident, although invented,
> Has happened, shall happen, must happen once to you.

Alfred Hayes has indeed lavishly bestowed on Eliot that sincerest flattery that consists in imitation. But the point that concerns us here is not merely that he has reproduced so many of the surface circumstances of Eliot's imagings, but that he has also pretty plainly spelled out what is the moral lesson of Eliot's "Fire Sermon" and of "Prufrock." And more than once throughout his work Hayes has given to this moral the religious turn which it has in Eliot. In *Welcome to the Castle* there is a very interesting account (in "The Angel") of a Jewish religious observance and of the effect of it on the feelings of a boy. In the tenement house where the family lives a glass of wine has been placed among the candlesticks in a ritual recalling the flight out of Egypt and other incidents in Hebrew history. The child awaits the coming of an angel.

> He has been told the wine is for Elijah, the door is open for
> Elijah, and he awaits the gigantic visitation of the angel.

He imagines the sound of great wings. He is paralyzed with anticipation.

> In *inconceivable terror* and inconceivable joy, unable to
> move, while his father chants the ancestral hymns,
> he watches the angelic mouth stain with the sweet wine.

One is reminded of Auden's initiating ceremony, the ancestral face and the archaic imagery. Hayes recognizes that the food and wine, "the language, is old, hieratic and magical," and "part of an enormous ritual." The terror that he experiences is religious, having the character of religious awe, and no doubt associated even in childhood with a sense of guilt. The Jews may not make so much as Christians do of original sin, and they may not, like De Quincey, trace their dream of the lion back to the fall of man, but the story of the Tree is their story, and sin with them is something more than a violation of human law.

Thus we find that in Hayes, as with so many recent poets, the fear symbolized by a beast lurking in a flowering bush or springing out upon his victim is something more than the psychological reaction to imminent danger, the rational fear of deep water, guns, or atomic bombs. It is rather the fear of moral danger half-buried in our unconscious and deep-rooted in the psychological experience of the race. It calls for penetrating psychological analysis.

5. THE HORROR! THE HORROR!

The emotion of fear (in all its synonyms) has of course been a favorite theme with imaginative writers everywhere since the beginning. "Tales of terror" were in great favor with Gothic writers in the eighteenth and early nineteenth centuries. The shivery sensation of fear is often a strong element of appeal in murder mysteries and in the stories of Poe, and has long been a specialty in the Grand Guignol theater and in certain types of moving picture. In a more

refined form of literature, the sensationalism of fear has been notably exploited by the philosophical De Quincey, and most of his
writings are peppered with the nouns *fear, terror, horror, anguish,
awe, dread*, and derivative adjectives. The tiger imagery is not infrequent. The mysterious Malay who appeared to De Quincey's
wife in their rustic kitchen seemed to her a tiger-cat; the third one
of Our Ladies of Sorrow moves with incalculable motions, bound-
ing, and with tiger's leaps; and in "The English Mail-Coach" we
read of the lady overtaken by the deadly coach that "suddenly as
from the ground yawning at her feet, *leaped upon her*, with the
flashing of cataracts, Death the crowned phantom, with all the
equipage of his *terrors* and the *tiger roar* of his voice."

In De Quincey, too, as we have seen, there is some effort to analyze the psychological causes of horror, as in the dream-of-a-lion
passage and the famous purple passage in the *Confessions* in which
he explains why the mysterious Malay had been for months "a
fearful enemy," and shows what trains of awful association are
evoked by Asiatic scenes.

But I think I have observed that during the later nineteenth century the emotional temperature considerably lowered so far as this
complex of emotions is concerned, at least in writing that pretended
to artistic self-restraint and the modesty of nature; and that there
was in the thirties and forties a notable resurgence of interest in the
subject of fear, most likely under the stimulus of the great wars,
economic and social changes, and other disturbing factors in religion and philosophy. And while De Quincey was decidedly aware
of the ethical and psychological factors in the fear complex, still, in
his inveterate passion for gaudy literary effect, he did play up much
more than our twentieth-century poets the specifically physical aspects of fear in the presence of imminent danger. Moreover, the
new turn of psychology since Freud which has so impressed our
imaginative writers, together with the revival of religion among our
poets in reaction against the prevailing rationalist unfaith among
intellectuals, has brought about a resurgence of ethico-psychologi-
cal interpretation.

I will begin my illustrations of the use of this theme in recent

American poetry by reference to a prose tale as famous as "The Beast in the Jungle" and one perhaps exerting as great an influence on the imaginations of later writers — Conrad's "Heart of Darkness." Readers of Conrad must all remember the scenes leading to the death of Mistah Kurtz, and particularly that in which Marlow, standing beside his deathbed, hears the dying words of this loathsome and mysterious ivory-hunter. Just at the end there came over Kurtz's features an appalling change. "It was as though a veil had been rent. I saw that on that ivory face the expression of sombre pride, of ruthless power, of craven terror — of an intense and hopeless despair. Did he live his life again in every detail of desire, temptation, and surrender during that supreme moment of complete knowledge? He cried in a whisper at some image, at some vision — he cried out twice, a cry that was no more than a breath — 'The horror! The horror!' " This Kurtz was a sort of incarnation of all the vices of civilization and those of savagery. He represented the horrors of the white man's cruel and heartless exploitation of the uncivilized native. He was an international figure, by race and by vice. We read earlier: "All Europe had contributed to the making of Kurtz; and by and by I learned that, most appropriately, the International Society for the Suppression of Savage Customs had intrusted him with the making of a report, for its future guidance." And the irony of this is that Kurtz had qualified for this mission by having "gone native" and practiced these abhorrent customs himself.

Conrad does not give us such a developed view of these savage customs as Robert Penn Warren does in his recent novel *Band of Angels*. But his characteristic impressionism builds up our notion of their horrid character by hint and adjective. And the same impressionism is used in the characterization of Kurtz himself. He has been under discussion in his remoteness during the whole voyage up the tropical river. We have a shadowy impression of him all along, but he only comes upon the stage for a very brief period at the end. His role is somewhat like that of Mrs. Newsome in *The Ambassadors*, or of Milly Theale during all the closing chapters of *The Wings of the Dove*. He is for Marlow a mysterious figure very hard to define, and Conrad never offers the one neat word in which his significance may be summed up. It would violate the integrity of Conrad's artistic method to make our own summing up by saying that he is the incarnation of inhumanity in its essence. And one might question the logic of making the man recognize the moral horror of what he himself stands for, and still be the same man. But such deathbed recognitions are a favorite convention of literature, even though a questionable fact of life. What we have here is certainly an impressive rendering of the notion that horror often has its origin in a sense of one's own abhorrent nature, and of the abhorrent nature of the human world in which he participates.

It may be worth making note in passing that, while Conrad is profoundly ethical in his interpretation of Kurtz and his world, and it is a *moral* revulsion that he records in invoking the sensation of horror, there seems to be no hint in this work of a disposition to associate his ethical interpretation with a distinctly religious understanding of moral values.

In my next case, on the other hand, everything is grounded in a religious interpretation of moral character. It is well known that Conrad had made a deep impression on Eliot and most certainly so in the case of this tale, from which Eliot took his epigraph for *The Hollow Men* (1925): "Mistah Kurtz — he dead."

Shortly after the tiger passages in "Gerontion," the old man describes the state to which he has been reduced by the loss of his love. It is well known, as a result of Leonard Unger's study of the rose-garden theme, that religious love and the abandonment of the spirit to this are closely related in Eliot's psychology to the passion of earthly love. So we are prepared for Gerontion's statement:

> I that was near your heart was removed therefrom
> To *lose beauty in terror, terror in inquisition.*

And we realize that the pitiful condition in the end is a spiritual condition and the terror which accompanied the process which led to it is essentially a religious terror. In *The Waste Land* when the protagonist says, "I will show you *fear* in a handful of dust," we realize that this is not simply fear of death but the more desolating fear of what follows death. And when the card diviner warns her client, "*Fear* death by water," we realize that death here stands not merely for drowning, but for the spiritual death suggested by the part water plays in the sacrament of baptism. In *East Coker*, it is in "the darkness of God" that one sees

> behind every face the mental emptiness deepens
> Leaving only the growing *terror of nothing to think about.*

And in *The Dry Salvages*, "the primitive terror" and "the pre-conscious terrors" referred to are not a matter of physiological fear in presence of an immediate danger. These are generalized inherited states of fear, referring back to the experiences of the race, "the backward half-look / Over the shoulder, towards the primitive terror." They may be given a psychological explanation in purely secular, or in magical terms, by reference to horoscope, sortilege, playing cards. One may

> fiddle with pentagraos
> Or barbituric acids, or dissect
> The recurrent image into *pre-conscious terrors* —
> To explore the womb, or tomb, or dreams.

But Eliot goes on in highly metaphysical terms to indicate the strictly religious origins of these sensations. As for the many references to horror and terror in *Murder in the Cathedral*, I will come back to them a little later.

While I am mainly concerned with a later generation of poets, who first came into prominence in the thirties and forties, we may well remind ourselves of two earlier poets in the United States who have dealt with fear in ourselves in the "modern" manner. First let us look at one who has played up the fear motive almost invariably, I believe, with a strictly religious reading of that emotion. Among other pieces in which fear is a central theme appearing in Allen Tate's *Poems 1928–1931* (1932), there is "The Eagle," in which that bird seems the very incarnation of religious revulsion from the evil of the world:

> Think not the world spins ever
> 'Tis only the gaunt fierce bird
> Flies, *merciless with fear*
> (Only the world has a year)

> Lest the air hold him not
> Beats up the scaffold of space
> Sick of the world's rot
> God's hideous face

The reminder that only the world has a year takes our fear out of the range of the finite into that of the infinite judgment. In the "Ode to Fear," Tate recalls the religious dread roused in Oedipus by the oracle's prophecy of his crimes to come — crimes which in him are links in a chain of evil going back to his remote ancestor Atreus. This religious fear, says the poet, haunts us all today throughout the world, and then, addressing the personified religious emotion he adds:

> You are the surety to immortal life
> God's hatred of the universal stain
> The heritage, *O fear*, of ancient strife
> Compounded with the tissue of the vein.

In *The Hamlet of A. MacLeish* (1928), that versatile poet gave a turn to the fear motive appropriate to his subject and, presumably, conformable to his own religious complexion. In Ophelia's mournful thoughts over her father's death, she is like a child needing to be comforted before she can go to sleep. What she needs to know is "the meaning of life," and to that question no one has given the answer.

From the very beginning Auden has been much occupied with the psychology of fear, only gradually passing over to a more religious interpretation. In his 1930 volume of *Poems* there are several rather cryptic pieces dealing with this theme. In number XII, beginning "We made all possible preparations," the reference seems to be to the revolt of the young against the forceful rule of their elders. Some interpreters, we are told, teach that there was no excuse for this. But

> in the light of recent researches
> Many would find the cause
>
> In a *not uncommon form of terror*;
> Others, still more astute,
> Point to possibilities of error
> At the very start.

One guesses that "the possibilities of error" refers to the older generation that insisted on a repressive and warlike policy, while the "not uncommon form of terror" refers to the moral terror of the young who sought for pacification in the world. In number XXI, beginning "On Sunday walks," the relation between fathers and sons is again played up, and we read:

> Not meaning to deceive,
> Wish to give suck
> Enforces make-believe
> And what was *fear*
> *Of fever and bad-luck*
> Is now *a scare*
> *At certain names*
> A need for charms
> For certain words . . .

(The natural and justifiable concern for anticipated dangers turns into a worked-up ideological scare at the mention of tribal enemies — e.g., Germany — or of social theories — e.g., socialism?) At this period of his writing, the extreme indirection of Auden's references may be accounted for, as in the case of Blake's prophetic books, by his espousal of "subversive" or revolutionary causes.

Two years later, in his ode addressed "To My Pupils," Auden refers to the generalized fears of men as a cause for the wars that have ravaged Europe. It is the fear psychology that begets militarism:

> What have we all been doing to have made from Fear
> That laconic war-bitten captain addressing them now?

It is Auden's special contribution to Marxian poetry to combine Marxian economic criticism of society with a strong tincture of English moralism, to prepare men's minds for revolution by a stern course of moral discipline (appropriate to the poet's function as master of a boys' school or boy scout leader), and to attribute political catastrophes to the corrupt state of men's hearts. Thus, in the ode to his pupils, along with fear and wrath, gluttony, acedia, and lust are cited as vices that sap men's strength and threaten defeat in the great struggle for which they are preparing.

47

Joseph Warren Beach

This theme reappears in 1935 in *The Dog beneath the Skin*, Auden's play written in collaboration with Isherwood. This play, a panoramic view of European degeneracy, is at the same time a manifesto of moralistic Marxism, and a preliminary sketch for the theme of *The Age of Anxiety* (1947). Anxiety (German *Angst*) is that diffused obsessive state of apprehension under which (according to some Freudian psychologists) all men labor, and which may be centered in certain neuroses upon some particular fear, as in claustrophobia or agoraphobia, but which in more favorable circumstances may be spread more thinly over the whole field of things that may be feared. It is vividly described in *The dog beneath the Skin* in an expository chorus:

> Man divided always and restless always: afraid and unable
>   to forgive:
> Unable to forgive his parents, or his first voluptuous
>   rectal sins,
> Afraid of the clock, afraid of catching his neighbour's
>   cold, afraid of his own body,
> Desperately anxious about his health and his position:
>   calling upon the universe to justify his existence.

In the psychological system of Otto Rank this general anxiety is traced back to the trauma of birth, which all men have suffered, and which is independent of postnatal conditioning. In other Freudian systems it is more likely to be attributed to traumas in early childhood, and above all to the child's relations with his parents leading to the silver-chord complex and to father-rejection, Auden is too much of a poet to dismiss any provocative idea and is an eclectic in regard to the causes of this obsession. The silver-chord theory is strongly emphasized in *The Ascent of F6*. The unspecified grudge against one's parents is referred to in the passage cited above. There is also an obsessive sense of sin derived from early sexual offenses.

Men's defense against their fears is flight; and many avenues of escape are here enumerated: in dreams of sexual enjoyment and of applause for one's feats; in reading in the papers of accidents and criminal convictions in which one is not involved; in the "time-honoured solutions of sickness and crime"; in good works, in devotion to such ideals as God, Beauty, Reason. Even the passion to

48

make money is more innocent than certain indulgences of personal vanity. The passage I have thus summarized is the table of contents to a popular psychological textbook. It is followed by a series of exhortations modeled, it might seem, on those uttered by the thunder in *The Waste Land* (give, sympathize, control):

> You have wonderful hospitals and a few good schools:
> Repent.
> The precision of your instruments and the skill of your
> designers is unparalleled:
> Unite.
> Your knowledge and your power are capable of
> infinite extension:
> Act.

Eliot has gone to the Upanishads for his world-wisdom. Auden has brought together three more recent voices: John the Baptist, Karl Marx, and Henry Wadsworth Longfellow.

6. THE ASSASSINS

Whatever Auden's preferred line of explanation, it is invariably from childhood that man derives the terrors of maturity. In *The Dog beneath the Skin*:

> So under the local images your blood has conjured,
> We show you *man caught in the trap of his terror,*
> *destroying himself.*
> From his favourite pool beneath the yew-hedge and the
> roses, it is no fairy-tale his line catches
> But grey, white and horrid, *the monster of his childhood*
> raises its huge domed forehead . . .

It is from childhood that come our fears and our universal sense of guilt — "the *web* of *guilt* that prisons every upright person and all those thousands of thoughtless jailers from whom Life pants to be delivered" (*The Ascent of F6*). And it is those far behind the lines, and not the men in the trenches, who are really to blame for the horrors of war. In *The Dog beneath the Skin*, a "famous author" makes his confession. "Yes, I and those like me. Invalid poets with a fountain pen, undersized professors in a classroom, we, the sedentary and learned, whose schooling cost the most, the least conspicuous of them all, are the assassins." It is not altogether clear whether the invalid poets and undersized professors are responsible for the war because, being weaklings and introverts, they are most subject to the psychological maladies that have infected mankind, or because, being the makers of books, they are in the most strategic position for spreading a vicious ideology. What we are concerned with is the complex of ideas which associates guilt and fear bred in childhood with the general state of mind that provokes the evils of capitalism and war. We are interested in the filiation of ideas in recent poetry, and we find that Auden and Isherwood, in their poems and plays, have been, in this and in other related matters, the nursing fathers of numerous later poets.

One of our more tangible clues in establishing paternity is Auden's use, in a very striking context, of the word *assassins*, and the following reappearance of this word as the title of a first volume of poems by Frederic Prokosch, in which there are numerous points of similarity with the poems of Auden. These include notions about fear and its psychological causes much like those of Auden set forth in close connection with the passage on the assassins. Frederic Prokosch was a young American who had taken a Ph.D. in English literature at Yale in 1932, who had been a teacher — research fellow there between 1931 and 1935, who was to take an M.A. in English in 1938 at King's College, Cambridge, and whose first two volumes of poems, 1936 and 1938, were published in London by Chatto and Windus, and his third volume in New York and London by Harper and Brothers. One's first natural conclusion would be that Prokosch had read *The Dog beneath the Skin* and had been so much impressed by the word *assassins* in its context that he decided to use it as the title of his volume of poems. This is a very probable hypothesis; but so far as literary filiation is concerned, it does not tell the whole story. It is quite possible, in this case, that, while the child is the legitimate son of his father, the child is also father of the man.

Let us review some of the circumstances suggesting that Prokosch was familiar with the work of Auden. *The Dog beneath the Skin* was published by Faber and Faber in May 1935, and in the autumn of 1936 Chatto and Windus brought out *The Assassins*. It was favorably reviewed in *New Verse* in the August–September number. In November 1937 *New Verse* brought out an "Auden Double Number," with a bibliography of Auden's poetry, and essays on him by many distinguished writers including Christopher Isherwood, Stephen Spender, Louis MacNeice, Cecil Day-Lewis, Herbert Reid, Edwin Muir, and Allen Tate. But anyone in the know in England would long since have been well aware of Auden as the most talked-of contemporary English poet. He was only nine months older than Prokosch, but already the leader of an influential movement. Prokosch would have known him not merely for his published volumes, but for poems appearing currently in such periodicals as the *Listener*, the *New Statesman and Nation*, the *Criterion*, and above all in *New Verse*, which was to England what *Poetry* was to the United States, only more consciously "advanced" in poetic techniques. *Poetry* had been rather impertinent in its strictures on *New Verse*, and *New Verse* had more than once given tit for tat. In reviewing Prokosch's *Assassins*, *New Verse* referred to "Paul Engle and the other posturing rhetoricians of the United States," and expressed the hope that Prokosch's talent would "take him much higher than most of the English and American chickweeds." Prokosch had several times had particular reason for taking account of Auden, when poems by the two men were featured in the same issue of the same magazine. This occurred in the October–November 1935 and in the February–March 1936 numbers of *New Verse*, and in the latter number there was also a review of *The Dog beneath the Skin*.

But some of these clues might well work both ways. If Prokosch would be likely to read the verse of Auden standing next to his own in the same periodical, Auden would have been likely to read poems of Prokosch standing next to his. And he might well have recognized in this poet, who had appeared before this in *New Verse*, the author of a highly interesting novel brought out by Harper and Brothers in the same year, 1935. This was Prokosch's first novel, *The Asiatics*; and if Prokosch might have been impressed by the peculiar use of the word *assassins* in *The Dog beneath the Skin*, Auden might almost equally well have been impressed by the peculiar use of this word in Prokosch's novel. This occurs in the philosophical tirade of a picturesque Russian, Krusnayaskov, while a prisoner with the hero in a Turkish prison: " 'There's no use giving up,' he'd say; 'don't let up while you're here. It's the same here as everywhere else. Life's got a lot of *little assassins watching you all the time.* They see everything you do, everything. There's no fooling them. . . . And if you do the rotten thing, by and by they'll get you, whether it's in the prison house or the grand hotel room. They'll haunt you. . . . *You become afraid of things.* . . . You start by looking at some simple object — a chair or a clock or a water jug — and quite unexpectedly it will *frighten you into a frenzy.* You begin to see faces and shapes, a warning finger.' " And he goes on to tell how these little fears will fasten on one like leeches and suck him dry, and soon he'll begin to smell like a corpse.

It will be observed that we have the hookup here between the word *assassins* and the topic of fear that appears in *The Dog beneath the Skin.* And Krusnayaskov's assassins would seem to be mythological symbols for the working of something like conscience in the individual who is possessed by them. But they are not identifiable as individuals or classes of people; nor do they have the Freudian quality they carry in Auden and in Prokosch's poems. They are Old World superstitious entities with some suggestion of an Old World ethic; they are mythological creatures designed to see that justice is done on men who "do the rotten thing." And the particular notion is thrown off casually by the philosophic Russian without a follow-up, not being further developed in the course of the narrative so far as I have observed.

It is interesting to suppose that the figure *assassins* was caught up by Auden from Prokosch's pages, and given a quite special turn; and that then Prokosch, who had invented the figure and set it going, when he encountered it in the pages of Auden, was impressed by the new turn given it — with the wider and deeper psychological possibilities it held — and decided to use the word for the title of his volume of poems.

In Prokosch's volume, "The Assassins" is the title of the opening poem as well as of the volume. In this poem there is no direct reference to the sort of people to which the term might apply; but the poet does speak of "our passionate and forever / Unregenerate spirit," and regret that under the physical loveliness of human beings there should be "such hostility to love, / Such horror and hate." In "After Midnight" the assassins are specifically referred to and their peculiar character suggested. And they are here discovered in the darkness of our own American land.

> But hush: follow these darker clouds and see
> In utter spiritual darkness the assassins.

He finds them in our brightly lighted cities.

> Make iron your nerves: the suffering, the insane
> Here plot their spidery and destructive fevers
> And wicked lovers yield.

"Invalid poets with a fountain pen" and "undersized professors in a classroom" have here become the "suffering," the "insane." In Prokosch's next volume, *The Carnival*, the silver-chord complex is resorted to as a cause of the sickness that produces the assassins ("Hesperides"). In the Americas, with our climatic violence, we are peculiarly liable to ever-new and violent passions.

> And hence the continual cry for another opiate,
> And the *blond assassin sprung from his mother's cradle*,
> And the frenzied poet to whom the vision at last
>   grew real and devouring.

Prokosch would here seem to be giving a more radically Freudian turn than even Auden to what he calls the "fever of the Spirit" that rages in our day throughout the world. It is, it would appear, the unsatisfied craving for love which begets the poet's frenzied vision, which in turn infects all lovers and drives them to violence.

> And the nameless dumbly accept on their bursting lips
> The wounding kiss of a vision . . .

In his third volume of poems, *Death at Sea*, in "War of Nerves," he even specifically names Freud and the movie queen Greta Garbo, along with the political Marx and Goebbels and the radio-inspiring Marconi, as among the abettors of assassination.

> Marconi, Marx, Miss Garbo, Dr. Goebbels and Dr. Freud
> *Huddle like assassins over the staggering void,*
> Faces illumined by the roving flames, they move
> > Their devastating glance,
> > Their empty lips and hands
> Exquisitely to and fro in the mimicries of love.

This association between love and violence is particularly marked in *The Carnival.* We read in "Song" of

> > Those whom *love drove forth to war,*
> > Broken heroes who must praise
> > Lies devouring all their days.

and in "The Balcony" of how in the ocean,

> > The night's drowned heroes sing
> > Of a destroying love
> > And through the corals move.

We read, in "The Castle," how

> > Power for violence, suffering for inertia,
> > Love for the serpentine caress of the selfish
> > > Carve the irrevocable channels,
> > > And the magic chain is severed.

Sexual perversion is but one of the forms taken by the general malady (in *The Assassins*, "The Funeral," "The Tragedians"). It is not so much, as in Auden and Spender, associated with a sense of guilt, but is rather one pitiful example of the prevailing degeneracy. In *Death at Sea* ("The Victims"), along with quarreling sailors, consumptives, mathematicians, "pudgy idealists in the swimming-pool," soldiers, surrealists, and raging politicians, are listed

> > The maniac smiling over the hedge and toying
> > > with his knife,
> > The syphilitic reflecting on his curious
> > > role in life . . .
> > They all pray to money or hate or an idol
> > > out of stone,
> > Overcome by a strange necessity; terribly alone;
> > All they thought they wanted was the look in
> > > another's eyes,
> > Lips meeting theirs, the touch of warm hands
> > > on their own.

This is not by any means the sole string to his bow — this theme of selfish and insatiable love as the source of our violence and misery. In "The Conspirators" (*The Assassins*) these are not the inventions of our age, but are an inheritance from our long past, as the intricate

> Languor of recollected centuries
> Descends with its terrible sweetness on our limbs.

In "The Festival" (*Death at Sea*), on the Danubian banks, among the archaic trees, "the restless dead / Dispel their homesick odours on the breeze," and we

> rediscover on this festive night
> The hatreds of a hundred thousand years.

Prokosch's vision of the world is far more desolating than Auden's. For one thing, there is no trace of the Marxian confidence that the ills of the world are economic and modern in origin and will be set right in our time. It is not the end of capitalism that Prokosch envisages, but the end of the world. In "Going Southward" (*The Assassins*) we read:

> This is the final dreading
> Of history ending, an end to living and terror
>   spreading,
> The dead destroying, the living dying, the
>   dream fulfilling,
> The long night falling and knowledge failing and
>   memory fading.

Poem after poem shows us Europe sinking into an Asiatic bog of languor, self-indulgence, cruelty, and indifference. The poet's imagination revels in scenes of arctic and African desolation; takes us to Pacific islands where the last men are dying of disease and despair. Prokosch is totally wanting in that Cockney humor that in Auden delights us with Gilbert and Sullivan sprightliness and jabberwocky burlesque. He does not amuse and shock us with a realism that dwells with cynical pleasure on the courts and brothels of Ostnia and Sudoland. His vision of mankind is purely tragic. In *The Dog beneath the Skin*, Auden lists the avenues of escape that men take from their anxieties, and we feel that we are in a jolly clinic of psychiatrists. In *Death at Sea*, Prokosch on the boulevard has a vision of mankind in the mass making their flight from life into death.

> All that they see, all
> That they do, whether in the cigarette-studded
> Silence of the attic room above the river, or the little
>   gas-lit bar near the docks, or the expensive Bach-
>   haunted solitudes of the concert-hall,
>
> Is a ceaseless flight: flight
> From identity, from guilt, from the fear of death
> Into death. A massive and critical longing for annihilation
>   cajoles all those who have lost their way across the
>   border . . .

He sees them in the city

>   passing down the street in the endless ritual
> of self-sacrifice to the gods of our civilization, the
> gods of vengeance, the faceless and serene.

Auden has, after all, in his Marxian phase, the cheerful view of humanity made possible by the economic interpretation of character and history. His moralism is the gift of "muscular Christianity" adapted to the Marxian program. Prokosch too has a moralism, but it is less cheerful than Auden's since, while it is colored by Freudian psychology, there is no suggestion, I think, of economic determinism in extenuation of the vices of his "wicked loves" and power-drunk dictators.

There is even a vague after-shine of dogmatic religion in Prokosch's occasional insistence that the dangers threatening civilization come from within. In "Fever" (*Death at Sea*), he represents the Fuehrer haranguing the populace in the square of a Carinthian town and urging the youth to join his movement, with its "new way of perceiving," for which

>   what is static is a lie . . . all change is truth,
> Victories, monuments, unfulfilled desires.

To this

>   the pastor of Dahlem replied,
> "O my brothers recall, continually recall
> How the real danger to us all comes from within,

And what is pure can be preserved only in its purity.
To sacrifice truth to stratagem, however benign,
To sacrifice God's power to human calculation,
    however agonized —
This and this alone will be our shame and our
    destruction."

And the poet goes on to make the very streams and rocks cry out a warning against evil power.

"Power: that is the real corruption
That sets the crime, the atonement, and the fall."

Again, in "The Athletes" (*Death at Sea*), beginning with "brutality, the exquisite resort of the cynic," the poet points to some wrong choice or yielding.

We too, each of us, made a single overwhelming
Error, crucially yielding for one split second

.   .   .   .

For which of us has desired without self-regard,
And which of us has been slighted without self-pity?

It is true that Auden, as early as 1937, in *The Ascent of F6*, had given his religious version of the origin of evil in the will and wrong choices, where his mountain-climbing hero, after his meeting with the Abbot in the monastery, soliloquizes: "There was a choice once, in the Lakeland Inn. I made it wrong; . . . Oh, You who are the history and the creator of all these forms in which we are condemned to suffer, to whom the necessary is also the just, show me, show each of us upon this mortal star the danger that under His hand is softly palpitating. Save us, save us from the destructive element of our will, for all we do is evil."

It is considered that *The Dog beneath the Skin* is peculiarly the monument of Auden's Marxian period and *The Ascent of F6* more especially that of his Freudian period. But they overlap, and the religious passage just cited is an opening wedge for the more frankly Christian period that was to come. Perhaps something of the same sort may be found for Prokosch in the passages so like them in sentiment. Only, with Prokosch, the poetic record ends with his third volume, and his subsequent production has been in the form of novels. And the strenuous religious note in the poet's quotation from the pastor of Dahlem is far from characteristic of the poems as a whole in their general tone. They are characterized rather by the sense of human nature as being passive to its doom, as if lying under an evil spell.

If we have regard to priorities in the poetic record, we must note that the strenuously religious passages are from poems appearing in *Death at Sea*, three years later than *The Ascent of F6*. But it is somewhat difficult, in the complex of themes we are here discussing, to establish priorities definitely and exclusively on one side or the other. These were the two poets in English most obsessed at the same time by the sense of that diffused and "nameless" fear, rising out of obscure psychological drives, which covers the whole landscape, the whole ground of human experience, and may be held responsible for the unexampled violence and destructiveness of their age — that all-pervasive anxiety which found its culminating expression a decade later in Auden's *Age of Anxiety*. If Prokosch was impressed by *The Dog beneath the Skin* and by *The Ascent of F6*, Auden was doubtless impressed by *The Assassins*. There was a two-way traffic in influence; and the two poets urged each other on to new psychological subtleties, to new and intensified visions of terror. In *The Assassins* we read of lovers who at nightfall wandered miles and miles, "knitting our hands in terror, trembling / With love, with grief" ("The Voyage"); of "The child whose hands, strangely equipped for love, / Turn like a leaf to terror" ("The Tragedians"); of drowned soldiers ("The Baltic Shore"),

> The huge and desolate eyes of the self-deceivers:
> They loved their land, they struggled and they fell!
> Now in their comprehending terror swaying
> On the immense and equalizing swell.

We read of those who have found safety in the freezing white ice of death ("Chorus"):

> Never again that clutching moment of error
> Beside the bed, the oath on the mound, the horrid
> Biting of buried flesh,

No, nor that fit of terror in the forest
Or the shrill drop of the net by the lagoon
Nor yet that melting

Thought, the awaited touch healing all wish for dying . . .

In *The Ascent of F6* we read of the Demon of the mountain: "He is — what shall I say? the formless terror in the dream, the stooping shadow that withdraws itself as you wake in the half-dawn. . . . You have felt his presence in the sinister contours of a valley or the sudden hostility of a copse or the choking apprehension that fills you unaccountably in the middle of the most intimate dinner-party." Then we come back to *Death at Sea* ("Elegy") and read of

Stray figures on the boulevard, suddenly
Rising out of the twisted fog appear
Like Aeschylean figures, hurled by a nameless fear.

In the archaic scenery, we hear

The small guilt-stricken whine of humanity
As the old walls collapse.

After the musicians finish playing at the inn, everything is quiet and peaceful, "Yet through this *single scene all human terror moves*." The "evil implicit in our age" is felt in the flickering sheaves of wheat as they are cut. It is felt in the singing faces of the reapers: ("The Reapers"):

For that is all our fever. It is a fever of the spirit,
And it lies deep. It will heal again, but certainly not soon.
We cannot localize it, we cannot even see or hear it . . .

We read ("The Sacred Wood") of

those tall rocks, those valleys
Fringed with our fears, those silent foam-entangled islands.

It would be interesting to speculate on why it is that Prokosch's poetry has not made more of an impression on American intellectuals and poetry lovers.

This section began with the word *assassins* in the special figurative use it has in Auden and Prokosch, as designating those characters whose neurotic fears are in part responsible for the often neurotic fears to which the rest of us are subject. The word recurs in similar contexts in several of our later American poets, and is perhaps a tribute to the assiduity with which our poets read one another. (Considering how small is the audience otherwise accessible to our poets, it is a comfort at least to realize how large a choir they make among themselves. If we assume that every other college student of English is a secret writer of verse, and that among their teachers every third one has seen his poems in print, we are encouraged to think that our better known poets need not see themselves as mute or inglorious Donnes.)

John Berryman in his "Boston Common" (*The Dispossessed*) reminds himself that anyone determined to be active in working for the common good need not feel himself unduly isolated. We are sure at least to make contact with enemies and assassins.

> None anywhere alone! The turning world
> Brings unaware us to our enemies,
> *Artist to Assassin*, Saint-Gaudens' bronze
> To a free shelter, images to end.

Alfred Hayes, in his "Heine: Biography of a Night" (*Welcome to the Castle*), pictures the German political exile in Paris during the time of revolutions (1830, 1848) meditating on his thankless and probably ineffectual occupation of poet, and on the general tension of war throughout Europe.

> And over Europe the wheel of disaster turned
>   in its grease.
> Though they sat in the cafes fierce about art
> *The assassins were preparing masterpieces* of their own.
> The people, as usual, relied upon their deputies and the police.

In Thomas Merton, it is not so clear whether the assassins are literal killers or belong to the tribe of ideological enemies referred to in this chapter. In "The Night Train" (*A Man in the Divided Sea*, 1946) he begins with an effective evocation of the quality of dead French towns as seen from the train window. Then he passes curiously to traveling diplomats waking to their fears, which include

> the undecoded names
> Of *the assassins they will recognise* too late:
> The ones that seem to be secret police,
> Now all in place, all armed, in the obvious ambush.

The Trappist poet would here seem to be trying something along the line of Kenneth Fearing, with his Houdini mystifications, the uncertainty as to identity of persons, as to friend and foe, with all-pervasive fear as the background; and doubtless, behind the material and political fears, the metaphysical and religious fears which give to the others their tragic force. Merton has other poems that symbolize the general state of fear of the times. Such as "Tropics," with its prisoners on a penal island in the jungle, the "chained and numbered men," and along with them the almost equally miserable guards. As night explodes like a bomb,

> Instantly the guards
> Hide in the jungle, build a boat
> And escape,
>
> But the prisoners of the state
> Do not cease their labor:
> Collecting the asphalt fragments of the night.

The alerted reader will have little difficulty in working out the symbolism of the poem — the jungle, emblem of life, nature, the world, with its evil; the sun, often as God or Christ or religious Truth; the prisoners, or sleepers, the unconscious, as opposed to the guards, the waking mind, seeking to arrest the wind.

And finally, to bring the figure of the assassins back full circle to its earliest use in Auden, there is a long (now suppressed) poem of 1936 (no. XVII of *Look, Stranger!*), in which young Auden reviews the ancient history suggested by his north country, the deceived "hopes of time," the "empires stiff in their brocaded glory, / The luscious lateral blossoming of woe," and, still earlier,

> intercalary ages of disorder
> When, as they prayed in antres, fell
> Upon the noblest in the country night
> *Angel assassins.*

Assassins are, as I take it, destroyers of the spirit, ideological inspirers of doubt; and such, in the old superstitious days, were supernatural visitants to those who went to the caves to pray for release from the evils of the time. Even the noblest, and most of all the noblest, were subject to these spiritual doubts, and turned away from the visioned good life here toward the promise of the perfect life beyond the grave.

7. NADA

Of all the precursors of the poets of the thirties, it is probably Conrad Aiken who most features the moral terror felt by men in contemplating the emptiness and futility of their lives. I call this moral terror in order to distinguish it from the fear experienced in the presence of physical danger. But it is abundantly clear that the revulsion recorded by Aiken is not, as in other poets, against the evil in men's hearts, their viciousness; that the sense of guilt does not enter into this feeling; and that there is not the faintest hint of what would ordinarily be considered theological implications. This, at any rate, is the case in the volume of poems from which I will take my illustrations, *Preludes for Memnon*, published in 1931. This is, in my opinion, Aiken's most continuously strong and beautiful writing in verse: it is the purest Aiken, in the fullness of his mature power. It is free from the experimental character of his psychological poetry. It never fails to be imaginative in its texture; and it conveys, throughout, a close-knit body of thinking on a central philosophical problem: the nature of the universe and of man's character and experience as part and parcel of the cosmic process.

It is always in relation to this problem — and to Aiken's vision of man's place in the cosmos — that the reaction of fear comes in. And it almost always makes its appearance in connection with aspects of nature and experience that reveal the absolute nothingness of man's life in a world of nothingness. Thus, in the melting beauty of a summer sunset (no. xxvII)

> *we see horrors there*, in a bright light,—
> A misery of waves, — a majesty
> Of incandescent and *defrauding void* . . .

Or the poet has a vision of his coming to "the shoreless shore of silence," where there are no seasons, no light, no time nor space, but "only nothing and the shore of nothing." And "I turned for terror, / Seeking in vain the Pole Star of my thought" (no. xxxIII).

One might say Aiken is here simply describing the emptiness of death, in which there are no senses and no consciousness to give content to the experience. But it is abundantly clear, as the lyrical utterance continues, that the nothingness he fears is not simply death, but the deathlike emptiness of the living experience itself, and all that lies about it. In an earlier lyric of the series (no. xiv), we have the same vision of "that sheer verge where horror hangs"; and in this case, as the poet looks down searching the darkness,

> *It is to self you come,* —
> And that is God. It is the seed of seeds:
> Seed for disastrous and immortal worlds.

This darkness and this horror come to lovers in their most intimate moments, when one becomes aware of "The fierce bright light of horror in the eyes" (no. xxxiv):

> Then it is that the moment falls between us,
> Wide as the spangled nothingness that hangs
> Between Canopus and Aldebaran.

And lover demands of lover how she came (no. liii)

> From darkness to this darkness, *from what terror*
> You found this *restless pause in terror*, learned
> The bitter light you follow. . . .

Or it is a child in the benign loveliness of sunset (no. liv):

> Suddenly he is frightened — for no reason —
> Something mysterious has chilled him, left
> Somewhere an opened door to darkness . . .

And even "god" is subject to the same fright as he contemplates events in the world of his creating. The witch will tell the children, frightened of sunset (no. liv),

> How *god was frightened*, when a pebble fell:
> Covered his eyes, because the plum-tree blossomed:
> And weeps for you, his sons, *who fear to live.*

The revulsion of terror and horror recorded in Aiken is thus almost invariably associated with the sense of nothingness of man's life. This sense of nothingness recurs many times in the course of this volume, with or without reference to the horror that it inspires. And it comprehends not merely men's own being, but the being of the universe as a whole and whatever "divine" power is involved in the cosmic process. We men are compounded of cosmic "accidents" and "idiot trifles" (no. XXIX). We are (no. XLIII)

> The clock that knows, if but it will, its tick
> To be a tick, and nothing but a tick.

The poet says to his neighbors that he has come "From a vast everything whose sum is nothing" (no. LII).

Sometimes he refers to our life as a meaningless interval of brightness between tracts of nothingness. In number XVIII:

> In the beginning, nothing; and in the end,
> Nothing; and in between those useless nothings,
> Brightness, music, God, one's self.

It is true that we, as conscious beings, have the illusion of being, of brightness and meaning. He returns several times to the image of intelligence as an angel, whose being is both glorious and null (no. XXIV):

> treader of bright thought, —
> Your being, which is nothing, in a nothing;
> And yet, are something, and are glorious;
> And make the godhead great.

This angelic thought is really dream-stuff —

> Great golden sum of dream whose truth is zero,
> Zero of thought whose truth is god, and life, —

and it is by virtue of this illusory dream that we wear "A brightness on the forehead of our terror." Sometimes the meaningfulness we feel in life is attributed to "imagination, aping / God," who is both "the supreme poet of delight" and the "supreme poet of despair" (no. XLV).

Aiken has, of course, read his philosophy and is well acquainted with idealistic systems of metaphysics. He can "propound / The subtle thesis of pure consciousness" — only in the next breath to "bow, and leave the world one wit the less" (no. XLVIII). He has in his time "drunk the waters of the absolute" (no. LIII), "Lived on the sea-moss of the absolute" (no. L), tried to answer "The insistent

question of the will-to-be; / The eternal challenge of the absolute"
(no. XLVIII). He knows that the *steeples* point to the absolute (no.
XLIII). But this is for him no more than "false nature in a mask"
(no. XLVIII). Much more insistent than the absolute is the voice
of time, with its continuous alteration of ourselves and everything
in our experience. In the "mid-waste" of his life, in his "dark
forest," trying to look the facts sternly in the face, he bids himself

> Stand, take off the garments time has lent you,
> The watch, the coins, the handkerchief, the shoes,

take off also the illusory "soul," and put aside the whole "Ridiculous chronicle, taste, touch, and smell" (no. XXVIII). He is forever
calling to witness the beauties of nature, the heavenly bodies, the
vegetable and animal life which he shares, and the "senseless rout of
atoms" in which they are all involved. The woman he loves is
"creature of the frost and sunlight, worm / Uplifted by the atom's
joy" (no. LIII). He calls upon the "lords of chaos, atoms of desire"
to hear his "brief cry of memory, that knows / At the dark's edge
how great the darkness is" (no. XXXIII).

I have had several occasions to cite passages referring to "god."
But we must not assume that there is here the remotest implication
of the meanings associated with that term in Hebrew, Christian, or
Islamic theology. Most often, in *Preludes for Memnon*, the word
god is not capitalized; and where it is, it is as if he were putting the
word in quotation marks. One must have some term for characterizing the whatever-it-is that acts (if it does act) on the whole process
of things, be it orderly or chaotic, meaningful or meaningless; or,
perhaps better, for summarizing the whole process. That is often
what he means by god. Or perhaps more often, he uses the term
to characterize the consciousness that man finds in himself and
makes him think he is a self — "It is to the self you came, — / And
that is God" (no. XIV). God is often identical with the angelic "bird
of bright dream," and so again with ourselves in our illusion of
meaningful selfhood. For we know (no. XXIV)

> We are but lightning on a sea of chaos;
> The flash on sad confusion which is god.

Like us, he is Narcissus, contemplating himself in a deceiving mirror (no. XXVII):

> Is there a god who knows and mourns himself?
> It is Narcissus and his glass is truth.

He is associated with the all-destroying process of time, and with the brief illusory flashes of meaning that time brings us (no. XXXII):

> And you, right flash of time, whose gentle hands
> Touch the divine in melody . . .

He is also, as time, the guarantor of final oblivion: "Divine time-thought / That brings the dead man home to underground" (no. XLIII). And since he shares with us the deceptive and flattering power of throwing a light of meaning over what is meaningless, he is finally reduced to the rhetoric that has so long been the bane of poetry. Very near the end of the whole series of poems, Aiken introduces Rimbaud and Verlaine agreeing over their beer that rhetoric is the great vice of poetry and that their one hope is to wring its neck. And the American poet calls upon us to describe that evening as it was, put in their places the atomic order of things, the powers that destroyed Rimbaud and Verlaine — "Time in the heart and sequence in the brain" (no. LVI),

> And let us then take godhead by the neck —
> And strangle it, and with it, rhetoric.

In this powerful set of poems we have, so far as I know, the most thoroughgoing elimination of supernatural religion from our *Weltansicht* that has ever been undertaken in poetry. And not merely that. Aiken seems to me to have eliminated from his vision of the world every last shred of ethical meaning; he has denied reality of any valid kind to our ideas of goodness and badness, either in the brute universe or in ourselves, and landed in the strictest materialism and even nihilism. The implied logical premise from which this conclusion is reached is, baldly, that whatever is passing in time (ideas, motives, acts) is devoid of reality and meaning simply because it does not persist in time. Even the consequences of acts, which may long persist and have some hold on temporal reality, since they may well in time come to nothing permanent, fail to qualify as real and meaningful. This is a premise (with its implied definitions of reality and of meaning) which I have never seen so uncompromisingly stated either in poetry or in philosophical writing, however "materialistic." Not certainly in Epicurus or Lucretius, or in the arrantest atheists of the Enlightenment. At any rate it is a premise the reader is not bound to accept, unless he is ready to agree that the "reality" of any ethical experience or value depends on the length of time that its manifestation endures in the subject's thought.

It is, of course, even harder for a poet to be entirely consistent than for a technical philosopher writing in prose. And it may be that other readers will find in Aiken many failures of consistency. But in most cases, the apparent inconsistency is resolved when we take full account of the author's skeptical irony. Thus he often recommends that, for want of positive faith, we at least look the gorgon full in the face, and die in a kind of triumph of the stern intellect. And this, he says, has its *nobility*. But in the very act of saying it, he takes it back (no. L):

> This were a death
> Noble indeed, enjoined of god, *for those*
> *Who think it noble and enjoined of god.*

It is also true that Aiken, looking into the depths of the human heart, uses terms of it that seem to imply a moral judgment passed upon the rottenness that he finds there. Thus in his own depths, he tells his lady, he finds (no. XXXIV)

> Such speed, such fierceness, and such glooms of filth,
> Such labyrinths of change, such laboratories
> Of obscene shape incessant in the mind
> As never woman knew.

Of his ideal lady, his Helen of Troy, he says that, as a phenomenon of nature, she is (no. XXIX)

> all that she has seen, —
> All filth, all beauty, all honor and deceit,

and that, of necessity she will know

> The lecheries of the cockroach and the worm,

> The chemistry of the sunset, the foul seeds
> Laid by the intellect in the simple heart.

Well, this poet, as a feeling man, is a person of gentle breeding and refined sensibilities, brought up in a Christian community, and is bound to give some ethical coloring to what he finds in human nature. Filth and obscenity and lechery are words referring to a human standard whose violation he shrinks from. But the philosopher in him is well aware that these are words that, in nature, have no pejorative connotation. Filth is simply dirt out of place in our domestic order; what is called obscenity or lechery is an incident to fertility in the animal kingdom; the ethical implications are out of place in referring to cockroaches and worms, and so far as we are creatures of nature, they are out of place for us. Honor and deceit are words of ethical reference; but what he is saying is that, of necessity, one is as much as the other a part of a woman's nature. The naturalistic *reduction* still remains, even when the author bids himself be sternly brave in facing the consequences of his theory.

These poems of Aiken do not strictly belong in my account of the thirties and forties. While they were published in 1931, they may well have been written before the end of the second decade. In any case, they are in the manner of an earlier time. They are characterized by a romantic diffusiveness and directness of statement and a frank indulgence in the old poetical music and rhetoric that had already gone out of style among the critics stemming from Eliot and Pound. And the extreme nihilism of the philosophy is something not characteristic of the later poets, nor is the stoic pride the author takes in his brave facing up to the facts of life. He is at one with them in the sense of horror he has in contemplating the world. But there is in his horror only the faintest tinge of ethical revulsion, and still less of religious feeling, unless indeed it be a lingering vestige of religious feeling that makes him shudder at the nothingness of things. Nor does he, at least in these poems, develop like Auden and others of the later men the psychological explanation of the pervading fear as going back to childhood misdemeanors. But I have included him here because, whether or not an influence on the poets, he does feature so strongly the "moral terror" one has in the face of life.

8. INTIMATIONS OF ELIOT, ETC.

Of our native American poets who took their start in the thirties Horace Gregory was one of the first to feature the theme of fear, though it is not clear how far the word carries in him the psychological, ethical, or religious connotations that it has in Eliot, in Tate and MacLeish, and in Prokosch and later men like Auden, Berryman, and Brinnin. The most striking passage in which this theme appears is in his *Chorus for Survival*, which was first published in 1935 and reprinted in part in his *Poems 1930–1940* (published in 1941) and in his *Selected Poems* in 1951. The passage in question is in the final section, beginning "For you, my son"; it was reproduced as section 16 in the 1941 *Poems* but was dropped out of the 1951 selections. *Chorus for Survival* is a series of episodic poems written at the height of the Great Depression, and is, taken as a whole, an effort to find a way out of the depression of mind which the poet feels at the thought of himself and his fellows, of the United States and the world, in this period of universal economic distress following upon World War I — to find the terms in which one may hope for the return of love to a world of hate, and the survival of those, like the poet, who have striven through all discouragements to "survive, outface despair, / *Terror and hate*" and to "build new fire / At an empty hearth." It is conceived within the general framework of the Whitmanesque tradition of "the American dream" as carried forward in our times by Sandburg, by Hart Crane, and by Paul Engle. But Gregory is not able to maintain the sanguine note of Whitman, Sandburg, and Engle; and addressing himself at the end to his son, as if from the grave, he can only characterize the condition of his own generation as one of fear:

> And this is *fear, fear,*
> The empty heart and the closed lung,
> The broken song . . .

This fear is characteristic of his time, and, as he says, his classmates are "a republic of old men." But the causes and quality of this fear are set in a somewhat different framework from that we find in so many other poets. Clues are given to the causes of fear when he writes of a classmate of his at a "German-English academy" who became a millionaire and took his own life after the crash; when he writes of London as "the dear dead city of ruined stone":

> Better to die
> Than to sit watching the world die
> Better to sleep and learn at last
> That *terror* and *loss*
> Have not utterly destroyed us
> That even our naked shades
> Still looked and talked like men . . .

or of Irish Wicklow and the poverty-stricken man with a broken nose who turned his venomous eye full on the poet —

> that venomous eye
> That is the manhood of my time,
> Whether at home or Wicklow town.

or of the sweepstake dream of millions and cars, and of all those for whom now

> it doesn't pay to work no more,
> until your hands grow cold
> and skin turns gray . . .

He shows the world breaking in him as

> flood, war and hurricane
> enter the narrow rivers of the brain.

They enter the brain, and threaten its extinction, but subside

> in darkness flowing with the warm blood-tide
> until I wake, ageless, the limbs walk free, —
> open my heart to meet my love again.

He refers to the tyrannical rule of the Caesars and the poverty of their subjects,

> There in the circus where they stared: the terror:
> the cry for bread
> and dark sky closed above them.

This is Whitman, singing of himself as the "ageless," prophetic voice of poetry which will survive the vicissitudes of his mortal life; it is Sandburg for whom "It is too early to sing and dance at funerals" ("All I can give you is broken-faced gargoyles") but who will make his appearance to later generations.

> It is early.
> I shall yet be footloose.

This is also, I assume, the spirit who, in section 18 of *Chorus for Survival*, apologizes for his intrusion on a scene that does not welcome such — this section not reproduced in either of the later collections. It is also the frustrated spirit of a New York poet, identified in 1941 as J. O. (James Oppenheim?), who is made to say

> I am the poet of the golden bird,
> The winged bough whose day is always spring,
> Whose fiery chariot is the song unheard
> Leaping the ashes of time's Illium
> From dark to dark . . .

It is also the spirit of Emerson, returned home to his Concord orchard from his visits with Coleridge and Carlyle, somewhat bitter when he thinks of

> The careful millionaire, the red frontier
> In city walls closed; and the hot mills pour
> Iron for guns, starvation, war . . .

But in spite of all that, he is unswervingly attached to his America, he retains his faith in the oversoul, and keeps his smile. For he feels that in his heart he is

> That angry ancient legend of a bird
> Who walked alive eating the ashes of his funeral urn.

And then, finally, this is the spirit that is half of the poet Gregory, the half of him that heeds Whitman's bidding to "loaf and invite the soul," that resists the material temptations to success and ease, and is again in touch with the phoenix-spirit.

> I mean that thing that walked with ancestors,
> and gave us blood, spirit, and god for which men die,
> that made this city and will destroy it,

It is in *Chorus for Survival*, when, we might say, Gregory had not quite found his own voice, that one is most conscious of his sen-

sitiveness to the influence of other poets — call it imitativeness, or
pious deference to great models, or a mere disposition to quotation
and allusion, conscious or unconscious. His verse is very free in a
manner that shows the influence of Eliot and Pound, as well as of
the Imagists. He is very fond of Pound's broken line, and one is not
always certain just how this is meant to serve the poetic effect. The
general method of composition is that of Eliot in *The Waste Land*
and Pound in *The Cantos*. I refer particularly to the interweaving
of themes from literature and history with those of the immediate
subject.

This was indeed a tendency evident in his earlier work, as in his
references to Macbeth, Oedipus, and Cassandra in his poem on hate-
ful New York ("New York, Cassandra," *No Retreat*, 1933):

> Somebody said that Macbeth went insane,
> Leaped thirty stories down to Birnam wood

or again,

> They say Macbeth embezzled funds, the market
> fell too soon, too soon the hands of Christ
> withered on the cross . . .

In this poem there is an even more daring parody of themes from
The Waste Land, with its Shakespearean reference, "Those were
pearls that were his eyes," and its telescoping of literature, legend,
and history,

> (her eyes are flowers
> blowing in the field down where the Lackawanna
>   railroad runs:
> flow softly rivers of coal and steam)

In "Valediction to My Contemporaries" (*No Retreat*) the influence of Crane joins with that of Eliot and Pound both in general
compositional method and in particular themes. We are reminded
of Crane in the rubrics set at the side of stanzas to furnish a gloss, as
well as in subject and rhythm —

> The course of empire westward to Cathay
> rides in the east: the circle breaks in fire:
> these charred remains of what we were expire,
> (O incandescent speed!)

72

In *Chorus for Survival* we are often reminded of Crane, and sometimes of Paul Engle, whose "America Remembers" was awarded the prize for the best poem about the Century of Progress Exposition in Chicago, 1933, by *Poetry*, and appeared in *American Song* in 1934. Thus in Gregory's account of the subway crowds (as in Crane's "The Tunnel")

> Under the stone I saw them flow,
> express Times Square at five o'clock
> eyes set in darkness . . .

Or again,

> Down traffic signals on Park Avenue . . .

With the later reference to the red and green lights, one may have echoes of both Crane and Dos Passos. Or

> Atlantis under hard blue skies,
> Thy Indian Summer bride is like the spring
> Roof-tree in light

Or

> Thou are Atlantis risen from the seas,
> Bride of the Indian Summer and the corn,
> The mountain forest, slow, unwinding plain . . .

In the final section (omitted in the 1951 selection), we seem to have a merging of Crane and Eliot influences, with Eliot dominant in the dream of the frightened millionaire:

> "The banks are broken, Gas has fallen;
> Consolidate Ice and Frigidaire
> Dropped down Chicago River;
> River swimming with rats, the poor . . ."

In section 7 the theme is the return home in hopes of finding the room where the poet was born, only to find that they have changed the name of the street and destroyed the chamber. And here pops up a curious reminiscence of a famous passage in *The Waste Land*:

> Hurry before police unearth the body
> and disclose the name.

The reader will remember

> That corpse you planted last year in your garden
> Has it begun to sprout?

Gregory's police have taken the place of Eliot's Dog, that friend to men. Here we must assume that the irony and the allusion are deliberate and a tribute to the Master.

The influence of Engle (if any) must be found in common items, Lake Michigan, the Dearborn huts, and the cross-bearing Jesuit inevitably encountered by their "forever westward-wandering people." As a strictly poetic influence it is entirely negligible; for Engle is still in what might be called the Whitman-and-Sandburg age of innocence, and while he also knows his Crane, he is not worshiping the same stern models of style and thought.

Whether effective or ineffective, Gregory's use of Eliot-Pound and Hart Crane methods of composition was deliberate, and his quotations and allusions were doubtless generally conscious. But there are echoes of earlier poets about which we do not feel sure that they were not inadvertent. Thus he has evidently been impressed with the curious repetitious arrangement of *face* and *faces*, *meet* and *meet*, in Prufrock's characteristic utterance, rendering so well his halting and irresolute nature:

> There will be time, there will be time
> To prepare a face to meet the faces that you meet.

He likes it so well that he tries his own variation on it in "Cymbalum Mundi" (*No Retreat*):

> Regret, return, do not return, retreat:
> The mouthpiece siren in my ears:
> these faces are too many faces in the street.

And when he has tried this he likes it so well that he must try it once more:

> down mirrors in the hall,
> the face is locked in faces in the street
> in places where all faces are the same.

Again, one does not know whether to assume an actual allusive quotation of Aiken's "Nocturne of Remembered Spring" when Gregory refers in *Chorus for Survival* to

74

> the lilac flowering
> In tombs that open when *remembered spring*
> Comes home again beneath the pine roof-tree.

One is left in the same doubt when, more recently in "Haunted Odysseus" (*Selected Poems*), Gregory makes his hero say that in Hades

> I saw hands reaching toward invisible *fruit*
> That once had *dropped through summer's heat*
> Above them.

Was he consciously paying his respects to H. D. by quoting her famous image in an anthology piece ("Heat," *Modern American Poetry*, ed. Louis Untermeyer)?

> *Fruit cannot drop*
> through this thick air —
> *fruit cannot fall into heat*
> that presses up and blunts
> the points of pears
> and rounds the grapes

Or had this striking image got lost in the deep well of the unconscious, only to emerge on a suitable occasion? And still another slight echo, at least for an old man steeped in Browning. Gregory is clearly quoting Keats's ode when he writes of "Athens, the urn, *Greek bride of quietness.*" But one is not so sure he is consciously quoting when, in "Venus and the Lute-Player" (*Selected Poems*), he makes Venus conclude an account of all she signifies to man by saying

> I am what you seek
> *And all you need to know.*

When Gregory speaks of London as "the *dear dead city* of ruined stone," has he actually forgotten, or never known, that in "A Toccata of Galuppi's," Browning dramatized himself as speaking to a player of old music about old Venice and its women:

> *Dear dead women*, with such hair, too — what's
>   become of all the gold
> Used to hang and brush their bosoms? I feel
>   chilly and grown old.

75

Or does he suppose that he can give another turn of the screw to these two adjectives by transferring them from dead women to a dead city?

It may seem captious on my account to pick out these instances of unconscious or ill-considered borrowings of what were good things in the original. It is something that any poet might do. But this sort of thing, where it is not brilliantly exceptional, is likely to give to poetry — as it gives to painting or music — a weakening air of the derivative. Eliot has certainly produced moving effects and deepened the tone of many passages in his writing by deliberate quotations from the classics. But this is a dangerous weapon in the hands of any but a very strong poet, and often makes his followers have the look of epigones.

9. THE FORMLESS TERROR

Meantime, Auden and Isherwood, in their symbolic drama, *The Ascent of F6*, had rung almost all conceivable changes on the psychological character of fear. The dangerous ascent of the mountain is clearly regarded mainly as a means of facing down fear by a resolute show of courage. The leader of the expedition, Michael Ransom, says of one of his followers: "David's always frightened when he climbs. Otherwise he couldn't climb. *Being frightened is his chief pleasure in life*." Of another companion, Ian, it is said: "You see . . . the ascent of F6 represents, for Ian, a kind of *triumph*, which he not only desires, but of which he's desperately *afraid*." As for Michael himself, there are numerous suggestions that his liability to fear is a part of the silver-chord complex. In one scene, his mother at home communicates in an extrasensory manner with Ransom. He is on the height facing the Demon of the mountain, and Mrs. Ransom whispers: "Michael darling, can you hear me? here, there. . . . It's all right. . . . There's *nothing to be frightened about*. Mother's with you. Of course she won't leave you alone, Michael, never. . . . Of course you'll get to the top, darling. Mother will help you. . . . Wasn't she with you from the very beginning, when you were a tiny baby? Of course she was! And she'll be with you at the very end . . ." Here the voice of Ransom is heard, very far off, frightened: "It's the Demon, Mother!" And his mother replies in rhyme:

> Michael, you shall be renowned,
> When the Demon you have downed

She promises to build him a cathedral and give him a lovely clean bed.

> You shall be mine, all mine,
> You shall have kisses like wine,
> When the wine gets into your head,
> Mother will see that you're not misled;
> A saint am I and a saint are you,
> It's perfectly, perfectly, perfectly true.

In another passage, Lady Isabel accuses Ransom of being afraid. But he replies: "I am afraid of a great many things, Lady Isabel. But of nothing which you in your worst nightmare could imagine." Obviously, Ransom's fears are of nothing so material as a steep mountain and death at the top.

This is true of fear wherever it pops up in this play. The Demon is, in his various subtle disguises, "*the formless terror in the dream*, the stooping shadow that withdraws itself as you wake in the half-dawn. . . . You have felt his presence in the sinister *contours of a valley* or the sudden hostility of a copse or the *choking apprehension* that fills you unaccountably in the middle of the most intimate dinner-party." Even for the mediocre people who stay at home fear is "the *menacing throb of our hearts*." People welcome heroic leaders in order "to be delivered from the *terror of thinking and feeling for themselves*." Because people desire evil they can thus enter the themes of guilt and unbelief. There is, says Ransom, "the *web of guilt* that prisons every upright person and all those thousands of thoughtless jailers from whom Life pants to be delivered — myself not least; all swept and driven by the possessive incompetent fury and the *disbelief*."

During the decade beginning with 1936 our poetry is particularly troubled by what Prokosch calls "the drumbeat of our governing fears" ("The Baltic Shore," *The Assassins*). In an earlier section we have found the theme of terror constantly present in his poems along with the many other symptoms of a decadent world — "the *final dreading / Of history ending*, an end to living and *terror spreading*" ("Going Southward," *The Assassins*). In many of the following sections we shall be brought back to this theme under other headings.

In *Death at Sea* ("Elegy")

> Stray figures on the boulevard suddenly
> Rising out of the twisted fog appear
> Like Aeschylean figures, hurled by a
>   *nameless fear.*

They are all driven by a fever of the spirit, which we "cannot localize," cannot even see or hear ("The Reapers," *Death at Sea*). In Robert Penn Warren we shall find the theme recurring in connection with his "Ode to Fear" and his "Letter from a Coward to a Hero." In Eliot's *Dry Salvages* we read of the haunting

> backward look behind the assurance
> Of recorded history, the backward half-look
> Over the shoulder, towards *the primitive terror.*

And we shall see how he dealt in *Murder in the Cathedral* with the various horrors that call for definition. Horace Gregory is early in the field, in his *Chorus for Survival*, characterizing for his son the era between wars that begins with bank failures and the Chicago River swimming with rats and culminates in a morally debilitating fear:

> And this is fear, fear,
> The empty heart and the closed lung,
> The broken song.

The theme of fear is naturally not confined to our American poets. It was strongly sounded in the forties by others of the English poets associated in the American mind with Auden. Thus Spender, in "The War God" (*Ruins and Visions*, 1942), reflects the psychological view of Auden and Prokosch that the conqueror

> Is an instrument of power,
> With *merciless heart hammered*
> *Out of former fear,*
> When to-day's vanquished

Destroyed his noble father,
Filling his cradle with anguish . . .

This highly involved set of figures, with their psychological analyses of fear, suggests both *Hamlet* and Blake's "Tyger," as well as the psychologizing poets of our day. The noble father must be Hamlet's, and the hammering of a merciless heart out of fear takes us straight back to Blake's poem.

And what shoulder and what art
Could *twist the sinews of thy heart*?
And when thy heart began to beat
What dread hand and what dread feet

Could fetch it from the furnace deep
And in thy horrid ribs dare steep
In the well of sanguine woe?
In what clay and in what mould
Were thy eyes of fury roll'd?

Where *the hammer*? Where the chain?
In what furnace was thy brain?
What *the anvil*? What dread grasp
Dare *its deadly terrors clasp*?

In "The Separation" Spender represents union with the loved one as the sole means of salvation for a man in our tragic times.

Shuttered by dark at the still centre
Of *the world's circular terror*,
O tender birth of life and mirror
Of lips, where love at last finds peace
Released from *the will's error*.

Error sounds much like a "rhyme word." And indeed it is a word that no poet can resist when looking for a word to chime with terror. Auden could not resist it, nor, as we shall see, could so fine and fastidious a poet as Hugh Chisholm. But in all three cases, the word *error* exactly suited the poet's deeper intention. For all these poets are agreed that the world's circular terror of our time is a product (and cause) of men's perverse willfulness. This is the case also with Day-Lewis in his "Ode to Fear."

But now, coming back to the American scene, we may briefly

note the appearance of the fear theme in certain other American poets of the forties. In Nemerov's "Trial and Death: A Double Feature" (*Guide to the Ruins*), we have a deep and subtle meditation on the psychological effect on our audiences of scenes of violence in the movies. His conclusion is that "these show murders gain a mortal weight."

> Our shrouding screen will shatter under wounds,
> And *horror drill the eyes in every head*
> *So deep the dry Platonic mind must bleed.*

And this is a stage in what he calls "the agon of our star."

Even more impressive on repeated readings are the references to fear in the poetry of Hugh Chisholm. In his "Elegy for All" (*The Prodigal Never Returns*, 1947), he compares the present disturbed mechanical age with the earlier quaint ages of faith and innocence and feudalism, and notes that, with all our new inventions, we

> who hear tenderness down a telephone,
> *inherited the terror of the heart*
> in spite of all our brilliant facts and figures . . .

In his "More Omens in the Evening," he associates the unsatisfactory experience of lovers hiding in the wood, whose emotion is as much hate as love, with the soldiers.

> singers marching in columns,
> Curling through olives and coiling their *uniformed terror*
> In and about the private heart of the evening.

Has it always been thus with lovers, he asks,

> Always the loins' insinuating,
> The leperous hope, the flight, the hating
> Heed of the lovers hiding in the wood?
> Always and always? and *the terrors,*
> *The trite contrition for the errors*
> Made and remade and never understood?

And he returns in the final stanza to the theme of inherited fear. After the days keyed to the lark's singing,

> Look at your lads, the lords, the critics,
> The great, the gods, the syphilitics,
> *Expert in fear, the lucky heirs that were.*

One grows tired of giving an account of poems with the citation
of mere fragments. And here I crave permission to set down an entire poem of Chisholm's, making the plainest and most moving statement of the spiritual state of a generation of men who were still
young at the conclusion of World War II. It is called "Lament of
the Lovers," and gears in with poems already referred to. But while
its overt subject is love with the heart gone out of it, it is really an
account of life with the heart gone out.

> We are already sick to death with death
> Who lived our youth between wars with a life
> That looked to count the bricks around the hearth
> And catch the twelve leaves on the autumn heath,
> To cut the pages with a paper knife.
>
> This latest year is bewitched, befouled, beloused,
> The old songs have no teeth, no eyes, no hair,
> The old roads twist and teeter and get lost,
> And ivy covers over even the least
> Resemblance here to there, to anywhere.
>
> Now only the old remember smatterings of glory,
> Moments and men and places touched with good;
> Only the old, the very old and weary
> Are near enough to the womb to hear the worry
> Of thunder under the clouds and under the wood.
>
> And the old are too young to care about a cure.
> And the young are too young to recognize a past,
> Too old to sing soprano in the choir.
> Despair is on the air, and across her sere
> And crooked landscape dying travels fast.

This poem seems to me eminently worthy of being given entire,
not merely for its pertinence to our theme, but because of the sureness of its artistry — the simplicity and directness and forward
movement of its statement, the fine selectiveness and evocativeness
of the items in the imaginative build-up (especially in the first two
stanzas), and the manly force of the poet's assertions about the
young and the old. (The poem is distinctly of our time, with no
suggestion of the special rhetoric or sentiment of the Victorians,
and at the same time it does not carry the manifest stigmata of cur-

rent fashions.) Though myself so far removed in age from the poet, and unable to verify from personal experience the emotional attitudes expressed, I still do not find them more exaggerated than good art and the situation call for, and am not aware of that self-conscious forcing of the note (or attitudinizing) which so often does impress me in poetry of this period.

In the case of Malcolm Brinnin, the references to fear and allied emotions are more controlled than usual by a resolute determination not to be swept off his feet in the general panic and landed in a philosophical bog. The dilemma is most acutely pointed up in "The World Is a Wedding" (*No Arch, No Triumph*), a poem dedicated to Delmore Schwartz and taking its title from a short story and a book of short stories by Schwartz. Brinnin candidly acknowledges that the prevailing horror is real and justified, and that it would be sentimental to deny it.

> *Wearing the stitch of horror on his heart,*
> Who can so dispossess himself to say,
> "In the midst of war there is a brotherhood,"
> And be not damned, and be not self-accused?

But still the world he envisages is one, though in the midst of crime and counter-crime "where justice shapes its final symmetry." His comfort is drawn from Shakespeare, who "retired from all tragedy, does not weep, but with a grim and rakish eye . . . *walks through our terrors at the side of Marx.*" So far as one can make out from his later writing, Brinnin has given up Marx for his walking companion, and has gone on, somewhat less bravely, with some more "spiritual" guide.

But in his period of "making faith," Brinnin realizes that fear is a dangerous malady, and one to be avoided if we are to look with a clear eye on the history with which we are confronted. In "Girl in a White Coat" (also *No Arch, No Triumph*) he takes his lesson, apparently, from an army nurse. In her ministrations to the crippled and wounded, he sees what humanity can do "against the imminence of atoms," and in her he loves "all that our faith must find, or wisdom give." In her "the local miracles come true,"

And manics whose important grief
Threatens their lives with years of stone
Read in your eyes *the excellence of life
Unfalsified by fear*, untaught by pain.

Here we return to the idea (of Prokosch, Spender, and the early
Auden) that fear itself may be a main cause of our tragic situation;
and more resolutely than Prokosch, Brinnin warns himself against
yielding to the falsifications of fear.

And now we are ready to take up a distinct new topic, but one
which in many cases involves a further effort to interpret the moral
implications of fear.

The coming of World War II was naturally the occasion for
much earnest reflection on the subject of fear. But in my reading of
poetry provoked directly or indirectly by the catastrophe of war,
I was impressed with the fact that fear seldom made its appearance
as the animal reaction to physical danger, either in the trenches or
still less in the accidents of travel at home. Almost always what the
poets were concerned with was the generalized moral fear to which
men are subject on searching their hearts; the political and economic aspects of contemporary history giving way to what we may
broadly call its "spiritual" aspects.

Thus it is in several reflective poems of John Berryman written
in the crucial years 1939 and 1940, to be found in his *Poems* (1942)
and *The Dispossessed* (1948). In "The Dangerous Year" (1 March
1939) he begins with the thought that we have so far in the United
States "come safely with our children, friends," though trying at a
distance

To make out the intentions of that man
Who is our Man of Fear

The Man of Fear is presumably Hitler, at least on the surface level
of meaning. But it may be that he is intended on a deeper level to
mean ourselves. For Berryman goes on to ask whether our sense
of safety is not temporary and in the end illusory. It is time, he says,
to forget the tinsel of our Christmas trees,

Forget the crass hope of a world restored
To dignity and unearned dividends.

Joseph Warren Beach

> Admit, admit that now *the ancient horde*
> *Loosed from the labyrinth of your desire*
> *Is coming as you feared.*

The dangers and miseries of the war become a symbol for all the dangers and miseries to which men are subject and which are the fruit of their own desires. Thus the perilous world situation of our times is at bottom a spiritual condition for which we are personally responsible. And he goes on to say that, while we need courage to meet the situation, courage is not enough. What we most need is spiritual insight.

> It's time to see how far you have been blind
> And try to prop your lids apart before
> The midnight of the mind.

This same solemn moral is further developed in "A Point of Age" (dated Detroit 1940). The somewhat cloudy theme of this poem is the need for a young man to move on from the city of his adolescence in strenuous ("Odyssey") pilgrimage toward some more mature and spiritually satisfying goal. At the end of the first section he says it is late and time to start:

> Settle the civic woe, deal with your dear,
> Convince the stranger: none of us is well.
> We must *travel in the direction of our fear.*

I cannot pretend to explain all his meaning in this context. But he is clearly suggesting that we are all suffering from some spiritual malady; and in saying "We must travel in the direction of our fear," he is doubtless carrying out the logic of the earlier poem. The evil that we fear is the fulfillment of our own wishes, and our spiritual quest must lead us toward the discovery of that within us to which we have been blind. The traditional hero, formidable to his enemy, is not what is here required, when in the violence of the storm he begins

> The climb, the conflict that are your desire.*

This line can best be understood by referring back to *The Ascent*

---

* In the later version of this poem in *The Dispossessed*, it has been variously, and not always happily, "improved"; and this line appears without the helpful comma: "The climb the conflict that are your desire."

84

of F6, where the "climb" is essentially represented as a means of facing the underground fears of the several climbers in the very act of facing their overt fears, and where the final chorus declares of one of the dead climbers:

> Free now from indignation,
> Immune from all frustration
> He lies in death alone;
> Now he *with secret terror*
> And every minor error
> Has also *made Man's weakness known.*

David's climbing was motivated by his liking for his fear. "Being frightened was his chief pleasure in life." For Berryman's hero, presumably, the fear in the climbing was prized because it makes man's weakness known, and so leads to a salutary self-knowledge. The poet goes on to ask:

> The animal within the animal
> How shall we satisfy? *With toys its fear,*
> With incantation its adorable trust?

Obviously not, is the answer. What will satisfy the questing hero at any rate is a knowledge of himself. And he takes the world conflagration for symbol of the moral conflagration that rages in the individual.

> All that a man has wished and understood
> Is fuel to the holocaust he lives:
> It spreads, it is the *face of his desire,**
> The tongue teeth eyes of your will and of mine.*

Here again one fancies one can trace an interesting line of filiation in literary symbolism leading back by three stages from Berryman to Joseph Conrad. Holocaust is "a burnt sacrifice; a sacrificial offering in which the whole is consumed by fire" (Webster). And the conflagration described by Berryman, caused by our desire and will, is instrumented by the destructive element of fire. In *The Ascent of F6*, perhaps under the influence of the Abbot on the mountain, the leading climber expresses himself in highly religious terms: "Oh, You who are the history and creator of all these forms

* In *The Dispossessed*, "It spreads, it is the famine of his desire."

in which we are condemned to suffer, to whom the necessary is also
the just, show me, show each of us upon this mortal star the danger
that under His hand is softly palpitating. Save us, save us from the
destructive element of our will, for all we do is evil." Thus Michael
Ransom, in the course of the climb, of the conflict that was his desire. "Destructive element" is indeed an image provocative of many
different meanings. For Stephen Spender in his volume of criticism,
The Destructive Element, it denoted one idea, and it denoted still
another to Stein, in *Lord Jim,* who said: "In the destructive element
immerse." It is at least amusing to consider the several possible suggestions in literature lying back of Berryman's holocaust that was
"the tongue teeth eyes of your will and mine."

In still another early poem, "At Chinese Checkers" (Grand Ma-
rais, 1939), Berryman was much occupied with the topic of fear.
Playing at Chinese checkers with young people, he asks himself
how we should

> counsel the unhappy young
> Or young excited in their thoughtlessness
> By game or deviltry or popular song?

And then he goes on to say most cryptically:

> Too many, blazing like disease, confess
> In their extinction *the consuming fear*
> No man has quite escaped: the good, the wise,
> The masters of their generation, share
> That pressure of inaction on their eyes.*

Here, alas, one finds oneself almost hopelessly baffled in one's effort
to read some plain meaning in these lines. How much in this is symbol and how much literal fact? Are the "blazing" and "extinction"
literal or figurative? Do they refer to young men in ordinary civil
life or to young men gone to lose their lives in war? And what is
the "pressure of inaction on the eyes" of the good and wise? Does
it mean that in the present holocaust of passions (the war in
Europe), the good and wise are forced to inaction by their consciousness that all military action is immoral? All that seems clear
is that the *consuming fear* which no man has quite escaped is that

---

* In *The Dispossessed:* "This pressure of inaction on their eyes."

moral horror of thinking men at the sight of a world immolating itself on the altar of its own unholy passions.

What makes it peculiarly difficult to make sense of these lines is that nothing in the context, the action of the poem, serves to throw light on these seemingly irrelevant observations. Perhaps it is in this poem that one is most conscious of Berryman's besetting sin — sin against the reader (a scornful disregard for communication); sin against poetic art, for which he has so great a talent if he would only not so hide it under a bushel. It is a many-faceted matter. There is, to begin with, the hopeless confusion between the direct and the oblique modes — between the literal and the figurative. There is the way of putting things together without indication of their relevance to one another. And this involves the habit of allusion, not to things of public note as in Eliot so much as to things known only to the poet and a few intimates — we might call it the private allusion. And along with these and related to them is Berryman's proneness to the eccentric and individual use of words, "dictionary words," as where a little later he says that, bewildered, he sees

> burnt faces rise and fall
In the recapitulation of their urn.

All this one writes in sorrow; for even in the course of this perversely obscure poem there are strains of arresting music, touches of real feeling, and an imaginative development that would add up to something important if the poet did not constantly so insist on being "different."

I will not try to list all passages in Berryman relevant to our theme, but content myself with one further example, from a poem later than the others considered, "Rock-Study with Wanderer." This is to be found in *The Dispossessed*, and apparently refers to the period immediately following the end of the war, when our foreign officers were still being gay in Europe, though that continent was no more now than a "ravished doll," while poets and thinkers had not yet found any reason to be more complacent with the state of the world, either political or spiritual. This present poet scans the horizon for signs of a political order more conformable to his ideal than any we have seen in the century of the great wars.

Joseph Warren Beach

> When shall the body of the State come near
> The body's state stable & labile? When
> Irriding & resisting *rage & fear*
> Shall men in unison yet resemble men?

For readers who do not have at their elbow an unabridged dictionary, I will note that according to Webster, *irrid* is obsolete for
deride, and that for *labile* the definitions most applicable here are
not "liable or prone to slip," nor yet "unstable in emotion or behavior," but rather "characterized by adaptability to change or
modification," or, more simply, "plastic."

10. DEFINITION OF TERROR

In the preceding section we have noted how, in recent American
poetry, the words *fear*, *terror*, and so on seldom refer to the emotion experienced when a man steps on a rattlesnake, wakes to find
himself in a burning house, or confronts an enemy in battle. The
fear that has concerned our poets is rather something not necessarily felt in the presence of imminent danger. It is a state of mind
more or less constantly present with us, carrying wide and involved
psychological or even religious implications, inviting the poet to
interpretative study. The present section is partly a continuation
of that theme. Only, here I would like to illustrate the proneness of
our later poets, in connection both with fear and with other subjects, to favor the words *define* and *definition*. I will begin with the
poet who uses the word *definition* most appropriately and unaffect-
edly in its context, and in poems of such unfailing imaginative
power that the slight taint of the metaphysical that clings to the
word is lost in the splendor of the total effect. This is Robert Penn
Warren, whose *Eleven Poems on the Same Theme* (1942) has left
many traces on subsequent American poetry.

I would not venture with confidence to pronounce the one word
which states the theme around which all these eleven poems revolve,
it is a theme so many-faceted, with half a dozen themes intricately
interwoven. Perhaps the word that best promises to lead naturally
into all the subsidiary themes is *guilt*, or, to use the term that makes
the title of one of the poems, *original sin*. Perhaps a shade better is

88

sense of guilt, for it is the (often vague and half-conscious) feeling of guilt that is in question rather than the positive fact of guilt. And the subsidiary themes are most helpfully phrased in pairs of opposites: guilt and innocence, or innocence and experience; time and eternity, as in "Bearded Oaks," since it is in time that guilty experience is had, and only in "eternity," beyond experience, that innocence may be recovered. And then, considering what it is that lures us forward out of innocence.into experience or guilt, we have the paired themes of happiness and peace, or to cover them both, "what the heart wants." There are also the related themes of heroism and cowardice, of courage and fear. These moral themes have their illustration, naturally, in such human activities as love and war and crime. And our concern with them here is primarily in connection with the frequent appearance of the idea of definition. To begin at the very center of the web, "what the heart wants," we find this developed with extremely subtle psychology in "Crime," where we are asked to envy "the mad killer who lies in the ditch and grieves." I will not attempt to deal with the psychological niceties of this subject, but come straight to the passage that is central for our study. What was it that led him to his crime; what is it, his hideous treasure, buried under the leaves, which he is too tired to remember?

> Happiness: what the heart wants. *That is its fond*
> *Definition,* and wants only the peace in God's eye.
> Our flame bends in that draft: and that is why
> He clutched at the object bright on the bottom
>   of the murky pond.

Is Warren thinking of Dante's theory that all men are drawn by the love of God, but in what they do are drawn aside by perverse conceptions of what it is they seek? The definition of what the heart wants is fondly given as happiness, whereas what the heart wants in the final analysis is the peace in God's eye.

In "Revelation" our word *definition* appears in connection with love. This poem deals with the discovery of love — of something important about it — by a child who has committed the offense of speaking harshly to his mother. This act of insubordination was followed for the boy by a preternatural and ominous illumination and animation of everything in nature — landscape, flora, and fauna. The description of these effects is one of the most beautiful and awesome of passages in American poetry, though frequently matched in Warren, and is one thing that by itself ranks him among the finest of contemporary poets in English. The present effects for the boy make him, or the poet, think of the supernatural omens of disaster in Rome when Sulla smote, as recorded by Saint Augustine, and in Dunsinane at Duncan's death. But his mother's kindness made of this frightening experience an apocalyptic revelation of the blessedness of love.

> But, oh! his mother was kinder than ever Rome,
> Dearer than Duncan — no wonder, then Nature's frame
> Thrilled in voluptuous hemispheres far off from his home;
> But not in *terror*: only as the bride, as the bride.

> *In separateness only does love learn definition.*

Love, as we all know, reaches its fulfillment in togetherness. That it should learn its definition, come to know itself, only in separateness is also a deep truth, but is one of those startling paradoxes loved by the seventeenth-century English poets even when they were not given over inveterately to the metaphysical system of writing. Warren was deeply immersed in seventeenth-century poetry at the time he wrote the poems in this volume and many of those that appear in his later *Selected Poems* (1944). His "Variation: Ode to Fear," however "modern" it is in detail and in its tone of wit and humor, is obviously modeled consciously on Herrick's "Litany to the Holy Spirit" — in form, in use of its refrain, in the frequent lines beginning with "when" ("When I lie within my bed"; "When I read in Charles A. Beard"), and, when all is said, in much of its substance and feeling. "Love's Parable" is metaphysical in its title and, all through, in its conceits and paradoxes:

> Love's mystery, then still unspent,
> That substance long in grossness bound
> Might bud into love's accident.

This is one of Warren's poems that becomes almost wearisome in its confinement to the intellectuality of the metaphysical mode. More generally, almost always, in Warren, the sheer play of intellect is duly subordinated to the imaginative effect. He may not be as "simple" as Milton would prescribe for poetry; but sensuousness and passion carry the day over geometry and wit.

In "Revelation," when he says, "In separateness only does love learn definition," he is consciously taking up the word of Marvell when he entitles one of his poems "The Definition of Love." In this poem Marvell is for him more than usually metaphysical all through, and the modern reader is inclined to think he is merely playing a parlor game with his subject; whereas in "Revelation" one is convinced that Warren takes his subject seriously, as more than an occasion to exercise his wit.

I cannot help feeling that "the definition of love" is a locution more in keeping with seventeenth- than with twentieth-century usage. However, our recent poets are not in agreement with me, either in England or the United States. The English Ronald Bottrall has a very fine and unmetaphysical poem, "Definition of Love" (*Farewell and Welcome*, 1945), in which he sets forth his notion of what goes to the making of an ideal marriage. W. S. Graham has an (unintelligible) "Definition of My Brother" (Kenneth Rexroth, ed., *The New British Poets*, 1949). Auden was characteristically early in the field, in the poem numbered x in his *Poems*, 1930:

> Love by *ambition*
> Of *definition*
> Suffers partition
> And cannot go
> From yes to no.

Warren perhaps, in all of his *Eleven Poems*, is concerned primarily with the definition of the virtues and vices invoked in our ethical theory — whether guilt or innocence, courage or heroism. In his *Selected Poems*, he uses the term in connection with *innocence* and *courage*. In concluding his tragic "Ballad of Billy Potts," he reflects on the tragic irony of this life-stained hero coming back

in the end to the innocence of "home" to find his death at the hands
of an old and evil father:

> And you, wanderer, back,
> For the beginning is death and the end may be life,
> For the *beginning was definition* and the *end may
>   be definition*,
> And our *innocence* needs, perhaps, *new definition*,
> And the wick needs the flame
> But the flame needs the wick.
> And the father waits for the son . . .

Here I have my own notion of what is meant by saying that the
beginning and the end are or may be definition, and that innocence
may need new definition. But I don't feel at all sure that my notion
corresponds to the poet's intention. And I wonder whether defining
the poet's word *definition* may not here require more translating
from one level of meaning into another than is generally the case
with dictionary definitions and more than is favorable to securing
the best poetic effect.

Perhaps this is also the case in Warren's "Ransom." Here he is
speaking of the continuing evil and violence in the world.

> What wars and lecheries! and the old zeal
>   Yet unfulfilled, unrarefied, unlaced.

He alludes to the unregenerate "Gerontion," evil old man: "At
night the old man coughs." Like Arnold in "Dover Beach," he addresses his "love" with such comfort as he can in view of the melancholy prospect of the world.

> Defeat is possible, and the stars rise.
> Our *courage needs*, perhaps, *new definition*.
> By night, my love, and noon, infirm of will
> And young, we may *endeavor definition*;
> Though frail as the claspéd dream beneath
>   the blanket's wool.

Well, let us not here put up pedantic objections! Taking this literally, as if it were prose writing, it is hard to see how the word
courage can have any other meaning than what it has for all of us
today according to the dictionary definition: "that quality of mind
which enables one to encounter danger and difficulties with firm-

ness; valor; boldness." But assuming the plain license of the poet, we may readily take this phrase, "new definition of courage," to mean redefinition, or new statement, of the grounds for courage, or new determination of what things are the gravest menace to man and most call for courage in meeting them. Then it is possible in religious terms to find grounds for courage not otherwise available, or to define *courage* as the quality of mind required for meeting spiritual dangers. Considering the allusion to Eliot's religious poem "Gerontion," and considering the ordinary religious implications of the title "Ransom," this would seem the most plausible interpretation. Perhaps to the strictly Christian reader, my explanations are not merely plausible but quite superfluous.

The context in Warren in which this idea of definition is most magnificently embodied in circumstance and imagery is the poem named "Terror." And it may be partly because so much of the imagery is taken from heroic exploits of early American volunteers in the war that this poem has so impressed other contemporary American poets. The poem begins with the difficulty heroic great men have in finding satisfaction for their thirst for dangerous adventure, which is for them the form taken by that universal "what the heart wants," whose "fond definition" was happiness. The fighting men in this poem are those who seek "what the heart wants" only in facing fear, like the climber in *The Ascent of F6*, of whom it is said: "David's always frightened when he climbs. Otherwise he couldn't climb. Being frightened is his chief pleasure in life." This is the sort of masochism that drives American volunteers to fight in foreign armies, in Spain or in Finland, and it does not matter on which side they are enlisted. In the North

> They fight old friends, for their obsession knows
> Only the immaculate itch, not human friends or foes.

It is a form of onanism, like the fury of the mobs worked up by the dictator demagogues in the Piazza or the Wilhelmplatz.

> Blood splashed on the terrorless intellect creates
> Corrosive fizzle like the spattered lime,
> And its enseamed stew but satiates
> Itself, in that lewd and faceless pantomime.

Nothing in civil life "suffices" their need, and they resort to the mere mechanical terrors of war, since they were "born to *no adequate definition of terror*."

We are here reminded of a striking passage in Eliot's *Murder in the Cathedral* (1935). While the knights are killing the Archbishop in the church, the chorus of old women exclaim over the special horror of the deed. They are accustomed to the fears of ordinary life:

> The terror by night that ends in daily action,
> The terror by day that ends in sleep.

But these sacrilegious acts mark a limit to their suffering.

> *Every horror had its definition*,
> Every sorrow had a kind of end:
> . . . .
> But this, this is out of life, this is out of time,
> An *instant eternity of evil* and wrong.

There are many distinguishable kinds of horror corresponding to the circumstances that arouse them, and many of them have no moral or religious character, since they involve no wrongdoing. But killing is a mortal sin and the killing of a priest arouses the special type of horror attaching to sacrilege.

It is possible that Warren is consciously alluding to Eliot's saying. At any rate he is here making a similar distinction among the occasions for terror. These men obsessed with the craving for deadly terror are not concerned with the moral, the human character of their killing: "their obsession knows / Only the immaculate itch, not human friends or foes." They were born "to no adequate definition of terror." And there follows a stanza in which he develops this idea. Their notion of fear is that of such trifling dangers as a kitten sucking a child's breath while he sleeps, so that he dreams of drowning. Some have not been satisfied with such tame fears, but have sought

> That immitigable face, whose smile is ice,
> And fired their hearts like pitch-pine, for they thought
> Rather flame than the damp worm-tooth of compromise.

One is here reminded of the sort of grotesque and ineffectual "hants" that, in "Original Sin," beset the uneasy but not terrified man wherever he goes. Nowhere is a state of mind embodied for the imagination in such an impressive, appropriate set of images as in Warren's account of the various forms taken by the man's bad conscience. It is not the consciousness of some particular sin that troubles him, but a vague diffused sense of guilt, perhaps inherited, but never coming to that intensity that would require that something be done about it. It

> . . . never came in the quantum glare of sun
> To shame you before your friends, and had nothing to do
> With your public experience or private reformation . . .

It is not involved with your love of women and children. It is something "out of life," "out of time." Its terror is subliminal, and is never resolved by a definite repudiation of "compromise."

This obscure sense of guilt is one side of the unfulfilled quest for happiness, or peace, referred to in "Crime," so impressively imaged in "Pursuit"; for purity and hope, so brilliantly dramatized in "Pursuit." In Warren's poems the prime desideratum for the spiritual life would seem to be this notion of a terror which can be adequately defined only in terms of a faith, according to which the most terrible thing we have to face is the evil within our own breasts.

II. THE WORD DEFINITION

Warren has been, and I suppose aptly, characterized as a religious poet, and his religion elaborately analyzed and identified with that of orthodox Christian theology. Whether he would agree to that identification I cannot tell. He has had his influence on contemporary poets of various doctrinal stripes.

The extended meaning of the word *definition* that we are considering is doubtless to be found in more poets of the forties than have come under our microscoping scrutiny. It appears, for example, in a rather late poem of Wallace Stevens, an illustrious holdover from the earlier decades. This poem is entitled "Examination of the Hero in a Time of War" (*Parts of a World*, 1942). There is nothing obscure or strained in Stevens's use of the word. He is forever defining and refining upon concepts which other people take for granted, and in a single poem he will use every type of imagery and of verbal formulation in the effort to track down the elusive essence. Here is the hero he is trying to define — not the hero as he is in his prose actuality, but as he exists in our imagination and our feeling. He has tried various metaphors or images; but then, he thinks, an image will not suffice:

> It is not an image. It is a feeling.
> There is no image of the hero.
> There is *a feeling as definition*.

The only way to get at the very essence of the concept, hero, is to define the feeling that we have for him. This, we must recognize, is as an entirely natural and felicitous use of the word *definition*. But it is doubtful whether it would have seemed natural in American or English writing of our century much before the year 1940.

A younger contemporary of Warren's who has made lavish use of locutions involving the words *definition* and *define* is John Malcolm Brinnin. It is quite certain that Warren had priority in the special use of these words, and it seems highly probable that Brinnin took up this use from Warren. Warren was well known for his poems published in "little magazines" in the middle twenties and for his volume, *Thirty-Six Poems*, published in 1935. In this volume Brinnin might have found *definition* in its extended sense in "Ransom" and *define* in "Letter of a Mother," where the poet speaks of a son "defined upon the superscription" of the mother's letter. *Definition* was used in striking contexts in "Crime" (published in the *Nation* in May 1940), in "Terror" (*Poetry*, February 1941), and in "Revelation" (*Poetry*, January 1942). All these uses antedate the publication, in 1942, of Warren's *Eleven Poems on the Same Theme*, and of Brinnin's *The Lincoln Lyrics* and *The Garden Is Political*, in which volumes the use of these words is at its peak.*

* *Eleven Poems on the Same Theme* was No. 3 of the Poets of the Month, and appeared presumably in March; *The Lincoln Lyrics* made No. 7 in this series, and appeared presumably in July; *The Garden Is Political* came out

The last instance I have noted of the use of the word in the poems of either Warren or Brinnin is in Warren's "Adieu Sentimentale," which appeared in *Voices* for September– December 1951.

Warren and Brinnin were almost certainly well acquainted with each other's poems, which often appeared in the same reviews and little magazines, sometimes in the same number. The most significant of such simultaneous appearances is that of Warren's "Terror" and several of Brinnin's Lincoln lyrics in *Poetry* for February 1941. The words in question do not appear in these Lincoln lyrics. But what is most significant in this connection is Brinnin's "Martha Graham," which appeared in the *New Republic* for May 26, 1941. In this poem Brinnin employs, in a single phrase, two of the words that Warren had most strikingly used. Of Martha Graham's dancing Brinnin says, rather cryptically, *"Pursuit has met its definition."* Flight-and-pursuit has all along been one of the leitmotivs of Warren's thinking. It made an early appearance in "Monologue at Midnight," where he refers to the belling of the windward hound and adds, with arresting brevity, "Then *what pursuit?*" Pursuit appears again as the subject and title of one of Warren's most forceful pieces in the volume of *Eleven Poems.* "Monologue at Midnight" (with its "pursuit" theme) was first published in the *Virginia Quarterly Review* for July 1936, and *definition* was already in print in 1935. It is a near certainty that both of these words were caught up by Brinnin from his reading of an admired contemporary, the distinguished poet and critic and editor of the *Southern Review.*

It was witty in Marvell to attempt a definition of love. When Warren suggests an adequate definition of terror or a new definition of innocence he is leading us into wide and rewarding fields of ethical speculation. When Eliot speaks of distinguishable horrors each with its own definition and of others which are "out of life," "out of time," he is saying something that speaks to the imagination

presumably in April, being advertised in the April 25 number of the *Saturday Review*. Some of the *Lincoln Lyrics* and the poems included in *The Garden Is Political* appeared in periodicals in about 1940 and in *Accent, The Best Poems of 1940.* But of those in which the words *definition* and *define* are used, I have only been able to trace "Martha Graham" from these original publications.

and the mind. When Brinnin (in *The Lincoln Lyrics*), thinking of
how noble words are used to justify crime and how

> Our law's anatomies of freedom like
> Anatomies of death, live deep in uncut
> Indices.

goes on to say that

> while innocents meet headsmen
> In the dawn, *those dusty definitions* serve
> Power and the taskmaster on wheels,

we are able to make out, without extreme difficulty, that the dusty
definitions refer to the neglected legal formulations of our consti-
tutional freedoms, and we remember that seventeenth-century poets had both. The general context and the title of the poem — "Liberty for Whom?" — suggest that he may be speaking of Negroes
under our free system of government. Somewhat more complicated
and farfetched is the use of the metaphor when Brinnin speaks (in
"Childhood and Wilderness," *The Lincoln Lyrics*) of the pioneer
children who learn the language of nature and to distinguish between hard fact and sentimental fancy:

> as clever with an axe
> As with *green definitions*, they will unlearn
> Bird-talk and daisies, accept the sober night.

This is farfetched enough. But what can you make of saying, in
connection with an allegorical mountain climb, that "definition
was that mountain" ("The Ascent," *The Garden Is Political*); or
that, in connection with Martha Graham's dancing, "pursuit has
met its definition" ("Martha Graham: A Dedication," *The Garden
Is Political*)? What can be meant by saying "The sun survives, and
many definitions / Meaning wonder"; or "The dignity of elegies /
Defines a premonition more valuable than praise"; or speaking of
"that commotion elegies define" ("A Salient of War," "Second
Sight," and "Mardi Gras," all in *No Arch, No Triumph*)? A mountain was definition? or definition was a mountain? Pursuit meets a
definition? Definitions meaning wonder? Elegies define a premonition, or a commotion?

The contexts sometimes help a little. In "The Ascent" Brinnin borrows from Auden and Isherwood the allegory of a mountain climb to plant a flag on the summit. He does not take over the psychological point of the play in relation to fear. He seems to use the mountain climb to symbolize the character discipline which a young man may secure by seeking higher things, overcoming difficulties, and shedding on his way the illusions of adolescence ("all the golden chateaux that he built"). Well, "whatever mountains meant / Before was tottering and uncertain."

> But definition was that mountain;
> Ubiquitous and blunt the rocky stair
> That drew the tyro there
> Equipped and now long competent with want.

The rocky stair was presumably ubiquitous because the mountain is defined as, or symbolical of, discipline wherever it is found. This is indeed moving mountains with a vengeance. "Competent with want," because discipline uses deprivation to develop character and competence, and the mountain is defined as discipline! Q.E.D. Then there is something about ruined castles and a new-appearing "rim of unique towers, structure / Of revealing future" — a structure, that is, that points to a better social order to come. For, we must assume, the man who learns discipline through climbing, he and the "love" he addresses are symbolic of the race that will realize the new social order.

As for Martha Graham and the definition of pursuit, I have quite given up any effort to trace the underground course of figurative associations there. In "Death of This Death" (*The Garden Is Political*), I think I can do better. The poet is, I believe, speaking of soldiers who have met their death in war, and who have made blueprints of a better world.

> Their *maps define*
> *The possible dominion of the free,*
> A calm community
> That, flowering in the culture of decay,
> Turns death to seed within our living day.

One would not quarrel with this, though it does take a little development of the terms used. Archibald MacLeish has a poem entitled "Definition of the Frontiers" (*Actfive and Other Poems*, 1948), where the words are put together strictly in accordance with familiar usage, and another in the same volume, with the same figure of speech, "Geography of This Time," in which he says:

> What is required of us, Companions, is the recognition
> of *the frontiers across this history*, and to take
>   heart: to cross over
> — to persist and to cross over and survive

It is clear enough in this context that the poet is recommending boldness and imagination in our ideology, and such progressiveness in action as will enable us to survive in a world of change. And it is clear, in "Definition of the Frontiers," that he is speaking of the line that divides our friends and foes, the former being able to distinguish among the ambiguities of character and opinion. For there are animals that belong to neither side.

> There are also the unnatural lovers the distortion
> of images the penetration of mirrors and the inarticulate
> meanings of the dreams. . . .

> Finally there is the evasion of those with whom we
> have come. It is *at the frontiers* that the companions
> desert us — that the girl returns to the old country
>   that we are alone.

This is didactic poetry, but it is all done in the oblique mode. The terms are all metaphorical or symbolic; but they are carried through with perfect consistency, all referring to the key symbol, definition of frontiers. And there is no violation of the conventions governing the meaning of words.

In Brinnin, the procedure is more pretentiously oblique. The maps of these cartographers of Utopia set down in its proper place and shape the country which the poet calls "the dominion of the free." They do not strictly define this territory, though they may properly be said to define its frontiers. To conform to prose usage, one would have to say, "define the frontiers of that country," or find some other way of stating what maps do for a territorial area. This is an instance of the telescoping of words so modish in certain poetic circles. But Brinnin is meaning more than this. He is taking advantage of the ambiguity of the word *dominion*. It may refer to a country, as in the Dominion of Canada; but it may also refer to the *dominance* of a class, as here in "the dominion of the free." Only, language has to be considerably strained to speak of *defining the dominance*. And of course this represents more telescoping; to make it clear to the grammatical-minded reader, it would have to be developed in some such way as this: These maps of the ideal free polity (or *blueprints* as he elsewhere calls them) outline (if you like, *define*) the nature of the ideal state or the conditions under which it can be realized. There are plenty of cases in which such telescoping, skillfully used, may be vastly more effective than the plain prose statement and subtend a wider arc of human interest or "truth." But it takes a genuine rare poetic instinct to do this effectively, and the poetic instinct means, for one thing, a strict sense of how ideas are naturally associated and of how words may best be used for adumbrating this association.

When Brinnin writes ("A Salient of War"),

> The sun survives, and many definitions
> Meaning wonder, meaning more than words
> May say,

one feels he is being guided less by a true poetic instinct than by the fascination of a modish word, which has rather lost its gloss. For example, there is this: "the living sign / Of that commotion elegies define" ("Mardi Gras"); there is also this: "The hand that lifts to action lifts to love / And will in its own definition live" ("Meditation on Tombs"); and finally: "The dignity of elegies / Defines a premonition more valuable than praise" ("Second Sight," all from *No Arch, No Triumph*), where he is admonishing us that elegies (reflections invoked by the deaths of heroes) look forward, if one has faith and a will to action, to "life in its plurality" (the ideal community).

I will not further strain the reader's patience with the strained use of this word in Brinnin, whether in the nominal or the verbal form, but simply refer him, for other instances, to the 24th, the 25th, and the 35th of *The Lincoln Lyrics*. In Brinnin's later volume

(*The Sorrows of Cold Stone: Poems 1940–1950*) from 1951, I have not observed instances of this use of the word.

1 2. SCATTERED INSTANCES OF DEFINITION

The case of Brinnin might suggest that this word *definition* has already run its course in our poetic age and is already falling into decay. But a few scattered citations will indicate that it is still in favor and may still be used with considerable appropriateness and effect and without any straining of linguistic usage. Howard Nemerov has an interesting poem, "Unscientific Postscript" (*The Image and the Law*, 1947), in which he develops an idea similar to those that so much occupied Wallace Stevens. It has to do with the distinction between the objective world of "things as they are" and the "dream" world of the Platonic cave where we see only the reflections on the wall and the forms we see are "neither real nor false nor subject to belief," but have the shining surface of an orchestral flare of "life." The poet is taking, I should say, a purely aesthetic attitude toward the show of things.

> It is not to believe, the love or fear
> Or *their profoundest definition, death*;
> But fully as orchestra to accept,
> Making an answer, even if lament,
> In measured dance, with the whole instrument.

We can readily apprehend how death is the profoundest definition of love and fear. It is what they both come to infallibly, and in that sense it defines them as mortal entities. Nemerov may well be taking advantage, too, of the ambiguity of the word *definition* by virtue of its affinity with the adjective *definitive* and the adverb *finally*. For obviously death is the most profoundly definitive of things, taking *definitive* in its first dictionary meaning, "serving to decide or settle something finally." The worst one could say of Nemerov's conceit is (along with the poem) that it is smart but not quite Stevens; the best one could say is that it is profound; the justest thing to say is that it is original, provocative, and witty.

Berryman, in "The Spinning Heart" (*The Dispossessed*), has a serious and ironical poem on the appearance in our age of the "triumphant animal." Among his instances of this species is

> Easterfield the court's best bore, *defining*
> *Space tied into a sailor's reef* . . .

If you are looking for one word to "define" this variety of animal, "l'homme moyen sensuel," you have but to name Easterfield, the court's best bore. As for "court," you can take your choice between tennis court and the royal court that always has its clown. The poem is quite good of its kind, and Berryman's conceit is in keeping with the tone of the whole.

In Mona Van Duyn's "Death by Aesthetics," earlier referred to in connection with her invocation of *ceremony*, reference is made to the doctor's "machinery of definition," an apt characterization of his instruments of diagnosis, and this too falls in well with the tone of the poem. Our word was still in favor in the year 1954, when this poem appeared in *Poetry* magazine.

So it seems that this word still has its appeal to our poets and they are still capable of giving it a witty or provocative turn. It is not yet clear how long or useful a life it has before it — nor how soon it may come to be shunned by those most in the know as smacking of cliché.

Here the joke is certainly on the writer of this pedantic treatise. He is himself a writer of poems, which he would devoutly hope to be original and as free as possible from affectation and cliché. He had long been conscious of the danger lurking in this word. But what was his horror, on completion of this section, to receive a magazine containing a poem of his own, and to discover that in the course of this one poem (rather long, to be sure) he had twice used the now cliché word *definition*! Naturally, he has tried to persuade himself that there is nothing obscure or strained in his use of the word. But for all that he cannot fail to be red in the face at finding himself in such a box.

13. PAYSAGE MORALISÉ

In the preceding section it was the topic word *fear*, in its character-istic psychological and moral sense, that led us into our discussion of the modish word *definition*; and it was in connection with *fear* (or one or another of its various synonyms) that we found this word *definition* most impressively and provocatively employed. In much of what follows, the word or concept *fear* will again be found closely associated with the particular symbol or topic word that we shall be considering, whether it be *island, journey, frontier, exile,* or whatnot. The word *fear* (*terror, horror*) is likely to be bound up in some relationship with each of these other words, and they are also likely to be linked together in a chain of association that leads from one to another. And thus the web of thought and image that characterizes the period in poetry begins to take form and con-sistency. We shall begin with a set of associated symbols for which Auden has given us our most suggestive phrase, *paysage moralisé.* This phrase appears as the title of a poem in sestina form included in the *Collected Poetry* (1945). It was one of the poems wisely chosen by Auden to be carried on from his earlier volume *Look, Stranger!* (1936), or *On This Island* (as it was entitled in the Amer-ican edition of 1937). In the earlier volume it appears without title simply under the number VII. But this poem was written at least four years earlier, and was published in the July 1933 number of the influential English literary magazine the *Criterion*. Here it took its title from the first line. Considering its importance as an influence upon later English and American poets, as well as its unmatched beauty in Auden's work, it seems desirable to give the poem in its entirety:

Hearing of harvests rotting in the valleys
Seeing at end of street the barren mountains,
Round corners coming suddenly on water,
Knowing them shipwrecked who were launched for islands,
We honour founders of these starving cities
Whose honour is the image of our sorrow,

Which cannot see its likeness in their sorrow
That brought them desperate to the brink of valleys;
Dreaming of evening walks through learned cities
They reined their violent horses on the mountains,
Those fields like ships to castaways on islands,
Visions of green to them who craved for water.

They built by rivers and at night the water
Running past windows comforted their sorrow;
Each in his little bed conceived of islands
Where every day was dancing in the valleys
And all the green trees blossomed on the mountains
Where love was innocent, being far from cities.

But dawn came back and they were still in cities;
No marvellous creature rose up from the water;
There was still gold and silver in the mountains
But hunger was a more immediate sorrow,
Although to moping villagers in valleys
Some waving pilgrims were describing islands . . .

"The gods," they promised, "Visit us from islands,
Are stalking, head-up, lovely, through our cities;
Now is the time to leave your wretched valleys
And sail with them across the lime-green water,
Sitting at their white sides, forget your sorrow
The shadow cast across your lives by mountains"

So many, doubtful, perished in the mountains,
Climbing up crags to get a view of islands,
So many, fearful, took with them their sorrow
Which stayed them when they reached unhappy cities,
So many, careless, dived and drowned in water,
So many, wretched, would not leave their valleys.

It is our sorrow. Shall it melt? Ah, water
Would gush, flush, green these mountains and these valleys,
And we rebuild our cities, not dream of islands.

By adding the title "Paysage Moralisé" in his *Collected Poetry*, Auden reminds us that the geographical or landscape features of this poem are meant to be taken in a symbolical and moral sense. But some of our poets had already realized this intention, and certain of the words recurring at the line-ends of this poem in accordance with the scheme of the sestina have been taken up by them and used in similar symbolic senses, with variations corresponding to the temperaments and moral maps of the several authors. I have not come on any full explication of this poem, and must attempt to make my own hesitant interpretation. But in this one is greatly helped by Auden's own use of the terms in later poems.

In an article on "The Dominant Symbols in Auden's Poetry" (*Sewanee Review*, Summer 1951), Professor Monroe K. Spears has given a brief, suggestive explication of the symbols used in this poem; but his statements sometimes need development and qualification in the light of this poem itself and of later poems in which the symbols appear.

This is particularly true of the mountain, which, according to Mr. Spears, stands for "action, decision." This is a meaning which could not easily be inferred from the present poem. We find that the mountains here are distinctly forbidding; and the reason for this seems to be that they are colored by feelings of the same deluded people who dream of islands instead of setting to work to rebuild their cities. The mountains are barren; they cast a shadow over the lives of those who dwell in valleys and cities; and they are places where men perish. On the other hand, there is treasure of gold and silver to be had in the mountains, and those who dream of islands can imagine them as green with trees (but this is illusory).

The mountains are indeed something of a challenge to those who look upon them. They are, for example, a challenge to climb, and as Mr. Spears notes, "mountains, because of their association with frontiers . . . suggest responsibility for decision, fear, difficult action and achievement." The only images in "Paysage Moralisé" that carry this suggestion are those of the gold and silver the mountains bear, and that of men reining their violent horses on the mountains. Men do penetrate the mountain passes in defending the homeland, or carrying the war into the enemy's country (and from that post they may survey both the alien and the home country): thus we have references in the early *Poems* to "control of the passes," to "the crux of the watershed," and to those who "crossing the pass descend the growing stream." But the actual frontier or border symbol is seldom if ever associated with mountains, as we shall see in our discussion on frontiers.

Mountains are indeed a challenge to the mind, and they make an appeal to those craving strenuous action more than to the passive and self-indulgent. In his "Letter to Lord Byron (IV)" (*Letters from Iceland*, 1937), Auden sees on the unrolled map of his youth "the *mental mountains* and the psychic creeks." But the mountains are by the same token "sterile" and "immature" ("Journey to Iceland"). They are also "ascetic" (*The Dog beneath the Skin*), and as such imply certain forms of escapism, to which the psychically sick resort.

> Some have adopted an irrefragable system of beliefs or
> a political programme, others have escaped to the
> ascetic mountains
> Or taken refuge in the family circle, among the boys on
> the bar-stools, on the small uncritical islands.

It is clear that, in this case, mountains are associated with asceticism as one avenue of escape from the universal fear, or *Angst*, to which guilt-ridden self-indulgent mortals are subject. In the same psychoanalytical vein, in *The Ascent of F6*, we have seen that the heroic Britons who made the arduous and dangerous ascent of a useless mountain on the borders of a British colony (urged on by politicians in their pride of nationalism) were personally motivated by their psychotic fear of fear, and their leader by a morbid condition produced by the silver-chord complex.

There is indeed one poem of a later date, cited by Mr. Spears, that presents the mountain in a more favorable light as symbol of the free choice of strenuous action enjoyed by natives of Britain. In this sonnet published in the *Listener* in November 1938 Auden speaks of the Northerner's craving for the easy life of the South.

> Wandering lost upon *the mountains of our choice*,
> Again and again we sigh for an ancient South,
> For the warm nude ages of instinctive poise,
> For the taste of joy in the innocent mouth.

But this softer, more archaic, life of the South, he goes on to say, is not for us.

> We live in freedom by necessity,
> A mountain people dwelling among mountains.

In this case the mountain life is indeed ascetic, but only in the sense of hard and self-denying, and as a condition for the political and moral freedom so highly prized by the British.

In poem xx of *Look, Stranger!* we have a variation on this view of mountains and the climbing involved, stressing the more effort required if we are to get beyond the ascetic or merely disciplinary phase (and its own self-indulgence) to the ideal life of men living socially. Here the speaker, "Fleeing the short-haired mad executives, / The subtle useless faces round my home," seeks to make his escape from this mechanical, morally indifferent way of life by "climbing the mountains of fear." It is an arduous climb, destined to take him across the passes to "the rich interior" country where one will find the good life free from fear. But this climber did not reach his destination. For he was going up with a companion, with whom climbing was easy; but when they reached the top,

> it was eyes we looked at, not the view;
> *Saw nothing but ourselves*, left-handed, lost:
> Returned to shore, the rich interior still
> Unknown. Love gave the power, but took the will.

In the general frame of Auden's writing, I take this to mean that the wrong kind of love, the private self-regarding love, prevented the companions from realizing the good life as conceived of in communal terms.

This view of the mountain climb as disciplinary, and as leading to the right kind of love and the right communal society, is found in Brinnin's poem "The Ascent," as I have earlier indicated in the section on *definition*. And I have there indicated how, starting perhaps from Auden and Isherwood's *Ascent of F6*, but without following up Auden's suggestions about psychotic motivations, Brinnin interprets the mountain climb in terms more conformable to Auden's symbolism in the last two poems considered. He defines the meaning of mountains in terms of social discipline.

> This path was *puritan*
> *And stern*, a real unkodaked
> Version of the challenge, sovereign fact.
> Climbing was the thing! Ascent accomplished
> More than all the *insular heart* had wished.

The insular heart was the heart like that of the lovers in Auden's poem just cited who looked at eyes and missed the view; and it will lead us shortly to Auden's island symbolism.

As for valleys, these are in "Paysage Moralisé" wretched places where the harvests are rotting, inhabited by moping villagers, who, for all their wretchedness, will not leave their valley homes. And they are places to whose dangerous brink sorrowing men are brought in desperation. But they are also variously conceived of as places "where love was innocent, being far from cities," where (on islands) there was dancing every day, and where if our sorrow would only melt, there would be greenness.

Turning to other uses of *valley* in Auden, we have, in *Poems* 1930, a reference to mountain climbers

> From the first dawn coming down
> Into a *new valley with a frown*
> Because of the sun and *a lost way*.

Again, in poem XVI, Auden, anticipating the "death of the old gang," sees them left "in *sullen valley* where is made no friend" — where the old gang refers to the thoughtless self-indulgent "lovers" not yet awakened to the strenuous obligations of the new day. In the "Epilogue" to *The Orators*, in apparent reference to the evils of our industrial system, we have "That valley is fatal when furnaces burn." In *The Dog beneath the Skin*, we have, more significantly for Auden's symbology, a reference to a man "ashamed / In the hour of crisis, / In the *valleys of corrosion*." In his "New Year Letter" (*The Double Man*), Auden speaks of the dominance in current society of "brotherhoods without belief" and "a butch and criminal elite,"

> While in *the vale of silly sheep*
> Rheumatic old patricians weep.

And again, valleys are roads, paths to precipices, but the signposts are illegible. The valleys are "silent" and we cannot "guess in what direction lies the overhanging precipice." In *The Ascent of F6*, still more suggestive is an account of a symbolic valley, which we might take to be the valley of spiritual death. For the speaker, the mountain-climber Ransom, says he is paying the "homage paid by the living to the unqualified and dangerous dead." He is descending to "the valley and all its varieties of desperation." These are then enumerated: "the calculations of shopkeepers under the gas-flares and the destructive idleness of the soldier; the governess in the dead of night giving the Universe nought for behavior and the abandonment of the prophet to the merciless curiosity of a demon; the plotting of diseases to establish an epoch of international justice . . ." Does he refer to germ warfare? It is all reduced to the "web of guilt that prisons every upright person."

The passage from which I have made these quotations is perhaps the most comprehensive and withering summary characterization of the spiritual emptiness and desperation of the modern world (as so many of our poets have conceived it) to be found in our poetical literature from Eliot down to Kenneth Patchen. The statement here is made in prose and without elaboration. It does not have the imaginative vividness of Eliot's *Waste Land*, nor the sustained funeral-march solemnity and detailed evocation of scenes and conditions that we find in Prokosch's poems and novels. (I have spoken earlier of the brisk hopefulness given to Auden's tone by his early Marxian doctrine and the lightening of the tragedy in him by an irrepressible wit, irony, and humor.) But it contains the germ of much poetizing in him and his American contemporaries.

There is perhaps an echo in Brinnin of Auden's "sullen valley," his "valleys of corrosion," his valleys where the harvests are rotting. And Brinnin's "rusted valley" carries a similar social doctrine. In "Second Sight" (*No Arch, No Triumph*) Brinnin, recommending action as against romantic indulgence in self-regarding sentiment, beginning at home with the task nearest, indicates how he may help save society from its decadence:

> The man of loving action, shouldering his paradox, signs
> For *the rusted valley* where his voluntary hands may claim,
> In time, their salvaged province.

The particular Auden symbolism of valleys seems not to have much impressed the poets who followed. There are, perhaps, some echoes in Prokosch, especially in *The Assassins*, where, as in his novel *The Seven Who Fled*, valleys are pretty uniformly places of mournfulness and desolation. In "The Voyage," which pictures a journey across more and more desolate regions until "we" come to "the world's long boundary" and nothing is left but "stars like snow on the endless prairie and a sea of snow," one stage of our journey takes us to a region where we hear "the whimpering of steers in the *yellow valleys*." "The Masks" is a still more frightening picture of the people one encounters in a survey of humanity which ends with the importation of opium to bring relief and Europe growing slim and pale. It begins with what sound like two lines right out of Auden's "Paysage Moralisé,"

> Some sit by ferns and *gaze across their valley*
> Counting the swallows loving on the gravel.

But it is in "The Sacred Wood" that the image of valleys appears in close association with Auden's key words *islands*, *dreams*, and *terror*, but with a musical, romantic build-up characteristic of no one in our day so much as Prokosch himself. What he is here evoking is the imaginative "Garden beyond all seas and hurricanes," with its groves of passion. What it most suggests in an earlier time is perhaps Böcklin's famous picture of "the Island of Death," which might have been seen by Prokosch as a schoolboy in Munich.

> What land is this? This land
> Is the land you have dreamed of, darling.
> Don't you remember those pale towers, those long
> And serpent channels, those tall rocks, *those valleys*
> *Fringed with our fears*, those *silent foam-entangled*
> *Islands?* This is the *empire of our dreams* . . .

Joseph Warren Beach

We shall come back to this collocation of symbols when we take up the symbolism of islands.

As for the end-word *sorrow* in Auden's sestina, we need simply say that it stands here for the universal distress of spirit with which, in a day of general unbelief and spiritual despair, men regard the *condition humaine* in general as well as their own particular want of happiness and satisfaction. It is this sorrow that has brought men desperate to the brink of valleys, has made them long for islands where every day was dancing in the valleys, which produces the sterility of mountains and valleys, but from which, if it only would melt, water would gush, flush green those mountains and these valleys.

The passage most difficult of interpretation occurs in the first and second stanzas.

> We honour founders of these starving cities
> Whose honour is the image of our sorrow,
>
> Which cannot see its likeness in their sorrow
> That brought them desperate to the brink of valleys

The clue to this, I believe, is the distinction between two kinds of sorrow, the public and the private. The sorrow of the city founders is public or social. Our sorrow is private or egocentric. It is too blindly self-regarding to see its likeness in their sorrow caused by the failure to realize their ideal for their cities. As for the line "Whose honour is the image of our sorrow," I can make no sense of this without resorting to some unplausible paraphrase, and must leave it to the greater acuteness of some other reader.

Prokosch has, in *The Carnival* ("Ode VII"), his own version of the predicament of those who live in the (spiritually) starving cities:

> What they desire is a god, and the old simple power
>   To send their implacable chorus of thoughts
> From the fragile and singular body out to the theatre
> Of *the collective father*. To trust and forget.

This poem ends with what is perhaps an allusion to Auden and Mac-Neice.

112

For it is the unfulfillable
Command to be loved which has now driven the vision
Out to the desert *and Iceland* and into the sea

Even less need be said of the end-word *water*. It is, of course, the same water of the spirit — the Biblical "water of life" — for want of which the desert of life is a Waste Land. "If there were water . . . but there is no water." This has deeply impressed all poets. It had appeared before Auden. In *The Hamlet of A. MacLeish* the melancholy Dane is repelled by the foreignness and miscomprehension of Rosencrantz and Guildenstern. They will not reply to his questions. They do not seem to "fear this place as I fear it."

As for the place I go to—
we seek water.
The water here is salt. We have seen neither
Birds nor green leaves since we found this country.

In Auden the sorrow of those who come to the city is comforted by the sound of water running past windows. Some of them believe that the gods come to them from islands across the lime-green water. And many, misled, careless, had dived and drowned in water. We may even be reminded of Eliot's ambiguous "death by water."

14. CITIES

And now we have left to gloss the two words that are the master keys to the symbolism of "Paysage Moralisé," *cities* and *islands*. It is clear from the concluding tercet that these terms are antithetical. If our sorrow is to melt (with, presumably, its causes), water would gush and make the earth green, "and we *rebuild our cities, not dream of islands*." Cities represent the ideal commonwealth, and their builders are to be honored. They are places of learning. The ideal is not fully realized and cities become starving and unhappy; they become dilapidated and need rebuilding. It is natural for their sorrowing denizens to dream of islands where there is dancing and greenness: they imagine lovely gods who come from islands and invite you to return with them across the water; there are always pilgrims describing these places of dreams. Some villagers are too apathetic in spite of their wretchedness to undertake the journey. Of those who do undertake it, many perish in the mountains, many but take their sorrow to other unhappy cities, many are drowned in the life-giving water (perhaps by their own will, like, say, Hart Crane). The thing to do is not dream of islands but rebuild the city, restore the social ideal.

This ideal is implicit in the many poems included in the 1930–1933 volume of *Poems*, in the 1932 *Orators*, including the "Journal of an Airman," and in the 1936 volume *Look, Stranger!* But in most of this body of poetry, the author is mainly occupied with the ruinous old order and with the personal discipline necessary for those lonely revolutionary spirits who were training for the struggle to reform it. His most frequent imagery is taken from the country and its neglected industrial works — "derelict ironworks on deserted coasts," "silted harbours," "strangled orchards," "shut gates of works." The poem in which both the industrial ruin and the moral decadence of Britain are spelled out in fullest detail and with the greatest heat is one not reproduced in the *Collected Poetry*; it is no. XXII in the 1933 edition of *Poems*, beginning

> Get there if you can and see the land you once were
> proud to own
> Though the roads have almost vanished and the
> expresses never run.

The specific symbolism of the ideal city is hardly to be found in this period except in "Paysage Moralisé." Where cities are mentioned, it is the actual cities of a world that denies the ideal. It is "our city — with the byres of poverty down to / The river's edge," a city "Built by the conscience-stricken, the weapon-making, / By us" ("Epilogue," *Look, Stranger!*).

It is in the years in which the threat of World War II became intensified that the ideal city of the earlier poem recurs as the Just City. In "Spain 1937" (*Another Time*, 1940) Auden, turning his back on the civilization and the superstitions of the past, and leaving in abeyance the hopes of the future for scientific research, for the expansive free pursuit of the arts and of love, insists upon the one immediate demand for militant action for the present political salvation of Spain. It is the life-force itself that speaks, urging the ego to constructive action in place of dreams and dilettantism. The life-force addressed the ego, offering it its choice.

> "What's your proposal. To *build the Just City*? I will.
> I agree. Or is it the suicide pact, the romantic
>   Death? Very well, I accept, for
> I am your choice, your decision: yes, I am Spain."

In the play *On the Frontier* written by Auden in collaboration with Isherwood (1938), the hero and heroine are citizens of rival nations at war. They are lovers separated by national dissensions but united in their dream of a world in which frontiers have been obliterated, and in the fight that each one wages for the ideal commonwealth. The piece ends with a dialogue between the spirits of these two devoted characters, one of them already in his grave. Anna speaks of those who in the darkness of Europe have worked to master necessity, and Eric defines the thing they have worked for —

> To build *the City where*
> *The will of love is done*
> And brought to its full flower
> The dignity of man.

One remembers St. Augustine's City of God; one remembers human dignity as the dominant ideal in Malraux's *La Condition humaine*. Anna goes on to ask pardon for the mistakes of these city-builders who "suffer for our sakes" and to conjure us to "honour, honour them all." And Eric concludes with the statement:

> They die to make man just
> And worthy of the earth.

In the poems that accompanied Auden and Isherwood's report on their trip to China in 1938, *Journey to a War* (1939), Auden contrasts the actual cities of his time, whose citizens "believed in nothing," self being their "one city," with the now fading dream of "the Good Place" and "the Juster Life," to which they are summoned by "the voice of Man,"

> Till they construct at last *a human justice*,
> The contribution of our star, within the shadow

> Of whose uplifting, loving, and constraining power
> All other reasons may rejoice and operate.

It is clearly totalitarian doctrine, as represented by Italy, Germany, and Japan, that is here identified as the most notable enemy of the truly Just Life; but it is totalitarianism that makes the most vociferous claims to this. Their propaganda declares that "Man can have Unity if Man will give up Freedom," and bids men:

> Leave Truth to the police and us; we know the Good;
> *We build the Perfect City* time shall never alter;
> Our Law shall guard you always like a cirque of
>   mountains.

It is against this fascist notion of the Perfect City that the voice of Man counters with its humanistic ideal of "a human justice" to be constructed as the special "contribution of our star."

The distinctive humanism of this passage has been overlooked by interpreters of Auden; and it is perhaps Auden himself who is responsible for this oversight. For in reprinting his poems "In Time of War" in the *Collected Poetry*, he made certain alterations obviously intended to give a distinctively Christian cast to poems not having that cast as first written and published. In the four concluding lines of the "Commentary" quoted above, the words *justice* and *whose* were both capitalized, and for "other reasons" in the last line the poet has substituted "human reasons." So that the lines now read:

> Till, as the contribution of our star, we follow
> The clear instructions of that Justice, in the shadow
> Of Whose uplifting, loving, and constraining power
> All human reasons do rejoice and operate.

In this altered form, the justice referred to is definitely that of divinity, and its reason is set in contrast to the merely and subordinate *human* reasons for cultivating justice.

In his article on Auden's poetry (see p. 106 above) Professor Monroe K. Spears has traced the further development of the city symbol in Auden, as the poet's secular humanism gives way before an orthodox Christian view of the world, as mere human love (the Freudian Eros) proves more and more inadequate to the establishment of social justice, and yields to the mystical Agape, following the dictates of the Logos, and as the dream of a Just City upon earth gives way before the assurance of justice in the City of God. One feels that he has been somewhat misled, so far as the earlier volumes are concerned, by the assumption that Auden, in this early period, was identifying all forms of nonreligious love with the Freudian Eros, and so with sexual love. It is certainly obvious that Auden from the very beginning was opposing mere self-regarding love (and so mere sexual love) to the love of one's fellows that leads to social well-being; or, say, the isolating self-indulgent love to the altruistic love of one's fellows. It is not until 1940, in his poem "In Memory of Sigmund Freud" (*Another Time*), when Auden was in transition to Christianity, that he contrasts "Eros, builder of cities" with "weeping anarchic Aphrodite." I see no advantage in reading psychoanalytic psychology into the earlier poems. The distinction that Auden here makes between selfish and unselfish love is something familiar enough in any humanistic system of thought.

Where he deals with Auden's work from 1939 on, Mr. Spears is more convincing and illuminating. He indicates the elements of uncertainty (as between secular and Christian views) in "New Year Letter, January 1, 1940," and the other poems of the same volume (*The Double Man*). He very plausibly suggests that "Auden's complete and final commitment to Christianity apparently took place in 1940." He traces the city symbol in *The Age of Anxiety* and, most distinctly of all, in a number of poems later published in *Nones* (1951), especially "Memorial for a City" — where Auden reviews the pagan city of antiquity, the New City (with a double meaning, secular and mystical) of the Christian order, the Rational City of the French Revolution, and finally the "abolished City" of our postwar condition, and leaves us at the end with a view of "Adam waiting for His City" (which is, of course, the heavenly City of God).

The transition from secular to religious is represented in "New Year Letter." Auden is now trying to do justice to both Head and Heart as guides to knowledge. Hence the title of the volume, *The Double Man*, referring to the duality or division in our nature described by Montaigne in the epigraph: "We are, I know not how, double in ourselves, so that what we believe we disbelieve, and cannot rid ourselves of what we condemn." This involves a slight modification of the associations attaching to the city symbol. This is felt in the concluding lines of "New Year Letter" by anyone who has read the poem through:

> O every day in sleep and labor
> Our life and death are with our neighbor,
> And love illuminates again
> *The city* and *the lion's den*
> The world's great rage,* the travel of young men.

In the Prologue to "New Year Letter," Auden has "the *philosophic city* where dwells / The knowledge they cannot get out of." But an explication of this ingeniously intricate poem would require a section by itself; and in any case, this philosophic city is more a city of the mind — and of the mind turning religious through doubt of itself — than it is the ideal commonwealth of the secularist. Auden is beginning to lose heart for the secularist vision, and if humanism is the faith that resists the seductions of Marxism on the one side and supernaturalism on the other, this is a faith which Auden seems not to have attained. This is, at any rate, not the Auden who furnished so many texts for the poets who followed him during the thirties and forties.

Among his followers it is Brinnin who most clearly reflects the city symbolism of the earlier Auden. This appears in the conclusion to "The Ascent," where the city is represented by "a rim of unique towers, structure / Of revealing future." But it is more unmistakable in the concluding lines of "Death of This Death" (which appeared in the *Virginia Quarterly Review* in the Spring number for 1941, and then in *The Garden Is Political*, 1942). The poet is here reflecting on the deaths of young men in battle and (like Hemingway in an impressive prose piece) on the unmistakable ugliness of their corpses, which gives the lie to the numerous apologists for war, whom he identifies with apologists for our lamentable social

---

* Obviously a punning distortion of, and slightly ironic commentary on, Shelley's "The World's great age begins anew."

order, with "their godlike reasonings for war and slum." He seems to suggest that the present war (in 1940) is a holdover from the obsolete "necromantic past," with its death's head like King Charles ("King Charles, and who's ripe for fight now?"). But he does admire the spirit of young men who are ready to defy death for an ideal. And the ideal worth dying for is that commonwealth which Auden envisages under the symbol of the Just City.

> Praise, then, the young whose cloudless willing hands
> *Blueprint a shoal of cities*, dear to turn
> From rotting acres of the dispossessed
> To meet life's penalty. Their maps define
> The *possible dominion of the free*,
> A calm *community*
> That, flowering in the culture of decay,
> Turns death to seed within our living day.

15. ISLANDS

We have already seen that, in "Paysage Moralisé," islands are opposed to cities as futile and self-indulgent dreams are opposed to the constructive and public-spirited activity of the builders of cities. Dreams are sensual and escapist. In this poem they are associated with the escape into supernaturalism. The lovely gods summon us across the seas to their imaginary islands and so lure us to our destruction. In some later poems of Auden and his followers, dreams are associated with love in its private aspect and even perhaps with the deviationist forms of love which do not have the social merit of uniting us with our fellows in the family. In earlier poets, at least the Americans, this disparaging view of islands is not marked. Hart Crane's peculiar mystique allows him to suppose that his private and homosexual loves lead him not away from but into the heavenly love, and his voyages among the islands are guided by "the seal's wide spindrift gaze toward paradise" ("Voyages" II, *White Buildings*, 1926). His Venus-sea is most favorable to the "pieties of lovers' hands." And, as he assures his companion,

> Adagios of islands, O my Prodigal,
> Complete the dark confessions her veins spell.

It is with a kind of religious fervor that he sings of

> islands where must lead inviolably
> Blue latitudes and levels of your eyes.

Archibald MacLeish, in an early poem addressed to Ernest Hemingway, invites his friend to sail with him to a westward island where the dead live and where they are to "trade [their] cargoes with the dead for sleep" ("The Voyage," *Poems 1924–1933*). This would seem to be a simple classical geography, without symbolical implications. Again, in *The Hamlet of A. MacLeish*, there is an impressive picture of tribal migrations, which would seem to be a sort of cultural history of the human race in its endless search for whatever it is that men are searching for over and above subsistence. In its geographical survey and in tone, it has a strong suggestion of MacLeish's own *Conquistador*, of Perse's *Anabase* (first French edition 1924) and "Exil" (*Poetry*, March 1942). One is teased by the items that often recur in Auden's poetry beginning with his first volume, published by Spender in 1928, and especially in "Paysage Moralisé"—the mountain passes, the "harvests of dry seeds," the rivers, cities, mountains, and the scattering islands. Taken as a whole the passage has a kind of symbolical association with Hamlet's own crazy discouraged search for meaning in the world. But individually the geographical features do not appear to be taken symbolically. And that is as true for the islands as for the passes, the harvests, the cities, or the mountains.

In the early poems of Auden, islands have pretty uniformly the special symbolic meaning as in "Paysage Moralisé" or some slight variation upon it. Islands are dangerous and to be avoided because, as etymology would indicate, they isolate us; they remove us from reality and from our fellows into a private dream world that weakens and betrays us. They may be associated with sensuality and with psychic illness. Most of these things are indicated in "The Voyage," a piece included in the *Collected Poetry* but probably much earlier in time of composition and publication. The poet begins by asking:

> Where does the journey look which the watcher
> upon the quay,
> Standing under his evil star, so bitterly enview?

Does it promise the "Juster Life"? Does it prove the real existence
of "the Good Place"? And then he answers:

> No, he discovers nothing: he does not want to arrive.
> *The journey is false; the false journey really an illness*
> *On the false island* where the heart cannot act and
>   will not suffer:
> He condones the fever; he is weaker than he thought;
>   his weakness is real.

But sometimes, when he sees real dolphins or a real island,

> the trance is broken: he remembers
> The hours, the places where he was well: he believes in joy.

As early as *The Orators* (1932), in the first of the odes, islands
are associated with sensuality and with childish dependence on one's
father. Auden is relating what he has seen in a troubled dream.
Among other things, he saw a number of kinds of "self-regarders."
And he saw the process of conditioning of the sick psyche.

> I saw the brain-track perfected, laid for conveying
>   The fatal error,
> *Sending the body to islands or after its father* . . .

In *The Dog beneath the Skin*, islands are associated with the ascetic
mountains as one alternative way of escape from reality, from fear.
Some

> have escaped to the ascetic mountains
> Or taken refuge in the family circle, among the boys on
>   the bar-stools, on the *small uncritical islands.*

Thus alcohol is listed as one of the promoters of escapism. Earlier
in the play we have the lying fish-stories and the stories of conquest
of "other men's wives," "when the ships from the *islands laden
with birds* come in."

In "Journey to Iceland" (*Letters from Iceland*), Auden recites
the many attractions of Iceland to the "lover of islands." He begins
with the traveler's hope that he may be "far from any physician."
This I take to mean that the lover of islands, being subject to the
psychic illness referred to in "The Voyage," does not wish for a
cure but for confirmation in his false dream state. The lover of
islands, says Auden, may see at last, "faintly, his limited hope." His

hope is limited to his wish to be freed from the pestering realities of "the world," which are hostile to the individual's sense of his own importance. The "world" it is that

> Asks all your questions: 'Where is the homage? When
> Shall justice be done? O who is against me?
> Why am I always alone?'

Well, the lover of islands can find much in Iceland to distract him, and he thinks, for a time, that this is owing to the absence of the world, of Europe.

> For Europe is absent. *This is an island and therefore
> Unreal.* And the steadfast affections of its dead
> may be bought
> By those whose dreams accuse them of being
> Spitefully alive, and *the pale*
>
> *From too much passion of kissing feel pure in its deserts.*

The island, then, is a place where the disturbing realities of the world are not present, and those disturbed by their erotic indulgences may imagine themselves pure again, their sense of guilt washed away. But he goes on to ask: "Can they? For the world is, and the present, and the lie." And all the features of the landscape make it "the natural setting for the jealousies of a province." So it turns out that Iceland is not a proper island in Auden's symbolical sense. The world of reality is too much present there for it to have the visionary unreality required by the lover of islands to make it his refuge.

It will be noted that MacNeice, Auden's traveling companion in Iceland, does not employ this symbolism, but gives to *island* an opposed and favorable meaning. His "Eclogue from Iceland," also published in the *Letters from Iceland*, puts into the mouth of the Icelandic hero, Grettir Asmundson, these words:

> There is only hope for *people who live upon islands*
> Where the Lowest Common labels will not stick
> And the unpolluted hills will hold your echo.

Here the islands are not the imaginary refuge of the self-indulgent solitary, but the one place where man may maintain the aristocracy of the spirit. And elsewhere MacNeice has used the image of the island in a favorable sense. In an "Ode" dated 1934 (*Poems*, 1937) in which he gives a rather rambling account of what it is he wants in life for himself and his son, he says that he wishes only a limited segment of God's infinite extension. He doesn't want a hundred wives or lives, or money like sand, or every sort of ability so as to show his power.

> I want a sufficient sample, the exact and framed
> Balance of definite masses, the *islanded hour*.
> I would *pray for that island*.

And thus again he is setting himself off from the "mob mania" for infinite experience.

Spender does seem to have adopted early Auden's pejorative associations with islands, in his interesting and in some ways admirable, much-admired and influential poem *Vienna*. That is, if I rightly read him; for the symbol occurs in the challenging but exasperatingly obscure section which he calls "Analysis and Final Statement." After his account of the attempted socialist uprising of '34, he wishes to register a judgment on the historical event. He begins with the diverse comments of five separate "voices," none satisfied, and then he makes his appeal to an imaginary "stranger," such as he would like himself to be. Only he must first list the kinds of persons his ideal commentator must not be. He must not be one of those easy critics soothing us with doom — cursing modern traffic and commerce and pseudo-progress. Then he has several varieties of persons dealing with love, and it is apparently here that his reference to islands applies.

> Those who hang about
> At jaws of lavatories, advertising their want of love
> Pilloried by their open failure: whose eyes are
>   still innocent
> Confessing a real disappointment. *Those who go to islands*,
> Whose salvaged happiness can greet their friends,
> A few worthy of jokes. Those who sell all
> Give to their first prostitute: or buy the most flashing
> Racing car or aeroplane . . .

The right word on the Vienna affair will not be spoken by any of these seekers after private satisfactions to make up for some inner emptiness and discontent. Islands seem here to symbolize, as in Auden, the selfish and personal as opposed to the collective interest; and the context also suggests strongly that the poet has in mind erotic and perhaps "perverted" satisfactions.

In other places in Spender, the socio-political and pejorative associations are lacking; and while the idea of unfortunate isolation is present, there is also the suggestion that islands (in love) are desirable places. In *The Still Centre* (1939) there are two melancholy analytic poems concerned with lovers separated by some fault of will or twist of the ego in the one who is speaking; and here there is much play with the island symbol. In all cases but one the island represents one or other of the lovers separately; but in the end it seems to represent the lovers united. In "The Separation," the lover at a great distance stares, beyond his "dark and climbing fears," to where

> Your *answering warm island* lies
> In the gilt wave of desire.

He images the far journey back to the other, but without hope of a satisfactory union. For

> when we meet — the ribs will still
> Divide the flesh-enfolding dream
> And the winds and the seas of time
> *Ruin the islands* with their stream
> However compassed be the will.

Yet he longs for the time when he shall be released from "the world's circular terror,"

> where love at last finds peace
> Released from the will's error.

Then, in the second of the poems called "Variations on My Life," the poet longs to return

> To the first loved friend, you
> Whose life seemed most unlike my own
> *As though you existed on an island*

> In seas of an archaic time,
> Hidden under birdsong and olive trees . . .

He goes on to give an attractive picture of the summer evening situation of the so different lover on his or her island. Then he outlines the psychological conditions (happiness and acceptance of self) on his part that would enable him to return and to be received. For he has this at least to offer:

> I was the sea, *I was the island*
> Where the casqued heroic head
> Lay and was remembered;
> My innocent crystal mirrored your heart,
> My mind was your legendary sky of love.

Then more conditions of improvement in his way of regarding himself, and finally,

> O, then my body would enter
> *Its island and its summer*
> The questions find their answer
> And my head its resting-place
> Where the other heart lies . . .

It is interesting to note the difference between Spender and Auden with regard to the locus of the sense of guilt. In Spender it is more often found in relation to a private love blocked by some perversity in the will or temperament of one lover and leading to what is generally called infidelity. In Auden it is more a matter of the selfishness of private love insofar as it gets in the way of collective love and action, as well as in the manner in which it tends to substitute self-indulgent dreaming for constructive action. In Spender I do not find that inveterate disparagement of the dream that is found in Auden; in Auden the dream quite regularly is synonymous with self-deception. Thus in poem xxx of *Look, Stranger!* addressed to Christopher Isherwood, beginning "August for the people and their *favourite islands*." In August people go to their favorite holiday resorts, and "lulled by the light they live *their dreams of freedom*." But, of course, it is suggested throughout the poem that under our present individualistic social order there is no genuine freedom. What we have is

> Beauty scratching miserably for food,
> Honour self-sacrificed for Calculation,
> And Reason stoned by Mediocrity,
> Freedom by Power shockingly maltreated,
> And Justice exiled till Saint Geoffrey's Day.

People's bourgeois dreams of freedom are ineffectual illusions. (Of course when it comes to the self-deceiving dreams in the period of *The Age of Anxiety*, the tables will be turned on the earlier Auden, and the illusory is found in another direction.)

In this same volume there is another poem (IX) in which there is a middle stand between Spender's and Auden's concepts of islands. The poet is celebrating his graduation from the illusory dreams of boyhood. He has left them behind in his voyaging:

> Lost in my wake the *archipelago*,
> *Islands of self* through which I sailed all day,
> Planting a pirate's flag, a generous boy;
> And *lost the way to action and to you*.

In Spender's poem, in his separate island, he has lost the way to "you," but nothing is said about action, that is, about participation in the larger collective life.

But after all, the island has always been for everyone the handiest of natural symbols. There is no opprobrium attaching to lovers of seclusion who set up their holiday retreats on islands. If you have enemies — as who has not? — the island is a most eligible position for self-defense, with a moat ready-made. Even in peaceful civil life, one is in need of self-defense against bores and philistines. The classical and the romantic legends are full of delightful islands — Atlantis, the islands of the blessed, among the Celts the Western Isles, the Isle of Women. It is true that in crossing water you enter the realm of magic. Islands are magical and deceptive. You stay three days on the Isle of Women, and it turns out to have been three thousand years; when you return to the mainland, if you are not careful — if you but eat an apple or set foot to the ground — you find that everything is changed, you are yourself a man of extreme age, you wither up and die. But for all that, the writers of romances did not take a stern view of islands and of journeys thither.

It is up to any poet to make what he likes of islands. And when
it comes to dreams, there are false dreams and true ones. So that
even Auden at times falls under the spell and represents his most
admired heroes as cultivating a dream — a true and proper one, to
be sure. Thus we have Auden and Isherwood's play *On the Frontier*. It is strong propaganda against nationalism and war. The hero
and heroine belong to adjoining nations that are dominated by in-
dustrialists and spoiling for a fight: the young couple are all for
conciliation, for ignoring boundaries. They yearn toward one another, but are kept apart. Only in spirit are they united. The stage
shows them in a small circle in the dark illuminated by the spot-
light. That is for them the good place where the air is not filled with
screams of hatred.

> Locked in each other's arms, we form a tower
> They cannot shake or enter. Our love
> Is *the far and unsuspected island*
> Their prestige does not hold.

Thus Auden would seem to have yielded to the romantic view of
islands as the secluded refuge of lovers. And, even more romantic
and Platonic is his resort to the figure of "the everlasting garden":

> This is *the everlasting garden*
> Where we shall walk together always,
> Happy, happy, happy, happy.

We may hardly suppose that *everlasting* is here used in the strict
religious sense of immortal, but rather in that of eternal, as used by
metaphysicians and by Romantic platonizing poets like Shelley,
with whom *eternal* means "in the realm of abstract ideas, which is
not subject to time." And when we come finally in Auden to the
word *dream*, we realize these playwrights have, for better effect
with their audience, stooped to the use of all these romantic words
not in the disparaging but in the favorable sense. Time, say the
lovers, will forget them, "but not the common thought that linked
them in a *dream*." Their dream was, as we have seen, that of the
city where the will of love is done — of building the city that is
symbol of the collectivity. So that in this case, talking the language

of the vulgar, the poets have raised islands and dreams into the realm of the socially admirable.

Prokosch is, perhaps, even fonder than Auden of the island symbol, and he is quite as aware of the danger of "going to islands." But he is tenderer with those who yield to their seductions. Auden, we are told, in his geographical excursions preferred the north. Prokosch is more in love with the southern isles. In *Death at Sea* he has a song in praise of "islands that I have loved." They are decidedly tropical with their colored birds and fruits, their rituals and mythology, all "calculated to put the heart to rest." He prays that his "dear" may be equally blessed with these natural joys, and with the tenderness of the sea and "her forgiving south." More often with him islands spell sorrow, tragedy, and death. But this is not clearly because the resort to islands means cutting oneself off from participation in the collective action of building the city, but more simply because islands stand for the illusory world of dreams, of wish-fulfillment, and whoever indulges in such dreams is bound to be cruelly disillusioned when he comes up against the world of everyday reality. This is, of course, an element in Auden's island symbolism, and one is strongly impressed with the Auden influence in Prokosch. But the terrible isolation to which men are doomed in their maturity is not so clearly social isolation, deprivation of the collective love, as the mere incapacity to find satisfaction for their private love, their craving for real union with the other party. However, there are hints of the public as well as the private isolation of spirit.

Audenesque, again, is the emphasis on childhood as the initial period of illusory dreaming. This can be seen especially in the earliest volume, *The Assassins*. Thus in "The Baltic Shore":

> O spires, O streams, O sorrows, O temptations,
> Those *quaint and charming islands of our childhood*!
> Sweet days of indecision! But approaching
> Crawls the curved drumbeat of *our governing fears*.

The root of our poison-tree is love. In "The Adriatic" we read of those

> Who out of sorrow *dream an amorous world* . . .

It was love that made us understand; love was the fever

> Summoned through miles of night by those long ships
> *Pointing toward islands* their eternal keels . . .

In "The Tragedians," this love fever, with its attendant sorrows and horrors, is variously compared to "gluttonous orchids," the "gigantic spurious mistletoe." We are shown

> Frail and enormous, hovering over the streets,
> Creatures of air, revolting dreams? Fragments
> Of night perhaps attending our nightly illusions?

In this poem emphasis is laid on perversions, especially in children, and, reminding us of Dante, him

> who lives in ice,
> Motionless, thoughtless, utterly alone . . .

As one reads more thoughtfully, one begins to see, however, that erotic love is celebrated not merely for itself but as a symbol of a broader love and faith which would make life worth living if one could find them in the general desolation of our spiritual life. When the poet sings, in *The Carnival*,

> O my world, O what have you done to me?
> For my love has turned to a laurel tree,
> The *axe hangs trembling over the Isles,*

we realize that it is not simple love dreams that are represented by the isles so menaced by the axe. In the title poem of this volume his vision spans the continents, and their sorrows, and recalls the age of faith.

> Yes, holy were bread and wine for some, and the peace
> Of evening, fallen from the hand of One
> Who whispered, Love, and gave to the word a
> Whole new world of tunes and meaning!

But in all directions, he sees only frenzy of fear and war.

> And southward, feuds. And *on the islands, caves.*
> What once was real is now degrading. Lost
> Utterly lie the onanistic,
> The lazy in *an age of falsehood.*

He goes on to state again that "this is the age of lies," to suggest how the phrase, the photograph, and written history "weave their deceptions," and to deprecate the falsities of art and the general decadence of the Old World.

This poem is peculiarly ambiguous, or ambivalent, and needs very careful reading. We are impressed by the nostalgic sympathy with which the poet recalls the ancient faith of Christianity. But he goes on to say that, in our time, "what once was real is now degrading." At first one thinks that the islands and the caves are actual geographical entities; but then one realizes that they may begin as such but end up as symbols of the deceptive dream world. Such also is the onanism, which surely refers to the "self-abuse" of "self-deceivers." We remember that in "The Baltic Shore" the self-deceivers began as those who "kissed once too often," but ended up as men who "loved their land" (who were taken in by the lie of nationalism) and whose drowned bodies now float in the ocean "in their comprehending terror."

It is in "The Sacred Wood" (*The Assassins*) that we have the closest approximation to Auden's position in regard to islands, dreams, and love. It is worth quoting a second time the passage that I have compared to Böcklin's picture, to remind ourselves how many of Auden's symbols are here brought together. This land, he says,

> Is the land you have dreamed of, darling.
> Don't you remember *those pale towers*, those long
> And serpent channels, those tall rocks, those *valleys*
> *Fringed with our fears*, those *silent foam-entangled*
> Islands? This is the *empire of our dreams* . . .

And he then goes on to bid his darling to flee from this illusory and deathly dream world

> Quickly from your remembrance carve all visions,
> All dreamed of kingdoms, of refuge after the dissolution,
> Of tenderness following despair, of life after death!

Here for once Prokosch is even sterner then the leftist Auden. He specifically includes the Christian hope of immortality among the lethal falsehoods of the dream world. Instead of this he recommends the Platonic timeless life of eternity.

All loveliness lies in the passing; yes, *eternity itself*
Swings over the moment of perfection: be strong,
Dismiss all terror, plunge into visible love
Your energies and powers, all night, all day.

Here surely love is meant to cover something more socially constructive than erotic indulgence. And while it may not have the collectivist slant given by Auden to his ideal, the call to the exercise of energies and powers frees it from the discouraged fatalism of Prokosch's more habitual attitude and establishes his kinship with — what shall we call it? — secular humanism.

16. NO MAN IS AN ISLAND

In American poetry of the forties the island symbol is fairly frequent, but perhaps not more frequent than one might expect of so tempting and universally accessible an image. And only occasionally are there unmistakable traces of the Auden or the Prokosch interpretation of islands as unhealthy states of mind, illusory dream worlds, dangerous refuges from reality, selfish isolation from the interests and hope of mankind. And this in spite of the reinforcement to the Auden symbolism which must have been given it by the striking epigraph from Donne that Hemingway put at the head of his *For Whom the Bell Tolls* (1940): "No man is an *Iland*, intire of itselfe; every man is a peece of the *Continent*, a part of the *maine*: if a *Clod* bee washed away by the *Sea*, Europe is the lesse, as well as if a *Promontorie* were, as well as if a *Mannor* of thy friends or of *thine* owne were; any mans *death* diminishes *me*, because I am involved in *Mankinde*; And therefore never send to know for whom the *bell* tolls; it tolls for *thee*." Thus early in World War II, by quoting an eloquent passage from a seventeenth-century sermon, Hemingway brought to everyone's imagination the figure of an island as representing the selfish confinement of a man's mind to his individual fortunes and the inevitability with which each man is, in spite of himself, involved with mankind as a whole.

Howard Baker in *A Letter from the Country and Other Poems* (1941) has conventional references to "fertile isles afloat on Grecian seas," where the image is symbolic only in the sense of carrying attractive associations, like the Goshen and the "terraced Babylon" that accompany it ("The Passing Generation"). Or again, his mind turns nostalgically to "lands in blue exile, / Of mazy coasts like *Pelops' Isle*," or the "adventurous strait / Where tufted isles stand alien to the shore" ("Destiny: An Ode").

In Wallace Stevens, the mental process and imagination were so inveterately original that he could be trusted to give a quite distinctive cast to any word or any concept invoked by other poets. Still, it may be possible to trace a broad analogy between his peculiar concepts, with the highly individual imagery in which they are invested, and those of less esoteric writers. Thus, in his "Asides on the Oboe" (*Parts of a World*), the opposition of the individual man-and-hero to the philosophers' man, the "central man," may be compared to Auden's opposition between the man "who goes to islands" and the one who engages in building ideal cities. Stevens speaks of

> That obsolete fiction of the wide river in
> An empty land; the gods that Boucher killed;
> And the metal heroes that time granulates . . .

This individualist, or "hautboy man," is contrasted with

> The impossible possible philosophers' man,
> The man who has had the time to think enough,
> The central man, the human globe, responsive
> As a mirror with a voice, the man of glass,
> Who in a million diamonds sums us up.

The frame of reference is quite different from Auden's. Auden has in mind *activity* for the realizing of the collective polity. He is concerned with the political consequences of the symbolic setup. Stevens (as "pure poet," or metaphysician as poet) has not come to the stage of political reference. He is concerned simply with the abstract philosophical concept of mankind as an undivided unity. And so when he brings in the island image it has a quite different feeling tone. It is, to be sure, the fatal catastrophe of war that starts him off:

> One year, death and war prevented the jasmine scent
> And the *jasmine islands* were bloody martyrdoms.

The jasmine islands must be taken to refer to the interior life of

individual men. They had naturally the jasmine scent, the sweetness
that our emotions lend to our living. But the war turned them into
bloody martyrdoms. That for the individual soldiers. But

> How was it then for the *central man*? Did we
> Find peace? We found *the sum of men*. We found,
> If we found the central evil, *the central good*.

O yes, there is in the end an ethical reference here. In the united
action of soldiers in war was found not merely the central evil (in
human perversity and the evil inherent in the conditions of living),
but also *the central good* — presumably, whatever is good in the action of men united in one ideal aim. He does not pretend that there
was not suffering for the soldier and for us, or that "the jasmine
ever returned." But we did realize our oneness:

> We had always been partly one. It was as we came
> To see him, that we were wholly one, as we heard
> Him chanting for those buried in their blood,
> In the jasmine haunted forests, that we knew
> The glass man, without external reference.

Thus in the end, there is the opposition between the individual
on his jasmine island and mankind as a unit, represented by the
philosophical glass man, who sees in his mirror all men united as
Hobbes sees them in his *Leviathan*. This is certainly not in the same
key as Auden's imagery; but it does, I think, clearly belong to our
poetic century and the post-Auden decade of American verse.

It is here, as with so many images, Brinnin who most sedulously
develops the symbolism of his predecessors — though here again, as
so often with Brinnin, some confusion in the imaginative handling
of his symbols makes it occasionally a great labor to trace in them
the precise direction of his thought in a particular context. We
have already seen how in "The Ascent," a poem in several details
reminiscent of the Auden-Isherwood play, the puritan discipline
of mountain climbing is found to be a more helpful initiation into
social action than the self-indulgence of the island life:

> Ascent accomplished
> More than all the *insular heart* had wished.

It is not improbable that Hemingway's epigraph from Donne has

entered here to reinforce the island image from Auden. Brinnin's
poetry is full of references to the social polity which is our political
ideal and crowded with admonitions in regard to the personal discipline which is necessary if we are to enter into the communal
movement of faith that is destined to realize this ideal. Like Auden
in the interbellum period of preparation, he can write an ode-like
poem "For My Pupils in the War Years" (*No Arch, No Triumph*),
and warn the soldiers of the mind against "romantic agonies" that
"become your lavish / Idea of a child playing bride on rainy days."
In "Second Sight" he warns against the pessimistic individualism
of literary genius, "the laurelled child /.Of honor and impeccable
ambition," who finds "Enchantingly dangerous routes to his most
simple ends," whose "tarnished eye distrusts the marriage of true
minds," who

> wins the world's exemption with his crooked smile.
> Silent, moving through self-distorting mirrors, he grows old
> Who might speak for us all.

As against the isolations, the self-regarding evasions of the individualist, he holds the vision of

> The *coming continent*, the long locality
> Of artless action without fault.

He warns that the achievement of the larger good is difficult:

> But once to hear *the melody*
> *Of life in its plurality*
> Is to know the dialect of the difficult.
> With the making faith we have we look toward its
> reality,
> For truth is a result.

There is in my summary, as there is in the poem itself, no adequate context of imagery to introduce the "coming continent,"
which starts out at once in all its bald confusion of the figurative
and literal. (Continents don't come, though new things may.) It is
a typical example of the unhappy mixture of the poetry of statement and the poetry of indirection that makes the work of Brinnin
so perversely hard on his reader. In the wider context of his thinking as a whole, we make out what it means, as we make out what

the poet means in "The Ascent" by his "rim of unique towers, structure / Of revealing future." Indeed it means the same thing — the ideal social polity to which we look forward. And it may well be that Brinnin's continent, like his insular heart, is an echo of, or an allusion to, Donne's lucid contrast of symbols: "No man is an *Iland*, intire in itselfe; every man is a peece of the *Continent*, a part of the *maine*."

In his earlier volume we have a lyric poem specifically devoted to island imagery, "Islands: A Song." The first stanza makes its meaning clear, almost without a gloss. The central idea is that

> *Islands of grief* refuse to tell
> *Their separating difference* ever . . .

They are inaccessible to sympathy. They stand as indifferent to others' opinion as a feudal castle. (The figure of a castle I am supplying by way of explication. Brinnin furnishes no image. He says with complete prose abstraction, "*Feudally* they stand.") In this stanza we recognize the familiar Auden-Prokosch symbol for isolation within our private emotional life. The second stanza is much more difficult, with many confusing details, and I do not guarantee my interpretation.

Here the poet is presumably underlining the contrast between the human isolation of islands and the communicability that characterizes what he calls "my island city"; he is making the same fusion of the two opposed images as Berryman was making at about the same time. In "A Point of Age" (*Poems*) Berryman is taking a very discouraged view of our hopeful political prophecies.

> To say that country, time to come, will be
> *The island or harbour city* of our choice
> Proclaims the sick will raving in the voice.

It is true that passage is no little obscure, even in the general context of Berryman's poem, and subject to a variety of alternative interpretations. Something depends on whether *country* and *time to come* are parallel items grammatically, *time to come* being in apposition to *country*, or *time to come* is an adverbial phrase, elliptical for *in time to come*. It is even possible that there is here an antinationalistic attitude implied, mere country or nation being too narrow a view of our ideal city. What now interests us is the combination in a single image of what in Auden are opposing ideas — island and city — the one an individualistic and dream-world state of mind, the other an ideal social polity in which we are not isolated from our fellows. It is probable that the intention is to take advantage of the most favorable associations of island, harbor, and city for suggesting the ideal polity, and to deprecate the notion that the attainment of this ideal will be easy. It may be that the poet wishes to suggest a state of things in which the personal gratifications associated with islands (love in the personal sense) would, in the ideal polity, be combined with the social relations (the larger love) associated with cities. But the reference to "the sick will in the raving voice" might mean that island and city are reconcilable.

In Brinnin's "Song," in the second stanza, there is an even greater probability that his "island city" is a deliberate fusion of Auden's opposed symbols. This island city is "furious"; it is "ample in its flashing pity"; the singer invites the lover, at a distance, to tune in on his radio and, "Sea-parted, share / This quickening fear." His compassionate island city is set in contrast to the islands of those bound up in grief by the communicability of its emotions. If the poem was written before we entered the war, the quickening fear might have reference to world events, and it might suggest the larger love of the social ideal. The city islander may represent one inspired by the communal polity. Or it may simply be that islands represent different personalities, some neither asking nor offering pity, and others with outgoing feelings. And then, of course, it is possible that island city, "Treeless and steepled," simply refers literally to Manhattan Island. But that would leave the whole poem rather without point. I give it up! Among our many alternatives, we can be sure only of the paradox in the phrase *island city*.

Some years later, however, Brinnin brought out another poem on islands — "The Fortunate Isles" (*No Arch, No Triumph*) — in which is unambiguously developed the symbolism of islands as representing the self-deception of those who dwell alone in a dream world. In the first stanza, he seems willing in his irony to let those who may find comfort in those summary atolls "Where flora is never a mere neurosis, / Nor clouds persuasions" and where "even the gods / Have godlike arms and godlike faces." But he goes on in the second stanza to signalize the plight of those who undertake to "come home" from that "climate of love." They are forever ridden with nostalgia; some grow old sailing the seas, foolishly hoping to return "with no illusion lost"; some, "in exile, learn at last, / Love is a backward look." There follows a stanza representing how their islands seem to their obstinate denizens the true home of truth and health. But it ends up with a clear indication of the way in which the island psychology lends itself to a ruinous passivity and the unprogressive backward look. Auden and Isherwood's uncritical islands have here become "irrational Isles."

> In those *sweet irrational Isles*, the past
> Takes to ruin with colossal ease,
> Wholly gives over to shells and leaves
> And the gem-like cultures of things that live
> Through epochs in a morning's mist.

The isolation of the islander is anatomized in the following stanza:

> A man with Fortunate Isles on his mind
> Is precipitously set between
> Marriage and exile, and marriage is difficult.

Marriage is difficult, but the islander is ingenious in adjusting himself to the single life.

> His imagination *makes a cave*
> *Of the world* and of solitude a cult.
> In the small rooms of his sorrowing,
> *Islands* and other places will hang
> Forever, *false* and full of love.

We have encountered "on the islands, *caves*" in Prokosch. In Auden we have encountered "the *false journey* really an illness / On the *false island*." "The small rooms of his sorrowing" is a gloss on Brinnin's earlier "islands of grief" that "refuse to tell / Their separating difference." The false islands, "full of love," recall Prokosch's heavy emphasis on love, especially perverted love, as the special illness that leads men to the island solitudes.

And then, finally, in the last stanza, Brinnin suggests the Freudian complex that lies at the bottom of so much island-seeking. Where are the Fortunate Isles, he asks; and answers the question by locating the prodigal's source of gratification in the mother's smiles:

> Because the boy of genesis
> Turned prodigal wants forgiveness,
> Wants the *maternal siren* with smiles
> And the attractive mouth of her daughter,
> Wants sleep and, most, self-sacrifice . . .

Thus Brinnin associates with the island symbol the whole psychoanalytical scheme that attributes to the silver-chord complex the variant forms of Don Juanism and saintliness. He even goes on from sleep to suicide.

> Locate the event and you will have the place
> Half way between atoms and stars:
> *Death in the throat of water.*

We do not need to determine whether "death in the throat of water" signifies spiritual death on a symbolic island, which is in the throat of the sea, or actual death in the throat of water, which may be the fate, say, of poets who "go to islands."

Here for once we may have the pleasure of noting in Brinnin the successful mastery of a coherent set of images for shadowing forth his thought almost altogether without confusion or obscurity. For three other poems, interesting for their thought in the present connection, we cannot quite say as much on the side of imaginative clarity. In "New Year's Eve" (*The Garden Is Political*), the poet describes the sadness that accompanies the traditional gaiety of the season at the thought that "Prague is two months gone." Amid the ruins of the great world he notes that his own "personal tower" still stands. He recalls a summer meeting of himself and his beloved when "*Night was our island*, love its enterprise." But then came the necessary parting, for

> The disparate heart must live
> Unfriended till the stonetraced pageant move . . .

The lovers must be separated, must leave their island, during these

138

stony days. And yet, he says, "Here was such reach of love" as might "in some other guise" have imposed treaties of peace,

> converted hangmen from their plans,
> Deployed the raiding planes,
> Put Christ in capitals and in the churches Marx,
> Rung in an Easter for the orthodox.

The point of this would seem to be that the quality of love which he shares with his mate (on their private island) is such as would be sufficient, under more favorable circumstances and applied on a wider scale, to bring about the reign of love and justice in the world.

In "This Voyaging" (*No Arch, No Triumph*), a later poem but with the war still on, the poet summons his dear to come out from her city home and walk the streets with him, to recall the stress and voyaging of their years together.

> Since all my choiring bridges lead to you,
> Come out, *my island in this island's stone* . . .

Here in a passage somewhat reminiscent of Hart Crane, this island would indeed seem to refer to stone-covered Manhattan. He then goes on to say, rather obscurely,

> For we have weathered here, anonymous,
> In death's frenetic house,
> The *empire of the human family.*

The human family is, presumably, the larger polity beyond their private island. They have weathered the storm of war and death. They have shared whatever triumph and freedom the human family had attained. But they have not escaped scot free.

> Since *none is insular,*
> Since none may go without his fitting wound . . .

"Any mans *death* diminishes *me*, because I am involved in *Mankinde*; And therefore never send to know for whom the *bell* tolls; it tolls for *thee*."

In "Observatory Hill" (also *No Arch, No Triumph*) the island image is, if possible, still more obscurely brought in. In this poem the warning is against the unrealistic optimism of a Whitman, and of all *those of single vision*, who are brought down,

> The mad, in furs, dead at the coldest poles . . .
> All hunters of a vision of white whales

engaged in a "self-destructive chase," who at length "find their graves in learned paradox." From this condemnation, looking close with telescopic eye, he is able to free certain other solitary geniuses — Beethoven triumphing in "his muffled room," Van Gogh, Joyce. Considering these examples,

> I knew forever then *the last frontier*
> Not to be reached by crossing over land
> Toward an Atlantic or Pacific strand
> But, like the *perishable isle of coral drowned*,
> In constricted channel found
> Lonely and not for long; for *the single traveler*
> Who greets it with penultimate despair
> *Frontier becomes exit and entrance there.*

I must confess myself pretty completely baffled by this complicated symbolism, and not much helped, if at all, by putting it alongside an almost equally difficult passage in Auden's ode "To My Pupils" (*The Orators*). In that poem Auden is speaking of "the youngest drummer" in a military outfit who

> Knows all the peace-time stories like the oldest soldier,
> Though *frontier-conscious.*

He knows, for example, about the tall white gods "who landed from their open boats . . ."

> *Before the islands were submerged*, when the
>   weather was calm,
>   The maned lion common,
> An open wishing-well in every garden;
>   When love came easy.

I have not undertaken to explain the symbols here, either the frontier or the submerged islands; and I cannot with any confidence explain the like symbols in Brinnin. What seems reasonably clear in Brinnin, however, is that the single traveler and the coral isle do represent the extreme and often fatal isolation of genius, but that

Words from Geography and Travel

there are cases in which, by some final rightness of vision, what seems the last frontier (what Prokosch calls "the world's long boundary"), and is greeted with "penultimate" (not *ultimate*) despair, does not mean merely exit, but also entrance into . . . what? into life? into understanding? Their lonely stay on the island is "not for long." They return, presumably to the *continent* or *maine* land.

In William Meredith's "The Islands of My Desire" (*Love Letter from an Impossible Land*, 1944) I find no traces of the Auden-Prokosch use of the island symbol. The islands of his desire are apparently his dreams of love in company with his faraway beloved. They are characterized in terms of the volcanic islands off the coast of Alaska, which in spite of the most unfavorable conditions, "grow a virtuous green." But for this airman caught up in the war, the "weather" does not favor his return to his love. He is "not for the islands yet." In "Love Letter from an Impossible Land," the metaphor is somewhat differently applied. He would seem to have gone to the actual physical islands and to be walking upon them, on their "unsettled mountains." Indeed, one is a little uncertain whether it is actual or symbolical islands that are in question.

> Combed by the cold seas, Bering and Pacific,
> These are the *exile islands of the mind.*
> All the charts and history you can muster
> Will not make them real as the fog is real . . .

Being islands of the mind, "impossible," and less real than the fog that veils them, they are presumably geographical entities vouched for by charts and history, and at the same time the islands of his desire, grown hazy by time and distance. Later they grow more definitely physical:

> Now I am convinced there is nothing to fear,
> Now *on these islands you are all I want* . . .

All that remains from the earlier symbolism is that islands are illusory and solitary places.

In Alfred Hayes there is more of a holdover from the Auden-Prokosch tradition. In "Union Square" (*The Big Time*), we have a picture of a young man in New York spending a night of cheap dissipation, concluding on a sharply ironic note with return home and dreams of innocence.

> Dream of a girl unlike all girls before . . .
> The hostess is covered with flowers, asleep in a
>   marriage bed . . .
> Doctor and druggist ask nothing in payment but smiles,
> They have padlocked the Automat, planted the
>   Square with grass,
> And the homegoing local is off for the *south sea isles*.

In other poems both Alfred Hayes and Hugh Chisholm have reversed Auden's terms of reference. The islands now stand not for the dreams of self-indulgent individualists but for the utopian visions of leftists and progressives. In his "Elegy for All" (*The Prodigal Never Returns*), Chisholm is being very severe on our modern boast of progress and enlightenment. Indeed, this poet takes a very dim view of the human scene whichever way we look. His irony hits both ways. He is not *laudator temporis acti*. He is not exactly recommending the filth and privilege of the Old World, though "there was elbow room." He is not recommending

> the diminutive,
> the window-view of life, with the mauve and green
> unquestionable hills beyond life . . .

But still, in this poem, his final grouch is against the present world of progress. We have

> inherited the terror of the heart
> in spite of all our brilliant facts and figures,
> even in spite of our traditional visions
> of porpoises and peace and *the praising isles*.

In Hayes's "Epistle to the Gentiles" (*Welcome to the Castle*) it is a utopian vision of a perfect community, impossible of realization under prevailing spiritual conditions, to which the island symbol refers.

> There is *a perfect island*, of course, some vacuum of
>   flowers and art, *simplest of communities*,
> but it exists nowhere for a common poison poisons all.

Thus we have seen how much a certain group of our recent poets

have been haunted by the image of the island as symbol of that isolation of spirit that individuals suffer, subjecting them to illusory
dream states, and often making them incapable of healthy activity
and of joining their fellows in the social community. This image has
served many of them well in developing various aspects of this
theme, which has been a dominant theme in the social philosophy
of the period. I do not know whether this image in general or in
the specialized sense has come by now to seem a cliché. It may be
that other preoccupations will have taken its place with more recent poets. Not all the poets reviewed have been equally happy in
its use. But this may not necessarily be because the image itself is
shopworn. Their failure to do poetical justice to it may sometimes
be the result of ill-judged poetical techniques — one of which is the
disposition to use an image simply as a conventional hieroglyph for
an idea, thus losing the benefit of an actual appeal to the imagination; and others are the confusion of the figurative and the literal,
the want of precision in the use of images, the confused telescoping
of separate images, all of which have so flourished in recent decades
under the cover of our general indulgence for the obscure in poetry.

17. EXILES: THE THIRTIES

We are now done with the island symbol, together with the other
closely related symbols employed by Auden in his moralized landscapes. But there are a number of other symbol images, again involved with these by close links of association in the tissue of symbolic images set going, most notably, by Auden. Most prominent of
these are exiles, journeys, and frontiers. We have already encountered them in their close connection with islands: as in Meredith's
exile islands of the mind, and in Auden's and Brinnin's bringing together of frontiers and submerged islands.

I will begin with the appearance of the exile symbol in early
poems of Auden, Spender, and MacNeice, and then consider two
famous uses of the word in prose writing which throw light on its
meaning in poetry and largely explain its vogue in poetry of our
time. In the number of the *Criterion* for January 1930 was pub-

lished the whole of Auden's "charade" entitled "Paid on Both Sides," which includes the chorus beginning, "To throw away the key and walk away," reprinted in the *Collected Poetry* under the rather misleading title "The Walking Tour." This chorus begins:

> To throw away the key and walk away,
> *Not abrupt exile*, the neighbours asking why,
> But following a line with left and right
> An altered gradient at another rate . . .

This walking away, the poet says, is not an abrupt exile about which the neighbors wish to know the reason — not banishment for political reasons as when the Athenians voted to ostracize a citizen considered dangerous to the state. But it is clear as the poem develops that it was a voluntary exiling of oneself as that word came to be commonly used in writing of the day. It meant learning more about the world than could be learned from maps at school; it meant getting a new view of the country from "forwarded posts." And it meant the trying isolation of one who takes up his home nowhere and makes no comforting human contacts.

> *Travellers* may sleep at inns but not attach,
> They sleep one night together, not asked to touch;
> Receive no normal welcome, not the pressed lip,
> Children to lift, nor the assuaging lap.

They make the arduous crossing through the *pass*, "descend the growing stream," and

> Reach villages to ask for a bed in
> Rock shutting out the sky, the old life done.

Travellers and *pass* I have italicized in anticipation of the associated themes of voyages and frontiers.

In the same volume of poems as "Paid on Both Sides" there is a better known and more haunting poem which sounds like another chorus from a play. It is the one beginning "Doom is dark and deeper than any sea-dingle," which has already been discussed above in section 3. The word *exile* is not here used, but the poem is a further development of the theme of his earlier chorus. It is a dark doom that falls on a man who leaves his house, unrestrained by "cloud-soft hand" of women,

But ever that man goes
Through place-keepers, through forest trees,
A *stranger to strangers* over undried sea,
Houses for fishes, suffocating water . . .

Perhaps we have at its best in this poem Auden's use of Old English alliterative measures and Old English kennings (houses for fishes) — what often becomes in later poems of some length a tedious undertaking leading him into stretches of mere burlesque. "Suffocating water" seems to echo an image in the earlier chorus. There the seeker of new views is not superficial in dealings with reality,

Not swooping at the surface still like gulls
But with prolonged drowning shall develop gills.

The symbolism is somewhat complicated and farfetched, but it may perhaps be unlocked by a reference to a famous passage in Conrad's *Lord Jim*, where the wise old trader Stein, having diagnosed Jim's spiritual malady as that of the romantic, explains to Marlow how that malady is to be cured. "One thing alone can us from being ourselves cure . . . A man that is born falls into a dream like a man who falls into the sea. If he tries to climb out into the air as inexperienced people endeavour to do, he drowns — *nicht wahr?* . . . No! I tell you! The way is *to the destructive element submit yourself*, and with the exertions of your hands and feet in the water make the deep, deep sea keep you up." Stein goes on to explain "how to be," how to live. He repeats his metaphor of the destructive element. " 'In the destructive element immerse.' . . . He spoke in subdued tone . . . one hand on each side of his face. 'That was the way. To follow the dream, and again to follow the dream — and so — *ewig — usque ad finem.*' " Auden does not refer to his exile's experience in life or in exile as a dream; but where Stein's swimmer keeps himself up by the exertions of his hands and feet in the deep water, Auden's, immersing himself and swimming under water, develops organs for breathing in the depths.

In the "Doom is deep" chorus the self-exiled seeker, wanting Moses' power to roll back the waves, must cross over undried sea, suffocating water, which does, for all that, provide houses for fishes.

He goes on with the picture of his isolation, where he may at night have dreams of home and wife,

> But waking sees
> Bird-flocks nameless to him, through doorway voices
> Of new men making another love.

And at the end he prays that he may be protected from all the perils of his lonely journey, and be brought safely home on "the day of his returning."

Two years after the appearance of this "charade," in the volume called *The Orators*, there is an ode, addressed to Edward Upward, Schoolmaster, which was reprinted by· Auden in his *Collected Poetry*, under the title of "The Exiles." * He begins with some account of the journey of persons "*On track to exile.*" The persons in question are of several different social and occupational classes — "Expert from uplands, always in oilskins," "Recliner from library, laying down law," and even "Owner from shire." The "shore" where they all meet sounds like a quasi-military training camp for boy scouts or young men at school. The items of their experience there are typical of Auden's symbolic poetry of this period. They "climb the cliff path to the coastguard's point." There are derelict docks, forts for sale, "the flare of foundries." The entertainment side of school life is represented by July picnics, skating and curling, charades and ragging at Christmas. But they are not there for a short term, but for life. "This life is to last, when we leave we leave all." It may be voluntary exile, but it is indeed exile. Though they are located "on the *border*," they are not actually arrayed against a foreign country, they are not in the literal sense in a state of war, and they need not fear "spy with signals for secret agent." As time goes on they are subject to moods of depression, "The slight despair / At what we are." The physical locality is left somewhat vague; it even admits their finding themselves at last in the streets of London, hearing the gaslights go out, and "Accepting dearth / The shadow of death."

It is clear that the exile into which these selected souls enter vol-

---

* In reprinting the poem, Auden omitted, for reasons not clear to me, four of the eighteen stanzas.

untarily is an exile of the mind and spirit. They are explorers of new worlds of thought and conduct. They have painfully torn themselves free from the culture pattern to which they were born, from the mores and ideology of home, and gone forth into a self-imposed loneliness. In their loneliness and adventuresomeness of mind, they might make one think of Wordsworth's Newton,

a mind forever
Voyaging through strange seas of thought, alone.

But the unmistakable model for the poetic exiles of the thirties and forties is a writer much nearer in time and carrying a much greater prestige than Wordsworth for the men of that generation. The unmistakable model for them was James Joyce in his life and (for the word and concept) in his prose drama *Exiles*. This play was written in 1914 at the beginning of World War I and first published in 1918, at the end of the war. But it was in the thirties, during the days of the Great Depression, when World War II was casting its shadows before it, and during the heyday of the socialist movement in England and America, that his concept of the exile began to catch on. In his introduction to the 1951 edition of Joyce's play, Padraic Colum has given an excellent account of its significance: "To break deliberately with an order one has been brought up in, a social, moral, and spiritual order, and, out of one's own convictions, to endeavour to create a new order, is to embark on a lonely and hazardous enterprise. Stephen Daedalus at the end of *A Portrait of the Artist as a Young Man* contemplates doing this. Richard Rowan in *Exiles* has attempted it. Through secrecy and exile Stephen Daedalus would forge the uncreated conscience of his race. He would go into his exile alone. Richard Rowan, going into exile, brought Bertha with him, and on two he left behind, Beatrice Justice and Robert Hand, he left the impress of his personality. The struggle on Richard Rowan's side to free friendship and love from all their bonds makes the drama of *Exiles*."

This edition of Joyce's play includes the notes on it written by Joyce in a blankbook, in which he underlines the hardships that must be suffered by those who go beyond the accepted moralities of the societies in which their lives are cast. Thus: "Why the title

Exiles? A nation exacts a penance from those who dared to leave her payable on their return. The elder brother in the fable of the Prodigal Son is Robert Hand. The father took the side of the prodigal. This is probably not the way of the world — certainly not in Ireland: but Jesus' Kingdom was not of this world nor was or is his wisdom." Again: "Exiles — also because at the end either Robert or Richard *must go into exile*. Perhaps the new Ireland cannot contain both. Robert will go. But her thoughts will they follow him into exile as those of her sister-in-love Isolde follow Tristan?"

One may be confident that we have in Joyce the primary literary influence in stamping the exile image with the shade of meaning that it has had in our poetry since the early Auden. But if this needed any reinforcement, it was supplied, especially in the United States, by Malcolm Cowley's book about American writers abroad — his *Exile's Return*. It is no insignificant coincidence that this book was first published in 1934, one year before the appearance in the *London Mercury* of Spender's elaborate poem "The Exiles," and only three years before the appearance in *Letters from Iceland* of Louis MacNeice's "Eclogue from Iceland," in which there is a long discussion of the nature of exiles and a listing of several notable Irish "exiles."

Spender's poem "The Exiles" was republished in his volume *The Still Centre* in 1939, in greatly revised and expanded form, and with an expanded title, "Exiles from Their Land, History Their Domicile." The revised form is a marked improvement over the original poem, especially in the matter of lucidity; it is much less difficult to make out what it is the poet means to convey in his strained and badly mixed metaphors and sentences that sometimes quite run off the track. Here is one sentence omitted in the second form — the poet is discussing the "accomplishment" of the returned exiles:

> How shall these severed lives
> Of spirit's hunger, spite's malaria
> — The hate-planted tree — to dissolve and re-form
> To a rosy finger's touch of history our creator?

It is very hard to determine the syntax of the second line. Are we to understand that the exiles' lives were severed *by* spirit's hunger, by spite's malaria? Are these parallel items, or does "spirit's hunger" refer to the hunger of the revered exiles' spirits, "spite's malaria" to a malaria emanating from the spitefulness of the envious? Then for "the hate-planted tree," obviously in apposition to either or both of the preceding, is it possible to realize imaginatively either hunger or malaria as a *tree*? And then we come to the adverbial phrase "to dissolve and re-form," which is left in the air with no predicate to hang on: "how shall these severed lives — *to dissolve* and re-form." And what shall we do with this squirming nest of figures: "to re-form our creator to a rosy finger's touch of history"?

The revised form, as I say, is an improvement, but it is still a sorry piece of writing, judged by any standards of either good prose or of verse as the vehicle of imaginative art. And it is not altogether irrelevant to our general theme to pause a moment over this fact. The poem was first published in a number of the *Mercury* devoted to the celebration of the jubilee (the twenty-fifth) anniversary of the reign of George V. It was accordingly a *pièce d'occasion*, and while Spender's sentiments did not fit in too well with those of the orthodox royalist nationalism, there was much in his tone reminiscent of the odes and rhapsodies associated with such occasions. You hear it for example in the concluding lines of the revised form:

> O utter with your tongues
> Of angels, fire your guns — O save and praise —
> Recall me from *life's exile*, let me join
> Those who now kneel to kiss their sands,
> And let my words restore
> Their printed, laurelled, victoried message.

We ought perhaps to make allowance for the lower poetic standards — the popularization of style — expected in poems written for public occasions by writers whose hearts are elsewhere — Tennysons or Masefields. But the truth is that Spender's stylistic faults in this piece are the faults generally characteristic of his poetry in this and later periods of his writing. And some of them are faults which are *les défaults de sa qualité*, or, we might better say, errors resulting from good intentions. He was trying for modernism in poetry without being altogether modernist in temperament. Some of the

failures of "communication" result from his effort at brevity, crisp-
ness — at getting rid of the prosy surplus of connective tissue. This
accounts for the tendency to elliptical statements; and it accounts
also, no doubt, for the messy confusion of metaphors unequally
yoked together, as well as for the clumsy misalliances of the poetical figure with the baldest prose statement. One feels that Spender
had fallen under the spell of surrealism, dadaism, abstractionism, and
kindred schools in poetry and pictorial art, and that he wished to
modernize his writing with "experimental" techniques not quite
natural to him. One feels that he is trying to be a symbolist when
he is by nature what Tillyard calls a poet of plain statement. Thus
he can refer to his returned exiles as

> Now no more rootless, for whom her [History's] printed page
> Glazes their bruised waste years in one
> Balancing present sky.

Or he can say of them, drinking "from cups of waves" on the seashore, that

> the translucent magnifying lights
> Purify the achievement of their lives
> With human bodies as words in history
> Penned by their wills.

I do not see how poetry could descend to lower depths of pretentious balderdash, and that in the hands of a writer whose early
poems gave promise of so much exactness of vision, sensitiveness of
feeling, and human insight. And yet Spender was a highly admired
member of a group of English poets who had great vogue and ex-
erted the strongest influence on American poets of the time, who in
their turn were eagerly taken up by important publishers and the
editors of influential high-class magazines. And Spender was accordingly an important influence in molding the language and di-
recting the line of interest of American poets of his time.

His conception of the exile, while not as subtle and intellectually
challenging as Joyce's or Auden's, has much in common with theirs.
Exiles were, more simply with him than with Joyce and Auden,
men who were unable to find a congenial environment at home and
who carried on their noble enterprises in foreign garrets and in

"back rooms with hot red plush hangings, / And all outside the snow of foreign tongues." He lists several varieties of such exiles, though not by name, who would doubtless be identifiable (including Joyce) by readers well acquainted with recent literary history. They were, of course, "freedom's friends." They are now buried on native soil, and they are "laurelled." They were harbingers of spring, whereas

> We, who are living, seem
> *Exiles from them*, more living: for we endure
> Perpetual winter, waiting
> Spring . . .

Most interesting, perhaps, is his inquiry as to what separates us who remain from those exiles whose integrated lives (as I interpret) made them unambiguously strong and worthy of their laurels. This passage is found in the revised poem. What, he asks, distinguishes our acts from our madness?

> Who recognizes
> Our image by the head and balanced eyes
> And forming hands, and not the hidden shames?

This reference to hidden shames of ours takes the place of a more open reference to sexual shames, or despair, in the earlier version.

> In the assertion
> Of glossing paper sky, where does the blemish
> Of sexual despair speck the clear dome
> With an ape's venery?

To tell the truth, the connection in the earlier version is so obscure that even a diligent reader is unable to determine whether this "sexual despair" (or hidden shame) is attributed to us the epigones (as in the second version) or to the laureled exiles themselves.

This is a question of some importance. For one has often the sense that this element in personal experience has an important part to play in the development of the concept of exile — either because of the odium widely attached to sexual irregularities, or because of a feeling of guilt on the part of the individual himself, or simply because it is a feature of his life and thought tending to cut him off from the traditionally more respectable members of society. This was, of course, an occasional factor of importance in the lives of those exiles treated by Cowley in *Exiles' Return*. And it is an interesting psychological speculation how far a consciousness of sexual irregularity or peculiarity may operate to develop in an individual a philosophy of life, and a social philosophy, considerably at odds with that prevailing in the social group to which he belongs by birth and nurture.

I do not mean to apply this speculation to particular writers under discussion — certainly not to MacNeice, whose concept of the exile is so much more radical and comprehensive than Spender's, so much more like Joyce's and Auden's. His "Eclogue from Iceland" represents two visitors to Iceland as having an encounter with the spirit of Grettir Asmundson, hero of a famous Icelandic saga, who was a famous outlaw and "exile" from the settled society of his time. He explains to them that he had been betrayed by women and wealthy men; and with "the best of us" driven out by "graft and aggression, legal prevarication," a condition of things which

> Secured long life to only the sly and the dumb
> To those who would not say what they really thought
> But got their ends through pretended indifference . . .

As an outlaw he had saved his pride and had a good life though one of hardship. The two visitors, one from Ireland and one (apparently) from England, confess that they too are exiles. The Irishman describes the Irish life of violence and vendetta, where

> Shooting straight in the cause of crooked thinking
> Their greed is sugared with pretence of public spirit.

The Englishman had been a tourist in Spain before the Civil War, but there had found nothing but the picturesque surface.

> Why should I trouble, an addict to oblivion,
> Running away from the gods of my own hearth
> With no intention of finding gods elsewhere?

They recall certain independent rebels at home — MacKenna, translator of Greek philosophy, "A brilliant talker who left / The salon for the solo flight of Mind"; Connolly, "vilified now by the gangs of Catholic action." To Grettir's question as to what they have found in Iceland, they reply that they have found "mere copy, mere surface." In Europe, Craven says, it is a "dyspeptic age of in-grown cynics," of men who go to war, drive fast cars and climb mountains simply "out of bravado or to divert ennui."

Ryan and Craven hear, what Grettir cannot hear, a honeyed mu-sic from Europe — Wurlitzer, Strauss and roses, blues — and are re-minded of the people at home who "work at desks" and seek enter-tainment in the sterile glossing of old texts or the worship of "tor-tured artists"; who indulge in self-pity and care not "If floods de-populate China"; of the inhuman stare they find everywhere in the faces of "Dictator, bullying schoolboy, or common lout, / Acquisi-tive women, financiers, invalids"; of unloving women on the make who, "half alive, invite to a fuller life," spending their thought on make-up and costume "All tributary to the wished ensemble, / The carriage of body that belies the soul"; of men apparently of good sense and dependable but ridden with fears

> For fear of opinion overtipping in bars,
> For fear of thought studying stupefaction,

who "are ready to plug you as you drink / Like dogs who bite from fear." (It is a pity to summarize, for the text is full of racy writing.) It is from all that that these men are trying to get away in their visit to Iceland. But Grettir bids them to go back home where they be-long, and live their own lives according to their own lights.

> go your own way, give the voice the lie,
> Outstare the inhuman eyes . . .

Their gesture may be minute,

> but it must be made —
> Your hazard, your act of defiance and hymn of hate,
> Hatred of hatred, assertion of human values.

That, he assures them, is their only duty:

> Yes, my friends, it is your only duty.
> And, it may be added, it is your only chance.

There is a touch of Robin Hood bravado in MacNeice's selection of the outlaw for his image of the exile. The Irishman thanks God

> For those who go their own way, will not kiss
> The arse of law and order nor compound
> For physical comfort at the price of pride:
> Soldiers of fortune, renegade artists, rebels
> and sharpers . . .

This may be, dramatically, out of deference to their Icelandic interlocutor; it may be for costume and color and getting away from prose. What the poet really has in mind is intellectual independence, ethical integrity. He is making his protest against the hollowness of so much in current European life — materialism, sensualism, disloyalty, and the sacrifice of all spiritual values to mere success and comfort. These are all sentiments to which a preacher might subscribe. There is something here of the puritan, the dissenter. Craven may be "running away from the gods of his own hearth," and declaring himself in favor of "human values." But this does not sound like "the transvaluation of values" that was undertaken by Ibsen or Joyce. Nor do we have much suggestion here of the social revolutionary that Auden was felt to be. One does not question that the men in this movement truly felt themselves to be "exiles." But one also has the feeling that it had come to be the fashion to be exiles.

Cowley in his *Exiles' Return*, while he was contributing to the popularity of the word, was really using it in a radically different sense from that we have been discussing, His exiles were writers who had cut themselves off from the moral and intellectual life of their home towns — their provincial Main Street — for reasons which, at least in his interpretation, were almost exclusively *literary*. They intended to be writers and they felt themselves superior to their schoolmates and families because they were literary and were accordingly masters of paradox. They cultivated what was called in a Pittsburgh high school the Second Convolution. This meant that in opinion they would always take the unexpected position. This was, of course, one manifestation of the militant individualism which these (at bottom) serious young fellows were opposing to the general conformism that made their American surroundings so stodgy and unrewarding. This conformism they found in their college teachers and classmates. College was hardly more than a school of traditional class-conscious good manners. American life as a whole they felt to be dominated by a gross commercialism and an ugly industrialism which they associated with philistinism as a chief menace to the freedom of the individual "soul" and especially to the soul of the "artist." They thus felt themselves to be exiles in their own homeland. Here the only escape from the pressures of philistinism was bohemia.

But there were other countries where the artist soul could thrive, and as many of these exiles-at-home as could took refuge in (mainly) Paris, and thus made themselves exiles in a quite different sense. They made themselves expatriates in hopes of finding themselves more at home. Many of them served in the war as ambulance drivers, etc. But this only served to make them aware of the hopeless jungle state of mankind. It introduced them to an even more reckless and irresponsible way of living, and a completer disillusion with the traditional faiths and ideals of their ancestors. Cowley emphasizes the fact that they were beginning, in their exile, to conceive a nostalgia for whatever it was they had left behind in their familial background, and had begun a frantic search for something that would take the place of that so as to make their escape from complete futility. Being by intention artists, they found this first of all in Art, with a very large capital A — in art-for-art's sake, in the most rigorous and limited sense of that term. And their inspiration here was largely French writers of the nineteenth century who had been in violent reaction against the progressive and "bourgeois" notions of their society, or recent English and Irish writers, like Eliot and Joyce, who had followed more or less in the train of the French. Some of them were serious and effective "artists"; some were weaklings or dilettanti. Few of them found full satisfaction in the religion of art, and many of them sought frantically for an "escape," in dissipation, in miscellaneous love-making, in drugs, and finally in death.

In the interests of brevity, I have been summarizing more or less in my own terms; but I do not think I have seriously misrepresented Cowley's thesis. What might confuse the reader in his book is the amount of attention devoted there to a minor literary figure named

Harry Crosby, scion of a wealthy Boston banking family, who entertained lavishly, had friends among the French aristocracy, made himself a place of some influence among the American and French literati, and even became one of the advisory editors of *transition*. He was, one concludes, an intellectual lightweight, a symbolist epigone, and a "soul" whose maladies might best be diagnosed by a priest, or still better by a competent psychologist. His was indeed a picturesque character and career, and one can quite understand how a literary historian would be moved to feature him at some length. He had a strong, muscular, sun-tanned body, and an insatiable appetite for dissipation and for the drugs which would enable him to keep it up. But he was also a bedeviled soul, and was capable of inventing a fanciful mythology in the framework of which he could "beautifully" and consistently end his life in a suicide pact in a New York Hotel des Artistes, only regretting that he could not take with him a large "band of followers into the Sun-Death."

Cowley is doubtless right in tracing through his career a consistent logic, and in suggesting that he was not altogether untypical of many others among his "exiles." But while he was a voluntary exile from a Boston which he rightly found stodgy, he carried with him into exile many of the most snobbish attitudes of his native culture-pattern, and notably his aversion to the populace and the poor. This, too, is germane to Cowley's thesis. But whether in the seriousness with which he took his own childish mythology, or in the complete absence in this life and thought of either an ethical-religious or a social scheme of values, he is a poor candidate for the title of exile as it applies to Ibsen or Joyce, to Auden or Spender, or even to Hart Crane.

Cowley goes on to show how many of his American exiles became commercially successful writers; how most of them came back to live in this country; how they settled down perhaps on a Connecticut farm within striking distance of New York. But they had all been subject to the process of deracination, not having succeeded in "reintegrating" themselves with the childhood culture-pattern from which they had cut themselves off. They were still exiles in the sense that they had not found a completely satisfying homeland of the spirit.

It is important here to distinguish between the original version of Cowley's book and the revised version published in 1951. In many respects the new work is an improvement over the original. It is much fuller in its biographical information about writers of the twenties belonging in the group. More allowance is made for variations in outlook and career. Cowley had in 1951 the advantage of a historical perspective not available in 1934. But there is one respect in which the later version loses point in comparison with the earlier. It is perhaps largely a matter of emphasis, but this is historically and theoretically a matter of great significance, and it is a matter of prime importance for his study of exilism. In 1934 Cowley emphasizes the point that for his expatriates the religion of art had proved a dead-sea fruit. Like love-making and other forms of dissipation it did not satisfy the craving for integration with something larger than the individual himself. But in 1934 there was one available means of escaping the soulless isolation of the artists. There was a world struggle going on between the classes in society, known to economic writers as the capitalists and the proletariat. Most of the writers were born into the former class, and it was there they had found their comforts, their friendships, their education, and their "culture." But actually this class had little to offer them. Its culture is available to very few. Its mellowness and liberalism "are merely the ornaments of its prosperous years"; in times of danger they give way to "brutality direct and unconcealed." Under it, individual freedom and the fostering of science are not secure: "Eventually it threatens the complete destruction of culture, since its inevitable and insoluble self-contradictions are leading it toward wars in which, tomorrow, not only books will be destroyed, but the libraries that contain them, and not only museums, universities, theatres, picture galleries, but also the wealth by which they are supported and the living people for whom they exist."

Well, whatever truth there may be in this, these are words that one no longer sets down in print in the United States; and they certainly do not represent the official point of view of our "working class." We are no longer so sure that "the present ruling class" consists of the bankers and manufacturers. We are fed up on the Soviet type of socialism. It is doubtless in all sincerity that Cowley has omitted passages like this from his revised version. But they were in 1934 necessary to his solution of the problem of the exiles, which was to find a way out of the suffocating spiritual isolation. In 1934 our best writers were in some fundamental sense "liberals." Our commercial culture did not satisfy their need for "integration." Their best hope then was to throw in their lot with the workers: "First of all, it can offer an end to the desperate feeling of solitude and uniqueness that has been oppressing artists for the last two centuries, the feeling that has reduced some of the best of them to silence or futility and the weaker ones to insanity or suicide. It can offer instead a sense of comradeship and participation in a historical process vastly bigger than the individual." It can even, he thinks, offer them a larger and more eager audience and quicker to grasp essentials.

Cowley was not suggesting that artists should turn to propaganda for their salvation. But he realized that the sharp dichotomy between art and life was no longer tenable — the opposition between aesthetic form and the interests we have as men; and he thought that art would be nourished and strengthened when artists were so identified with the interests we have as men that these would naturally make themselves felt in the artist's work.

We no longer think in America of the class struggle as the means by which the just and happy state is to be brought into being. And Cowley could not in all conscience leave in his book ideological statements that reflect an outmoded point of view. But in making these inevitable revisions he did of necessity weaken his book. In any case, he could not keep the happy ending by which writers were encouraged to identify themselves with a movement that might have finally brought about their return from exile to their native home of the spirit.

And now we return to a writer of the thirties who seems never to have entertained the hopes associated with the Marxian ideology, and who, while he was much of an expatriate, did not pre-

sumably regard himself as an exile of the sort described by Cowley. In Prokosch the word *exile* has not the implications of brave
and resolute remaking of one's system of values that it has with
Joyce — after the pattern, say, of Nietsche or Ibsen, of self-imposed
discipline in preparation for some great ideological struggle that
it has with the earlier Auden. It is not a question of maintaining
one's individual character in the face of philistine pressures as in
MacNeice and Cowley's exiles. It does imply great isolation and
loneliness in the world, as with many of these, of homelessness and
deracination. The peculiar note in Prokosch is the utter hopelessness of his exiles in a world that is rotten and going to pieces, the
need for escape from the horrors of this world and the irresistible
craving for annihilation. I will first illustrate his use of the word
in poetry and then cite passages from his novel *The Seven Who
Fled* that will fill in the background of thought and assist in the interpretation of the poems. In *The Carnival* there is a "Song" in
which are listed certain characters in the human scene upon whose
crimes and sufferings the gentle star Hesperus sheds his rays.
Among these are the exiles, and — identical with them or of the
same general class — those who have "lost the wish to live." Hesperus

> Sheds his mild solicitude
> Where the *sickened exile* stood;
> Calms but never can forgive
> Those who lost the wish to live —
> Blinded travellers on the slope
> Who at last abandoned hope . . .

Here also appear those "broken heroes" — "those whom love drove
forth to war" — referred to earlier in another connection. And this,
of course, suggests another motive for exile than that of the general state of the world. In still another "Song" of similar tenor are
listed various happenings at dusk as the "cruel moon moves higher."
Among these:

> When drums cry out and trumpets blow,
> And bombers split the town apart,
> When *exiles march to still their woe*
> *With bullets in the heart* . . .

These are again "those whom love drove forth to war," and the bullets are the anodyne and not the cause of their woe.

In *Death at Sea* there is a haunting and teasing poem entitled "Going into Exile." It represents a party landing on a granite coast and being soon "touched by the fever of that land." The fever of that land is the impulse to kill. As stated by a cripple sighted by them before landing,

> "The only law
> Is that whoever conquers must also kill,
> Who kills must sicken and die by his own hand!"

And they did find fighting and kissing and parting in that land; and there was one of them "who kept his word, went mad, and finally died." It might at first seem that this land symbolizes simply war, but as one reflects upon it, one realizes that war is here but one typical aspect of life itself — of the struggle for existence in which we survive by the destruction of others by one means or another. In any case, in landing upon that shore, we become exiles from humanity, and the final logic of it all is self-destruction.

This interpretation is confirmed by the set of life histories given by Prokosch in *The Seven Who Fled*. They are the histories of seven persons of various races and conditions traveling together by caravan eastward from Turkestan across central Asia. Some of them are held, for obscure political reasons, in the town of Aqsu, either in the prison or in the filthy caravanserai; and others go on to distant places in Mongolia and China. Most of them find their death in one way or another, and accept it unresistingly. And there are several gloomy Eastern philosophers met by the way who dilate at length on what are the dominant drives in the Western world. Thus the Russian Mordovinov: " 'Their whole life, all of "civilized" life' — and he uttered the word with a violent spasm of disgust — 'is a subtle and degraded *escape*. Music, paper, print, oratory, fast movement, alcohol, crowds, racial and economic theories, and all the rest . . . . Marxism, fascism, yes, all of them — some on a fine, idealistic basis, to be sure, others on a terrifying legendary basis — but it's all the same deep down. O yes! they can't bear modern living, they try desperately to make it into something endurable. But they can't quite!' " And again: " 'They talk of war and money and starvation and injustice and all the rest. But the reality is much bigger, more profound, more terrible than these by far. Do you want to know what it is? It's this. *The love of death*.' " He goes on to name their distractions — books, women, etc.: " 'But only one thing really matters with these western people like you and your friends. The desire for annihilation.' "

Prokosch does not confine this view to Westerners, however. In his first novel, *The Asiatics*, he had already taken his readers on a tour through southern Asia — Turkey, Iran, Afghanistan, India, Burma, Indochina — in company with an adventurous young American, full of life, and given us the fullest display of a civilization extremely far gone in decay, with every imaginable variety of physical degradation and moral degeneracy, and with the love of death even more impressive than among the Westerners of the later novel. The main points of difference were the greater passivity of the Asiatics to every form of misery in life and to the lure of death, and the greater disposition to find escape in some form of superstitious mysticism.

In *The Seven Who Fled*, it is in connection with the cultivated English explorer Layeville that the image of the exile is invoked. He and the wealthy Chinaman, Dr. Liu, are discussing the status and characters of their fellow travelers in the caravan. Of one of them Layeville says, "An exile . . . a man without a home . . . looking for a place where he can lose his identity," Dr. Liu wants to know if he is a fugitive from the Soviet; but Layeville cannot answer that. (Being a political fugitive is clearly not the defining character of an exile.) Then Dr. Liu politely asks about Layeville himself. " 'And you? . . . why are you here. Here in desolate Sinkiang? . . . *Exile*? Fear? Exhaustion? Langour? Adventurousness? Ambition?' " Layeville silently considers this. "Suddenly he perceived his body as something apart. A pale, slender *island* in the sea of humanity. A snow-flecked island, surrounded by winds, an *inaccessible and solitary island* in an endless sea." He looks toward the sunny peaks in the distance covered with snow. "Beautiful it looked, pure, icy, incorruptible. The end of all things; all things ended. 'No,' he murmured, half to himself, 'None of those.' "

None of those. Not adventurousness. Not fear in the ordinary sense of the word. Not exile in the sense of one seeking to lose his legal and social identity. But certainly fear and certainly exile in the more radical, the symbolic sense of the word. As Layeville lies down in the snow in some remote valley of Mongolia, and lets it rise up and caress his cheeks, his lips, his eyelids, he has been reviewing his own life and the young men he had known in the capitals of Europe: "the shadowy young people who had spent their whole lives in trying so desolately yet fastidiously to devise some reply to suffering, unalleviated and degraded youthful suffering, the most perilous of all. And then, the desperate *longing for purity*, the detestation of cities, *the fear of humanity*, the *recognition of escape*." And then – and here comes back in all its fullness the symbolism of the island – "Then he closed his eyes and slid back upon the past once more, *that consoling little island, the past*."

The longing for *purity* would have its significance in a religious scheme of things, and would doubtless be a main key to any psychological interpretation to this poet's form of exilism, along with the fear of humanity, the need to escape, and the island symbolism. But we are literary people incompetent to enter the difficult realm of psychology. We must simply note that, while the sense of isolation is a prominent feature in the exilism of Ibsen, of Joyce, and of Auden, their exilism looks in a very different direction. Theirs is a fighting program in the interest of life. Layeville's is a passive exilism leading straight to death.

18. EXILES: THE FORTIES

Our instances of the exile image thus far have been taken from poetry of the thirties. The image persists through the forties, though often with a distinct loss of the comprehensive significance it held in poets like Auden and Prokosch. In Auden himself it has undergone a sea-change in its direction of reference. Thus in *The Age of Anxiety*, when he has long since put behind him the secular ideology of his earlier poems, we have Rosetta speaking of the likelihood that she may soon be called for some new exile. In an age of anxiety, all men live in exile cut off from the saving Truth. For, as we know from *The Double Man* (in "The Quest" and the "Epilogue"), they have chosen the "Negative Way toward the Dry" instead of the positive way, which leads to the Truth whose various symbols are the Waters, the Garden, the Word, and whose character is "One immortal one infinite Substance." Rosetta had come to America, which was "the best place to come to if you had to earn your living," and had done well as a buyer for a big department store. She had hoped to find love in the person of Emble. He had enlisted in the navy while a student in a midwestern university, and he "suffered from that anxiety about himself and his future which haunts, like a bad smell, the minds of most young men." He had come home with Rosetta from a party, and it looked as if they might find love together. But instead he fell into a drunken sleep, and she was left to reflect on how their "ways had crossed and our words touched / On Babylon's banks." She anticipates that he will build here and be satisfied soon,

> while I sit waiting
> On my light luggage to leave if called
> For *some new exile*, with enough clothes
> But no merry maypole.

Thus the status of exile has declined in Auden from a brave self-imposed isolation and discipline in the interests of a new thought and a saving way of life for men, to the dreary and anxiety-ridden loneliness of one who, by accident or want of vision, or simple perversity, has taken the wrong turning, and who in his nightmares sees ("The Third Temptation," *The Double Man*)

> Approaching down a ruined corridor,
> A figure with his own distorted features
> That wept, and grew enormous, and cried Woe.

The war naturally gave currency to the image of exile as the soldier's lot, whether or not he embraced it with faith in its nobility or with a sense of its hideous futility. Thus we have Meredith's *"exile islands* of the mind," which may refer simply to the fact that he is separated from his loved one. Karl Shapiro, in "Homecoming" (*The Trial of a Poet*, 1947), begins with the same use of exile to characterize the soldier's enforced separation from normal living.

> Lost in the vastness of the void Pacific
> My *thousand days of exile*, pain,
> Bid me farewell.

But as the poem proceeds, the word takes on a deeper coloration from a more critical view of war, its causes, and its effects. He is unable, in the ocean mist, to smile

> And ask forgiveness of the things that thrust
> Shame and all death on millions and on me.

As he describes the shipload of the sick, the lunatics, and the majority of the healthy, who

> stare with eyes in rut,
> Their hands a rabble to snatch the riches
> Of glittering shops and girls,

he grows angry, and stands alone, hating

> the swarms of khaki men that crawl
> Like lice upon the wrinkled hide of earth . . .

He leans outward seeking to pierce the fog and find "our sacred *bridge of exile and return*." Thus, echoing, perhaps, the title of Cowley's book, he rises to the concept of exile as an alienating state of mind from which one may hope to return home. He is also, perhaps, echoing the title of Auden's book, "gnawing the thin slops of *anxiety*." And as the boat enters territorial waters, he records that "terrible burst of joy" that will

> liberate in that high burst of love
> The *imprisoned souls* of soldiers and of me.

For him exile was not the mere banishment of bodies but an imprisonment of men's souls.

Hayes's *Welcome to the Castle* is throughout a bitterly disillusioned picture of the European soul as seen by those whose business it was to occupy Europe after the war. Hard-boiled cynical materialism is its leading feature, along with a decadence that includes both the Italian and the American characters. It is quite in key with

the other poems in this book that he should give us a picture of
Heinrich Heine during the dark days of his "exile" in Paris:

> Though he loved this city of boulevards and the Bastille
> Still *the exile always has a strange haircut.*

He thinks nostalgically of Düsseldorf, Frankfort, Göttingen, and
his early loves, and then of himself, writing German in Paris. "Marx
was in England; Gautier was his friend; Goethe was dead." There is
reference to his mistress, Matilda, who "was good to him though
she had never read Hegel." There is a threat of war in the air:

> And over Europe the wheel of disaster turned
>   in its grease.
> Though they sat in the cafes fierce about art
> The *assassins* were preparing masterpieces
>   of their own.

Perhaps Hayes had been reading Auden and/or Prokosch. He gives
Heine a prophetic vision of our own time:

> We will all, he brooded, be *exiles* soon.
> Because we were unlucky enough to choose
>   the wrong father
> Or because of a remark made in an open cafe.

Since Heine the Jews in Europe have been mostly either liquidated
or sent into exile; and that has been pretty much the case with anyone injudicious enough to express the wrong political sentiment.
We are living, thinks Heine, in "Europe's declining afternoon."
And then with a symbolism more marked than usual with Hayes,

> Travelling on the false passport we arrive at
>   the tropical harbor,
> Unload our baggage in the diseased towns
>   of the equator.

I will not venture to put a specific interpretation upon these symbols. They make one think of the island and exile imagery in Prokosch. But still more, perhaps, they make one think of various characters in Conrad who have lost their identity in sundry diseased
towns of the equator. Heine belongs, certainly, to the species of exiles who set themselves off deliberately from the intellectual world
of the philistines. He was one who earnestly sought to bring about

Joseph Warren Beach

a *rapprochement* between the French and the Germans. Hayes makes him think of Marx, now in exile in England. And he also makes him think of those whom race and opinion send off to the dead ends of jungle and tropical harbor.

It is Malcolm Brinnin who, in the forties, most persistently labored to give a constructive ethical and social significance to the image of the exile. It appears in several of his most challenging poems, and here one must acknowledge that, for all their forbidding thorny texture, like the hedge that surrounded the Sleeping Beauty in the fairy tale, there is a force and bite to much of his writing, and a sturdy determination not to give in to a weak romantic disillusion in the face of world disasters, that brings one back to them in spite of his frequent obscurity. But it has taken me many strenuous readings to make out in each case just what meaning to assign to the word *exile* as it appears in its several contexts and I do not offer my gloss with any great confidence.

It is with three poems in the 1945 volume, *No Arch, No Triumph*, that we have to do. In "A Sail" Brinnin shows us a phantom yachtsman sailing straight across the harbor's mouth, since there is no sign or haven on that coast, and he is one who dreams "of white boats in blue air / Drawn by the gentle shores." We are then informed that, if he had landed there, he would have found a dreary province, full of men "bent like headstones" and women who

> marry young and in white houses
> Die through the snows and roses
> Of little seasons pleasure cannot fill . . .

There are many other signs of decadence and of sentimental pretense of well being. The "golden poets . . . weave of exhausted sun / The rakish haloes of senility," and "The glory grins / From platforms like a patriotic whore." So much for the country where the "exile" cannot see a haven to put in at. Then there comes a lift of wind to delight "the exile and his sail." The wind does not hold out. But no matter.

> The yachtsman, and he may be a Jew,
> Fares on illegibly through the ancient haze

166

> As through the branches of dead trees
> And seals the view.

The Wandering Jew was long since the prototype of the perpetual exile, and at the moment Brinnin was writing, the Jews, when their lives were spared, were still the world's most lamentable exiles. One also remembers the figure of "the abstract Jew" in Warren's "Original Sin," and "the feverish old Jew" who "stares stern with authority" in the doctor's waiting room in "Pursuit." But none of that makes clear the further symbolism of the exile. In the framework of Brinnin's writing as a whole, and in the light of the two other poems where the exile appears, it seems probable that he stands here for the intransigent high-minded idealist who, in a world of lies and ruins, instead of staying at home and applying himself actively to reconstruction, sails off to the Fortunate Isles and loses himself in private and deceiving dreams.

This is clearly enough the sense the word has in "The Fortunate Isles" — a poem we have already considered in connection with the island image. In Brinnin's account there of what becomes of persons coming home from "that climate of love" represented by the Fortunate Isles, there are some who, "in *exile*, learn at last / Love is the backward look." It is a backward and hopeless look instead of a forward and hopeful one. The poet then goes on to say that a man with Fortunate Isles on his mind,

> Is precipitously set between
> *Marriage and exile*, and marriage is difficult . . .

At first one thinks of marriage in the literal sense; and everyone knows how true it is that marriage is difficult. But in this particular context and in the general framework of Brinnin's thought, one decides that marriage is symbolic. Marriage means signing up for good with society and the world as they are, with the intention either of making the best of them on their own terms or of making them *better* in terms of one's ideal. And we have already seen that, in this poem, the exile "makes a cave / Of the world and of solitude a cult," and that

> In the small rooms of his sorrowing,

167

Joseph Warren Beach

> Islands and other places will hang
> Forever, false and full of love.

"Second Sight" is perhaps the fullest and most impressive exhibition of Brinnin's philosophic stand in the face of the war and the postwar world. It is a strong and brave stand, and a strong and brave poem, and gives one the best notion of why so many editors and publishers have considered him important. And here again the exile image appears in a highly significant context. Brinnin begins with an elaborate critical analysis of the writer's psychology in this age of disillusionment. He is exhibiting the psychology of the writer who is not strong enough to bear up against the ugly facts of the modern world, and who takes refuge in a sentimental extravagance in the use of lying words. Above all "the laurelled child / Of honor and impeccable ambition" takes refuge in sentimental self-indulgence. He is complex, self-pitying, and self-willed, when what the world needs is a clear eye free from egoism and "the simple operations of accomplished hands." And so our writers, whom we so much need to speak for us and express our continuing faiths, fail us. The "laurelled child"

> wins the world's exemption with his crooked smile.
> Silent, moving through self-distorting mirrors, he grows old
> Who might speak for us all.

The poet then goes on to characterize our world as one of wasted energies.

> Waste and the images of waste — the *exile*, the slum,
> The dog in the limousine, the juke-box coin of sex . . .

He distinguishes two types of reaction to this situation. There is the "man with question," who looks askance, is moved by irrational pity, and "like a grim draftee leaves home." And there is "the man of living action" who,

> shouldering his paradox, signs
> For the rusted valley where his voluntary hands may claim,
> In time, their salvaged province.

This is the same "stolid province" where, in "The Sail," the men were like bent headstones. This rusted valley is presumably the same as Auden's in his mournful *paysage* — "hearing of harvests

168

rotting in the valleys." They are like the lands of the South wasted by one-crop farming, but capable of being salvaged. The grim draftee comes in a little later, where

> the soldier-poet, in a metamorphosis
> Of militating sense, falls to an emphasis
> On inner order, and attains
> A *vision of exile* for his pains.

The inner order is a private and sentimental order, suitable to a man in exile, not the outer and public and "truthful" order of what Brinnin calls "the melody / Of life in its plurality." To realize this melody it takes effort and action, and it takes a "making faith."

> With the making faith we have we look toward its reality,
> For truth is a result.

Thus Brinnin seems to give to the exile image essentially the same meaning as Prokosch, but he sets over against it the unsymbolized "man of loving action." He shares Auden's early faith in "life in its plurality." But with him the exile is not one who voluntarily breaks with the current ideals (or lack of them) in order to realize ideals not yet generally accepted; he is instead the discouraged and egotistic man who "goes to islands."

19. EXILES: FRENCH VERSION

Meantime, while English and American poets were celebrating, under the image of the exile, those whom war and nationalism and race prejudice condemned to isolation, those who chose loneliness as the price they must pay for the enterprise of transvaluating values in the realm of ethics and social organization, and those who sought out the islands and caves of solitude in order to maintain some private dream of love or death, an eloquent French poet was carrying the term into the wider and higher, the more abstract level, in which it refers to all those who, in a self-imposed solitude of the mind and heart, were keeping alive that all-comprehending dream of human meaning and value in a brute world entirely indifferent to all things human, made up of forces continually busy in destroying and obliterating the works of men. I refer, of course, to Saint-John Perse (Saint-Léger Léger), and mainly to his poem "Exil."

I do not have it in mind to prove a direct relationship of literary influence operating here between poetry in the English and French languages; nor on the other hand to rule out the possibility that such influence may have been in operation. As early as 1928, fragments of certain of Perse's early poems were published in English translation in the American magazine in Paris, *transition*, and in 1944 a whole volume of the early poems was published in English and French, in New York, with an introduction by Archibald MacLeish. Perse's *Anabase*, first published as a whole in 1924, was published in 1930 in London, with an English translation and preface by T. S. Eliot, French and English on opposite pages; and later editions including Eliot's translation appeared in New York in 1938 and 1949. What is still more important for our present study, Perse's "Exil" was written in the United States and made its first appearance, in French, in *Poetry*, March 1942. Various other late poems of Perse were published in translation in the *Sewanee Review* and *Briarcliff Quarterly* between 1944 and 1946; and *Exile and Other Poems*, with translations by Denis Devlin opposite the French originals, was published in New York in 1949. There was also an edition of these poems in French, with a preface by Archibald MacLeish, published at Buenos Aires in 1944.

The theme of exile was momentarily sounded by this French poet in the beginning of his *Anabase*. He is about to raise the "song of an entire people" — the people of the desert. As poet, he addresses the various sorts of people who visit the desert on business or pleasure, explorers or mere "finders of reasons for moving on from where they are," and he boasts that none of them do business in a "stronger salt" than he,

> when in the morning, forecasting kingly realms and dead waters suspended high above the smokes of earth, *the drums of exile* awake on the frontiers the eternity that yawns above the sands.*

* Here and in later quotations from "Exil" I make my own translation, with less regard for the exalted style of the original than for the precise meaning.

But little effort is made in this early poem to develop the character of the exile. He is, to be sure, the Stranger or Foreigner (*L'étranger*), inhabiting the solitude of his thoughts, and "there is no more substance of man left in him." But what absorbs him is not so much the "dreams" of a poet as the people he is observing — "all sorts of men in their ways and fashions."

In "Exil," the poet is not much concerned with the ordinary ways of men, of desert tribes — their migrations, feuds, wars and settlements — but rather with the visionary minds that carry men's thoughts beyond their primitive ways and concepts of living:

> Those who went on crusade to the great Atlantic Indies, those who smell out the new idea in the coolnesses of the abyss, those who blow their horns at the gates of the future
> Know that in *the sands of exile* whistle the high passions coiled beneath the whip of the lightning . . .

The exile here is the Stranger, and the Poet, and the Foreigner (*Le Pérégrin*); he is also the Outlaw or Banished One (*Le Proscrit*) and the Prodigal (*Le Prodigue*). And sometimes he is called the Prince of Exile. He is never represented as dwelling, though a stranger, among the peoples whom he visits and being entertained by them, as the poet in *Anabase*. But he is pursued by a symbolical Beggar Woman, who is a sort of personification of the clamor, the splendor, the lamentation that fill the world, like "an insurrection of the soul." He is pursued by the great repudiated and unloved girl whom the ancient priests called courtesan, but who dwelt in the green caves of the Sibyls; his name was called by this prophetic figure. Whatever was written was soon erased and lost to memory; and the impure offerings and objects of superstition were burned. But he went on composing "a pure language without ritual" and "a great poem that might be blotted out." There were times when everything seemed to fail one, and "many centuries veil themselves before the lapses of history." But again he cries: "Here I am restored to my native shore . . . There is no history but that of the soul, there is no satisfaction but that of the soul."

What the poem is celebrating is, to put it in the bald language of prose, the inveterate aspiration of a noble soul in the face of the mere phenomena of nature and the great wastes of history. My feeble summary of the first five sections of the poem might give the impression of a somewhat inflated rhapsody, with little content drawn from the rich offerings of actual life. The aspirations of men seem thin and empty of all but feeling. "Exil" is so far in contrast with *Anabase*, which though expressed in much the same lofty style is most colorful in its evocation of the ways of life among nomadic peoples and the natural scenery in which Asiatic history was enacted. "Exil" was written during the early years of World War II, but there is in the whole poem but one clear reference to this overwhelming event. *Anabase* was written some years after the close of World War I, soon after Eliot's *Waste Land*. And while it refers to ancient times and semiprimitive people, there are circumstances having to do with dynastic wars that might be thought to parallel the recent experience of Europe. Thus, in a general vision of wars and alliances and displaced populations, of

> needy captains in immortal paths, the whole male population come in crowds to do us obedience with their gods on staffs, and the princes fallen in the Northern sands, their daughters tributary swearing fealty to us, and the Master saying: I have faith in my destiny,

we have this realistic account of the way wars are deliberately started by politicians:

> For us who were there, we provoked upon the frontiers exceptional accidents, and spurring our selves into action to the limit of our powers, our joy among you was a very great joy.

But as we read on in "Exil," we find that the title of exile is not limited to poets and visionaries of the mind, and here we find that the later poem greatly surpasses the earlier in solidity of specification, in moral seriousness and elevation, and above all in interest for us who live in an age of science at its peak and of advanced mechanical civilization. In each of these poems, toward the end, there are long passages given over to the listing of occupations characteristic of the stages of civilization under discussion. In *Anabase* they are all occupations or even types of idleness to which men turn in the millenary search for happiness. And we have a picturesque and comprehensive showing of characters and activities that flourish among the mostly nomadic and mainly illiterate populations of the Near East, where the organization of life is tribal and military and the common life is subject to the changes of climate on the edges of great deserts. Their skills have to do with the care of horses and camels and the performance of sacred rites for the propitiation of the powers in nature, the arts of the soothsayer, of husbandry, all crafts of building and the making of clothes and of beautiful objects of use, the trader's arts, the military arts (for "a great principle of violence dictated our fashions") and, with more book learning, the arts of the astronomer and the lexicographer, and always, along with these, the arts of women for giving men pleasure in their times of relaxation. And these activities are for the most part carried on publicly and without severance from the life of the community.

In "Exil," the activities listed are all such as are carried on in solitary places and with lonely concentration of mind and spirit, and almost always for the furtherance of knowledge or the preservation of life and security under conditions of high civilization. There is

> the man who wanders at midnight, along the galleries of stone
> to determine the rank of a beautiful comet; he that watches,
> between two wars, over the purity of the great crystal lenses;
> he that rises before dawn to clean out the fountains, and it is
> the end of the great epidemics . . .

There is the man who cares for the insane; the one who paints warning signs on high headlands and reefs; the one who, drawing charts, is shut up in the closed circle of the cyclone; there is the forest ranger, after the storm, dispelling the funereal smell of burning brambles in the woods; the one who, "in sterile places, watches over the fate of the major telegraph lines"; and the reader of seismographs in the catacombs and sewers under the city. There are those who save from rioters the Botanical Gardens, the Offices of the Mint, and other public services, and who, in times of crisis, safeguard the tall liners "held under seal." Above all, there are the solitary intellectual workers, as well as those who provide funds for their researches:

He that opens a bank account for the researches of the mind; he that enters the arena of his new creation, in an exaltation of his whole being, and for three days no one may look upon his silence but his mother, no one have access to his chamber but the oldest of his servants; he who leads his mount to the springs but does not drink himself . . . he who, like (the conqueror of India) Baber, who between two great manly exploits, puts on his poet's robe to pay homage to the beauty of a terrace; he who falls into revery during the dedication of a nave, and there are crockets in the spandrel, like ears, walled in for the acoustics . . .

All these, and many others equally dedicated to lonely and elevated pursuits of the mind, are, the poet says, *Princes of Exile*, and have no need for his song; since they are, he implies, the exponents of the same vision with him. They are, like him, "*Strangers upon all shores of the world*, without audience or witness." They are "precarious guests on the fringes of our cities." They will not "cross the threshold of Lloyds, where their word has no currency and their gold no value." And as with the poet, their mothers and wives must pay the price of their association with exiles, must give up their men to their solitary undertakings.

All these, save Baber, represent the civilization of Europe — postdating the invention of telescope and microscope, the harnessing of electricity, the development of medical science, and the scientific pursuit of climatology and meteorology. If I have chosen my example too much from theoretical and applied science to please the literary and artistic mind, I will hasten to add "the man who, when armies move in, goes up to the organs in their solitude," and the one

whose concern is with the accidents of phonetics, with the alteration of signs and the great erosions of language; who participates in the high debates of semantics . . . he who determines the hierarchies in the great rituals of language . . .

But that, too, I fear, will not satisfy our modern poets and literary critics. Phonetics and semantics sound too much like science, and science is with them the scapegoat for all their grudges against our "mechanical age," all their fears that empirical knowledge threatens to wither away our spiritual life. But there, to be sure, is where, for the most part, they most show their want of vision and their loss of nerve. And one is happy to find at length a distinguished poet doing justice to the scientist and to those who safeguard the application of scientific knowledge to the machines that support our modern structure of civilization. It may be a surprise to us that this reverent view of science and technology is found in a representative of Old World civilization, one learned in medieval and Asiatic lore; and, at that, a "purer" poet than most of ours, who writes in an exalted "classical" (or Asiatic) style. One would have welcomed it most in an American poet, inheritor of our traditions and special accomplishments and master of our more down-to-earth manner of writing. But perhaps the lesson is that we have not yet lived long enough with our own inheritance to unselfconsciously be proud of it.

20. THE STRANGER

Wherever the exile may be, he is a stranger, for, as Alfred Hayes has Heine say, the exile always has a strange haircut. He is not at home though he be at home, for his language is not understood. The stranger is, as Perse says in *Anabase*, "clad in his new thoughts, and making himself partisans in the ways of silence." However well he is made at home in the villages where he stops, his thoughts are already "encamped under other walls." His hosts elicit from him a song, but, he says, "I have not told anyone to wait for me." Indeed, "I hate you all in my gentle way." And he is always rising before dawn to leave for another destination.

Perhaps even more than *exile* the word *stranger* carries with it the human emotion attaching to this condition. Auden says of his Wanderer,

> No cloud-soft hand can hold him, restraint by women;
> But ever than man goes
> Through place-keepers, through forest trees,
> A *stranger* to *strangers* over undried sea . . .

The stranger is a traveler, and as such he is a foreigner and stranger to the ways of the country where he stops momentarily, or in which, as exile, he must find a home. Foreigner is the primary meaning of the French word *Etranger*. And in poetry voyageur (traveler) is often identical with exile and stranger. He follows the roads of the world seeking the seeds of poetic intoxication: "O Traveller in the yellow wind!" He goes alone. Perse writes:

> Solitude! I have told no one to wait for me . . . . I am going wherever I wish . . . ." And the Stranger, clad in his own new thoughts . . . And the earth in its winged seeds, like the poet in his discourse, *travels* . . .

And so in Auden,

> Travellers may sleep at inns but not attach,
> They sleep one night together, not asked to touch;
> Receive no normal welcome, not the pressed lip,
> Children to lift, not the assuaging lap.

And he on whom doom falls, dreams in strange places of

> Kissing of wife under single sheet;
> But waking sees
> Bird-flocks nameless to him, through doorway voices
> Of new men making another love.

In Prokosch ("Song," *The Carnival*) the star Hesperus looks down with mild solicitude upon "the sickened exile,"

> Calms but never can forgive
> Those who lost the wish to live —
> *Blinded travellers* on the slope
> Who at last abandoned hope . . .

To the traveler himself it is the inhabitants of the foreign country who are strangers, and a menace to him. Prokosch ("The Assassins" in the volume of the same name) bids us remember that under physical beauty in man or nature hides "Such hostility to love, / Such horror and hate," and consider,

> in the hours
> Of tenderness before sleep
> By *each beautiful stranger*
> Whether of word or flesh
> What everlasting danger is there hidden.

In another place the "hairless stranger" who enters the central wood and encounters the horrors of nature in Africa, is, of course, the Caucasian traveler. Some of the most moving passages of recent poetry involving the image of the stranger are found in John Berryman's "At Chinese Checkers" (*Poems*) and Randall Jarrell's "On the Railway Platform" (*Blood for a Stranger*, 1942; first published in *Five Young American Poets*, 1940). In Berryman's poem he places the writer "*Sitting with strangers* by a Northern lake," playing the game with marbles called Chinese Checkers with a group of excited young people. He is only half there: his mind wanders to the old lumbering days before the woods were gutted by exploiters; to the days of his childhood far from there, to the dear remembered young people playing this same game in a "low and country room" in the South, to his friend Delmore lying sleepless in "the unfriendly city"; and, presumably, to men on the battlefield. He is frequently recalled to the play by "insistent voices." They are the voices of strangers, and his is a "crowded travelling face."

> What prophecies, what travel? *Strangers call*
> *Across the miles of table*, and I return,
> Bewildered, see burnt faces rise and fall
> In the recapitulation of their urn.

Something in his train of associations calls up the vision of seas and Simonetta's grave "Deeper than the dark cliff of any tooth, / Deeper than memory." But

> The man across the table shouts an oath,
> The sea recedes, *strangers possess the house.*

But he hears again "Delmore's magic tongue," *

> What the sea told
> Will keep *these violent strangers* from our room.

I have commented earlier on the obstinate obscurities of this poem, which many readings will not clear up. But here I would dwell on

---

* The exact text is "Issued from the tomb, Delmore's magic tongue." If, as one assumes, this Delmore is the poet Delmore Schwartz, and if it is he who is referred to in the following stanza as "his taken friend," one is completely at a loss to understand how these words can apply to a man still living.

the great beauty of the poem as a whole in spite of this heavy handicap. I would be reluctant to admit that this may be partly attributable to the air of romantic strangeness that derives from the teasing obliquities. Without them it might have been a truly "great" performance. But in any case, there is the beauty of rhythm in the verse movement, the imaginative power with which the particular scene is invested, and above all, the strong emotional effect that rises from the sense of alienation imprinted on this "crowded travelling face" by the insistent interruption of his train of thought and feeling by the "violent strangers" in the room.

But far the most beautiful and effective evocation of the image of the stranger, the traveler, the journey, to be found in our poetry is Jarrell's "On the Railway Platform." This too is "difficult" reading from the simple fact that it is all done by the indirect means of symbolism, with rigorous economy of word, and that the symbolism is intricate and rich in its interconnections. But the interconnections are all made clearly enough; the individual images are distinct and sharp; and the implications of thought, while far ranging, are not too esoteric for a reader to follow, once he has been captured by the more obvious emotional appeal of the imagery. It is always a pity to summarize, or to try to render the sense of a poem by small isolated fragments. It would, of course, take an anthology to do proper justice to the poetry one discusses. With so fine a poem as this, one feels compelled to give it in its entirety:

> The rewarded porters opening their smiles,
> Grapes with a card, and the climate changing
> From the sun of bathers to the ice of skis
> Cannot hide it — journeys are journeys.
>
> And, arrived or leaving, "Where am I going?"
> All the travellers have wept; "is it once again only
> The county I laughed at and nobody else?
> The passage of a cell between two cells?"
>
> No, the ends are hardly indifferent, the shadow
> Falls from our beaches to the shivering floes,
> The faces fail while we watch, and darkness
> Sucks from the traveller his crazy kiss.

The tears are forming; and the leaver falls
Down tracks no wheel retraces, by the signs
Whose names name nothing, mean: Turn where you
  may,
You travel by the world's one way.

And the tears fall. What we leave we leave forever:
Time has no travellers. And journeys end in
No destinations we meant. And the strangers
Of all the future turn their helpless gaze

Past the travellers who cannot understand
That they have come back to tomorrow's city,
And wander all night through the unbuilt houses
And take from strangers their unmeant kisses.

This poem marches straight forward without interruptions and
without allusion to situations with which the reader has no means
of being acquainted. Suppose we say that its subject is journeys,
what one hopes to find at one's destination, and the inevitability,
since the situation forever changes, in an irreversible time process,
of one's being sadly disappointed. And let us assume that the journey is symbolical of something much more comprehensive than
mere travel to distant places; it symbolizes all experience, for all
experience involves a seeking after something which, by our very
nature, we cannot find, since "tomorrow's city" is always different
from that with which we are familiar and that which we anticipate.
The various symbols, it should be noted, are not given abstractly
as so many hieroglyphics to be decoded, but with a physical realism that makes them at once visible to the imagination.

The beginning of the journey and its hopeful mood are embodied in the images of porters smiling with gratification on receiving
their proper tips, the going-away gift of grapes with the donor's
card, and the change of climate as one passes from sunny bathing
beaches to icy Arctic floes. All of these things arouse one's hopes.
But they cannot disguise the truth, stated with such piquant final-
ity, that "journeys are journeys." Every move we make is destined
to bring disappointment, the new move necessarily involving alteration, whereas we are bound to carry with us our old selves — "the

shadow? Falls from our beaches to the shivering floes." Our hopeful expectations are embodied in the faces and kisses that we are always missing, but hope to find in the new place, but these "fail while we watch, and darkness sucks from the traveller his crazy kiss." The traveler is on the verge of tears as he "falls down tracks no wheel retraces," and passes signs that have for him no recognizable meaning except that he travels "by the world's one way." He may expect to return to the county he had laughed at; that is, after all, his native setting. However, that he cannot do, for once he makes a move he has unalterably changed the situation. "What we leave we leave forever." "Time has no travellers." We may be swept along in the flood of time; but we cannot keep pace with time's changes. These are the *lachrymae rerum*; "the tears fall." "*Journeys* end in / No destinations we meant"; we cannot realize our best intentions. The future is always there where we expected to find the present, or perhaps it is a very future which we cannot recognize. The places that we arrive at are full of strangers, who "know not" us. And we do not understand them. They turn their gaze helplessly

> Past the travelers who cannot understand
> That they have come back to tomorrow's city,
> And wander all night through the unbuilt houses
> And *take from strangers their unmeant kisses.*

There are in this poem a number of images that take us back to earlier writing. Coming back to tomorrow's city may remind us of "Rip Van Winkle." One well versed in the early work of Auden will be reminded of the sadness suggested in many passages dealing with voyagers and strangers. Especially he may remember from the two choruses how travelers "sleep one night together, not asked to touch," receiving "no normal welcome, not the pressed lip," and how the man doomed to exile wakes in the morning to "voices of new men making a new love." In "The Exiles" he may remember the same definitiveness asserted of the "leaver" — "This life is to last, when we leave we leave all." As for the unmeant kisses, we may remember how in "The Exiles," "We live like ghouls / On posts from girls / What the spirit utters / In formal letters," and this other riddling reference to the "love" allotted to the exiles.

Here we shall live
And somehow love
Though we only master
The sad posture.*

And there are still other passages in the early Auden that might
have some bearing on the crazy and unmeant kisses in Berryman's
poem. Thus in *Look, Stranger!* poem XXIII (which appears in the
Collected Poetry under the title "It's So Dull Here") the speaker
is asking his "darling" whether she can bear "to settle in this village
of the heart." They have returned to the "hall" full of childhood
memories, but now turned into a "licensed house for tourists, /
None too particular." The whole neighborhood has changed and
vulgarized. And he asks her whether she can really see this as home,
and not depend

> For comfort on the chance, the sly encounter
> With the *irresponsible beauty of the stranger?*

Going even farther afield, some analogy might be found with the
passage in *Anabase* where some woman of the tribe (apparently a
prophetess) says of the Stranger, entertained and honored in his
tent,

> At night they bring him tall barren woman . . . and perhaps
> of me also will he take his pleasure. (I know not what are his
> ways with women.)

But whether or not any items of imagery from earlier poets may
have sparked the imagination in Jarrell, he cannot in any disparaging sense be regarded as "derivative." Anything that he may have
caught up from his reading has been thoroughly assimilated to the
body of his own creation. It is the *emotion* attaching to the stranger's feeling of alienation from the things and the people he encoun-

* This image I do not understand. It sounds like some code word for those
who do understand, especially when we take it together with Spender's use
of the word in his *Vienna*. He is speaking in praise of normal sexual love and
apparently of some fear he felt for this. And he blames his disability on his
father. "It was surely my father / His dry love his dry falling / Through
dust and death to stamp my feature / That made me ever fear *that fortunate
posture.*"

ters that has here been brought to its highest pitch and given its classical expression in this poem.

It is in truth the "purest" of poetry. We know that in Jarrell's thinking and imagining there is a rich background of abstract theory and factual observation. He has been the most outspoken of our poets in his pacificism, his hatred of war and of the social system that breeds war. And there may well be, tucked away in the symbolism of this poem some reference to these ideological attitudes. But for its appreciation there is no need for any such interpretation. The poem does not depend for its force or significance on any such reference. It stands there quite sufficient through its appeal to universal experience and emotion. This is true of several other poems on related subjects included in the same volume of *Five Young American Poets*, later appearing in *Blood for a Stranger*: "The See-er of Cities," "When You and I Were All," "A Poem for Someone Killed in Spain," and "Love, in Its Separate Being." In the last-named there are poignant evocations of the images of exile and stranger. And in later, more realistic poems on the war, Jarrell makes probably the most successful combination of actualities and symbolism of any American poet of his age group.

21. JOURNEYS

The image of the voyage and the traveler (*Voyageur*) is dominant (along with that of the exile) throughout Perse's two great poems. *Anabase* takes its name from Xenophon's famous history of the expedition of the ten thousand from Cunaxa in Mesopotamia, up the Tigris, through the wilds of Kurdistan, and through the highlands of Armenia and Georgia, to Trebizond on the Euxine. It does not touch on Xenophon's expedition, but does picture the country and the life of semibarbarous and largely nomadic peoples who might have been encountered in those parts of the world. It is full of the mass migrations and the wars of Asiatic peoples, and there is much suggestion of the motives that drive them on in all their movements. These are mainly the lust for power and for that vaguer end called happiness. One might say that the theme of the poem is the blind search for happiness and glory and the evanescent character of all human life. One cannot help thinking that there is some parallel intended by the poet between the millennial violence, the tribal ambitions, the alliances and debacles of these Asiatic peoples, and those that came to a head in Europe in World War I. And the poet, while he seems at times to identify himself with the people with whom he lingers, and to be celebrating their exploits and the vividness of their life, is really expressing his dissent from their own view of themselves. He is like a prophet ironically praising and covertly denouncing the error of their ways and declaring his own separation from them. He says he dwells in a pure robe among them, for another year among them. Then we hear the voice of his hosts followed by his own critical comment:

"My glory is upon the seas, my force is among you!
    This breath of other shores to our promised destiny carrying beyond the seeds of time, the *splendor of an age at its height* on the beam of the scales. . . ."
    Calculations hung on the layers of salt! At the sensitive point on my brow where the poem takes form, I inscribe this song of a whole people, the most drunken,
      to our dockyards drawing eternal keels . . .

Here Eliot translates "un peuple *le plus ivre*" "the most rapt god-drunken," on perhaps good authority. But drunken with what god? And is it possible to read in 1924 of "the splendor of an age at its height on the beam of the scales" without thinking of the Wheel of Fortune and the inevitable doom of whoever is at its top; and is it possible in that year, reading of the tribal wars and alliances and disasters of Asiatic peoples, not to think of the war so lately concluded in Europe and the uneasy balance of power that foreshadowed another war within a generation? Amid the conquests and exultance of these great people, and amid their moral perversities, the prophet's thought is much on the dead and the coming doom.

    And perhaps the day does not pass but the same man has burned with desire for a woman and for her daughter.
    Knowing laugh of the dead, that this fruit be peeled! And so! is there no more grace in the world under the wild rose.
    There comes from this side of the world a great purple doom upon the waters.

Even in the abundance of the barley harvest, he thinks of the dead, lying under "the sand and the urine and the salt of the earth . . ."

> And my soul, my soul keeps loud vigil at the portals of
> death – but say to the Prince to be still: on the point
> of a lance, amongst us,
>   this horse's skull!

The voyage of the poet is another thing from this materialist search for sensual happiness and power. And it must be carried on in solitude. "O traveller in the yellow wind, taste of the soul!" This separation from the world is even more marked in "Exil":

> My glory is on the sands! my glory is on the sands! . . .
> And it is no mistake, O Peregrine,
>   To desire the barest eyrie [or area] for assembling on
> the perilous sands [*aux syrtes*] of exile a great poem, a poem
> made from nothing.

The role of the poet is doubled by the two figures of the Beggar Woman and the temple prostitute, the Sibyl. The Beggar Woman: "O wandering force upon my threshold, O Beggar Woman on our roads and on the trail of the Prodigal!" The Sibyl: "World-wanderer was her courtesan's name among the priests."

The great poem may be made from nothing, for it is made from the spirits longing for the ideal; and if the "night's poems" are "disowned before the dawn," it is because the poet will be content with nothing short of "a pure language without ritual [usage]"; and "there is no history but the soul's and no contentment but of the soul." This may seem an insubstantial program for the soul's voyage. But we have seen how well, in the end, the poet has filled in the picture from instances taken from the modern devotees of the mind's search for knowledge and security.

There are in Archibald MacLeish two notable instances of tribal or mass anabases, in which it is possible to conceive the possibility of influence from the French poet. One is his brilliant epic of the conquest of Mexico, *Conquistador* (1932). And the other, of greater interest to us here, is found in section 9 of *The Hamlet of*

A. MacLeish (1928). This poem is a very modern version of the theme of doubting Hamlet — following, but in its own highly individual manner, Laforgue's treatment of it in his *Moralités Légendaires*. It is not so *fin de siècle* as Laforgue — not so cynical, ironic, and nihilistic. And it is more "poetical." Almost all the action passes in the mind of Hamlet, and it represents a frantic and unsuccessful effort on his part to solve the problem of faith in life, as stated by Ophelia, "How shall we learn what it is our hearts believe in?" Hamlet, reminiscent of *The Waste Land*, is seeking water. He knows there is an answer somewhere to his questions. He cannot find the secret word.

> only these shapes of things that seem
> Ways of knowing what it is I am knowing.

Everywhere "there are signs and I cannot read them." He has traveled widely, and all the places named are in Asia Minor, in a country much like that in *Anabase*. He hears "voices calling the small new name of God." He has intimations from mountains and leaves, but they do not quite make him "remember."

> It has always been secret like that to me.
> Always something has not been said.

Fully half of the poem has for setting the platform at Elsinore, where Hamlet has his meeting with his father's ghost and vainly hopes to hear the secret word from him, and what it is the ghost wishes him to swear to. There is a passage of some four or five pages devoted to an account (from the Welsh Bleheris) of Gawain's quest for the Holy Grail, the long journey to the bare chapel; and then the vision of a dead hand closing about the grail, and a great cry of mocking laughter that sends him scuttling. Another long passage is devoted to an account of journeyings in quest of something not named.

> We who have followed the clouds by day and by darkness
> The march of the wandering fires, we who have watched
> Bird signs in the sky . . .

He is speaking to the ghost, and he wants to know, "where wilt thou lead us?" They have followed him to the "farthest verge," to the "ultimate sea," where men in former times have had messages "from the leaves of future-telling oaks" and "from dolphin-ridden surf." These things have been vouchsafed to "poets, speakers in the earth." But for us,

> Always this blank of silence like a dial
> That counts but will not keep our journey hours.

Almost immediately following the platform scene is that of the play enacted to catch the conscience of the king. But instead of the stages of the play scene, as given in the rubrics in the margin, what we have is a long passage recounting the great migrations of the race since the beginning, or at least since mankind was "the Cloth-Clad Race, the People of Horses." Their progress westward over the face of the earth is sketched in broadly with staccato strokes, in a style that is poetic, by virtue of its mannered simplicity, as in *Conquistador*. There is nothing of the dithyrambic and visionary quality of Perse's narrative. The language is Biblical, without the prophetic note of high passion. The sentences are short, the terms simple and objective, with an almost complete suppression of emotional and impressionistic descriptive words, and of the explanatory connective tissue characteristic of prose history. Important action is often left unstated, but indicated by its effects. It is not said that they made campfires and set up tents in unfamiliar locations, but "Their smoke hangs / Under the unknown skies at evening." Everything is given in the dramatic present, and the present that covers many instances.

> They come to the rivers.
> Before them cities stand in the cool of the date palms.
> The walls go down. There is smoke. They wait for the
> summer
> Watching the streams fail.

The essentials of life and all movements over the earth are given. They are by necessity much the same as in *Anabase* and in many of the early poems of Auden. There is the westward movement with the sun, the coming down through passes to the hot lands, the begetting of children, the destruction of cities and dwelling in the cool of the date palms, the crossing of rivers, the dearth of water, the coming to mountains and the rich plains beyond, the ruthless conquests —

> Taking the lands, killing the male, consuming
> The fat earth. They live in the land. They are
> lords there.

They can never be still. At length they come to the land's end; they build ships and sail to the scattering islands. They dwell at the last shores.

They have their culture, their laws, their language — names for the mountains, for the planting of corn — their theories of origins, their religion and art. "They kiss their hands to the sun and the moon." They leave "the shape of the bird god who delivered / Men from the ancient ill." And, with all that, "they vanish. They disappear from the earth."

> I say there were millions
> Died like that and the usual constellations.

This chronicle is recited while the players enact the king's crime and the dumb show enters. As the disappearance of millions is recited the king rises and lights are called for. It is evident that for Hamlet there is a connection between the king's crime and the endless chronicle of man's barbaric progress through the world. They both make up the world of facts from which Hamlet strives in vain to derive some answer to his moral questioning. "What is the meaning of life? No one has answered us."

The marches of animal man across the face of the earth is one type of journey; Hamlet's quest for meaning and Gawain's search for the Holy Grail are others.

Of all our poets of the thirties and forties it is Auden who returns most often to the image of the journey, and it is for him the symbol of several different types of seeking. In his earliest poems, as in the two choruses discussed under the heading of exiles, it is to underline the loneliness and resolution of one who leaves his native home of the spirit to seek the truth for himself. In the 1930 *Poems*, no. xxv, he complains that such a man is rare.

> Who will endure
> Heat of day and winter danger,
> *Journey from one place to another?*

Most are content to lie all day on the headland "between the land and sea."

> For no one goes
> Further than railhead or the ends of piers.

No one will even send his son further than a certain point where the gamekeeper with dog and gun will shout "Turn back." In the earliest poems he is compassionate for those who make these ideological journeys, but highly approving the journey and the courage of the traveler. Somewhat later he tends to associate journeys with the false islands of sentimentality. In these cases the journey itself is false and deadly. "The journey is false; *the false journey* really an illness / On the false island." In "Paysage Moralisé," those were "shipwrecked who were launched for islands." In "The Journey to Iceland," the traveler hopes to find in that island a refuge. But

> Tears fall in all the rivers. Again the driver
> Pulls on his gloves and in a blinding snow storm starts
> Upon *his deadly journey*; and again the writer
> Runs howling to his art.

In a poem called "The Traveller," published in *New Statesman and Nation* in 1938, one is not quite certain whether he approves or deprecates this type of voyager:

> Holding the distance up before his face
> And standing under the peculiar tree
> He seeks the hostile unfamiliar place,
> It is the strangeness that he tries to see.

By 1940, Auden had gone a long way on what he calls "the emigration of beliefs." Settled down now in the realm of eternity, he no longer celebrates the youth who had taken the *left* way to truth and gone into exile.

> following a line with left and right
> An altered gradient at another rate.

He has now only a sort of condescending pity for "The voyages of hopes and griefs," and for that to which he had himself been so subject, "The world's great rage, the travel of young men" ("A New Year Letter"). He has seen enough of

> the births and deaths
> Of pious hopes, the short career
> Of dashing promising ideas . . .

In the same volume, *The Double Man*, Auden has a set of poems entitled "The Quest," which represent symbolically the search for truth and a true way of life undertaken by a would-be hero, who is bound to fail since he has chosen to go "the Negative Way toward the Dry" instead of the positive way suggested in the (following) epilogue, which would lead him to discovery of the Word, whose attributes are those of "One immortal one infinite Substance." "The Garden" furnishes another image for the true end of man's seek-ing; for it is there that "all journeys die." The poems included in Auden's "The Quest" are not among his finest in quality, but they have great interest in connection with his "emigration of faiths," as well as with his symbology and various allusions to the poet's wide reading: in "The Way," "The way through the waste to the chapel in the rock"; in "The Second Temptation," "He threw away a rival's silly book, / And clattered panting up the spiral stair"; in "The Adventurers," "Still praising the Absurd with their last breath."

A more extended quest is featured in *The Age of Anxiety* in the cross-country expedition of four bewildered worldlings. Emble even wonders if everyone sees himself, like him,

> as the pilgrim prince
> Whose life belongs to his quest
> For the Truth, the tall princess,
> The buried gold or the Grail . . .

But the association of the Grail story with the fairy-tale motives of the tall princess and the buried gold betrays the burlesque in-tention; and the sophisticated Emble knows himself that his "end-less journey" is not toward eternal truths, but has its joy in passing sensations, "the whirr of wheels." Malin has earlier suggested that "the incessant Now of / The traveller through time" means that he is really "in quest of his own / Absconded Self yet scared to find it." When Emble invites Rosetta to be their Beatrice guide, she disclaims having any gift of direction justifying her in taking charge of an expedition that is in essence a "Journey homeward," or in other, more psychological terms, the "Regressive road to Grandmother's House." And the poet himself reminds us, in his stage directions, that their journey has been simply one long flight from the world. They have been in flight from the world because they have not been willing to face the truth embodied in a sacred person whose pronominal designation is always spelled with a capital H.

Thus Auden has come to the end of his journey, unless indeed he should take off again on "the emigration of beliefs." He has come at length to a mystical realm, where it is harder to follow him with the imagination than with the terms of metaphysics and theology.

Other American poets have written poems entitled "The Journey," "This Journeying," or "Voyages." But few of them employ this symbol in Auden's way.

Before Auden, Hart Crane had written his "Voyages" (*White Buildings*), impassioned, desperate love poems, in a brilliantly imagined Antilles world of seas and archipelagoes, in which his human love is conceived of as carrying through death into a mystical paradise in which all mortal grief and evil are caught up into the good that is the final truth of things. These poems celebrate his journeys into the heart of love. In the third one of them, in a confused tangle of images, drawn mostly from sea and sky, he represents himself as winding "ribboned water lanes" on the journey to his beloved; the poem ends with the line "Permit me voyage, love, into your hands . . ." where the language is, as often with Crane, rather startlingly strained and unidiomatic. Crane does not here capitalize the word *love*, and the identification of his human with the heavenly love is not explicitly made. But this identification is implicit here, as generally in Crane's writing. And an enthusiastic admirer of Crane and his philosophy, James Agee, takes from this line the title of a volume of poems, *Permit Me Voyage* (1934), including a piece with the same title. This poem ends with the concluding

line of Crane's, without change except that here *love* is capitalized.
The poet has signed up without reservation for Crane's philosophy
and his view of the poet's prophetic mission:

> And how this world of wildness through
> True poets shall walk who herald you:
> Of whom God grant me of your grace,
> To be, that shall preserve this race.
>
> Permit me voyage, Love, into your hands.

Few poets have been graced with such wholehearted discipleship!

Prokosch has many poems recording the melancholy voyage of
the spirit through a world of horrors, leading inevitably toward
death for the individual and the race. Such are, in *The Assassins*,
"Empty Provinces" and "Going Southward." I have earlier referred to "The Voyage," in which "they" promised us that, "beyond the torrential islands," we may at last "find the concerted
will / And the quiet heart, and the sure and sharpened spirit." But
instead we found misery and mourning in crumbling towers and
desolate sea-marshes, "the whimpering of steers in the yellow valleys," and "wild-eyed longing" among the sea birds. And at length
the land grew white, and beside the sea at "the world's long boundary," there is no sound at all, and to be seen "only stars like snow
on the endless prairie and a sea of snow." In *The Carnival*, in "Journeys," we find white pilgrims rising from their beds and seeking
"through years of blackness / Their chapels lost in prayer and ice."
And nothing

> Can stop our tears, they cover us like veils.
> No peace? No. Never. Not
> Till the power has vanished, not till the heart fails.

In Malcolm Brinnin, the image of the voyage makes its appearance. In "Afternoon of a Faun" (*The Garden Is Political*) there is
a picture of a frivolous "bourgeois" tea-party, somewhat in the
vein of Eliot's early poems, which arouses only boredom and disgust in the writer, and he bids us

> Say, Mine is *another voyage*
> When the dark surrounds the dark,

> Say, I Love, against the money and the talons,
> Like Ruth in the Bible hugging sheaves.

His voyage has a more serious destination than that of the soulless uncles and aunts; and he feels like "Ruth in tears amid the alien corn." In "This Voyaging" (*No Arch, No Triumph*) the figure is applied somewhat vaguely to the uninterrupted commerce of spirits between him and his "dear."

In Karl Shapiro's *Trial of a Poet* there is a poem very little characteristic of this writer, entitled "The Voyage." It involves an elaborate and highly complicated symbolism of, I think, love-making, where "the ship of my body" has "pierced to the center the heavy embrace of the tide." It is now morning and the "she" of the poem lies still in the underseas dreaming of their love. Then the odor of love in the sun and wind awakes "*the stream of our voyage* that lies on the belt of the seas," and the man sails at his ease

> Where the sponges and rubbery seaweeds and flowers
>   of hair
> Uprooted abound in the water and choke in the air.

Shapiro is a very fine poet, but I do not think it is in this "metaphysical" vein that he is at his best. And at any rate, his metaphor of a sea voyage does not seem to fall within the range of the travel symbolism we have been discussing.

Probably the same thing is true of the voyage and stranger figures to be found in several arresting poems of Jean Garrigue, all in the third series of *Five Young American Poets* (1944), two of them reprinted in *The Ego and the Centaur* (1947). The most intriguing and the most difficult of interpretation in detail is "Journey to the Last Station." The imagery consistently refers throughout to a railway journey from the mother station in Harrisburg through a bleak and frightening snowy landscape to some final station in the dark. I suppose that the journey by train symbolizes the poet's journey of the spirit, and I suspect that the last station must signify death. This passenger is "briefest of travelers." But there is much in the symbolism that I do not understand, such as "that fish-shaped train, green headed," and I am prepared to be corrected by some reader better instructed in, say, iconography. Voyages and strangers appear again in this poet's "Letter from Song" and "The Stranger." The stranger in the latter poem one takes on first reading to be an actual person whom the writer allowed to escape her when the stranger turned a corner in Denmark and disappeared for good. But as one grows more familiar with the poem, one suspects that she is the personification of something abstract, perhaps poetry. In "Letter from Song," if the letter writer is indeed Song, or Poetry, the "dear Stranger" is presumably poetry of an earlier age, — is it possible? — or the poet herself at an earlier age, and song the poet, the singer, in her maturity. They both have made "journeys piratical," and the adolescent is bid go

> Where old Bohemias, shipwrecks, recommend
> Adulthood to its innate comedy
> And what you were tells my identity.

All three of these poems are interesting and imaginative; but they are marred by an inveterate and irritating way of "telescoping" images, as where the writer says that she will, on capes and ledges, patrol

> The ghost or spectre of a rose
> Our parley bears the emanation of.

It takes a very lively imagination to conceive of the process of patrolling a rose, or of a parley bearing the emanation of a rose. In any case, the symbolism of the stranger is not in this poet along the line of thought of those who sing of exile.

Before we leave the voyage symbolism, it might be worthwhile to refer to the use of this, in the variant form of the quest, by a British poet of the same period. MacNeice in a volume of radio scripts includes "The Dark Tower" (*The Dark Tower and Other Radio Scripts*, 1947). The title at once suggests that this is more of nineteenth- than of twentieth-century inspiration. It is a modern version of Browning's "Childe Roland to the Dark Tower Came." But, being directed very deliberately to the "gross public" of the radio, it is not MacNeice at his best. It is a very simple allegory, in which every character and object is as plainly ticketed as in Bunyan. Leaving his mother and his girl friend, Sylvie, Roland takes ship for the Further Side of the Sea, for the Dead End of the World, and the

Bourne of No Return. (This *is* Auden but without his comedy.)
On the boat he has an affair with Horace and Milton's Neaera, who
makes fun of his romantic notions. She assures him:

> You never believed in this Quest of yours, you see —
> The Dark Tower — the Dragon — all this plague.

Neaera is frankly labeled pleasure but not happiness. Upon landing he finds Sylvie and is married to her by a priest who informs
him that the original sin is doubt. He goes on to find the Chapel
closed, but a priest is there who bids him go

> Forward through the gibbering guile of the forest,
> Forward through the silent doubt of the desert.

Here again we have allegorical alliteration à la Auden, but without
the wit or the impudence. In pursuing his quest he has to give up,
as bidden in the gospel, his mother — for the sake of Free Will! —
like others before him

> Who went to their death of their own Free Will
> Bequeathing Free Will to others.

Coming at length to the Dark Tower, where his father and brothers
are incarcerated, he unslings his trumpet and summons the evil
Dragon.

> You, you Dragon, or whatever you are
> Who make men beasts, come out — here is a man.

The Sergeant-Trumpeter bids Roland hold that note. And the note
is enriched and endorsed by the orchestra.

It all brings vividly to mind the hopeless predicament of the poet
in our day of universal education. If he writes like poets in our
time, he will have an extremely limited audience. If he aims at a
mass audience, he must spell out his meaning on the Sunday School
blackboard, and he will not be remembered beyond his generation.

22. FRONTIERS

Since 1914, there have been very good reasons why we should all
be acutely conscious of the importance of frontiers. Passports and
visas and iron curtains have had their effect on all of us, and those
who go to war have had the hotter consciousness of trenches and

barbwire fences. The poets have not missed the imaginative appeal of this word, and they have not failed to give it a symbolic extension of meaning. In Perse's *Anabase*, first published in the same year as *The Waste Land*, the word appears in both its literal sense and in a sense in which it is perhaps taking on symbolic overtones. We have already referred to both passages: that in which reference is made to the provoking of incidents on the frontiers in order to start a war of conquest, and that in which the poet, boasting of his superiority to ordinary tribesmen, exclaims that for him, "the drums of exile wake upon the frontiers the eternity that broods over the sands." There is here the suggestion that the poet, in order to attain his vision of eternity, must make himself an "exile" by crossing the frontier between the settled regions and the unsettled wastes of the desert. And so the frontier is not merely geographical or political but spiritual or ideological.

Auden's numerous references to the frontier are ideological and ethical. And anyone who undertakes to be explicator of this fascinating body of symbolic verse should realize that he is rushing in where angels fear to tread. If this is Marxian propaganda, as we are led to suppose — and this is surely suggested by Auden's own "line with left and right / An altered gradient at another rate" — it has more often the tone of the YMCA, the Sunday School, and the military training camp, and would remind a well-read Englishman of Dr. Thomas Arnold and Rugby School. It is as if we were trying to get the sense of secret documents that have to be decoded. Well, the fact seems to be that, as Francis Scarfe tells us in his book on Auden, this poet was a serious moralist from the start. And in many of his early poems Auden seems even more concerned with the moral discipline and the risk involved in any revolutionary movement than with the exact nature of the revolution contemplated.

Thus in the first of his odes, while the Jewess flees southward and the drunken Scotsman salutes the rising moon, there is Christopher, "in the middle of Autumn destruction," standing

> his face grown lined with wincing
> In front of ignorance — "Tell the English," he shivered,
> "Man is a spirit."

In the ode addressed "To My Pupils," we are in a training camp for recruits, living under the strain of guarding against mysterious enemies encamped not so far distant and under the pressure of officers constantly asking, "Are you in training?" We are being urged to make haste with "that rifle-sight you're designing"; and warned that all leave is canceled tonight, for

> We entrain at once for the North; we shall see in the morning
> The headlands we're doomed to attack; snow down to the
> tide-line . . .

Who the enemy may be is rather a mystery. They would seem to be of an old order, the "good old times," with customs established by the tall white gods from across the water, when the weather was favorable, "An open wishing-well in every garden," and "When love came easy." And they have scarecrow prophets denouncing us in the name of their Lord and urging them on to be more wise and courageous as their might lessens and to fight till they "lie down beside the Lord" they have loved. But apparently we too are blessed by the bishop in a cathedral service and exulting in our victories over an enemy that "fought against God." And when it comes to naming the leaders among the enemy, they turn out to be the vices of Wrath, Gluttony, Acedia, and Lust, who all threatened to mislead us and sap our strength.

The young recruits in this camp have heard all the peacetime stories about the old days, but are frontier-conscious; they are aware of the dangers besetting their party on every side. They talk about *things done on the frontier* we were never told." And they are particularly warned against fraternizing with the enemy as was done once on Christmas Eve, when on both sides they walked about on the skyline, exchanged cigarettes and the foreign words for "I love you." Do you think

> You can stroll across for a smoke and a chat any evening?
> Try it and see.

However ambiguous this may be — for does not this list of vices have a somewhat "bourgeois" sound? and would not a true leftist recommend fraternization (at least under actual military conditions)? — it is clear enough that these schoolboys or soldier volunteers are living in a world divided into ideological camps, and that for their side to win, it is necessary for each of them to keep in training and cultivate the standard moral virtues. And there are strong intimations that the other side represents an old (though in its way attractive) social order.

This is more obvious in certain poems which were included in the 1930 volume. There is, for example, the long reflective poem, numbered xvi, in which the poet is shown walking at Easter in the public gardens, and in which he comes to the conclusion that

> It is time for the destruction of error.
> The chairs are being brought in from the garden,
> The summer talk stopped on that savage coast
> Before the storms, after the guests and birds . . .

He addresses one whom he gladly walks with and touches. But now, he warns, more is needed than this loving relationship. Love now

> Needs death, death of the grain, our death,
> *Death of the old gang* . . .

Who the old gang are Auden spells out in a slam-bang fighting poem on England going to pot industrially — capitalist exploiters and wealthy playboys, those who say "What was good enough for my father was good enough for me," those who lecture "on navigation while the ship is going down," and in general people beset with terror at the coming insurrection of the workers, but too comfortable to do anything about it. There are also presumably our "bourgeois" poets and prophets:

> Newman, Ciddy, Plato, Pascal, Bowdler, Baudelaire,
> Doctor Frommer, Mrs. Allom, Freud, the Baron, and Flaubert.

This poem, with its vivid description of damaged machinery and abandoned mines (symptomatic of, and symbolic of, the breakdown of capitalism), has its light to throw on several others in this volume that bring in frontiers, and (what are synonymous with them in this symbolism) passes and watersheds. In number xi, someone, having left behind the "crux of the watershed," stands

looking down on various evidences of "an industry already coma-
tose." And we learn of several ambitious men who had tried to
rehabilitate the old machinery; and of one who, finding "the fells
impassable," met his death not in his own village, but after nosing
his way through long abandoned levels, "in his final valley went to
ground."

(Auden's fascination with the features of nature, and of the relics
of industry, in the North country where he grew up, and the
child's sense of mystery and adventure with which he invests
them — like Huck Finn with his Mississippi River surroundings —
are so infectious that I cannot forbear bringing them in at greater
length than the subject requires. They are a large part of what
caught the world's imagination in the work of his first ten years of
writing, and even leave their traces in so late a work as *The Age
of Anxiety*.)

In the latter half of this poem, the poet bids his "stranger" by
the watershed go back home, though "frustrate" and vexed. Here
he has passed beyond the borders of his own world. "This land, cut
off, will not communicate." Only, he feels that, in this to him so
foreign country (though so familiar), near him taller than grass,
"Ears poise before decision, scenting danger."

In another difficult but intriguing poem, number III, the speaker
is apparently some impersonation of nature or fate or that inevitableness in the process of history that, according to Marxist theory,
decrees the evolution and decay of successive cultures and social
orders. This conductor of historical evolution is addressing someone who has decided "to begin to-day" — to begin, as I understand
it, the reform of himself. But his mentor is no more inclined to encourage him in this project of conversion than, say, a Catholic
priest to encourage a Baptist or a Presbyterian to embrace his alien
faith. The man has been too self-indulgent and comfortable and is
too much conditioned by the habits of a lifetime. Even if he feels
his safety threatened by the new order, even if he feels anguish at
the thought of "goodness wasted," this only

> Means that I wish to leave and to pass on,
> *Select another form, perhaps your son* . . .

The cosmic process is too vast for the old order to cope with, but it will go on without its conversion, and history will leave it and pass on. It will select some other form, perhaps the very son of the old order; and so the future will automatically replace the past. And it is here that the frontier symbol is brought in. History warns the old order that it cannot even voluntarily yield to the new:

> Do not imagine you can abdicate;
> *Before you reach the frontier* you are caught . . .

This would seem to be a warning against the notion of "gradualism," or at least the gradualism by which a Tory can make himself over into a social revolutionary. Perhaps this is Marx against the Fabians? Others have tried before "To finish that which they did not begin." The fate of all such is

> To suffer the loss they were afraid of, yes,
> Holders of one position, wrong for years.

The ideological significance of the frontier in Auden may take on even more subtle and recherché disguises or provocative strangeness of costume. In number xviii we have what is at first sight a poem on love:

> Before this loved one
> Was that one and that one . . .
> Was much to be done,
> *Frontiers* to cross . . .

This is not an anthology, and I cannot give the poem in its entirety. And while we all agree, as has so often been insisted, that the prose paraphrase can never give us the poem in its peculiar essence, it is also true, and above all in this type of indirect or oblique writing, that without the paraphrase we shall be so lost that we shall miss the poem altogether. There is surely no "explication" without summary and paraphrase. In this case, I take the poem to refer to superficial liking between people who are, after all, across the border from one another in their social philosophy. There is family and ancestry and standard of living involved in the matter, and frontiers have to be crossed before there can be a true meeting of minds. "Touching" may be "shaking hands / On mortgaged lands." And our polite greeting does not constitute a "real meeting."

We must realize that what we have to do with, at any rate in the early work of Auden, is no crude form of political propaganda, and certainly no bald simplification of thought in regard to the complexities of the human spirit. What we have to do with is a temperament prone to adventuresomeness in thinking, seriously drawn to the idea of social progress and improvement, and even to the idea of moral discipline. We have a man at odds with the social tone of his time and country, and perhaps at odds with himself, and youthfully attracted to the romantic role of the rebel against convention. He was a poet with a very lively imagination, and this in combination with what was ethically serious and temperamentally romantic, accounts for the instant and wide appeal of poems that were irritatingly (or to many readers flatteringly) obscure and esoteric, at the same time that they were startlingly fresh and original in conception.

When it comes to the plays he wrote, some years later, with Isherwood, that is something else again. *The Dog beneath the Skin* and *On the Frontier* are both rather bald allegories, with the meanings often spelled out in abstract prose terms (the poets make their own paraphrase), intended, like MacNeice's radio plays, for a popular audience. The first has to do mainly with ideological or ethical frontiers, the other mainly with the frontiers incidental to national rivalries and traditional hatreds. The somewhat fantastic and confused plot of *The Dog beneath the Skin* is concerned with a young English heir to a baronetcy, named Francis, who has disappeared from his home town; he cannot be located though several envoys have been sent out through the world to find him. The last one sent, Alan Norman, in his search for the lost baronet, is often helped by a mysterious and sagacious dog. When he comes back having given up the search, the dog comes too. He is really the lost Francis, and he nows throws off the dog's skin, which he had worn as a disguise so that he could size up the world, including his own townsmen. After six months of travel he hadn't wanted to come home. "You see, I had begun to regard you in a new light.

I was fascinated and horrified by you all. I thought such obscene, cruel, hypocritical, mean, vulgar creatures had never existed before in the history of the planet, and that it was my office and doom to record it." But he has with experience and maturity ceased to hate them. "You are units in an immense army: most of you will die without ever knowing what your leaders are really fighting for or even that you are fighting at all. Well, I am going to be *a unit in the army of the other side*: but the battlefield is so huge that it's practically certain you will never see me again." He has really come home to recruit volunteers for his "side" in the worldwide division of minds. The curate immediately takes the other side, though Francis's side sounds so much more Christian. Francis is labeled by the General "a disgrace to his class and his family," and the press refuses to recognize these disgraceful incidents as ever having taken place since they do not fall into any "artistic category" which they recognize. The chorus commiserates with the benighted people of this village for inability to make up their minds, and urges them to take their place,

> not this that we have lately witnessed: but
> another country
> Where grace may grow outward and be given praise
> Beauty and virtue be vivid there.

I have not observed that the word *frontier* appears in this play; but we have the synonym for it when the Vicar sends Alan forth on his mission and authorizes him to

> *Cross any border* in sand or snow,
> Will you do whatever may be needful
> Though people and customs both be hateful,
> When mind and members go opposite way . . .

Perhaps *customs*, in its association with *border*, has a double meaning. And *border* itself in the context has a vaguely symbolic coloring.

In *On the Frontier*, in addition to the title, the image of the frontier is given scenical representation on the stage. One recurring scene is "the Ostnia-Westland room," in which two separate families are shown on the same stage, one belonging to Westland and the other to Ostnia, each carrying on a conversation exhibiting its own local prejudices but a mental set identical with its enemy across the imaginary line that makes the border. Then in a lighted circle within the darkened stage, we have the youth Eric, a Westlander, and the girl Anna from the Ostnian family united in their love and their common hatred of these traditional hostilities. Later when he has lost his son in the inevitable war, Eric's father, Dr. Thorwald, is shown reflecting that he had been wrong in his inherited view "that a man's greatest privilege was to fight for his country." He finds that war is beastly when it actually happens. "Perhaps 'country' and 'frontier' are old-fashioned words that don't mean anything now. What are we really fighting for? I feel so muddled."

In our discussion of *islands* we have seen how the ghosts of Anna and Eric came together in the end, anticipating the new order in the future where,

> Others like us shall meet, the *frontier gone*,
> And find the real world happy.

Throughout this allegorical play, then, *frontier* stands for that more or less artificial barrier of traditional rivalries, hatreds, and misunderstandings that separates social groups and national groups, though we are all so much alike, and has its ugliest and deadliest manifestation in war.

Prokosch is, as we have seen, one of the American poets who most dogs the footsteps of Auden, but one who most regularly gives a new and individual turn to the symbolic images they have in common. Crossing the border appears in him as a symbol for getting hopelessly lost in the doubts and fears that befog our time, and more than that, a symbol for the sort of mental alienism that Prokosch everywhere finds. And so we have:

> A massive and crucial longing for annihilation
> cajoles all those who have *lost their way across*
> *the border.*

Prokosch also extends the frontier image ("boundary") to include the commonest use of *frontier* in our country, familiar from the beginning and given great literary currency by the historian Turner through his *Frontier in American History*. The frontier in American history has been not so much the boundary between two states as the final point reached by settlers in the wilderness, or, in a sense, the line that marked the end of civilization. When the frontier was finally closed, that meant the end of opportunity for landless citizens to find land for nothing. Prokosch's variation on the theme is, in "The Voyage," that his unfortunate travelers come at last to "the world's long boundary," where there was nothing to be heard but stillness and nothing to be seen but "stars like snow on the endless prairie and a sea of snow." All that betrays an American note here is the endless prairie.

Gregory and Brinnin come nearer to the typical American frontier à la Turner. Gregory refers (in *Chorus for Survival*) to the blank hopelessness of his generation (in the early 1930's) as

> Window and door open to empty air
> Echo in darkness of *the lost frontier*.

And he has Emerson think bitterly of seeing

> the *red frontier*
> In city walls closed, and the hot mills pour
> Iron for guns, starvation, war . . .

For Brinnin in the Lincoln lyrics, "Frontiers are hopes," etc., and in the brutish and perishable frontier village of New Salem, he has the rail-splitter learn wisdom and drink in "a love / Explosive to the mind's most winglike touch." In "Observatory Hill" (*No Arch, No Triumph*), we read that, in looking through the great telescope, he felt "My *settled shore and frontier* struck from view." Later he figuratively turned the telescopic eye down on certain specimens of artist humanity, and

> knew forever then *the last frontier*
> Not to be reached by coasting over land
> Toward an Atlantic or Pacific strand.

And, in an intricately figured passage, he shows us a traveler coming to an island where "*frontier* becomes exit and entrance" — crossing that leaves one intellectual realm to enter another.

Joseph Warren Beach

One of the most effective of poems dominated throughout by the image of the frontier in what we might refer back to as the Auden sense, and a poem well organized and peculiarly free from the obscurity so often found in symbolic poetry, is Berryman's "The Dangerous Year" (*Poems*). This poem is dated New York, 1 March 1939. It was written under the cloud of the coming war, and it passes ingeniously but naturally from the literal to the figurative sense of the word *frontier*. The first half of the poem is taken up by the false sense of security that we have this side of the Atlantic.

> Our factories and homes, the man next door,
> Our dear upholstered memories, are safe . . .

And then we are ready to start on our weekend pleasures (the italics are Berryman's):

> *The car is still upon the road*, we say.
> What road? Where will you sleep tomorrow night?

And so we are brought back to the concept of ideological frontiers.

> It's *time to see the frontiers as they are.*

He gives a fine original version of Auden's poem, cited above,

> It is time for the destruction of error,
> The chairs are being brought in from the garden . . .

We must now give up the Christmas tree and summer resort notion of our American culture,

> Forget the crass hope of a world restored
> To dignity and unearned dividends,

and realize that the catastrophic events of our time that we so much fear are really "loosed from the labyrinth of your desire."

Frontiers are redolent of geography, and, as in Perse, of desert and difficult places. Archibald MacLeish has a special feeling for geography and for places marked by the special winds there, places on the far borders of experience, which have their own symbolic meanings. And from far back he has been concerned with the feeling qualities of different ideologies. It will be appropriate to close our show of poetical frontiers with some (presumably) late lyrics of MacLeish's. In "Geography of This Time" (*Actfive and Other Poems*) he impresses on us the importance of knowing where we actually stand in history, for one period is not the same as that which preceded or that which followed. "What is required of us is the *recognition of the frontiers between the centuries*." Men's ideas change, and the world changes with them. Many people have no perception that such change is come about and are "killed in the place between" the old and the new. They are to be pitied as victims of accidents, but "their deaths do not signify." Many have supposed that "the time went on, the years went forward, the history was continuous." They "came to *the frontiers between the times* and did not know them," did not find the familiar features — sentry boxes, barricades, etc. "We are very far." We have come to where the roads end.

> What is required of us, Companions, is the *recognitions of the frontiers* across this history, and to take heart: to cross over
> — to persist and to cross over and survive . . .

In this last poem we are companions on a great adventure — comrades it might have been some twelve years before when MacLeish wrote *Public Speech* (1936). We are making history, we have to have the courage of our recognition, we have to cross the frontier in order to survive. "The old order changeth yielding place to new." In "Definition of the Frontiers," the poet builds up our sense of the sinister and disquieting features accompanying our approach to the form — and the penalty we pay for beyond the comfortable bounds of the familiar. He devotes three of his prose paragraphs to characterize the wind that blows from the other side — its "persistent pressure," its strange odor, and its "bitter and sharp taste like rust on the taste of snow . . ." "When the air has this taste of time the frontiers are not far from us." Then there are all the unfamiliar wild animals that "belong neither to our side nor to theirs," and threaten "the violation of custom and the subversion of order." And there are still more unpleasant things — "the unnatural lovers the distortion of images the penetration of mirrors" (shades of Alice!)

205

and "the inarticulate meanings of the dreams." And finally there is "the evasion of those with whom we have come."

> It is *at the frontiers that the companions desert us* — that the
> girl returns to the old country
>   that we are alone

Here comes in again the note of exile, and we are back with Joyce, with the early Auden, and with Perse. Frontiers are ideological, companions are few, and not to be trusted too far, and when you cross over you are pretty sure to find yourself alone. All alone, too, we have been *en voyage*, whether we were going to islands, or into the desert, or into the enemy's country. It is not surprising that these poems on frontiers should be followed in the same volume by a "Voyage West," and the speaker should sound like Christopher Columbus in his days of bitterness after his experience with kings and courts and with weak and faithless companions. He is addressing some Señora, and telling her with disillusioned irony that the "time for discoveries" is past — the maps all made and the last lands peopled.

> A man would better never have been born
> Than find upon the open ocean flowers
> Drifted from islands where there are no islands.

It is a great misfortune for a man

> To lift along the evening of the sky,
> Certain as sun and sea, a new-found land
> Steep from an ocean where no landfall can be.

MacLeish has his own secret recipes for evoking imaginative and tonal effects nostalgic, mysterious, and a trifle *fin de siècle*, penetrated with the magic of wind and rain, with the sense of sea, mountain, and desert, and of the special local qualities of landscapes. He is quite of our time in his insistence on a realistic view of facts, and his generous use of "prose" language to save poetry from being "literary." He long since set out in *Conquistador* to give poetic form to the American saga. In 1944 he turned out *The American: Ten Broadcasts*, which were heard over NBC, featuring Columbus, Amerigo Vespucci, Montezuma, and other figures representing "the experience common to the Americans of the early settlements and voyages, of whatever race." These radio scripts were done in prose, but brilliantly in a style worthy of a poet. Considering the time, these were no doubt partly designed to be morale-boosters for our side in a world conflict of cultures. But they were certainly not jingoistic, or in any disparaging sense the carriers of propaganda or ideology. But the three lyrics here discussed are certainly in a broad sense ideological, and may serve as a sort of recapitulation of the poetic themes with which we have been concerned in the last four sections.

◀§ *THE HERO*

23. THE HERO AS FEELING

The twentieth century as a period of great wars has been peculiarly concerned with heroes. They were the theme of much poetry during World War I, and again during the period of the Great Depression and the socialist movement. This topic reached a climax in the early years of the second war, and its echoes continued to sound throughout the forties and even into the fifties.

Hero is a peculiarly literary term. Webster begins with its meaning in mythology and religion as "a man, especially a warrior." His second definition is "A man honored after death by public worship, because of exceptional service to mankind, and usually held to be in part at least of divine descent." Then comes poetic literature with "the principal male personage, usually of noble character, in a poem, story, drama, or the like . . . as Achilles in the *Iliad*, Odysseus in the *Odyssey*, etc." And hence we have, in general, "a person of distinguished valor in danger, or fortitude in suffering," and finally "a prominent or central personage in any remarkable action or event . . . hence, a person regarded as a model of noble qualities; as, Washington is more than a national *hero*."

Our subject here is the concept of the word *hero* as it appears in American poetry during the second half of the period of the great wars (up till the present). Now, it so happens that this is, in our poetry, a highly critical age, in which traditional ideas have been steadily under fire; a time of realism and disillusionment, in which many words traditionally used for exaltation have been subject to ironical criticism or applied in new ways that mean the negation of old values. The question has been raised, what is the hero in fact? or to what sort of person should the old word be applied?

208

Meantime one distinguished American poet, Wallace Stevens, at the highest point of interest in the subject of the hero, offered a set of fourteen sonnet-length poems entitled "Examination of the Hero in a Time of War" (*Parts of a World*, 1942). But we must note at once that "examination of the hero" does not here mean examination of the facts about the hero as an actuality, or of his qualifications to meet our ethical requirements, but an examination of the *image* of the hero as it is created by the popular imagination. The poems are accompanied by a note in prose distinguishing between the consciousness we have of "the violent reality of war" as it exists objectively (the fact itself) and the poetic imaginative consciousness, "heroic fact," of "what we wanted fact to be." Stevens begins in the first poem with the elements of danger and suffering noted by Webster in his definition of the hero, "a person of distinguished valor in danger, or fortitude in suffering." Stevens makes the hero say that he is not at home in the humdrum of the centers of civilization, Roma, Avignon, Leyden. He is a creature of fate, devoted to "The brightness / Of arms, the will opposed to cold." His angel is the brilliant and colorful angel of explosives, "convulsive shatterer, gun." We are sick of the "old romance"; the spirit calls for that "whose whispers prickle the spirit" and causes sight to hang "heaven with flesh drapery." In the hero, "the eccentric / On a horse, in a plane, at the piano," what we want is a *virtuoso*. The submarine blows up a sea-tower, a sea-mountain, and "the pinnacles frisson. / The mountain collapses. Chopiniana." It is true that "the common man is the common hero." For there is a common fortune, which we share with the hero

> induced by nothing,
> Unwished for, chance, the merest riding
> Of the wind . . .

We have to believe in the hero, or there will be nothing to believe. Whatever you make him of, mud or ice, he is our north star. For he represents for us

> the extremest power
> Living and being about us and being
> Ours, like a familiar companion.

Joseph Warren Beach

There have been many bourgeois heroes, who are "the classic changed." Statues are an unsatisfactory representation of the hero, but they do represent "The idea of things for public gardens." You may have a statue of Xenophon, which does not need to be a realistic picture of what he was. But you need the name, for the marbles of the statue are "Like a white abstraction only" until you call it Xenophon. The emblem of the hero must "stand taller than a person stands." Everything about him is greater than life size. He is well presented by street parades, circus parades, with drums and trumpets and hip-hip-hurrahs:

> The elephants of sound, the tigers
> In trombones roaring for the children . . .

For the hero is by definition a thing of feeling — "a man seen / As if the eye was an emotion." It is through this emotional vision that "we have and are the man." The hero exists in his actions, and they are the actions of his people.

> Say that *the hero   is   his   nation*,
> *In him made one* . . .

This oneness is poetically developed in terms of musical harmonies. In the following poem, we rise above even the nation. The hero is now mythologized, deified. He is the "highest man with nothing higher / Than himself." He becomes "man-sun, man-moon," etc. In a mere study of the wallpaper and the lemons on the table, he "Arrives at the man-man   as   he   wanted."

Thus shamelessly I paraphrase — as prosily succinct and exact as possible, with no pretensions to "rendering" the "poem," but with here and there a phrase in quotation marks to give the reader some hint of the quality I do not render, to justify my prose statements, and to trace through its seeming sinuosities the unwavering progress of the thought. For Wallace Stevens, while the most tenuously fanciful, most splendiferous, most whimsical of our poets, is also the coldest, most unrelenting thinker who ever pursued an ontological idea through the mazes of poetical imagery.

In these poems he is giving the anatomy of the folk concept of a hero, with full awareness that he is dealing with a mythological creation, with something in the psychology of all times that corresponds with that which operated in the age of magic and the age in which the magical powers are deified. The hero is man at his highest power "with nothing higher than himself." He might be Aristotle's Nicomachean man, except that Aristotle is concerned only with so many faculties and virtues that are social and "moral" whereas Stevens, in the folk tradition, is concerned only with what exalts the man and gives us, who identify ourselves with him, the feeling of exaltation. In his final poem, he attacks what is the almost invariable problem of all his poetry, the problem of the real and the ideal, the fact and the fiction, in human thinking and imagining. He points out that false things have their day and come to an end, like summer flowers withered in autumn.

> After the hero, the familiar
> Man makes the hero   artificial.

He thus raises the question of the realist: since the hero is a creature of the imagination, must we not condemn him as false? Does not autumn give the lie to summer? But Stevens declines to render a judgment, as Stevens, in his dualism, always declines to do. He is too "cold" for that. He states the case for the realist. And then he asks, "But was the summer false?" He wants to know how we came to think that "autumn was the veritable season." And he ends up with a summer-colored backdrop for "the large, the solitary figure."

One is often tempted to say of Stevens that he is our purest exponent of "pure poetry." But one must be very careful not to be misunderstood. He is certainly not a realist in any literary sense, though it is clear enough that he will admit the objective reality of the outside world to anyone who will admit with him the subjective reality of our consciousness. He does not live in any familiar world, whether of Hartford or the Florida sea coast, though he may take his departure from some sensation felt by him in those places. He does not feature cities or machinery or slums. He does not write poems about people or render their speech with meticulous faithfulness. He is not a moralist, and he makes no propaganda for political or social doctrines, though he exercises the "right" to free play of mind and imagination claimed by the individualist, and he can sing of collectivity.

> Supple and turbulent a ring of men
> Shall chant an orgy on a summer morn
> Their boisterous devotion to the sun . . .

But as some writers interpret "purity" in poetry, he is decidedly impure. His imagination is always working, but it is always working under strict intellectual control. And it is always playing the game of philosophy. What saves it from impurity, if it is saved, is that, while it plays the philosophic game, it does not use the chessmen of philosophy. The men of philosophy are abstractions; Steven's men are images and sensations. Instead of realism he says the sun; instead of idealism (or romanticism) he says the moon. Or it may be any one of the seasons for either of these. For romanticism it may be summer (as above), or spring, or even autumn, according to the special effects associated with these seasons. In "The Motive for Metaphor" (*Transport to Summer*, 1947), he says to his romantic soul

> You like it under the trees in autumn,
> Because everything is half dead.
> The wind moves like a cripple among the leaves
> And repeats words without meaning.

In the following stanza, he tells him why he likes it in spring and by moonlight. In the concluding stanzas he shows him shrinking from "the weight of primary noon, the A B C of being."

He does not use the abstractions of metaphysics, and he does not maintain the colorless objectivity and justice of philosophical discussion. He begins "The Motive for Metaphor" in tones suggestive of satire on the romanticist for his shrinking nature; but he changes horses in midstream, and describes the horrors of the noonday view of life (the realistic view) in terms that put him squarely on the side of the romantic. It is not quite suddenly that he changes sides. For this poet is really on both sides at once. From the beginning his irony is everywhere present, and it is by gradual steps that he passes over from mockery of the romantic to horror at the realist.

Such irony is out of place in a strictly philosophical discussion.

212

But it is the very making of a poet, where he has any touch of intellect. It is the intellect illuminated by the imagination and powered by personal feeling. It is a poor psychologist who thinks he can separate these three "faculties"; a poor critic who assumes that our thoughts do not color our feelings and affect our vision. If that is what "pure poetry" wants, then it cannot have the allegiance of any reader who is emotionally affected by what he thinks. For any reader fond of philosophical speculation and at the same time sensitive to imaginative effects, Stevens is bound to be one of our most highly prized poets. I would have said "most precious" if I had not feared that people would think I was running him down for his "preciosity."

In his treatment of the hero, Stevens is almost unique. There is, however, one other American poet of the same period who, if I read her rightly, shares his general point of view. Only, Marianne Moore is so much more feminine in her reactions — so unaccountable and variable in her points of view (*donna e mobile!*) that it is sometimes very hard to trace the course of her thought with any confidence through a poem of any length. In her *Selected Poems* (1935), there is a poem of half a dozen stanzas named "The Hero" (included under "Part of a Novel, Part of a Poem, Part of a Play"). She begins by noting that there are kinds of places where we do not like to go ("where the ground is sour," etc.). There are, she says, some things we do not like; and that she says, is true of the hero —

> going where one does not wish
> to go; suffering and not
> saying so; standing and listening where something
> is hiding. *The hero shrinks*
> at what it is flies out on muffled wings, with twin
> yellow eyes — to and fro —

She seems to say that even heroes fear the same things other people fear, and she seems to like them none the less for that. Then she goes on through three stanzas developing the idea that there are kinds of people that others do not like — even such estimable people as Joseph and Cincinnatus and the inveterately hopeful Pilgrim.

And we are presumably to take it that the hero is like others in this matter. It is only in the final stanza, by some esoteric turn of thought, that she comes to what may be considered the heart of the matter.

> It is not what I eat that is
> my natural meat,
>   *the hero says*. He's not out
> seeing a sight but the rock
> crystal thing to see — the startling El Greco
> brimming with inner light — that
> covers nothing that it has let go. This then you
> may know as the hero

I would not undertake to trace the devious course of thought by which Miss Moore arrives at her conclusion, even if I thought I could. But it does appear that, where she first refers to the hero, she has in mind the dictionary definition of him as "a person of distinguished valor in danger, or fortitude in suffering," but wishes to humanize him by saying that the hero doesn't really like to suffer silently or to stand up against the hidden danger, or even to be sent to places he doesn't like. One thinks infallibly of the soldier, who is obliged to do all these things, and who somehow manages to do them all. It is the great merit of the heroic soldier that he is not naturally courageous. The next time she refers to the hero, there is not necessarily any reference to the soldier. The heroic man is here someone who does not live on the surface of things. His "natural meat" is not what he eats, or what, as a tourist, he happens to see. His natural meat is what underlies the surface of common experience, the "rock crystal thing." It is the inner light that illuminates an El Greco. El Greco is famous for his spiritualizing touch among more superficial religious painters. The hero is the man that sees the ideal essence of experience. Well, the category includes more than soldiers. But ours has been an age of soldier heroes, and the soldier hero is presumably the man who knows what he is fighting for. What that has been Miss Moore has told us distinctly in her poem "In Distrust of Merits" (*Nevertheless*, 1944), written in the early years of World War II.

I do not mean to say that Marianne Moore, like Stevens, was consciously anatomizing the mythical folk hero. She is not so aloof and objective in her examination of this phenomenon. She is indeed warmly backing the hero as an agent of ethical and social values. But neither was she, like so many of our poets, examining the concept of the hero with a critical eye with intent to deglamorize it or to redefine it in terms of a new ideology.

One is less certain where to place Warren's treatment of the hero image. The hero with him would seem to be, quite simply, the man who has the courage to face fear in its extremest forms: and to such courage he seems to give, at times, the highest rating. Thus in his "Letter from a Coward to a Hero" (*Selected Poems 1923–1943*) the writer of his letter represents himself as "gun-shy," one who dislikes loud noise, "Drums beating for / The big war," or "clocks that tick all night, and will not stop." But his unqualified admiration goes to the companion of his youth, in whose childhood somehow "courage was early caulked," who comes out strong in times of disaster. Of him he says, "I have not seen your courage put to pawn." And in the conclusion he shows him, in the small hours of the night, when other people lie awake overcome with griefs, regrets, and uneasy consciences, calmly reclining

> Clutching between forefinger and thumb
> Honor, for death shy valentine.

In this poem Warren does not even inquire in what cause the hero exercises his courage and whether the death he is ready to meet so bravely will contribute anything to the sum of human good. His honor consists simply in not yielding to any fear, possibly even in not actually feeling fear in the face of danger. The extremest danger is death, and to that the hero shyly offers up his honor as a lover sends a valentine to the object of his affection.

It is only in the light of later poems that one begins to wonder whether there may lurk some ambiguity in this praise. This figure of speech does not invest the transaction with the conventional exalted tone of heroism. Is it possible that the coward who sends this letter is unconsciously defending himself against his humiliation by some thought of the boyish simplicity of the hero's attitude?

The sense of ambiguity takes on full strength with the presum-

ably later poem "Terror" (*Eleven Poems on the Same Theme*).
Here again there are two parties, the "you" addressed by the poet,
corresponding to the letter writer in the earlier poem, and the
"some" referred to who are seekers after the thrill of danger and
correspond to the "hero." The ambiguity lies in the fact that neither
of these parties has the poet's unqualified approval. The "you" is
"born to no adequate definition of terror," and nothing suffices to
still the gnawing of his conscience and bring him the happiness he
seeks. He is the same halfhearted and compromising soul who is
the protagonist in Warren's "Pursuit," "Original Sin," "End of
Season," and whom in "Crime" he bids "Envy the mad killer who
lies in the ditch and grieves." He is certainly no hero; but neither
is that word applied to the "some, unsatisfied and sick," who "have
sought / That immitigable face, whose smile is ice,"

> whose passionate emptiness and tidal
> Lust swayed toward the debris of Madrid,

and, after fighting there, go North

> to seek that visioned face
> And polarize their iron of despair . . .
> They fight old friends, for their obsession knows
> Only the immaculate itch, not human friends or foes.

What they hug is "truth which cause and conscience scarcely
reach." Courage and honor are still absolute values, but when they
merely serve to fill a moral void and drown the pain of an incurable
psychic malady, many readers, and even the poet himself, may not
prefer them to the ineffectual sense of guilt which leaves the "you"
to sit cracking nuts "while the conscience-stricken stare / Kisses
the terror."

In a still later poem, Warren returns to the subjects of fear and
the hero; but with all the simple clarity and impressiveness of writing, the moral ambiguity is not lost. In "Variation: Ode to Fear"
(*Selected Poems*), Warren runs the gamut of human fears to which
he confesses his subjection; and all fears are but surrogates for the
all-comprehending fear of death. In the dentist's chair and under
the surgeon's scalpel, "*Timor mortis conturbat me.*" And the same
fear disturbs him when he gets a notice of an overdue account at

the bank, or watches a friend disappear with the departing train, or thinks of national bankruptcy ahead, or thinks about sculldug- gery among the Founding Fathers, about neuroticism in Milton or in St. Joan, or about Christ suffering from T.B. in Gethsemane.

This poem, in verse form modeled on Herrick's "Litany to the Holy Spirit," has the wit and irony of other seventeenth-century models, together with a humor and realism of our own day. The spiritual predicament of our day has come in with this disposition to rewrite history in terms of economic maneuvers and religion in terms of the new psychology. With the war and the feats of air- men, the writer realizes that he is "no hero." It is his knees and his stomach that tell him this. The seriousness steadily grows, though without abatement of wit and humor. Night fears and time are represented by the "breath of the clock" in the dark, breath of a "clock that's never slow." His spirits reach their comforting nadir with the realization that he is not "the first or last of men," but

> That various men in various ages
> Have *dispensed with hero*es and with sages,

have dispensed indeed with absolute standards in religion and fi- nance,

> And though they found the going hard
> Did without Jesus or the gold standard.

And so the writer decides that, in spite of "the beast that sleeps be- side the bed," he need not throw up the game. He can still

> put on my pants and vest, and go
> Down to eat my breakfast, though
> *Timor mortis conturbet me.*

The present writer must confess that, when Mr. Warren showed him this poem in manuscript in, say, 1943, he did scant justice to its brilliancy, its gaiety, its subtlety, or its emotional depth. He was not prepared to take it in its frame of reference. Being Victorian in birth and conditioning, having sat under an Andover pastor for whom religion was pretty well summed up in Watts's hymn and who never touched on original sin or Adam's expulsion from the garden, he was unprepared for the state of mind that has prevailed in so much poetry of our time. Eliot he could indeed readily absorb and appreciate; for as a man he had read the books and attended the services and studied the monuments of Catholic Christianity. He had read Dante and felt the might of his poetry before ever Eliot had come to tell us that, with imagination, one can appreciate this poet, without sharing his religion. He had even read Canon Henson of Westminster Abbey, and knew that the creeds might be taken as symbolic of spiritual truths. And he had read Warren's *Eleven Poems on the Same Theme* and been charmed by his dealings with guilt and innocence, time and eternity. He relished him in his metaphysical vein. But it was at first hard for him to bring together in one climate of thought the fear of death, the "conscience-stricken stare," and the bright, sardonic humor.

But live and learn — that is the motto of the literary scholar. This reader is now steeped in modernism in all its forms, and has long since been convinced that this poem of Warren's is one of the finest of our century, and one of the most representative of a broad current of sensibility and thought.

As for the hero, it is clear enough that Warren has clung rather tenaciously to his notion of the man of courage as typical hero, and that while in the case of the "unsatisfied and sick" heroes who have so desperately sought "the immitigable face" he can be very critical of their motives, he finds it hard going to live in a world that has "dispensed with heroes and with sages." For that reason I am putting him here under the heading of the hero as feeling.

24. THE HERO DISCREDITED

We might here begin by reminding ourselves that, before World War I, there were poets of distinction in England who could write "The Song of Honour," which was, not merely the song of those who fought in "holy war," but

> The song of fighters great and small
> The song of petty fighters all
> And high heroic things.
>
> RALPH HODGSON

And in the first war, there were distinguished poets in America who could write poems in praise of heroic soldiers fighting holy war like Sandburg's "The Four Brothers," where the soldiers are agents of God's will in rubbing out the Kaiser and the Czar. And there were even good poems written in the soldier's faith that, "if I die,"

> this heart, all evil shed away
> A pulse in the eternal mind, no less
> Gives somewhere back the thoughts by England given . . .
>
> RUPERT BROOKE

But among poets still well remembered, and they are mostly English, there is little featuring of heroism in the common soldier:

> In the great hour of destiny they stand,
> Each with his feuds and jealousies and sorrows
>
> SIEGFRIED SASSOON

and still less featuring of heroism among the officers —

> If I were fierce and bald and short of breath,
> I'd live with scarlet Majors at the Base,
> And speed glum heroes up the line to death. . . .
>
> SIEGFRIED SASSOON

The best English poets were very realistic in depicting the misery, the horror, and the pity of the soldier's life and death. And they were ironic and satirical in their titles — as Wilfred Owen's "Dulce et decorum Est," "Arms and the Boy," bent on debunking the ideal of the military hero that prevailed from Virgil and Horace down to Collins and Tennyson.

But it was later that poets in England and America began their really critical examination of the ideal of the hero as warrior in terms of its social and psychological implications. Here, as so often, Auden was among the very first to give the cue to later writers in England and the United States. In his first volume of poems, there is a characteristic piece (no. xxiv) in which "The tall unwounded leader" is shown looking down from a height on one side upon a happy valley and on another upon a wilder region where his "doomed companions," "Fighters for no one's sake," lie buried — those who "died beyond the border." They were "*Heroes . . .*

who did not believe in death," whose bravery was proved by their scorn for death in fighting with the enemy. But bravery now is

> Not in the dying breath
> But in resisting the temptations
> To skyline operations.

"Skyline operations" may refer to military operations on the border, at the watershed or pass; but I think it must also refer to fighting undertaken for romantic ideals. Such fighting is showy and glamorous, especially when it is at the cost of self-sacrifice. (Death is for the common soldier, *bien entendu*, not for the commander, the Leader. He is the "unwounded leader of doomed companions.") Such sacrifice for the Leader used to be glorious, but it is now a temptation. There are more important, more realistic ways of being glorious and serviceable than such "skyline operations." And even the leader seems to be involved in the new program. Lights and wine are still set for supper by the lake.

> But leaders must migrate:
> "Leave for Cape Wrath to-night."

And the host, who had been waiting to entertain his Leader, will have to put out his lamps and "pass / Alive into the house." Giving up one's life for the "Leader" is now outmoded, and summer visitors to the country will no longer *"Find heroes in the wood."*

Auden's "Journal of an Airman" (*The Orators*) is one of his blindest and most amusing performances. It consists of passages in prose and verse and mere diary notations of personal doings and reminders, of military orders on both sides, those of the "enemy" intercepted and decoded, of psychological tests (with geometrical figures) to distinguish friends and enemies, and charts to trace ancestral traits on Mendelian principles. And there are many glossaries of terms used by the airman or the enemy. It is all written in a code, or in several codes, which one cannot hope to understand with certainty if one has not attended an English boys' school in the early thirties and acquired inside information on the "ideology" of Auden and his intimates at that period. What is most clear is that it has to do with some course of training for action against the "enemy": but the precise character of the enemy is left very unclear. There are many indications of a socio-political reference, and that it is a luxurious English social order fast going to pieces that has occasion to fear the enemy: "The band is leaving the Winter Gardens by an emergency exit. A lady has fainted. Time for lunch. There isn't going to be very much lunch unless you all wake up." There are mysterious references to beautiful spies presented by the vicar with "a handsome eight-day clock," of a "registered package" brought to the vicar by the gardener, of treaties arranged, and of "agents" that "smile for a moment and then turn back to their charming companions."

But one must be careful not to jump to conclusions too readily where the symbolism is so private and esoteric. There are many intimations that the enemy is as much moral as he is socio-political, and that those most dedicated to the good cause have particular need to be on their guard against this moral enemy. The all-important thing is to be in training. There are what we call vices to be eschewed and bad habits to be overcome, and they are sometimes vices and habits to which teenagers may be especially prone. Thus we have recurrent references to "hands" as offenders and to the need for reform: "Yesterday positively the last time." One can hardly avoid assuming that the reference is to sexual offenses. But here again, how can we be sure that this is not a private code, and serves as a symbol for something in the "ideological" realm?

It is difficult to take this piece seriously as a literary performance, or even perhaps as a social document. It is all great fun to anyone who loves riddles, and must have been very great fun for Auden and those of his acquaintances who were qualified to read it with understanding. Indeed, this riddling style — with its dark hints of danger and disguise familiar to the departments of "intelligence" and counterespionage — as well as the presumably serious undercurrent of "ideological" thinking — must have been a main point of appeal to the reading world in all the early poetry of Auden. Perhaps this is one of the unconscious motivations of modern writers in their poetry of symbolism and indirection. Psychology has served it well with Jungian theories of unconscious symbols passed on from generation to generation in the "racial consciousness." Even our religious poetry has made a profit from the same source of mystery and awe.

I am not proposing to throw out the poetry of Auden or Dylan Thomas or whomever you please on the grounds of this "childish" motivation. We have been told too often that the poet is one who retains in maturity the spirit and imagination of the child. But in the case of this "Journal of an Airman" we are too much aware of the "cops and robbers" mentality — and too far from 1930 — to take a solemn pose and declare that this is "great poetry." In any case, this is all a preliminary to quoting Auden's definition of the cockpit from "The Airman's Alphabet":

> *Soft seat*
> and support of soldier
> *and hold for hero.*

Well, the airman is *the* modern hero, whom we all admire, schoolboy or schoolmaster — admire and envy. But the time has come when our schoolmaster even is allowed to show himself unabashed, so that we can refer to the place where he operates as soft seat.

In the same volume, we have in the second ode * a poem in serious praise of the *discipline* that enables students to win victory for their school and bring home the cup. They are each generously praised by name for their particular feats. The airman is already in mind as the typical hero. In their attack, they are "aligned like a squadron of bombers." There is also commiseration for the defeated team, who had to return in a drizzle to a hushed school. As the poem proceeds it grows more thoughtful and "moral." The fathers of these boys are congratulated on the splendid fellows they have begotten. Auden admonishes the boys of the need for *resistance* to keep them fit and effective:

> Whether at lathe-work, loading, reading, to resist
> Rather! the torsion, the tension, the list

* It is addressed to the Captain of Sedbergh School, Spring 1927.

and he sees "joy docked in every duct" coming at night "to the right sleep."

This schoolmaster-poet feels full responsibility for the character of the boys entrusted to his care; he has as full a sense of the puritan, the spartan, virtues as the New England college professor who wrote that

> Something accomplished, something done
> Has earned a night's repose.

Auden has here no ideological ax to grind. He has full sympathy for the boys returning successful from the game, having "the time of their life." One might perhaps detect the faintest hint of irony in his extravagant reference to the school flags: "The flags are flushed, *would die at their heroes' feet.*"

When it comes to *The Dog beneath the Skin* the psychological, analytic method has taken over. His philosophic chorus is approaching an urban "centre of culture" with its detached suburban villas, and proceeding to "Section these dwellings: expose the life of a people / Living by law and the length of a reference."

> See love in its disguises and the losses of the heart,
> *Cats and old silver inspire heroic virtues*
> And psychic fields, accidentally generated, destroy
>   whole families.

So! love in its various disguises and the losses of the heart may be the real inspiration of the soldier. His heroic virtues may be the sublimation of his frustrated sexual urge. And whole families may be destroyed by psychic maladies generated by some accident incurred in erotic experience.

In *Look, Stranger!* the hero image appears in the socio-political context doubled by the psychological. Number xvii is a long meditation of the poet on a high place with "England below me." He thinks back to a time when, though alone, he thought of a distant lover and was happy. This scene is no longer one of innocence but of isolation and fear. But England is "the body of the absent lover, / An *image to the would-be hero of the soul.*" The best gloss for this phrase is, perhaps, Rupert Brooke's thought, if he dies in the European war,

> That there's some corner of a foreign field
> That is forever England.

Brooke is here the type of the would-be hero of the soul, to whom England is an image, as it were the body of the absent lover. But that, the poet seems to say, will not hold water. "For private reasons I must have the truth." The past years have been years of sorrow, hunger, and a Europe grown "anxious about her health." He develops at length the picture of a self-indulgent, decadent England. And the voice of dead soldiers speaks to him, reminding him that

> the major cause of our collapse
> Was a distortion in the human plastic by luxury produced,

that, instead of "the disciplined love which alone should have employed these engines," they had espoused hatred, which "promised an immediate dividend."

> Unable to endure ourselves, we sought relief
> In the insouciance of the soldier, *the heroic
> sexual pose.*

And he concludes the poem with quotations from Wilfred Owen and Katherine Mansfield and a call to a loving instead of a hating kind of action. Thus we have the traditional noble hero reduced to a "would-be hero of the soul" engaging in sentimental "skyline operations" and even striking a "heroic sexual pose" to impress "the little ladies."

This takes us back to *The Dog beneath the Skin*, with its heavy emphasis on psychic maladies and guilt complexes deriving from emotional disturbances in childhood, and leading the "assassins" to provoke the horrors of war. And it takes us forward to *The Ascent of F6*, which is entirely devoted to the analysis of heroism as exhibited by daring mountain climbers. We have seen earlier that the courage of these men is, as with Warren's volunteer airmen, a kind of desperate need to face their fears, that their fears lie much deeper than any physical danger incurred in their exploits and, in the case of the leading "hero" of the story, are tied up closely with the silver-chord complex. As for the socio-political background of their exploits, the whole play is a heavy satirical attack on militarism, caste, nationalism, colonialism, and political careerism. The unvisited and haunted mountain named F6 lies exactly on the frontier between British Sudoland and Ostnian Sudoland, and the territory is claimed by both Britain and Sudoland. It is to secure the title to this useless mountain that our heroic climbers are sent out to reach it first and plant their flag. The chief man, Michael Ransom, has no faith in this nationalistic ideal, and does not believe that the capture of this mountain will serve to promote Virtue and Knowledge. Great poets have been regarded as the exponents of these high values. Such was Dante. But, thinks Ransom, "Who was Dante — to whom the Universe was peopled only by his artistocratic Italian acquaintances and a few classical literary characters, the fruit of an exile's reading — who was Dante, to speak of Virtue and Knowledge?" Dante was a soul turned bitter by involuntary privation. It was neither Virtue nor Knowledge that he could pray for, it was Power. It was the power motive in British nationalism, and nothing ideal, that sent these fine men to their deaths on the haunted mountain. It was British colonialism in its decadent stage, represented by Lady Isabel, who had lived as a child in "poor darling Sudoland" and who is outraged that stern and bloody measures are not used to put down rebellion of the Sudoese hillmen as would have been done in her father's day. The General, wholly sympathetic to her point of view, has to remind her that in her father's time "a British Governor was required to rule, not to coddle a native population according to the sentimental notions of a gang of home-bred politicians." Sir James Ransom resents this slur on the government. "You are apt to forget," he says, in his democratic cant, "that we are only servants of the public." But one is not led to take any stock in the elevation of his motives or the humaneness of his sentiments; and one is reminded that he is a man jealous of his brother's brains and manliness, and of his mother's love for him, who is sending his brother off on this perilous venture, for the furtherance of his own political career. As for the common run of people in the country, while they turn on the wireless when it is time for news, they are "sick of the news," of politics

— "Talk about treaties, talk about honour, mad dogs quarreling over a bone." The politicians really care nothing for the people, and pay attention to them and flatter them only when there's a war. "Then they will ask for our children and kill them; and sympathize deeply and ask for some more."

As for heroes and heroism, these are mentioned only by these common people and by the cynical power-hungry politicians making speeches:

> MR. A. Turn off the wireless; we are tired of descriptions
> of travel;
> We are bored by *the exploits of amazing heroes*;
> We *do not wish to be heroes*, nor are we likely to
> travel.

It is the politicians who strike the right tone of awed reverence in which to invest these words. Lord Stagmantle fears the bodies of the dead mountain climbers will never be recovered, "but while our thoughts are naturally *centred upon their leader*, their *devotion to duty* and *their quiet heroism* must never be forgotten . . ." As for the leader, it is the jealous brother, Sir James, who sent him to his death, who pays unctuous tribute to his talents in all directions, his hatred of publicity, his unwillingness to take high office in the state. And he is interrupted by the Lord, declaring: "Their names are the latest but not the least on that *long roll of heroes who gave their lives for the honour of this country*." In so putting the sacred words in the mouths of politicians and publicists, the poet has brought them to their lowest point of degradation.

In Auden's "Spain 1937" (*Another Time*) in his long listing of the ways and accomplishments of yesterday as opposed to the struggle for freedom which is today's business, the hero is definitely relegated to yesterday's limbo of outmoded things. Yesterday were heresy trials, water divination, miraculous cures, the installation of dynamos and turbines, and the extension of railway lines through the desert.

> Yesterday the belief in the absolute value of Greek;
> The *fall of the curtain upon the death of a hero*;

Yesterday the prayer to the sunset,
And the adoration of madmen. But today the struggle.

On the whole romantic past of Spain — delusions and devotions, imperialism and material progress — and on all civilized activities of the future, we must now turn our backs and concern ourselves with the one present task — the freeing of Spain from fascist tyranny, or we shall have missed the historical occasion.

In his "fall of the curtain upon the death of a hero," Auden may have been thinking of any number of plays and operas. But he was almost certainly thinking also of Spender's *Vienna*, with its section entitled "The Death of Heroes." He was probably thinking, with Spender, of Beethoven's funeral march and Wagner's opera inspired by the death of heroes. And he was suggesting that, in our time at any rate, we cannot afford to spend our time romanticizing the hero. There is a job to be done in the world, and that is a matter of acts and not words.

The hero image continues to appear in Auden after his conversion from socialism to religion, as will appear later, but without restoration of the hero to his ancient stature. Meantime Spender, in his *Vienna*, had impressed on the poets' imagination the theme of "The Death of Heroes." For Spender those who fought for the socialistic uprising were heroes in the full sense of the old word. But not all were heroes, and the word actually appears only in ironic or negative connections. Many people "suffered from the destruction of houses / More than from death of men." For

> *Heroes are instantly replaced*: civilization
> Wears concrete sides . . .

Those who ran away from the fight and reached the frontier could only tell of their defeat.

> The desolate
> Praise mocked the defeated "*You're heroes.*"

Lucky were those who were "killed outright"; unlucky those who survived and went underground, "Burrowing survivors without '*tasks fit for heroes.*'"

A few years later, as we have seen under another heading, Pro-

Joseph Warren Beach

kosch was uniformly regarding our heroes as victims of the madness of our time: *"Broken heroes* who must praise, / Lies devouring all their days"* ("Song," *The Carnival*). The sight of the sea makes him think of "The *night's drowned heroes*" who "sing / Of a destroying love / And through the corals move" ("The Balcony," *The Carnival*). Again, he sees ("The Victims," *Death at Sea*) the waves thronging shoreward,

> offering themselves as *forms of heroism or escape*
> To those who loved too privately or suffered too long.

The madness that destroyed them was nothing new. On the seashore ("The Sand," *Death at Sea*)

> *The Consecrated*
> *Heroes and madmen of the Middle Ages* rise and stand
> Screaming and terrible among the inlets.

What they had always craved was some ethical formula

> Making slaughter acceptable in a justice fully planned,
> Catastrophe fruitful and death a concluding harmony . . .

Throughout history, heroes were those who succumbed to what Auden called "the temptations / To skyline operations."

World War II found many of our American poets looking sourly on the traditional hero. Brinnin asks sadly ("Heroes," *The Garden Is Political*):

> Where are the *heroes promised in the books,*
> Coming with dignity, riding the crowds,
> Sharing the air with plumed, commanding looks?

And he answers his own question: "They are not here. Only the clowns are proud." He finds that "Time's pictured heroes are not anywhere." In his poem dedicated to Martha Graham (*The Garden Is Political*), he speaks of a trust he means to keep

> in spite of *heroes who,*
> With loosening courage, apparently *request*
> *The least of honor,* or *in fear undo*
> *Tower* and *manifesto.*

In the same year, in his "Boston Common: A Meditation upon

228

the Hero" (*The Dispossessed*), Berryman finds that war is no theater for true heroism. It is the

> Congress of adolescents, love in a mask,
> Bestial and easy, issueless . . .

He asks, what ceremony shall a man find "loose in the brothel of another war"? Question, he says, "your official heroes in a magazine." What you will find is dereliction,

> Lust and blood lust, error and goodwill, this one
> Died howling, craven, this one was a swine
> From childhood . . .

Let honor, he says, be

> Consolation to those who give,
> *None to the hero, and no sign of him* . . .

Referring back to "the death of heroes," he speaks of "the chivalry and defenders of our time" — Spain, China, Leningrad, Syria, Corregidor — as Beethoven variations on a primitive theme, consumed in fiery night.

Hugh Chisholm has a "Death of a Hero" (*The Prodigal Never Returns*), duly ironic and naturalistic. "His guts / foul his boots." Heroes, he says, "escape / into hope / whenever a star / swims too near." But now tonight "a god / entered his side / with the plain truth / of death."

> and now
> he is in the know
>
> whether he likes it
> or not

Howard Nemerov is even more resolutely ironic and more grimly naturalistic. He has a poem celebrating not the death of a hero, but his mutilated survival, "The Hero Comes Home in His Hamper, and Is Exhibited at the World's Fair" (*Guide to the Ruins*). His hero has lost his arms and legs and the power of speech and hearing. And he reflects,

> And I was made the utter solipsist.
> My happy state! These thoughts, within their bound,
> Although they go not out, go round and round.

Joseph Warren Beach

Another poem of Chisholm's is a letter "To a Friend Gone to Fight for the Kuomintang" (*The Prodigal Never Returns*), in which he defends himself against his friend's accusation of pessimism, and asks him to let him know

> *Are there yet heroes. Do they wish to kill?*
> What is the will of the dead we dying do?

Somewhat in the same tone of smart, disillusioned postwar writing with Chisholm and Nemerov is Weldon Kees. In his "White Collar Ballad" (*The Fall of the Magicians*, 1947) the hero appears not as the soldier-victim of the wars, but as the comfort-giving cynosure of our eyes on the silver screen. The burden of this ballad is the boredom of a world in which there is nowhere any love to be found. There are plenty of places to go: the club, the movie,

> Plush-and-golden cinemas that always show
> *How cunningly the heroine and hero rub.*
> Put on your hat, put on your gloves.
> But there isn't any love, there isn't any love.

This is the absolute nadir in the descent of the hero from his once revered status.

But the American poet that gives us the most complete review of heroes in all their kinds, and the most sharply analytical account of how each one has failed to satisfy the need of our time, is Archibald MacLeish. And this is done, in *Actfive*, without cynicism, in the tone and spirit of a poet rendering man's tragic sense of destiny. He gives it, too, the visual appeal of a stage performance, a pantomime. All the world's a stage, and every piece must have its hero. In his first scene MacLeish gives us The Stage All Blood, and he asks, "And who shall *play the hero in the piece?*" There must be someone to "utter the soliloquies / Sole upon the ramparts in these stars." There was once the God, a creature of our dreams, "That gave the meaning for the wonder and the fear to find." There was the King, and the King's son,

> Concealed at birth, his consequence made known
> By wrenching sword from chock of stone,

"In whose must the pain the death the dearth had justice," and who,

230

under extremest suffering and wrong, "gave wrong its right." There was Man, "earth's creature," "gentled by labor," peace-loving, forbearing, who "gave history its reason." But now man has been murdered, the throne is empty. Who then shall be the hero in the play; who now shall make us men, shall "make us whole"?

The second scene is the Masque of Mummers, representing the Heroes of Each Age as they have passed. For all the drapery and curtaining of the past has been torn away. And now we have in turn heroes for the fairy stories, for the infant's dream; "The *Science Hero* with the secret box," the key that "unlocks / All the golden answers"; "The *Boyo of industry*"; "The *Revolutionary Hero with the Book*, / Cleansed of every feeling"; the *Great Man* —Führer of the wetted bed" — who will see you through every trouble and weakness; the *Victim Hero*,

> Citizen who never knows
> Why the hurt and why the blows . . .
> Scapegoat who redeems the time
> From every duty, every burden . . .

There is the Visitor, the immigrant, one form of the victim, who comes to live with us and subject himself dutifully to every rule and pipe-dream of state and church. There is the infallible State; the big I, the self-indulgent Ego; and last of all the Crowd, with whom one identifies oneself so as to be indistinguishable, never lonely, and always victorious and big.
Only

> The many added together are not more but
> Less than each since each one fears
> And all are only each divided
> By the fears of all the others . . .

It is proper that MacLeish should be the one to bring down the curtain on this exhibit of heroes discredited. All along, he has been the most accurate barometer, the most sensitive register of weather, in the world of poetry, whether on the side of form and style or on that of attitudes taken toward public affairs. He has certainly been a liberal in his social-political thinking, and he has certainly not been an "irresponsible." But he could not be insensible to the waves of disillusionment that have swept over the minds of poets, whether in the early days of philosophical skepticism, to which the whole world was heir, or in the later time, when a half-century of fatal and desolating wars have brought so many staid minds to a state of almost hopeless gloom. And it is natural that he should be the one to dismiss with most precise gestures and with most comprehensive sweep history's whole family of heroes, with all its genera and species, as unfit to play the leading role in life's tragic drama. There remains, in his third tableau the Shape of Flesh and Bone; but that we shall leave to the following section, on the Hero New Style.

It is hard to find a place in my classification of attitudes toward the hero for Horace Gregory's review of variant attitudes in his "Voices of Heroes," found in the 1951 *Selected Poems*. The whole piece is indicated as a sort of colloquy "Overheard in a Churchyard Dedicated to the Memory of 1776." We have a series of meditations on the soldier as hero, first, it would seem, in World War I and then in World War II. We hear that because the bones of soldiers lie in this graveyard, "the bleak earth glows with sunlight from their eyes," and "their voices speak among us at their will." This view is corrected by a review of the usual "human commonplace preoccupations of living heroes; then there is a picture of them disillusioned, as the spirit that fed their hearts is gone —

> Gone with the vanished hope of richer farms,
> Or brighter towns, or countless money . . .

But then, in World War II, we are reminded that they "died fighting for what you are," that it was "better to die / Than to sit watching the world die," that they were game to the end, since "terror and loss / Have not utterly destroyed us." And then, when the poet seems to have granted them a certain immortality, he reminds us that it is only war that is immortal — "old wars remain unfinished," that "flesh is mortal / And in a world at war, only the wars live on." Thus Gregory runs through a great variety of views of the concept the soldier-hero, and ends up with a rather limp version of Sandburg's famous "Grass." ("I am the grass. I cover all.")

25. THE HERO NEW STYLE

The word *hero* has been thoroughly discredited in these later years because of derogatory associations that it has taken on — because the typical hero has been too often "the unwounded leader of doomed companions," or the doomed companion himself, the victim of vainglorious leaders, who have led him into mistaken crusades, and for whom the term *hero* is a mere consolation prize for the loss of everything else; because the hero, whom we need to give meaning and moral significance to life, has failed to perform that function, and is no better than the figment of fairy tales; has failed to give us a model of greatness and nobility with which we can identify ourselves and feel good about ourselves. This doesn't mean that our poets have all given up the concept of nobility, the ideal of courage in the face of danger or fortitude in suffering. And many of the poets who have been hardest on the traditional hero have been most earnest in their search for nobility even if they apply to it some term less redolent of the platform.

Thus Brinnin, who cannot find the heroes promised in the books, for war has no longer the trappings of chivalry and we no longer take pleasure like a Malory in the sight of warriors knee deep in one another's blood, can find the movement of heroism in those who "recount our difficult and common life" ("Heroes," *The Garden Is Political*). For it is the simple who are "imperial today." And most often in him it is the "faith" in a social ideal that heartens him when faced with the degradations of our time. Though "With wicked gifts of steel we are undone" ("Mardi Gras," *No Arch, No Triumph*), we are saved from utter defeat, when

> We find *some smoky hero breathing yet*,
> And tend his wound, and teach him second faith . . .

This "second faith" is one with the "second sight" that is the subject of one of Brinnin's most serious poems which we have already studied at some length, mainly under the rubric of the exile. In his "Meditation on Tombs," the poet comes from the tombs of Lenin and Lincoln, where he has "been kin to *those heroic*." But he takes himself to task for the easy optimism begotten in him by this identification with heroic statesmen, and that throws him into an easy and self-flattering pessimism, and he fancies himself

> as Byron, wounded, beautiful,
> Asserting ego in its sovereign seat
> And its luxurious pride . . .

And so he withdraws from public concerns, wraps himself in "glory and distress," and

> I tasted mortal zero,
> Felt the moving shadow and origin
> Of the first enduring sin,
> *Became the first hero.*

But this is just what is wrong with the old heroic ideal. It means the triumph of the individual, of the ego over the "superego." And, as Brinnin has it in another of his most serious poems ("In Season of Actual War," *No Arch, No Triumph*),

> In season of actual war it is good to declare
> Death of the false and individual,
> The visions of an old cosmology . . .

In "Meditation on Tombs" what recalls him from selfish dreams is the faith that leads to action, to love, and to life. And the hero drops out of the picture or finds himself in "the melody of life in its plurality."

Berryman is down on the traditional hero for the same reason — his unregenerate egotism. In "A Point of Age" (*Poems*), dated Detroit 1940,

> *The Hero*, haggard on the top of time,
> *Enacts his inconceivable woe and pride*,
> Plunging his enemies down the mountainside.

This is the old image of the hero whom the poet must repudiate. And he must repudiate in the name of another and more Christian image.

> We are come to learn
> Compassion from the last and piercing scream
> Of who was lifted before he could die.

In the following stanza we have again "Animal and Hero": "where you lounge the air / Is the air of summer, smooth and masculine."

But darkness and storm take over, and the hero begins "the climb, the conflict that are your desire." This figure is left without development, and we can only guess at the application intended. It must presumably be taken in the framework of the poet's reference to Christ. And it may help to place it in the framework of Brinnin's somewhat later poem, "The Ascent," discussed earlier, and of Auden and Isherwood's *The Ascent of F6*.

The image of the climb, with which we are all familiar, of course, from Ibsen's *Brand* and from Longfellow's "Excelsior," is rather frequent in the early Auden. In "Paid on Both Sides" (1930 *Poems*) one of the characters refers to the paternal wisdom we all inherit, the "lies" our fathers taught us.

> They taught us war,
> To scamper after darlings, *to climb hills*,
> To emigrate from weakness, find ourselves
> The easy conquerors of empty bays.

In two of the odes in *The Orators*, the symbol appears. In one place, among the activities of the recruits in training is "to *climb the cliff path* to the coastguard's point." In another, the writer's pupils are warned that there is imminent danger of war —

> Passports are issued no longer; that area is closed;
> There's no fire in the waiting room now at the
> *climbers' Junction*.

In *Look, Stranger!* there is a sonnet, reprinted in the *Collected Poetry* under the title "The Climbers," in which the poet, addressing his love, says, "Upon the mountains of our fear I climb." We have already seen, in another connection, that this mountain climb is here associated with a selfish indulgence in private love that is opposed to the virtuous ideal of collectivity.

Taking these passages altogether, and in connection with the treatment of the climbers in *The Ascent of F6*, it seems clear that, while the imagination of young Auden is intrigued by the symbol of the climb, associated as it is with disciplined effort, adventure, and elevation, and so with romantic idealism in general, he felt constrained to warn against the self-deception and vainglory involved in such "skyline operations." And so with him the climb became

a symbol for what was discredited in the old-line hero. With Brinnin, on the other hand, the climb symbolized just what the discredited heroism and insularity did not generally involve, self-
discipline and modest hard work in building up the structures of
the ideal city. And this I take to be the attitude of Berryman in his
obscure reference to "the climb / the conflict that are your desire."
At any rate this poem concludes with a reference to this desired
"island or harbour city of our choice," and with the sober reflection
"we have a work to do," and the suggestion that this, rather than a
glorious death on the battlefield, will bring "a grave / At last for
the honourable and exhausted man."

This Carlylean emphasis on sober work is more extensively developed in Berryman's "Boston Common," along with an insistence
on the idea that it is not the conventional military hero who will
make us hear "the heart of the Future beating." The image of the
true hero is for him the common man lying beneath the bronze
stallion in the statue of Colonel Shaw. The common man, "common
character," the "casual man," "the *possible hero*" in this poem are
opposed to "your *official heroes in a mazagine* . . . loose in the
brothel" of a war, who turn out, individually, so unworthy of admiration when closely examined, and who move in an undifferentiated mass where "the will is mounted and gregarious and bronze,"
and where it is actually "tanks and guns" that "move and must move
to their conclusions." We look far off for our heroes, and they are
right here under our eyes, quietly going about the arts of peace —
"fishermen, gardeners," and simple, unpretentious, fabulous men
like Lincoln and Mao Tse-tung and Tracy Doll, "tracing the
future on the wall of a cell." There is the individual standing firm
against the mass. There is

> The face towards which we hope all history,
> Institutions, tears move, there the Individual.

There then we have the "possible hero," who is to replace the
standard hero of the past.

> Farewell the plumed troop, and the big wars,
> That makes ambition virtue! O, farewell! . . .
> Pride, pomp, and circumstance of glorious war!

If the reader finds in my summary paraphrase something of obscurity and confusion, I can only plead that I have done my best to render the several items of Berryman's thought in this poem and to indicate such connections among them as are suggested in the poem but not developed with the coherence of prose discourse. Brinnin's emphasis is more on the collectivity (the harmony in the melody), Berryman's more on the individual who resists the leveling trend of mass action. But in both of them the man admired, without the title of hero, is a plain man, a hard worker, a man devoted to a better future, not seeking his own glory, in whom "love" is the guarantee that it is the good of all for which he labors.

But it is MacLeish, who, having most thoroughly discredited and dismissed every type of specious, showy hero on whom men have pinned their faith and worship in the several ages in which each has been dominant, most sturdily clings to what remains in man to admire, though he does not call it heroic. Of all our modern poets, MacLeish is the one who, without cynicism, has most bravely faced a world deprived of supernatural hopes and sanctions. MacLeish and Jeffers are the two major poets of our time in whom there would appear to be no "aftershine" of Christian, or even theistic, assumptions. But MacLeish has never fallen in with Jeffers's scornful view of humanity itself. In *Actfive* we are confronted with a world in which

> the King unthroned, the God
> Departed with his leopards serpents
> Fish, and on the forestage Man
> Murdered,

and with all the traditional heroes dismissed as of no help, there is nothing left but The Shape of Flesh and Bone. The third tableau is devoted to this mere residue of humanity and to the situation in which he finds himself in a world completely ruined and no dreams left in which to take refuge.

> The city of man consumed to ashes, ashes,
> The republic a marble rubble on its hill,
> The laws rules rites prayers philters all exhausted,
> Elders and supernatural aids withdrawn . . .

MacLeish does not here envisage the possible extinction of man in some future war. He assumes the survival of man on our planet, but of all his traditional "sanctions" he has made *tabula rasa*. What is left is simply animal man. But animal man is still *man*, and the "mortal flesh and mortal bone" are still endowed with two faculties — will and love.

> And yet the will endures: the boy dies
> Believing in his death and in the others.
> The woman tells her son to act the man.
> The heart persists. The love survives.

Those who consider that this is impossible without supernatural sanctions will find here a crass contradiction in thought. But those who believe that man's faculties are the product of a natural evolution, that will is inherent in his animal nature, and that love is an inevitable function of his family life, will not find it so hard to accept the paradox. Within the framework of his thought, MacLeish can even write lines that sound like Hemingway:

> The blinded gunner at the ford — the rest
> Dead: the rest fallen: none to see:
> None to say the deed was well done: no one.

And he can write lines of a bravado that would not suit Hemingway's ideal of understatement. The poem ends with a picture of mortal flesh and bone left in utter darkness, and yet

> know the part they have to bear
> And know the void vast night above
> And know the night below and dare
> Endure and love.

Most critical readers will, I fear, regard this way of writing as grandiloquent and theatrical. But this may be simply because they cannot conceive of any alternative to a religious cosmology except the complete surrender of our humanity. It is not a time when critical suffrages will go to a poet who has nothing to offer in the way of mythology.

In any case, it will be remarked that, in his substitute hero MacLeish agrees with Berryman and Brinnin in finding his hope for the

future in the "common man" and in one guided by "love." In his
"New Poems (1951–1952)" (*Collected Poems, 1917–1952*) he has
a poem entitled " 'Common Man' (the Century of)" in which he
celebrates the

> *Nameless, faceless hero* who
> Loves for us in humankind
> What we cannot find to love,
> Whom we love and cannot find!

FACE OF THE AGE

26. THE AGE OF . . .

All ages since literary history began have put labels on themselves or been labeled by their successors as the age of this and that. The Greeks looked back to the age of Saturn, which was a golden age, and distinguished ages of silver, iron, and lead as intervening before the expected cyclical return of the Golden Age. The eighteenth century has often been called the Age of Reason, or Enlightenment. Shelley, in the tide of revolutionary enthusiasm, in his anticipation of a century of liberty and justice, sang:

> The world's great age begins anew,
> The golden years return,

though before he had finished singing, he fell prey to disillusioning thoughts:

> O cease! must hate and death return?
> Cease! must men kill and die?
> Cease! drain not to its dregs the urn
> Of bitter prophecy.

Tennyson, in a long age of peace, took up the strain of prophecy, dipped into the future, visioned bloody wars in the air, and saw in the end an age when

> . . . the war-drum throbb'd no longer, and the battle-flags
> were furl'd
> In the Parliament of man, the Federation of the world.

Our poets since World War I have been extremely liberal in putting names upon their age, and almost completely unanimous in assigning derogatory names to it. They pretty much all agree with Ezra Pound who, in 1920, asking what our soldiers had fought for in the first great war, called our culture "an old bitch gone in the teeth," "a botched civilization." It was in about 1936, when the second war began to threaten a ruined world, that our later poets began to call names. For Prokosch ("Port Said," *Assassins*), our age was comparable to

> *that age of ice* like a sheet over
> The terrified towers and windowed cliffs and over
> The flowerlike bodies deprived
> Of spirit, gently covering
> Their solitude like a lover.

He also called it "the Age of Passion," which now had "killed the spirit" ("Empty Provinces," *Assassins*), and also "an age of falsehood," "the age of lies" ("The Carnival," *The Carnival*). For Brinnin our age is "this mechanic's age." In *The Asiatics*, Prokosch has one of his characters call our age "the age of inversion, the negative age," anticipating Auden's adventurers in "The Quest," who "went the Negative Way toward the Dry."

In this matter of labeling the age with a phrase, Auden came later with his now classic *Age of Anxiety*. He also, in that work, called ours "a tawdry age." He also talks of "the ages of anguish" in a passage where it is not quite clear whether he is referring to ages of the world or ages in a man's life. Alfred Hayes comes along with a similar ambiguity, where in his *Welcome to the Castle*, the cynical old man assures his young friends that this is an honest age (whether in his life or in the world) — meaning an age in which we may candidly confess the worst of motives. For MacLeish ours is the "faint age of fear" (*Actfive*). Kenneth Rexroth, when he tunes in on the radio, listens to "the sentimentality / Of an age more dead than the Cro-Magnon" ("Un Bel Di Vendremo," *The Phoenix and the Tortoise*, 1944).

One may even find in E. E. Cummings a highly disparaging characterization of the age. But he is a bird of a quite different feather and approaches the subject from a peculiar angle. He is another poet who was well established during the twenties, one of the Cowley "exiles," a veteran of World War I, the main bulk of whose work falls within the thirties and forties. His poetry is not primarily

socio-political or ideological; it is primarily personal and philosophical. His philosophy might be summed up in terms of the gospel: "Consider the lilies of the field, how they grow" (Matthew
5:28). For what concerns him is not what society has and achieves,
but what a man feels, how he "grows" and is alive in his "soul." But
as he continues to "sing," under the pressures of history, he becomes
more and more biting in his comments on certain features of human
nature very prominent in the modern world, under the nefarious
effects of "civilization." He is not exposing the decay of civilization, like so many other poets of the time, but rather the triumph
of civilization over the "soul." So that he is capable of writing
toward the end of the thirties (*Fifty Poems*, 1940) that if

> than all mankind something more small occurs
> or *something more distorting than socalled*
> *civilization* i'll kiss a stalinist arse

And even earlier (*No Thanks*, 1935) he was moved to write, having in mind the triumph of Progress and Gadgets and the weakening of manhood:

> King Christ, *this world is all aleak*;
> and life preservers there are none:
> and waves which only He may walk
> Who dares to call himself a man.

This sour note represents, of course, only the "negative" side of his
world view; and we must make allowance for the unfailing play-
boy and billboard vividness of his style. He is in the main a very
cheerful writer — a daring young man on a flying trapeze. He never
puts off the cap-and-bells that is an extravagant version of Gertrude Stein. And he is an extreme romantic in his indulgence in
sentiment. Every other poem is a sonnet to his lady's eyebrow or a
moonlight sonata, and he is chronically in a state of swooning
ecstasy over the beauty of the world and the stirrings of his "soul."
But through all his writing runs a consistent critical philosophy that
makes him impatient with most people's attitudes toward life, and
we shall have occasion in later sections to illustrate several facets of
his thinking (though he disapproves of thinking) on the subjects
of progress, science, etc.

242

The most withering account of the age was given by a poet not yet mentioned, Kenneth Fearing. It is seldom that Fearing directly characterizes the times in his own words, but he has one poem from the period 1935–1938 in which he does characterize the twentieth century in ironic but unmistakable terms. It is called "C Stands for Civilization" (*Collected Poems*, 1940). It refers to the great achievements of modern science, in electrical measurement, effective bombs, and above all in the marvels of television, which can bring us directly the details of a lynching or of disasters photographed from Lockheed monoplanes. In each stanza we have, in capital letters, the poem's refrain, " THE TWENTIETH CENTURY COMES BUT ONCE," in one case with the sardonic addition, "Once too soon, or a little too late, just once too often."

The hundred-odd pieces included in Fearing's *Collected Poems* cover the work of fifteen years, beginning with 1925. He is thus the earliest, as well as one of the most incisive, of American verse commentators on the modern world during the period we are considering, and deserves some brief notice here. One hesitates to call his work poetry, or even to consider it over-seriously as "literature," though it is extremely clever and displays much ingenuity in phrasing and in organization for effect. It is written in verse form and in irregular stanzas for which, presumably, Sandburg was the chief model. But the language is very deliberately and persistently that of prose — the prose of the street, the tavern, the stock exchange, and gangland. There is almost no hint of the lyrical and musical quality of Sandburg, or Sandburg's awareness of the beauty and "mystical" appeal of the world. I suppose Fearing's method of presentation is best characterized as that of skillful advertising, though he has nothing for sale but an intensely cynical view of things. One assumes that his revulsion from the world as it is, is in terms of some implicit notion of what it might be like. But he is very careful not to sketch in any ideal frame of reference against which the actualities of the world are felt as sickening.

His earliest poems represent the 1925–1929 period, when, in the United States at least, things were booming. They are taken up with the lives of criminals, of unscrupulous money-getters, of lovers "in taxis bound for bright cabarets," and of men in the street whose emptiness is expressed by the words "We didn't know what we wanted, and there was nothing to say." There are drunks assuring themselves that "there were reasons for having lied and betrayed and cringed," and businessmen putting themselves to sleep with the halfhearted assurance of their own importance. "Go to sleep, you are a gentleman, McKade, alive and sane, a gentleman of position." There is also the Dos Passos *U.S.A.* awareness that private and public life are interrelated. The killer protests his innocence as the electric current is turned on; and the headlines read, "SEE U.S. INVOLVED IN FISHERY DISPUTE / EARTHQUAKE REPORTED IN PERU."

The poems of the second group (1930–1935) are written on a background of bankruptcy, suicide, breadlines, political corruption, and large dividends in the United States, republican movements in Italy and Spain, Hitler dictatorship in Germany. The most dominant themes are men's subjection to illusory dreams and to the promises of quacks — quacks in politics, in finance, in philanthropy, in religion, and in literature. The poet's irony falls evenhanded on the D.A.R. and People's Gas, on Father Coughlin, Aimee Semple McPherson, and H. L. Mencken, on the Guggenheim Fund, Mr. Hoover, Will Hays, Al Capone, on popular magazines and on "that genius, that literateur [*sic*], Theodore True, / St. Louis boy who made good as an Englishman in theory, a deacon in Vaudeville, a cipher in politics" ("American Rhapsody (1)"). There is something of the preacher's note in "Twentieth-Century Blues," as he asks people what they have won when they have got their successes — speculative plunger, the salesman, the irresistible love — what in the end have they "really, finally won?"

> Question mark, question mark, question mark, question mark,
> And you, fantasy Frank, and Dreamworld Dora and hallu-
> cination Harold, and delusion Dick, and Nightmare Ned.

And the moralist is heard beneath the irony of "Winner Take All," as the loser makes his alibi and proclaims his innocence.

> You've got to have what you've got to have, you're going to
> do what you've got to do,
> And you are innocent of what has to happen.

In the third group (1935–1938), the pitch rises to a climax and the drums beat louder as things grow more sensational on the public stage, and the next war is anticipated in all its horror. In "The Program,"

ACT ONE, Madrid-Barcelona,
ACT TWO, Paris in springtime, during the siege,
ACT THREE, London, Bank Holiday, after an air raid,
ACT FOUR, a short time later in the U.S.A.

There follow the lists of millions dead and wounded, with advertisements of chocolates, brassières, tobaccos, and cocktails. In this group are found his most effective pieces, as the general tension rises, and fears become more acute as the ambiguities multiply. What most deserves inclusion in the anthologies is the macabre "Hold the Wire," where the frantic householder, suspecting that he has been followed, is uncertain what to do or expect when the doorbell rings, or what to think of the man at the other end of the wire.

Who are you, who are you, you have the right number but
 the connection's very poor;
We can hear you well enough, but we don't like what you're
 saying;
Yes, the order was received, but we asked for something
 else . . .

The ambiguity is multiple, for, in the complications of irony, we are not sure who the speaker is, whether he is on the side of the angels, and in the general confusion — agents and counteragents, propaganda and counterpropaganda, everyone in disguise and the "samples free" — we are all in a state of frantic bewilderment.

HOW DO WE KNOW YOU'RE THE PERSON THAT YOU SAY?

By now, our fears and / or hopes are centered on one terrible figure.

If it's Adolf Hitler, if it's the subway gorilla, if it's Jack
 the Ripper,
SEND HIM IN, SEND HIM IN, IF IT'S JOLLY JACK THE RIPPER IN A
DOUBLE-BREASTED SUIT AND THE SAMPLES ARE FREE.

It would be a mistake to assume that what Fearing is mainly concerned with is the political and economic situation in the world and the United States. "Hold the Wire" is obviously symbolic of the moral situation — the moral or "spiritual" bewilderment and fright. In "Manhattan" (significantly dedicated to Alfred Hayes), he reviews certain aspects of American politics — "the missing judge, the bigshot spender, and the hundred dollar bills," "the reform party and the gambling clean-up (a ten-day laugh)." He touches on our baseball mania, on abortion and rape, and assorted private ambitions and misfortunes; and then he breaks out in a momentary Waste Land strain that betrays a deeper intention —

> City, city, city,
> Eye without vision, light without warmth, voice without
>   mind, pulse without flesh . . .

"Radio Blues" is a pitiful picture of someone tuning in on various higher and higher wave lengths, with the recurrent question, "Is that what you want to match the feeling that you have?"

Perhaps we have arrived here at the very center from which Fearing makes his sardonic survey of the modern world. There is some right feeling that we all vaguely and ineffectually search for, but without the means within us to find it. This is the most impressive note in his fourth group of poems (1938–1940). In "American Rhapsody (4)" we have the picture of some woman exhibiting the symptoms of approaching madness.

> But first, baby, as you climb and count the stairs (and they
>   total the same) did you, sometime or somewhere, have a
>   different idea?
> Is this, baby, what you were born to feel, and do, and be?

And there is Mrs. Raeburn, the spiritualist operator, reminiscent of Aiken, Eliot, and the Tarot Cards. There are several false roads to the right feeling which fall under his scornful notice. We go to the doctor with our fears and phobias. The doctor's task ("The Doctor Will See You Now") is to enable us to "adjust."

> To adjust the person to his gods, and to his own estate, and
>   to the larger group.
> Adjust to the conventions and the niceties. That is, by infer-
>   ence, to the Chamber of Commerce, to the local police,

to the Society of Ancient Instruments, and to the West
Side Bicycle Club.

And then there is the psychoanalytic way, considered by the "Gentleman Holding Hands with Girl." He thinks "of Freud, of Krafft-
Ebing for a moment. Of Havelock Ellis (must read, some day, in
full)."

If Fearing is a moralist, he would seem to be a purely negative
one. Perhaps he was impressed with the dreariness, the shabbiness
of spirit exhibited by Eliot in "Prufrock" and *The Waste Land*;
but there is no sign of the "way out" already suggested in *The
Waste Land* by the allusion to St. Augustine and the voice of the
thunder over Himavant. These poems of Fearing's were written in
an active period of socialist doctrine, but, in spite of his scorn for
commercialism, I find no hint that he found spiritual satisfaction
in the repudiation of capitalism.

In Fearing's later volumes of poetry there is no marked change
in theme or attitude. *Afternoon of a Pawnbroker and Other Poems*
(1943), written at the height of the long-expected war, and
Stranger at Coney Island and Other Poems (1948), in the postwar
period, make perhaps less of the outward scene and more of the
inner emptiness, anxiety, loneliness, and ineffectual questioning of
the "soul" in a world of machines that cannot answer our questions. We now hear of a mysterious stranger whom we have long
sought and who alone "can solve these many riddles we have found
so difficult," a "terrible stranger" who "puts, to each of us, a question that must be answered with the truth." And there is even a
Kafka-like symbolizing of a decision and sort of last judgment for
which we go to the "assistant secretary" in a long, the "right,"
marble hall, and then to "The authoritative man with those powerful but delicate photo-electric eyes, / Perception like radar, a cal-
culator mind."

Fearing is obviously not enthusiastic about the mechanical civilization from which his imagery and décor are drawn, and he tries at
times to supply something more "elevating" for contrast and ad-
monition. Sometimes this is drawn from children's fairy books. His
travelers on their Long Journey do not realize that beside them on

the train are Sinbad the Sailor, Jack the Giant Killer, and "the Princess of the Diamond Isles in love with Captain Wonder." Sometimes he goes higher in the mythological scale. The pawnbroker has among his pledges the Fountain of Youth, Pandora's Box, and Gabriel's Trumpet; and sometimes he wonders why he has never taken advantage of these talismanic properties. These things are meant to suggest the more "spiritual" life, from which our age infallibly turns away. But so sophisticated an artist cannot afford to be caught out in what might appear sentimentality, and must always give any such images a fanciful and burlesque turn. The angel Gabriel is "Mr. Gabriel," and the Fountain of Youth is, like other pledges, "in good condition." This sort of thing has a sure-fire appeal to magazine readers who pride themselves on their smart modernity but have a low tolerance for more rigorous effects of poetry. It is a sweetening ingredient in that sauce of wistful pathos, red-pepper sarcasm, and paradoxical wit with which he serves up his raw slices of contemporary life. The whole dish is skillfully compounded to suit the popular taste. The wistfulness is a stronger note as the world's tragedy intensifies. We read in "Finale" (*Afternoon of a Pawnbroker*):

How cold, how very cold is the wind that blows out of nowhere into nowhere . . .
Bearing away to nowhere and to no place the very especial sins and virtues that once were ours . . .

The question mark is much in evidence — what Sandburg calls the "beautiful unanswerable questions." Only, for Sandburg they are truly beautiful questions; whereas here they are the somewhat maudlin questions we ask ourselves after midnight when gazing into the barroom mirror. The endless iterations are like the iterations of machinery, or, as Fearing himself notes, of a cracked phonograph record.

All it has to do is to, do is to, do is to, do is to start at the beginning and continue to the end.

He is here referring, ironically, to the *mind*, but rendering its operation in terms of the cracked record. It is an ingenious trick, and may be regarded by some as a proud reflection on the prevailing materialism. But it is also the clue to what it is that makes us question the artistic soundness of his poetic method. His battle against materialism is carried on with the weapons of materialism; in the end it leaves us gasping for a breath of fresh air. It is a case of the dyer's hand subdued to what it works in.

Not even the author of *John Brown's Body* was immune to the pessimist infection in the period of Barcelona and Madrid, Vienna and Munich. Stephen Vincent Benét came into the thirties as a veteran celebrator of the American dream. Though he did not take hope from Marxian promises, he was well fortified by the democratic faith. But as a poet of common life and of public affairs, he was, as it were, in duty bound to reflect the gloom and despair that reigned in serious minds even in our relatively hopeful and protected world, and he laid himself out in *Nightmare at Noon* (1940) to cover this topic. It is true that he fought hard to find the silver lining to every cloud. In his "Ode to the Austrian Socialists" he can point the moral inherent in the tragedy:

> When you do not build
> To make one man rich, you can give people light and air,
> You can have room to turn around . . .

In his "Ode to Walt Whitman" he can point out that even Whitman witnessed odious passages in American political life.

> I have seen the rich arrogant and the poor oppressed . . .
> The democratic vista botched by the people,
> Yet not despaired, loving the giant land.

In "Litany for Dictatorships" he can say the obvious things about the horrors of the police state. In "Nightmare, with Angels" he can have an angel point out that even totalitarian states — as under the Incas — have had their day and passed into oblivion.

But he does here allow himself a note of something like cynicism as another angel seems to include even us in his sweeping prophecy.

> "You will not be saved by General Motors or the pre-fabricated house.
> You will not be saved by dialectical materialism or the Lambeth Conference.

You will not be saved by Vitamin D or the expanding universe.
In fact you will not be saved."

And this angel goes on to sow the earth with metal seeds. "Where
he sowed them, the green vine withered, and the smoke and the
armies sprang up." And there are several nightmares more horrify-
ing than this. There is one in which the termites, in the metropolis,
quit eating wood and begin eating the steel itself ("Metropolitan
Nightmare"). There is one in which the machines take over and
do away with men; there is some hope that they will find they
need us men to provide oil and spare parts ("Nightmare Number
Three"). There is another nightmare in which, in World War III,
the women take over and smash every government in the world:
"And since then, there just aren't any children" ("Minor Litany").

This is, of course, the poetry of fantasy, and it takes a Jonathan
Swift, a Samuel Butler, a Franz Kafka (writing in prose), to give
it its full point. Benét is perhaps more effective when he writes of
how private citizens feel in the modern city — the desolate feeling
of loneliness (in "Notes to be Left on a Corner Stone"), and the
anodynes that the lost people depend upon ("Minor Litany"):

> This is for those who wait till six for the drink,
> Till eleven for the tablet;
> And for those who cannot wait but go to the darkness;
> And those who long for the darkness but do not go . . .

27. REVOLUTIONARIES

It was presumably the tuba and saxophone proletarian note that
gave its great vogue to the poetry of Kenneth Patchen, beginning
in the middle thirties with his volume *Before the Brave* (1936), and
extending persistently down through the forties and fifties. This is
something very different from the cynical and sophisticated note
of Fearing, since it is supported by a jubilant belief in the salvation
possible within the Marxist faith, and the muse here deliberately
wears the blue jeans of the laboring class in field and factory. His
poems, like Fearing's, were eagerly sought after by publishing
houses that exploited "modernism," but the modernism here is

largely a matter of crude naturalism and a violent emotional expressionism. It is not against the age that Patchen fulminates, nor against the inveterate emptiness and wistfulness of the human soul; it is against the brutalities of capitalism and its minions, and the miseries of the poor that flourish under this system. But his proletarian ideology makes him understand that, in their state of social benightedness, "Americans have learned neither to live nor to die, but they have / made an art of being loudly between the two." It is liberalism that is the deceiver and betrayer, and the poets "with death on their tongues." But *"The fat nonsense will end. / You will drown in your rot."* And again, *"The slimy hypocrisy will end. / You will go down in your filth"* ("A Vision for the People of America," *Selected Poems*, 1946; italics in original).

On the jacket of *Before the Brave*, we were informed that "with this book, an American poet takes his place in the company of three left-wing poets of the younger generation — Stephen Spender, W. H. Auden, and C. Day-Lewis." But three years later in *First Will and Testament* (1939) Patchen was making all kinds of fun of S.L.A., or Mr. Triumvirate, as he calls them. He has a lot of fun as well with Mr. Eliot and with another triumvirate, Gregory MacLeish Millay, who is made to say over the telephone: "H'lo, England? I want to be remembered when I die and even after I am dead because what lips I kissed last make me feel very very empty inside" ("The Old Lean over the Tombstone"). There are Joycean dialogues with people like Ben Johnson and John Donne and Matthew Arnold, and other less recognizable characters, in which almost the only word of sense uttered is by Nikolai Lenin: "There is no darkness when men know what they are fighting for." This poet is equally down on the "capitalism of democracy and the capitalism of fascism," on the church of Rome and the church of Stalin. Those well acquainted with the movements of the past twenty years will know exactly where that places him politically and ideologically.

There are two wise characters in his Joycean dialogues named Kek and Nolly. Kek says, "The world seems sick as though man had grown tired of being shut up in himself and was trying to get out." But, he adds, "There isn't a Goddamned place for him to go." Nolly says, "There never was." But, says Kek, "only a few knew it." And Nolly agrees, "And they were the good guys."

28. MYSTICS

Robert Fitzgerald is a much less sensational poet than any of these, and his singing voice is much less forced and strident. He is not aiming at modernism in any of its forms, good or bad, and has certainly not much enlarged the bounds of poetic art. He has not strained himself to be the poet of his age. He has not been unaware of what he calls "the great night and murmur of the age" ("Testamentary," in *A Wreath for the Sea*, 1943). He has gently touched on the inadequacy of all those to whom we might think of going for wisdom in our present need — the businessmen, the philosophers, journalists, priests, psychoanalysts, doctors, musicians, historians, stylists. These all have their merits, but are condemned not by what they are, but somehow by something which they are not. He does not fail to deal with the bewildered, distracted denizens of metropolis ("The Imprisoned"):

> Against the shine of windows, visual
> Madness of intersecting multitudes,
> Their speech torn to bits in the torrent.

It is his religious faith that, as would appear, enables him to keep his voice down in the general chorus of lamentation. We read in "Testamentary":

> The mind comes to its flowering time
> The senses achieve morning
> By charity and hope. Let it be known
> In the great night and murmur of the age.

There are a number of good poets of the thirties and forties, and others significant enough for serious consideration though we cannot call them good without qualification, who do not call for comment here because they are not really concerned particularly to characterize the age. And that for the simple reason that they are essentially mystics; it is the "eternal" order of thought and

feeling in which they dwell. Such are Richard Eberhart and Muriel
Rukeyser, than whom it is impossible to imagine two more different writers in style and method of composition. What they have
in common is that they write altogether from spiritual insight or
intuition, and the objects and incidents of contemporary history
are for them strictly incidental to their vision. Eberhart can write,
in "A Meditation" (*Song and Idea*, 1940):

> Of the mind of God, rising like a mighty fire
> Pure and calm *beyond all mortal instances* . . .

He can write of himself as not subject to the caprices of the seasons ("The Scarf of June"):

> For I am where no sun shone yet,
> And am earth's inner being keeping,
> Locked in this lone discipline
> Against the world's decay.

He is, to be sure, a nature poet, as Blake and Wordsworth and Hopkins were nature poets, and he can write feelingly and sometimes
wittily about people. But the Wordsworth he may suggest is the
poet in that "serene and blessed mood," when

> the breath of this corporeal frame
> And even the motion of our human blood
> Almost suspended, we are laid asleep
> In body, and become a living soul.

If Blake is suggested, it is the Blake who wrote

> To see a world in a grain of sand,
> And a heaven in a wild flower;
> Hold infinity in the palm of your hand,
> And eternity in an hour.

Eberhart's religion, though it may be a "discipline," holds no suggestion of dogma. He is prone to meditation on death, but without
gloom. All times are alike to him. "The Fury of Aerial Bombard-
ment" (*Mid-Century American Poets*, ed. John Ciardi, 1950) makes
him think

> You would feel that after so many centuries
> God would give man to repent . . .

and to speculate

> Was man made stupid to see his own stupidity?
> Is God by definition indifferent, beyond us all?
> Is the eternal truth man's fighting soul
> Wherein the Beast ravens in his own avidity?

The nearest reference to the times that I find is the adjuration of the skull to man ("A Meditation," *Song and Idea*):

> You are imperfect, will never know perfection,
> You must strive, but the goal will recede forever,
> That you must do what the great poets and the sages say,
> *Obeying scripture even in the rotten times.*

Muriel Rukeyser is in her way as much of a mystic as Eberhart, as much "above the war." She is, indeed, very much of her time, and her "God" is not, like his, "above all mortal instances." Her greatest inspiration was presumably Hart Crane, and she is as eager as Crane to incorporate the products of the mechanical age into the body of her faith. But again, like Crane, her structures of steel and aluminum are symbols from the start — in her a social system that is "spiritual" framework and essence. The airplane gives her the two dominant symbols of flight and contact, where flight is revolutionary aspiration and contact (in the starter) is power and social solidarity, joining together, like Crane's Brooklyn Bridge ("Preamble," *Theory of Flight*, 1935). The gyroscope is symbol of the centrifugal power of the mind, the outward widening circles, out and back, God and man, the soul's polarity ("The Gyroscope"). Here comes in again the symbol of contact; earth and sky are brought together as in Crane. In contrast with Crane, and with Eberhart, her religion is social and revolutionary. Her idols are da Vinci, discoverer, and Shelley, rebel. (Shelley figures with her as Whitman figures with Crane.) Marx suggests the dialectic of thesis, antithesis, and synthesis. This operates between citizens in the state, and between men and women in the freedom of sex life. Desire is a motive that should be encouraged in an expansive universe and an affirmative ideology. Jesus and Icarus are almost identical symbols for the positive and progressive attitude ("Theory of Flight"):

Icarus' phoenix-flight fulfils itself
desire's symbol swings full circle here,
eternal defeat by power, eternal death
of the soul and body in murder or despair
to be followed by eternal return, until
the thoughtful rebel may triumph everywhere.

Thus she manages to include even the death-and-resurrection "myth" in her comprehensive symbology ("The Lynchings of Jesus: I, Passage to Godhead"). "The Committee Room" is the assembly of those who vote against the rebels and discoveries; it is all one with the synagogue, the journalists, the school, with its negative teaching of history. "The Trial" starts with the Scottsboro case, representative of age-long oppression of subject races and dissenters. Her leading themes are developed in "The Structure of the Plane," which ends with an effusive peroration in favor of an affirmative attitude toward life, without benefit of dogma and superstition:

O be convinced without formula or rhyme
or any dogma   ;   use yourselves : be : fly.
Believe that we bloom upon this stalk of time.

In her poetical product of the forties, there is a very marked toning down of the revolutionary note — almost a complete disappearance of this, though not, I should say, a repudiation of those instinctive philosophical attitudes that underlie all her work. Public history and private living have sobered and mellowed her utterance and given it a less propagandist turn. As she says herself in "This Place in the Ways" (*The Green Wave*, 1948):

Rage for the world as it is
but for what it may be
more love now than last year
and always less self-pity
since I know in a clearer light
the strength of the mystery.

The whole of *The Green Wave* is a jubilant affirmation of the animal faith which is, one may suppose, the abounding source and effect of her abounding vitality. In "Easter Eve 1945" she notes the shining of the leaf, the wing, the stone deep in the mountain, the drop in the green wave:

> Lit by their energies, secretly, all things shine.
> Nothing can black that glow of life;   although
>   each part go crumbling down
>   itself shall rise up whole.

The poet writes much of the maternal vocation which she has found. This enables her to identify herself most feelingly with the eternal world-process of *becoming*, as opposed to mere static *being* which from the start appealed so strongly to her imagination, and which made Hegelian Marxism so congenial a theme. She grows more convincing as she grows more personal. Two of her finest poems, considered as imaginative expressions, are "Mrs. Walpurga" and "Green Limits." The one is a consistent and effective build-up of Freudian symbolism — she is dreaming of loves in the grove, and makes rich use of natural imagery supporting her theme of coupling lovers. In "Green Limits" she goes back to an incident of childhood when two aunts dragged her frightened and unwilling into high waves on the beach. Her fear of the waves is a symbol of personal isolation; her final immersion in the waves means the transcendence of the limits of self.

> Green limits walled me, water
> stood higher than I saw —
> glass walls, fall back!   let me
> dive and be saved.

It is often said that Hart Crane failed to complete the soaring cathedral of his faith. One reason for this was obviously the destructive compulsions that ruled him as a man; but another was surely the rigorous critical standards he set for himself as a poet. He could not force himself to fake anything in the overambitious task he set himself. In the case of Muriel Rukeyser it was not her inhibitions that stood in her way — no critical sense of what it takes to make a poem. It was just the other way with her. She could rush in fearlessly where angels fear to tread. Her notions of form were improvised as she went along. She had the inspiration to seek for symbolism that would give her work the force of images. But she did not have the patience to weave her symbols into a consistent pattern. She could not resist the temptation to patch up her symbolism with the mortar of prosy abstractions: and here she constantly ran into the baldness of cliché. What is needed to give proper effect to such outlandish combinations of tone and reference as are found throughout *Theory of Flight* is a solvent capable of assimilating them all to itself — such as irony, for example, in the later Auden. Without that one is frequently repelled by the raw gobbets, the unstyled crudities of rhetoric and self-revelation.

There is also the bustling personal note that so often intrudes, "— I am in love / with rivers," and (in *Theory of Flight*) the confident self-assurance of the young woman taking on the Whitman mantle of prophecy. Somehow, in Whitman, one feels that the "I" of the poet is actually *possessed* by his prophetic vision and raised out of himself; he is merely the challenger of old shells of thought, and the vehicle or medium through which the revelation declares itself. Besides, he has no confidently worked-out ideological system like Miss Rukeyser's revolutionary doctrine. He does not have anything like so pretentious a program, and is not so prone to take his own personal vitality as the proof of this and that social dogma. It is the uncritical cheekiness of this young woman that does much to prevent her from writing really fine poetry.

This is much more the case in *Theory of Flight* than in her later work. Where she is merely rendering her feeling toward herself and the world we have no objection to the sureness of her affirmations, and the personal tone has its appropriateness. It was, however, in her first volume that she had the most interesting things to say about the social problems that were so pressing in her time. It was there that she might have been tempted to pass a smart, facile sentence on her age. And it was, precisely, the wider views that her prophetic vision gave her that saved her from succumbing to that temptation.

With Kenneth Rexroth something of the same sort is true. In *The Phoenix and the Tortoise*, however, he contrasts the days spent in childhood with his mother in Italy, hearing the music of Puccini and Verdi, with listening to tinny music on the radio. He refers to "the sentimentality of an age more dead than the Cro-Magnon" ("Un Bel Di Vendremo"). "It is a terrible thing," he says, "to see a world die twice." The first time it died it was in tragedy, "the second as evil farce." It is also true that, in *The Dragon and the Unicorn*, while bicycling through southern France and Italy after the war, he took a very sour view of some decadent types of modern humanity (especially the homosexuals), and that on his return to the States he could pass a more crudely sardonic commentary on things at home.

> A ruined country and a
> Ruining people, the world
> Would be better if Kansas
> Were not in it.

But throughout most of his writing, he has been too much occupied with the age-old ontological problem of free will and necessity, and with developing a positive philosophy of love, to make it a primary concern to elaborate on the local features of our times. Like Jeffers, he thinks in terms of geological, of solar ages. Something of Jeffers's scorn for the race in its mass meanness has entered into his feeling. Alone in his Sierra mountain hut or by the shores of the Pacific, he can spare a moment to glance at men in cities (*The Phoenix and the Tortoise*):

> The State is the organization
> Of the evil instincts of mankind.
> History is the penalty
> We pay for original sin . . .

He can realize the helplessness of men in the flux of forces, unable to grasp the ABC of metaphysics:

> The atoms of Lucretius still,
> Falling, inexplicably swerve.
> And the generation that purposed
> To control history vanishes
> In its own apotheosis
> Of calamity, unable
> To explain why anything
> Should happen at all.

But he himself has a glimpse of the existentialist open-sesame to individual being:

> Value, causality, being,
> Are reducible to the purest
> Act, the self-determining person,
> He who discriminates structure
> In contingency, he who assumes
> All the responsibility
> Of ordered, focused, potential —
> Sustained by all the universe,
> Focusing the universe in act.

He has also his formula for a love which is not possessive and destructive of both itself and society (*The Dragon and the Unicorn*):

> The lover and the beloved
> Rise above the levels of
> Appetite, discursive knowledge,
> Consequence, probability,
> And enter into each other
> Directly. Knowledge of each
> Other becomes a mode of
> Being, and through each other
> The being of all the others.

Rexroth is not Auden. But, like the author of "New Year Letter," he has done his reading in metaphysics and the philosophy of science. He has worked out for himself an original approach to the problem of will and the definition of love. He is more technical in his vocabulary than Auden and more individualistic or "modern" in versification and composition. For the duly equipped reader, he is often a challenging and stimulating writer. He stands more aloof than Auden from this particular moment in time, and is not so sedulous a weathervane for the veering contemporary wind of doctrine.

29. TWILIGHT OF THE GODS

The poets of the thirties and the forties do not use the Wagnerian phrase, for they do not think of the protagonists of their drama as anything like gods. But a considerable chorus of them sing in unison of ours as a dying world. In Gregory's "Voices of Heroes," he refers to those who "sit *watching the world die*" (*Selected Poems*). Most prominent in the forties is Prokosch, who constantly dwells in a Ragnarok atmosphere of the last days and the furthest margins ("Going Southward," *Assassins*):

> This is *the final dreading*
> *Of history ending*, an end to living and terror
> spreading . . .
> *The long night falling* and knowledge failing and
> memory fading.

In Prokosch's novels there are many references to the dying world. In *The Seven Who Fled*, an Asiatic says to a European, "You are as lonely as I, my friend . . . We are *part of a dying world*, both you and I." In *The Asiatics* a Dutchman says to an American that what he sees at the end of their tunnel is darkness — "The *dark ages coming over* us like an ocean."

Prokosch's landscapes, in his poems, are full of ruins — often ruined towers or ruined castles that represent the old dead or dying order. In one poem he notes, "The *senility* of the Tuscan castle, / And the sobbing, fitful pulse of the faithless" (title poem of *The Carnival*).

The consciousness of our world as dying naturally grows stronger after 1939 and 1941. It is in *The Big Time* that Hayes speaks of the dying world, and he is thinking of the boom days that followed the first war and marked the second. His *Welcome to the Castle* shows us many scenes from the ruined, chaotic, cynical, and writhing Europe. His title for the volume and for the poem of the same name may have been suggested by a poem of Weldon Kees in his volume *The Fall of the Magicians*. "The View of the Castle" is a sardonic ballad symbolizing the old dead order under the image of a castle going to pieces, being visited by some sentimental tourist. The three first stanzas begin, "The castle is mortgaged now, my dear, / The mortgage is overdue," "The castle's been cracking for years, my dear," "The princesses were whores, my dear." And it ends with the ironic summary: "This is the castle, then, my dear, / With its justly famous view." Perhaps this poem offered a suggestion, also, for Nemerov's "Guide to the Ruins," which gives its title to the volume in which it stands first. Castles (or towers) are frequently associated with ruin in these decades as symbols of an old order that has passed. It is even found in Eliot in "The Rock" — "the Church disowned, the *tower overthrown*," and was used by Auden in "The Quest" (*Collected Poetry*):

> Nor all his weeping ways through weary wastes have found
> The *castle* where his Greater Hallows are interned;
> For broken bridges halt him, and dark thickets round
> Some *ruin where an evil heritage was burned.*

In Kees and Nemerov these ruined castles are tourist attractions, and the guide in Nemerov exploits commercially the prestige attaching to the old culture. But in Kees the castle is cracking and mortgaged and its princely possessors were actually in their time no better than they should be. In Nemerov's ruins and the temple groves, one admires "the gods with their noses knocked off."

Hayes presents many characters who witness to the decline of heroism and virtue in his dying world. Kees and Nemerov are particularly impressive in the invention of material symbols for the crack-up of modern society. In "Aunt Elizabeth," with her *National Geographics*, a little reminiscent of Eliot's early poems, her hideous ancestors leaning in frames along the fading wall,

> "And when the 'phone rang, Paul,"
> She says, "I answered. There was no one there;
> There was no one there at all."

There is some suggestion here of the sinister menace of ambiguous things in Fearing's "Hold the Wire." And this is true of other disturbing images. In one of his sprightly Villanelles, "The crack is moving down the wall. / Defective plaster isn't all the cause." This macabre refrain recurs the prescriptive number of times until with jittery nerves we read the final stanza!

> These nights one hears a creaking in the hall,
> The sort of thing that gives one pause.
> The crack is moving down the wall.
> We must remain until the roof falls in.

This is a good variation on Fearing's formula, and reminds us of

Charles Addams' macabre pictures in the *New Yorker*. Other symbols of the crack-up are "That spot of blood on the drawing-room wall" widening and moving like a fish ("Conversation in the Drawing Room") and (more and more fearsome á la Fearing) the walled-in corridor where "no messages will come" (fourth Villanelle); the insane detective Le Roux, screaming that "all the world is mad, that clues / Lead nowhere" ("Crime Club"); and the people in an earthquake who "blink in darkened rooms toward exits that are gone" ("Xantha Street"), where we have an echo of Sartre's famous play representing hell. These are neat little contraptions, with the imagery sharply etched, perhaps a trifle frivolous in their ironic lightness of tone and not rising to Arnold's "high seriousness," but somewhat of a relief from the soggy solemnity of the current elegies and odes in which the imagery is drowned in reflective morality.

In Nemerov there is much similar symbolic imagery, more weighted with sardonically toned moral implications. Such is that of his first "Still Life" (*Guide to the Ruins*) in which an oyster on a plate against the background of marble wall suggests that "all man had been / Castrated with a single knife," or his "Elegy of Last Resort" which begins:

> The boardwalks are empty, the cafés closed,
> The bathchairs in mute squadrons face the sea.
> Gray cloud goes over, the baffled involved brain
> Of the old god over the vacant waters:
> The proprietors of the world have gone home.

Here the imagery deepens in tone till we reach "the last / Steep fall of time into the deep of time" and "the perplexity of a sour world / Whose mighty dispensations all are done." Similar is the progress in "Trial and Death: A Double Feature," from his panorama of ruined houses, walls, broken aircraft, etc., to the concluding image:

> So we attend the agon of our star
> That burns, on the dusty and tarnished air,
> The helpless light that is its only speech.

Kees and Nemerov are peculiarly sharp in their commentary on

what is a central theme of nearly every poet of the time — the sui-
cidal futility and wickedness of war. This reaches its cruelest pitch
in Nemerov's "The Hero Comes Home in His Hamper, and Is
Exhibited at the World's Fair," and shows a sharp edge of irony in
Kees's Villanelle with the refrain: "The truce was signed but the
attack goes on."

Even where the poets will not baldly declare that the world is
dying, they agree that it is "sick unto death." It is a decadent world
even where its decadence is the prelude to its recovery and death a
prelude to rebirth. Thus we have Brinnin's brave vision of the coming world of freedom, in "Death of This Death" (*The Garden Is
Political*):

> A calm community
> That, *flowering in the culture of decay*,
> *Turns death to seed* within our living day.

The decadence of our world is imaged in various forms of disease, physical and psychological. Prokosch's dominant image is of
fever: in "The Assassins," the "blood and fever" of our unregenerate spirit; in "The Carnival," "The rattling fever which condones
all crimes;" in "Epilogue" to *Death at Sea*, "the pause in the onrush
of fever." And one recurring symbol of our psychological decadence is sexual perversion. For Berryman our malady is paralysis,
"busy with society and souls" seeking oblivion of pain. We read in
"Rock-Study with Wanderer":

> Paraplegia dolorosa   The world rolls
> A tired and old man resting on the grass.

With Chisholm it is our *impotence* that is betrayed by our crim-
inality ("The Road," *The Prodigal Never Returns*):

> The while we school our limbs and cells to kill
> And steal exclusively — no use to wonder
> Why these precipices, palms, and stars
> So studiously proclaim our impotence.

With Hayes, it is "the exhaustion of spirit that is not Rome but
Europe" ("The Fall of Rome," *Welcome to the Castle*). And it is
the general "sickness of being man" which he acknowledges to be

his constant theme and what accounts for what his friends complain of as the sour note to his music ("The Sour Note").

30. PROGRESS

How far our poets have been from representing the popular view of the time is clearly seen, I think, in this notion that ours is a sick and dying world. Since 1950, with the perfection of the atom bomb, and the realization of the possible lethal effects for whole populations of an atomic war, the general public has come to envisage the possibility that man may be wiped out and civilization come to an end. But that is not generally taken to mean that our culture is decadent. The destruction of the race by the aftereffects of atomic bombing is regarded as a colossal accident to which we are liable as a result of the forces of nature set off by some political maniac. It is no more proof that the world is sick and dying of its own rottenness than the sinking of the *Titanic*. Anyone who reads the newspapers or the literature of popular science or the speeches of political leaders must realize that our age is generally regarded as the culmination of several centuries of steady progress toward the good life. The common man still reflects the tradition of Volney and the optimist program of Condorcet in his *Esquisse d'un tableau des progrès humains* — a current of hopeful thinking that has run strong throughout the civilized world from the time of the French *Encyclopédie* down to the present year.

The concept of progress was very comprehensive, covering every aspect of human well-being, social and individual. Men's reliance in this matter was, first, upon democratic institutions that might be expected to ensure justice and opportunity for the humblest citizen, and for citizens of both sexes. It was, second, on universal education, which would enable each citizen to develop his native capacities and realize his potentialities in thought and action. Education, too, might be relied upon to clear away the handicaps of prejudice and superstition. Their reliance was, third, on social measures, undertaken privately or under the sponsorship of government, that would ensure the financial security of each citizen even in old age and the care of his health, and the elimination of slums. And back of all this and making it possible was the limitless advancement in scientific knowledge, already well started and heavily featured in the *Encyclopédie*. This would include the basic laws of nature as they might be applied to the improvement of our minds and of our living conditions and the enlargement of our productive capacity, and above all to improvement of agriculture, so as to provide food for the increasing populations of the earth. It was also anticipated that the advancement of medical science would go far toward the prevention and cure of disease and the prolongation of life. Along with all this, there was great confidence that improved knowledge and improved social and political conditions would bring about in time the elimination of the causes of war and a general reign of peace throughout the world. And these improvements in the conditions of living were expected to conduce to men's happiness and tend to greater gentleness and refinement in their manners and morality.

Such was the program and hope of what is called "liberal" thought throughout the last two hundred years. It was the almost universal hope of the common man, and has, I think, continued to be so. And for him it would certainly seem to have considerable justification in the historical facts. Democratic institutions are well established in the United States and in most European countries, and they have worked fairly well in freeing the citizenry of all classes from the condition of peonage that prevailed everywhere before the growing up of the free cities during the late Renaissance. In most countries women have a voice in choosing their rulers, and it is possible for them to find gainful employment where necessary or desirable. There is a very large measure of justice and protection of the underdog in our judicial procedures. There is no class in democratic societies that is positively debarred from improving its levels where opportunity and affluence are attainable. Education has everywhere been extended to all classes, and there are democratic countries in which literacy is almost one hundred per cent. It is everywhere taken for granted, and by all political parties, that the state is in large degree responsible for making provision against poverty, unemployment, and old age, and for providing public help where necessary in hospitalization and the care of health. Every city of any size in the more enlightened democracies has housing regulations and programs for the elimination of slums. Science in all its branches has gone forward beyond the wildest dreams of the eighteenth century: and their applications to human convenience are such as would be unbelievable to Diderot or Sir Thomas More, let alone to the philosophers and epicures of Greece and Rome. The wealth of our world is something never known before on the planet, and its distribution through all classes in Europe and America something unknown to antiquity, the Middle Ages, or the Renaissance. The production of food per capita, in Europe and America, has multiplied several times. The proudest citizens of the ancient world would be dazzled and enchanted with the way our streets and homes are lighted, with our means of loco-motion and communication. Of all branches of knowledge, it is perhaps medical science that has advanced most. Many diseases have been practically eliminated, prevented, or controlled: infant mortality has been reduced and the general length of life enor-mously increased over that, say, of Elizabethan England.

We are still somewhat subject to commercial depression and periods of unemployment, but the effects are not to be compared with those of the famines and pestilences of the Middle Ages, when half the population of a country might be wiped out. Even in the incidence and extensiveness of war, the comparative rate of mortal-ity and destructiveness, having regard to the numbers of the popu-lations involved, it may be that we do not show up badly in com-parison with antiquity, the Middle Ages, or the Renaissance, though the relative peacefulness of the eighteenth and nineteenth centuries has made the world wars of our century the more shocking and scandalous. Former ages took chronic war for granted and ideal-ized the status of the warrior. It is an age whose moral sense is out-raged by the existence of war that has made our reaction to our two world wars so violently censorious.

In the whole view those who have held the faith in progress would seem to have been amply justified in all respects except the assumption that human progress inevitably tends to human happiness and the improvement of morals and manners. On that point it is difficult to argue the case on a basis of statistical data. A careful historical study might help to determine whether vice and crime are more prevalent now than in the Middle Ages or the Renaissance. As for happiness, that is indeed a most elusive entity, hard to measure by any means available to sociology or psychology. How far the beauty of our surroundings may determine our happiness is difficult to determine; and it may be equally hard to determine whether the ugliness of many American cities is greater in its way than the ugliness and squalor of London in Chaucer's or in Pepys's day. There remains the extremely elusive subject of refinement of manners. In such matters a mere unreasoned preference for the ways of the past (and in the past, for the privileged and the aristocratic) might well determine one's judgment.

In the United States, at any rate, the man in the street today would hardly question that great progress has been made in human living since the Middle Ages, and that it is still being made; nor that this is a substantial good and a subject for rejoicing. And the man in the street would find it a little odd that our poets hold so contrary a view.

It was in the forties that our poets were so much occupied with the subject of progress and so much inclined to take a dim view of the notion of progress. It is true that they had, somewhat earlier, the distinguished example of Eliot. In his choruses from "The Rock," there is a solemn passage of lamentation over men's ungodliness, in which every aspect of men's enthusiasm for progress is touched on and dismissed as evidence of an unreligious spirit. He deprecates men's concern with "arts and inventions and daring enterprises," with "schemes of human greatness thoroughly discredited." They are so busy "bidding the earth and water to [their] service," "engaged in devising the perfect refrigerator." His satirical wit is lavished on even so innocent and awesome a science as astronomy — "Dividing the stars into common and preferred." The notion of happiness is degraded by associating it with drinking and rowdyism — "plotting of happiness and flinging empty bottles."

And all these errors of godless man are listed side by side with the root error of men "engaged in working out a rational morality." Men's devotion to the ideals of race and humanity are sneeringly referred to as "fevered enthusiasm" engendered out of spiritual "vacancy."

This whole passage is one of the few spots in Eliot's *Collected Poetry* really open to adverse criticism on aesthetic grounds. It does not measure up to the standards of good writing which he and Pound held at the time when he wrote *The Waste Land* and Pound helped him to cut out the surplus matter. The propagandist intention is too baldly displayed, and the prose meaning too nakedly stated. But it has the merit of making very clear the motive for his almost phobic reaction against the concept of progress. Eliot is of course not opposed to scientific research, or to the enlightened effort to improve humanity, or to applying reason to morality; man's reason cannot bring him to a true morality unless guided by supernatural revelation. But his religion makes him feel that men's exaltation of the grandeur of their minds and the glory of their actions stands in the way of what alone can save them, the worship of God. His scorn for the faith in progress is rooted in his hatred for secularism. The ideological basis is baldly stated a little later in the choruses. Men, he says, deny and at the same time invent new secular gods to worship,

> professing first Reason,
> And then Money, and Power, and what they call Life, or
> Race, or Dialectic.

The root crime of all crimes is that of the French Revolution, the setting up for worship of the Goddess of Reason, with its modern equivalent of the Marxian dialectic.

It is significant that Auden's attack on the idea of progress does not appear until his revolutionary hopes have given way to a religious faith. The same ethical preoccupation inspires them both, but with the coming in of supernatural religion, we first begin to hear of the "intellectual sin" of "Reason's depravity" ("New Year Letter"). It is perhaps a part of Auden's irony that the argument against reliance on reason should be made in witty Hudibrastic

couplets out of the Age of Reason. Or perhaps we might say that
he has turned from the romantic irregularities of his enthusiastic
youth to the classical form and style appropriate to his conformist
maturity. His "New Year Letter" is the kind of poetry of direct
statement favored by Pope and Gray rather than the poetry of
symbolistic indirection favored by Donne and Eliot, and there is
not even the irreducible minimum of decorative metaphor and description found in Gray and Thomson, Wordsworth and Scott.
But to say it is plain statement is not to imply that it does not have
its fine subtleties of irony and involution. In his undermining of the
notion of progress, he is infinitely more subtle than Eliot in "The
Rock." Thus he defends the religious attitude by highly ambiguous
references to men as open to disparagement as Blake and Rousseau,
Kierkegaard and Baudelaire. Baudelaire, he says, "went mad protesting / That progress is not interesting." And, even worse, he

> thought he was an albatross,
> The great Erotic *on the cross*
> *Of Science*, crucified by fools
> Who sit all day on office stools . . .

But when it comes to Reason, Liberty, Progress, and Science, it
turns out that the madmen were right. What the worship of these
secular gods has led to is

> Man captured by his liberty,
> The measurable taking charge
> Of him who measures . . .

His useful facts

> Become the user of his acts
> And Chance the choices of his soul . . .

And then we have that almost invariable association of science with
the invention of mechanical conveniences in which the poet is in
agreement with the man in the street. The difference is that for the
ordinary man in the street this association is honorific to both members, whereas our recent poets all represent man as the slave to his
conveniences, and in their dislike for "materialism" science itself
is degraded. So Auden shows us factory-trained boys "feeding
helpless machines," "girls married off to typewriters," and "homes

blackmailed by a radio set." And there is a still further association generally present — the association, or identification, of mechanical conveniences and materialistic commercialism. Thus we have in Auden the one holdover from his "liberal" period — the theory of the fatal contradictions of capitalism — "old men in love / With prices they can never get" —

> Children inherited by slums
> And idiots by enormous sums.

This constellation of distinct but associated ideas, in which each one is supposed to imply all the rest, proves a hardy and prolific weed, full-blown in *The Age of Anxiety*, where the intellectual wit and philosophical dialectic of "New Year Letter" have given place to music-hall burlesque. There are two extensive passages in which Auden's *Angst*-ridden characters are made his mouthpieces in a wholesale condemnation of the age in all its multifarious aspects. It is perhaps surprising that these last characters should themselves be able to give so detailed a diagnosis of the malady of the age. But let this pass for a dramatic convention. Let us assume that since they are in this mess, "they should know!" The constant feature of these pictures is that they are all confused medleys of disparate things supposedly on the same level of importance. In Malin's first ironic account of human evolution, after a round of drinks, Progress is represented by

> Tidy utopias of eternal spring,
> Vitamins, villas, visas for dogs
> And art for all.

And on the same level with utopias and visa'd dogs, and subject to the same sarcastic denigration, we have the marvels of nature secured to us by science through the lenses of telescope and microscope. Later Emble, Quant, Rosetta, and Malin vie with each other in their disparaging account of "this tawdry age." Its commercialism is represented by making people market-made commodities; its entertainments by juke-box jives, its conveniences by escalators, democracy by the loss of personality, as one after another loses his

> essential self and sinks into
> One press-applauded public untruth

and all march in step to the music of the juke-box. And above all there is the inevitable identification of science with mechanical playthings and appliances:

> vile civilities vouched for by
> Statisticians, this stupid world where
> Gadgets are gods . . .

Still later in the play Malin comes back to the attack upon our "facetious culture." Medical science is shown in intimate association with political economy, with

> the medicine men whose magic keeps this body
> Politic free from fevers,
> Cancer and constipation.

And this facetious culture is matched by the facetiousness with which the poet (or his mouthpiece) lists the items that make up its dubious attractions: "Publishing houses, pawnshops and pay-toilets." This is all very amusing, but it does not have the solemn wit of Alexander Pope when he characterizes mankind as "the glory, jest and riddle of the world."

It is in a very different tone — in a tone of wistful sadness — that Hayes meditates on our scientific progress and our utopian hopes in "The Doctor's Here Now" (*The Big Time*). His sympathy is altogether with the young doctor in a charity ward doing what can humanly be done for people who come "relying on a knife and a surgical guile," and pitting all his learning and devotion

> Against the great forms of death, gangrenous and obscene,
> Never quite certain *what paradise our knowledge is*
> *moving towards*,
> What inconceivable wounds, incredible epidemics
> lie in between.

And Hugh Chisholm, in his "Elegy for All" (*The Prodigal Never Returns*), is actually divided in feeling between the past, with its comfortable privacies, the "peacock vanity" of the privileged classes, and its

> window-view of life, with the mauve and green
> unquestionable hills beyond life,

and the present, with its mass pressure against individualism of character. For the present has

> inherited the terror of the heart
> *in spite of all our brilliant facts and figures,*

and

> *For all our progress* we have antagonized
> and twisted the patient crowd's affection to
> revenges, where the same is the good, is the millions.

But in Chisholm's "Notes on Progress" (*The Prodigal Never Returns*) we have a more biting satire on the prevailing ideals, and more of the items of condemnation that are featured by Auden. He is very sour on the "speeches and publications," the belching of the big boys. Our manner of living is determined by our machinery.

> Nuts and their bolts copulate
> At five thousand revolutions per,
> And out of their well-oiled fornications
> The laws for living pour.

"Trucks whip their drivers," chairmen of the boards are crucified on their dynamos. Commercialism and crookedness reign.

> It was all in the cards, the advances, the lunches,
>   the bids,
> The crooked contracts, the manufactured hate
> Dumped on the market.

We pride ourselves on our liberation from savagery, but we really move in rhythm

> With paleolithic drum and prophetic fife
> Whose music we refuse to fathom.

We deny that the same forces move us, and we turn our backs resolutely on the creations of mythology — centaurs and angels.

This may not be as brilliantly original a poem as Auden's *Age of Anxiety*, but it is an impressive performance. It does not have Auden's facetiousness, but it is not lacking in his wit. It is a serious, well-organized, and imaginative poetical arraignment of the sort of progress by which our commercialism and mechanical inventions brought us into the most destructive of all wars. And it gives us a clue to what it is that ranges our poets so commonly against the notion of progress and makes them so down on science. It is a culture that has deprived us of our primitive mythologies without having weakened the savagery of our passions.

Of all our poets, the most vociferous, abusive, and comprehensive in his denunciation of progress is E. E. Cummings. I say comprehensive, because the word *progress* by Cummings is made to include almost everything in our material, our social and political, and our "spiritual" life, especially in l'Amérique, which is included under the general head of our civilization and culture. If we begin at the material end, progress refers to the worship of gadgets, and gadgets seem to comprehend everything in the way of mechanical appliances that adds to convenience in living and extends the range of amusements for the mass of our population, or what Cummings calls "mostpeople." In the Introduction to his *New Poems* (1938), Cummings flatly states that his poems are definitely not for mostpeople, who have less in common with "ourselves" than "the square-rootofminus one. You and I are human beings; mostpeople are snobs." (A somewhat daring extension, or inversion, of the nineteenth-century, the Thackeray, use of the word *snobs*.) The trouble with mostpeople is that they are not alive, but simply interested in "the socalled standard of living." We read in *Poems 1923–1954*: "What do mostpeople mean by 'living'? They don't mean living. They mean the latest and closest plural approximation to singular prenatal passivity which science, in its finite but unbounded wisdom, has succeeded in selling their wives." "Singular prenatal passivity" is, of course, the condition of the human embryo or foetus before it has properly come to life, but is entirely secure, snug and unsocial, in the mother's womb. Cummings is fond of this image. In a poem of this volume he prays that his young reader may be spared from ever thinking,

> for that way knowledge lies, *the foetal grave*
> *called progress*, and negation's dead undoom.

And in an earlier volume, *No Thanks*, a sharply satirical poem
against progress is shortly followed by another beginning

> çi gît 1 Foetus(unborn to not die

> safely whose epoch fits him like a grave)
> with all his toys(money men motors "my"

The foetal state is one in which the organism is concerned exclusively with its comfort and security; in mature life comfort and
security are represented by our possessions, our toys (money men
motors "my"). The organism is still exclusively concerned with
these things, and so with itself, but what it does not have is heart
or soul (*One Times One*) —

> of all the blessings which to man
> *kind progress* doth impart
> one stands supreme i mean *the an*
> *imal without a heart.*

And this heartless and soulless animal lives in ideal comfort and
security in the modern "democratic" state. This is an "Ever-Ever
Land," the creation of social science, a place (*New Poems*)

> that's measured and safe and known
> where it's lucky to be unlucky
> and the hitler lies down with the cohn)

Unfortunately it is a place where the individual is entirely submerged in the hoi polloi, in a "peopleshaped toomany-ness far too"
(*Fifty Poems*), where "sameness chokes oneness, / truth is confused
with fact" (*No Thanks*), where (*No Thanks*)

> their heels for Freedom slaves will click;
> where Boobs are holy, poets mad,
> illustrious punks of Progress shriek;

In short, in his violent reaction against the monster Massemensch,
Cummings makes a clean sweep of all the old liberal ideas — not
merely of Utilitarianism (which is materialistic and soulless), but
of Humanity (which is tainted with Collectivism), Humanitarianism (which is mechanical), and even Benevolence (which has too
wide a social horizon to be individualistic). He is all for "love" and
the Individual. But since he notes himself (in *Fifty Poems*) that

274

>   there are possibly 2 ½ or impossibly 3
>   individuals every several fat
>   thousand years,

and it would be "dumb" to expect more, there remains no hope for improvement, and no gleam of satisfaction to be taken in the hu-man scene except in the person of an occasional "poet" who has escaped from the net of sameness and peopleshaped toomany-ness.

Into the philosophical roots and social flowering of this world-view we shall go a little deeper when it comes to the poet's revul-sion against science.

A rather raw but lively illustration of the same attitudes, and the last one I will note under this heading, is Peter Viereck's "Progress: a Dialogue" (*Strike through the Mask!* 1950). It is a ballad in three stanzas. In each stanza there is question and answer, contrasting the lost mythologies and romantic feelings of the past with the purely, and vulgarly, material gratifications of present-day culture. In the first stanza, Question: "What do you see in the holy dread of the moonlight?" (Diana the huntress?) Answer:

> *Clambakes, clambakes on cranberry bogs:*
> *Cans piled up to the moon.*

(Italics in original.) In the second stanza, it is unicorns of delicate loveliness in the question, hamburgers in the answer; in the third, drunkenness with the wine of the moon in the question, gumdrops in the answer. Here we have reduced to its simplest terms the feud between poetry, with its nostalgia for the old mythologies, and the materialism of an age of progress.

31. SCIENCE — AND NOVELTY

Why is it that for our twentieth-century poets science has taken the shape of an ogre? For eighteenth-century poets and many of their preachers it was a chief support for their conception of a divinely ordered world. And it remained that for poets like Words-worth and for many nineteenth-century religious philosophers who found in the purposive dispensations of nature another proof of the teleological view of the world of which they were independently assured by revelation. Newton's theory of gravitation had persuaded them that nature is not chaotic but well designed and subject to the same unitary law as the spiritual world. In the early Wordsworth there is scarcely a trace of the characteristically Christian dualism. It is true that there is physical motion and spiritual motivation, but these are two parallel manifestations of the same power, which is operative in inanimate nature and in the mind of man. Thus he can speak, in "Tintern Abbey," of

> *A motion and a spirit*, that impels
> All thinking things, all objects of all thought,
> And rolls through all things.

And in the "Ode to Duty," identifying this spiritual law, or obligation, with the law of gravity, he apostrophises Duty:

> Thou dost preserve the stars from wrong;
> And the most ancient heavens, through Thee, are
> fresh and strong.

This monism was current among theological liberals in his day, and it was not by any means a strictly materialistic philosophy, for it did not *reduce* the operations of the "spirit" to those of matter. It rather identified the two. The Unitarian preacher who was the discoverer of oxygen considered that "spirit" and matter were inseparable, and anticipated the modern reduction of physical matter to physical energy. Priestley represented a very subtle and refined form of Deism, which was the foster-mother of natural theology. Natural theology was extremely popular in the early nineteenth century among both theologians and professional scientists, and a very influential foundation encouraged the publication of scientific treatises in which the active power of God was demonstrated by examples of purposefulness both in the inanimate and in the animate world, where many biological structures were interpreted as being divinely planned to perform their specific functions.

But the deistic monism that underlies this philosophy could not withstand the inveterate dualism of orthodox Christianity, especially as the scientists were not satisfied with the teleological interpretation of natural phenomena. Darwinian evolutionism started with variations (or mutations) which were not regarded as having a purpose, but rather as favoring the survival of the individual, in whom they occurred by chance or as the effect of natural causes not yet determined. By the end of the nineteenth century, there was a general disposition to consider that the primary assumptions of science were not to be reconciled with the primary assumptions of theology.

But again, in the present century, there was a marked tendency among the more philosophical theorists of science to abandon the notion of a strict demonstrable and coercive chain of causality. The philosophers of science had read their Hume, and the skepticism of that eighteenth-century agnostic promised to give great comfort to the type of thinking that has so long prevailed among our poets. This does not, however, mean that the scientist gave up the idea of an orderly relation between antecedent and consequent in the natural world. The practical test of scientific validity is prediction, and prediction is possible only on the assumption that a certain specific set of phenomena is regular, followed by a new specific constellation that corresponds with it point by point. And all scientific experiment and prediction is predicated on the general presumption that if the antecedent set of phenomena can be strictly limited and defined one may expect that the set which corresponds to it point by point will follow.

For the most part our poets would not object to this way of thinking where the inanimate or the lower animate world is involved. They are not inclined to question the soundness of scientific predictions in the realms of meteorology, of chemistry, or of agriculture. It is mainly where an effort is made to extend scientific method into the study of human nature that they cry out against it. And then they begin to note, as the subtlest philosophers of science have noted before them, that, while in its proper realm, in the practical manipulation of natural forces, and within the range of our present knowledge, science does work amazingly well and predictions have a very high percentage of justification, and while the point-by-point correspondence between antecedent and consequent does hold in principle, science has not been able to explain *why*, in any given instance, this particular antecedent should be followed by this particular consequent — why, for example, the coming together of hydrogen and oxygen in specified proportions under certain specified conditions should result in the appearance of water, with its peculiar characters and type of behavior. All they can say — and that satisfies their needs — is that the specific characters of chemistry of oxygen and hydrogen are such that, under the right conditions, they form a composition known as water. And there are certain crucial points in the natural process at which "novelties" more mysterious than the appearance of water come under our notice. There is the appearance of organic life where there had been only inanimate matter; the appearance of consciousness where there had been only irritability; and there is the appearance of mental faculties more specific and extraordinary than mere undifferentiated consciousness. And I suppose that in some sense any mutation occurring in any vegetable or animal species is a "novelty." In regard to the "why" of the relation between any twó events, and in regard to the great crucial novelties of life, irritability, sensitiveness, and consciousness, science is nowadays more modest, or less ambitious and dogmatic, than theology. It is less fond of underlining the mysteries of nature and at the same time less confident in defining the occult causes. And contemporary poets greatly prefer the mysteries of "metaphysics" and the confident solutions of theology.

Well, the poets have rightly been impressed with the former dogmatism and naiveté of scientists. In the nineteenth century there were plenty of scientists who did not even recognize that there was an *unanswered why*, a something unaccounted for in their chain of causal relations. And our poets are no better satisfied with the attitude of the empirical positivists of the present moment. They are not content, with Meredith, to call these questions of *why*, "questions that sew not nor spin." They argue on logical grounds that these questions are factitious, or meaningless in effect, since there is in the nature of things no possible way of finding evidence that would lead to an answer.

This, our poets think, is the basic error of science. It cannot explain the "novelties" that constantly appear in nature. As Auden has it in *The Age of Anxiety*,

> The laws of science have
> Never explained why novelty always
> Arrives to enrich.

And he adds that the questions put by science are such as arrive nowhere.

> (though the wrong question
> Initiates nothing.) Nature rewards
> Perilous leaps.

Here, in portmanteau fashion, Auden runs together two separate meanings of the phrase *perilous leaps*, or what philosophers call *saltus*. The context suggests that he is thinking of the discontinuities in the natural process by which nature arrives at its novelties, or what he calls, in "New Year Letter," "discontinuous events." It does so by leaps across or beyond the unexplained gaps in the "causal chain." But before he has done, he has introduced a distinct and separate meaning of the metaphor, the leaps beyond the known which the scientist or philosopher must make to arrive at the truth. He is thinking, perhaps, of Newman's "illative sense," in *The Grammar of Assent*, which in any reasoning process carries us beyond the line to which strict logic has brought us, and by following the converging lines in our thought out in the speculative area to the point at which they presumably intersect.

This process is indeed present in all scientific construction of hypotheses, and is the "perilous leap" taken by the scientist in passing from the ascertained data to the speculative theory to account for them in terms of natural "law." Nature does reward such perilous leaps when the right questions are put. But Auden reminds us that "the wrong question initiates nothing." And it is clear that by "the wrong question" he means any question that ignores the metaphysical problem of the *why*, and confines itself to some theory of the *how* suggested by the empirical data already possessed, and subject to confirmation by empirical data that may be obtained by further research. For the peculiarity of the scientific *saltus* is that it is always tentative and hypothetical and subject to confirmation

or rejection as data obtained by further research and experiment
tend to confirm or invalidate it. Whereas the metaphysical *saltus* is
made once for all in terms of logical inference from assumptions
made, and is not subject to confirmation in terms of empirical data,
since it refers to what a scientist might call "occult" entities lying
behind or above all empirically ascertainable facts. For Auden the
right question has reference to these "metaphysical" or "spiritual"
entities and the corresponding truths.

But Auden does not confine himself to the defense of metaphysical entities or truth, but carries his attack boldly into the enemy
country. He has informed himself in regard to some of the scientific
doubts and puzzles that have come into so much prominence in the
wake of relativity, the quantum theory, and discoveries of physics
in the behavior of atoms and their submicroscopic constituents. He
is aware that a different geometry than the Euclidean is required
for determining the behavior of light at great distances; and that
when an atom is bombarded and electrons are dislodged and take
their place in some one of several wider orbits, it is not possible to
determine (at least for the present) in which of the wider orbits the
individual electron will take its place. He knows that even Einstein
has not succeeded in reconciling two rival and equally necessary
schemes of physical behavior. And so the laboratory scientists are
doomed to defeat in their overambitious undertakings and with
their naive reliance on natural "laws." They are like Kafka in his
efforts to chart the economy of heaven. As Auden wrote in "New
Year Letter":

> In labs the puzzled KAFKAS meet
> The inexplicable defeat:
> The *odd behavior of the law.*

It is, of course, the scientists themselves and their sympathetic
philosophical exponents, trained in scientific method, who have in
our time shown the most undogmatic and open-minded spirit. It is
they who have given up the uncritical interpretations of the concepts of "law," "determinism," and other offensive articles of
nineteenth-century thinking. It is they who, by their admirable
candor, have undermined the authority of the old Church of Sci-

ence, and have exposed to the vulgar public, ill-equipped to understand the real issues, the theoretical difficulties encountered in the passage from Newtonian to Einsteinian physics. And the least philosophically critical of them have given great comfort to the lovers of mystery by their hasty assumption that there is a basic *indeterminism* in nature itself. One would expect our poets to be grateful to modern science for giving them, with its broader interpretation of natural law, so much more room to move around in. But instead they seem to think that critical modern science has simply given them ammunition to use against an earlier and essential science, which, being simpler, is easier for them to understand, and will better serve as an enemy to be fought.

The Eddingtonian doctrine of indeterminism is, as Auden knows, grounded in the assumption that the predictions of science can only be made in large groups of facts subject to statistical study. It is impossible to predict in what orbit any individual electron will land, but it can be predicted what proportion of a group of electrons will land in any specified orbit. And this same principle is apparent in the behavior of social groups. It is no doubt the sociologist's extension of this statistical method to human behavior that so arouses the poet's scorn for science as a whole. Thus Auden, in "New Year Letter":

> Our million individual deeds,
> Omissions, vanities, and creeds,
> *Put through the statistician's hoop*
> *The gross behavior of a group.*

No one objects to the statistical method of prediction when it is applied to material phenomena. Every object that can be seen and touched is a vast congeries of individual constituent microscopic elements. In the early Eddington days people used to say that our tables and floors must be flimsy and insubstantial because they are made up largely of empty space — the vast distances which, on a microscopic scale of measurement, separate atom from atom and electron from electron. But experience has shown us that tables and floors can be relied on to support our weight provided that the legs of tables have not been broken or come unglued or the wood of the floors become rotten or their underpinning given way. And so with animal organisms. Dogs have their individual peculiarities; but properly trained we find that police dogs can to a very large degree be depended on to guide the blind through the streets and fields without mishap. We cannot know whether our individual organism has that stoutness of resistance to disease that will enable it to live beyond forty or sixty. We cannot predict at what age we shall cease to live. But life insurance companies would all go out of business tomorrow if actuarial statisticians could not shrewdly calculate what number of us will die at twenty, at sixty, or at a hundred.

But behind all these minor grudges against physics or sociology there lurks the frightful phantom of psychology to provoke this storm of rage and scorn in the breasts of the poets. For psychology is trying in our day to bring the personal behavior of men within the range of study as natural phenomena, and the poets are in a panic for fear the operation of their "souls" may turn out to be subject to the coercion of natural "law." They are afraid it may be found that their "will" is not "free" to make choices according to its whim. And it is true that many psychologists are highly uncritical in their philosophical notions and, in their "scientific" way, simplify the problems raised as much as the poets do in their "mythical" way. It is here not so much science that is the culprit as a half-baked scientism. And what the scorners of science oppose to this is a sort of half-baked "spiritism" grounded in a philosophic dualism whose final motivation is to take man and his behavior out of the world.

One traditional way of taking man out of the world is the hocus-pocus of time and eternity, in which Eliot performed his feats of wizardry in his *Four Quartets*. Thus Auden (again in "New Year Letter") assures us that

> The intellect
> That parts the Cause from the Effect
> And thinks in terms of Space and Time
> Commits a legalistic crime . . .

and that

> Our best protection is that we
> In fact live in eternity.

Well, the word *eternity* has many meanings. With Plato, living in
eternity meant living in the Ideas, which by definition are the inherent generalized meanings and so are not subject to space and
time. But living in the Ideas means exhibiting the ideas in our living,
and since our living is done in space and time and in our relation
to persons and objects existing in space and time, the notion of
eternity is not incompatible with the existence of space and time
or whatever it is that we apprehend under these forms of thought.

32. SCIENCE — AND FREEDOM

One suspects that much of the fuss made over "determinism" and
"free will" derives from the ambiguity and confusion attaching to
the supposedly opposed terms *determined* and *free*. Everybody
agrees that, living in the world, and physically constituted as we
are, there are many things that we are unable to do. We can't do
the impossible. And there are many things that we have to do, as
living organisms, and are constantly doing unconsciously, such as
breathing or responding to the movements of our vegetative nervous system. Short of suicide, we are obliged to go to prison if the
police insist. It is only in our choices that we are free. We are not
obliged by any external compulsion to kill or steal or commit adultery. And even science has given up the notion that, even in the
physical world, things are simply forced to certain actions entirely
through external compulsion. Things act according to their own
nature, and in fulfillment of their own nature, in reaction to the
external conditions in which they find themselves. If we extend this
conception to animal and human nature, determination means again
acting according to one's nature in a certain set of conditions. If
we hold a certain ideal of good with sufficient intensity, then we
are determined to act in conformity to this ideal. All education depends on the assumption that people can be so conditioned that it
is their nature to act in conformity to certain ideals of what is best.

But we are composite in our nature, and there are within us

283

many competing ideas of what is to be preferred. In the conflict that arises when certain aims are incompatible, the final decision will depend on which ideas are in the ascendent, and this is as much as to say that we act in accordance with what elements in our nature are dominant. Even our effort to stop and take time in order to concentrate upon the problem so as to come to the right decision, to make a considered choice, derives from our character as it is, and our character as it depends on many diverse factors — of heredity, of training, and of habits of thinking already formed through previous actions taken. We are free from external compulsion, we are "morally" free, to make our choice, as we are free to choose what type of house we wish to build, within the limits of our taste and our pecuniary means (or even in defiance of our means and our taste if other considerations are in the ascendent). But in thinking of such choices, many people seem to consider that we are not free unless we are totally unaffected by all such considerations, that we are free to act independently of all such motivating reasons or considerations. To be free in this sense would mean to be acting in a void, and the word would have no comprehensible meaning.

But this fictitious and incomprehensible freedom, which in the moral realm would mean complete amorality, is what many people think they must have, and they are prone to blame science for ruling this out. At any rate our poets are perpetually on the alert against the threat that science constitutes toward the notion that people or things are free to act independently of their own nature. And this they find everywhere in the modern world, and see "in every bush a bear."

In World War II, what Berryman sees (in *The Dispossessed*) is

> Misled blood-red *statistical men.*
> Images of a *conduct in a crucible.*

I do not mean to suggest that Berryman is not protesting here against actual abuses in current thought that do lead to disastrous consequences; but the passage will serve to illustrate the many ways in which, with our poets, "science" is made the villain in the piece. The great sins of science in our day are making men the subject of laboratory research (conduct in a crucible), and treating the individual man, with his personal acts of will, as but an item in a statistical mass: the sins of science in psychology (behaviorism) and in sociology. The result of the two sins compounded in the political field is making men dispensable in mass warfare, where their eyes are "nameless" and "The will is mounted and gregarious and bronze" ("Boston Common," *The Dispossessed*). These sins of psychological and sociological science are represented again in "New Year's Eve" (also *The Dispossessed*), in which we have Miss Weirs whispering her international fears, spiced with psychoanalysis and Kinsey.

Brinnin in "A Devotion for John Milton" (*No Arch, No Triumph*), feeling that there is no advantage in referring, as Milton might, to a religious sanction for morality, notes:

> Our *laboratories sabotage free will*
> And we are leased certificates to lust
> With no taskmaster now to bear us ill.

Chisholm notes that the statisticians have not saved us from our fears. We have not overcome our inherited terror of the heart "in spite of all *our brilliant facts and figures*" ("Elegy for All," *The Prodigal Never Returns*). He finds that we have given up our poetic mysteries for the not more satisfactory explanations and consolations of science. In "You, Horse"

> lust is dusty
> With intellectual complications, death with
> *scientific theories*

Jean Garrigue makes the same complaint of the loss of poetic mysteries, or myths, which seem to be identical with the "absolutes" of philosophy and the promises of religion. In her "Broken-Nosed Gods IV" (*The Ego and the Centaur*) she is mourning

> Extinction of the hope we can't endure
> Where Absolutes outside of time, compute
> With their pure fixities, our desperate shifts

And in the third poem of this series, she finds that, when spring comes with its brutal green, she is "like the dead that nourish not one dream," and "mythless as a scientist or beast."

Many of our poets, like Chisholm, are hung up between the comforting "mythical" order of which they have been deprived by the scientists and statisticians and the new order offered by science which leaves them no room for voluntary choices. Such is Nemerov, who is left as gloomy by contemplating our insoluble metaphysical dilemma as by the wars and disorders and moral decadence of the times. He has evidently been reading Rexroth's *In What Hour* (1940), and has taken the title for a philosophical meditation in verse from Part III of that volume, entitled "The Place of Value in a World of Facts." Rexroth's title is taken from Wolfgang Köhler; and his poems here are characteristic efforts to define the elusive freedom of the will — in this case in terms suggested by what he sees in the country landscapes round about him — terms taken liberally from both science and metaphysics. Rexroth is cheerful enough on this theme; for he greatly enjoys this intellectual game, confident that he has the clue to the world's millennial puzzle. Nemerov takes up the intellectual game with zest, and makes interesting use of a style in verse suggestive of Rexroth's; but he is not cheerful. For, as in another poem, he tells some protesting friend, he has a mind "cancered (as you say) by the worm I worship in the mystic rose" ("To a Friend Gone to Fight for the Kuomintang," *The Image and the Law*); and he does not think that he has the clue to the puzzle. In "The Place of Value" (also *The Image and the Law*) he writes:

> The "place of value in
> A world of fact" is to supply
> Cohesiveness, weight, stability,
> And to give reason and point
> To the particular screams
> Which otherwise merely would
> Echo between empty buildings
> Or make bubbles in the water.

Lower animal organisms live on a level of physiological reactions that do not require conscious attention. But

> The rest of us,
> Amazed mice, face the neurosis
> Of the continual choice on which

All depends; or play the hopeless
Shell game against the cheerful
Healthy statistician, who knows
"Pretty well" the final result.

For these poets science is the gloomy fellow who has taken away
our comforting myths and absolutes. For the Catholic poet James
Agee, the scientist has, the other way around, deluded us with his
own myths — his "strict allegories." In his dithyrambic prose dedication to his volume *Permit Me Voyage*, he dedicates his poems,
among others, to "those who have been *deluded of their dignity as
men and of their good knowledge* into the practise and advancement of transient matters: to those whom love, or despair, or mild-
ness, or magnanimity, or greed; or cloudiness of mind congenital
or premeditated; or *the strict allegories of science, have thus deluded.*" The strict allegories of science are evidently scientific theories that contradict our "good knowledge." Our good knowledge
is represented by the truth-seekers of all time; they include Mark
Twain, Walt Whitman, Ring Lardner, Hart Crane, Lincoln, as
well as Joyce, Chaplin, Picasso, Housman, Roy Harris, Einstein,
and Scott Fitzgerald. These are presumably truth-seekers because
they are creative, constructive, positive spirits. Whereas science,
with its reduction of everything human to material terms, is simply
a maker of delusive allegories, or "laws."

Satirical poets have, of course, many points that can be made
against scientific researchers. Their interest in their own research
involves, naturally, some concern for their own personal success
and prestige, and may lead them to a certain indifference to their
laboratory subjects. And where these are living organisms this is
particularly open to attack on the part of tender-minded onlookers. Weldon Kees takes advantage of every opportunity to hit off
the unattractive side of research scientists in a smart little ballad
called "Report of the Meeting" (*The Fall of the Magicians*). Here
the scientists perform their operative experiments on an antiseptic
stage. Their operations are always successful, however disappoint-
ing their results humanly speaking. The scientists are satisfied, but
the people mumble, "Fake."

Joseph Warren Beach

> The scientists
> Returned, annoyed and puzzled, to their homes,
>
> Where they wrote monographs on every phase
> Of the affair, constructed graphs and charts and plans,
> Cut up the lion, placed its parts in pans,
> And did not venture on the streets for days.

To do the poet justice, his satire strikes both ways, against the self-satisfaction of the scientists, their professional pretentiousness, and their way of regarding living creatures indifferently as subjects for experiment, and against the ignorant people who regard it all as "fake" (that is, assuming that the poet does not entirely share their point of view). Perhaps we need not take too seriously what is perhaps just a piece of fun-making. Scientists are human; they have their weaknesses and their funny side. But one cannot help wondering how the poets would look if the scientists had their literary gifts and could reply in kind. Considering an invidious painting of a lion, Chaucer notes that it is not done by a lion, and asks shrewdly "Who painted the lion?"

Horace Gregory is another of our poets who has recently come to the defense of poetry against the supposed encroachments of science. It is in a labored piece of irony entitled "Opera, Opera!" (*Selected Poems*). The poem is put in the mouth of "an Investigator," who is somewhat worried over the extraordinary things disclosed by opera glasses as the lenses are brought to a new state of refinement — such things as Parsifal in unattractive costume stirring headache powders in a cup, Eurydice kissing the reflection of her lips in a mirror, and other invidious figures of mythical heroes. As a result of the investigation carried out it was decided that these lenses looked both too near and too far.

> If the glasses were a 'work of art,'
> They should be destroyed, but if 'scientific' . . .

well, if scientific, they should be brought to the utmost perfection. They might be devoted to expert uses

> Among ourselves, among friends and enemies
> In restless peace and all-pervading war.

This somewhat muddle-headed Investigator is supposed to represent the mentality of the scientists; and this poet seems to have fallen for the widespread notion that it is science that is to blame for the deadly destructiveness of modern war. He overlooks the fact that the loudest voices raised against the use, or even the development, of nuclear weapons were those of our most distinguished scientists. It is the voice of the politician that promotes our wars; and it is only very recently that poets have taken to questioning the wisdom of the politicians. It was not in the days of Homer that poets were down on war; nor in those of Dante and Chaucer, or of Shakespeare, or of Tennyson. Tennyson may have dreamed of a day "when the war drums throb no longer." But it was a kind of mouthpiece of his in "Maud" who welcomed the Crimean War in which even the money-grubbing merchant struck, "with his cheating yard-wand, home." Even in the days of Rupert Brooke the poets were not unanimous in their deprecation of war. And it is precisely in our day that science and poetry have taken the same side on this moral question. Wars are the product of ideologies, and ideologies have not always been the exclusive products of politicians. Even Auden and Isherwood, in *The Dog beneath the Skin*, have identified as the original "assassins" "Invalid poets with a fountain pen" and "undersized professors in a classroom."

33. SCIENCE—AND THE POET

Among our contemporary poets, perhaps the most radical and the most *simpliste* in his revulsion against science is Cummings. We have seen earlier that he is down on science because he blames it for men's slavery to the domestic conveniences which it has made possible. But his objection to science is much more far-reaching than this. For these mechanical appliances are but one example of the material possessions which are the chief enemy to the soul's life. *Having* in his elastic vocabulary is the direct antithesis to *living* and *growing*, which are of the essence of the soul's being. And the *knowing*, which is the essence of science, is itself another unspiritual form of *having*, and is death to the self. In *Fifty Poems* we read:

> *all knowing's having* and have is(you guess)
> perhaps the very unkindest way to kill
> each of those creatures called one's self

In spite of his special vocabulary, Cummings has obviously read some philosophy. He seems to have in mind the German distinction between being and becoming (*Sein* and *Werden*), and he is all on the side of becoming, though he has reversed the ordinary uses of the two words. For with him becoming (*Werden* instead of *Sein*) is the realm of eternity, infinity, etc., where the soul is at home. He is penetrated with the philosophical distinction between time and eternity. He realizes that eternity is the homeland of the higher metaphysics, whereas time and place are the stamping ground of science and what used to be called common sense. His victims of the scientific attitude are *wherelings* and *whenlings*, they are slaves to other qualifying aspects of the factual world as charted by science.

> *wherelings whenlings*
> (daughters of *ifbut* offspring of *hopefear*
> sons of *unless* and children of *almost*)

Above all, they are slaves to *why* and *because*, which are of the essence of scientific explanation, and directly antithetic to the interests and action of the soul.

> *why coloured worlds* of because do
> not stand against *yes* which is built by
> *forever* & *sunsmell*

"Whycoloured worlds" suggest the confining causal chain. They are negative and deathly, whereas the soul lives in eternity (forever) and in the direct intuitions of the senses (e.g., sunsmell). Scientific explanations (why) explain nothing that is important; for

> only Nobody knows
> where truth grows why
> birds fly and
> especially who the moon is.

Cumming's distrust for science has its social, political, its theological, and its ethical implications and corollaries. Science is lethal in the social realm because it endeavors rationally to construct the social fabric in which freedom is promoted, and to replace God's fiat by man's reason. In *One Times One* (1944)

> that strictly (and how) scienti
> fic land of supernod
> where freedom is compulsory
> and only man is god

His theology has its limits, and his ethics might well be judged antinomian by an orthodox critic. For theology has its laws as strict as science, and Thomistic theology includes natural law as well as divine. They both have their *oughts* and *musts*. Cummings begins with rebellion against scientific limitations and goes on to ethical anarchism (*No Thanks*):

> let *must* or *if* be damned with whomever's afraid
> *down with ought* with *because* with every brain
> which thinks it thinks, nor dares to feel

It is but one step from scientific to ethical "freedom." "Never the murdered finalities of wherewhen and yesno, impotent non-games of *wrongright* and *rightwrong*."

The "scientific attitude" is peculiarly repulsive and "godless" to Cummings when it comes to speculations and explanations on the subject of love, as in the psychoanalytic system of "frood / whom [someone] pronounces young"; "hear / ye! the godless are the dull and the dull are damned" (*Fifty Poems*).

Thus even considerations of right and wrong come under this poet's ban against science; for they involve thinking and knowing and having, "greedy anguishes and cringing ecstasies of inexistence" (*New Poems*). All knowing is dull and deathly. It is only in "feeling" that we are "living." And where shall we find "feeling"? In the poet and the lover. It is only in love that we are "growing" and "becoming."

Love is a word that subtends a wide arch of human experience; and a poet of rich enough experience and imagination might manage to make it comprehend almost everything in our life of feeling and sensation and fellow-feeling. It might be made to include caritas and benevolence; and with some help from the structures of the mind, it might be made the keystone of a philosophical system. But one must confess that, in Cummings, when all is said, the word *love* has a certain thinness about it, except as it applies to the "love-making" of man and woman, and is colored up by associations with, well, moonlight and roses. It never comes near carrying the weight of eighteenth-century benevolence or of Gospel caritas. The "mostpeople" whom he relegates to "inexistence" with so cavalier a raising of the eyebrow, so confident a shrugging of the shoulders — these are, for Utilitarians, "brothers," and for Christ they are "children of God." For the humble Negro singer "all God's chillen got wings." But this poet does not seem to have the least sympathy for the mostpeople in their passionate attachments to one another in a great variety of relationships, their responsibilities, their despairs, their sufferings, their courage, their games, their sonfulness (both secular and religious), their worship, and their aspirations after the "good life." The bookkeeper that denies himself every luxury to send his boys to college, to pay for the house and keep up his life insurance, is readily dismissed as sunk in materialism. The brilliant surgeon who impoverishes himself inventing appliances for the treatment of heart disease and disease of the prostate, and who gives them free to the world, lies under the double imputation of scientist and humanitarian. The housewife who, in living within the family income, does her own washing — dishes and bedding and clothes — and makes her own dresses, and to this end makes use of washing machines and a sewing machine, is guilty of a soulless passion for gadgets.

There are, of course, as there always have been, vain, shallow, and greedy people, people who have never grown up, and those sunk in anxious concern for the mere comforts of life; and these are fair targets for satire. But the mass of men do not call for the pharisaical smugness that breathes forth from so much of this poet's writing. I am not of course referring to him personally, a man of whom I have heard nothing but good. It is when he dons the robes of poet and gospeler that he gives such an impression of emotional immaturity. He has apparently no real acquaintance with those who do the work of the world — who provide our eggs and potatoes and bring our milk to the door, who build our houses and make our cars run so that we can get to the country, who make our trains run and dispose of our sewage, let alone those who make it safe to live in our cities. It is as if he had never seen more of life than what can be seen from a table in the Café du Dome. His is not the genuine voice of Saint Francis, or even of Wordsworth, or Hardy, or Sandburg — all like him exponents of plain living and high thinking.

Well, no. High thinking! The most curious thing about him is his constant denigration of the whole world of thought and knowledge — which certainly is what we mainly mean by civilization. If we took him at his word, we should have to give up not merely Marconi and Edison, but also Newton and Einstein; not merely Newton and Einstein, but Spinoza and Aristotle; not merely Spinoza and Aristotle, but also Pascal and Descartes and Socrates. Anybody with the rudiments of philosophy knows what Cummings is driving at when he says that

> only Nobody knows
> where truth grows why
> birds fly and especially who the moon is

It is the old metaphysical hocus-pocus of the *how* and the *why*. Science gives us the how, but only Nobody knows the why. Well, we do know how birds fly, and with that knowledge we have taken ourselves to flying. As for "who the moon is," who since J. M. Barrie or Robert Louis Stevenson would raise that question? Whoever wants to know *who* the moon is speaks with the voice of a child or a savage. And that was never quite the voice of our great poets. It is not the voice of Homer or Dante or Shakespeare or of Eliot or Frost or whomever you rank as great in our own time.

34. THE DOCTOR

One of the most striking paradoxes of our time is the contradiction between the popular view of the doctor and that presented by our poets of the thirties and forties. Since the appearance of *Arrowsmith* our greatest popular hero has been the doctor as presented in fiction, in plays and moving pictures, in the newspapers, and (with some exceptions) in prose fiction. And this high regard for the medical profession is reflected practically in the great sums donated for hospitals, clinics, and for research in the cause and cure of tuberculosis, polio, heart disease, and cancer. The doctor is regarded with the highest admiration for his devoted labors in the advancement of medical science; for his self-denying labor in the care of the sick, the alleviation of human suffering, and the prolongation of human life. And even where doctors come in for severe criticism, it is simply because they are, in many cases, mercenary and self-seeking in their practice of a profession that calls for supreme dedication to altruistic ideals.

But our poets are for the most part incorruptible. In an age of low standards of value, they are perpetually on their guard against any taint of materialism (in both the metaphysical and the ethical sense of the word). For them *vox populi* is very far from being *vox Dei*, and they are resolutely determined not to yield an inch to popular clamor. The worship of doctors and medical science is, for them, part and parcel of that sentimental humanitarianism that threatens to take the place of sound doctrine in spiritual matters. And it means for them the worship of materialism in the strict metaphysical sense of the word.

Auden and Isherwood are here, as so often, in the forefront of the movement, in this case the movement to deflate the pretensions of medical science. And this is not even in the service of supernatural religion. For *The Dog beneath the Skin* was presumably written before Auden had undergone his conversion from a secular to a religious philosophy. His opposition to the reigning economic order was in the name of an ethical idealism but not of supernatural religion. In their burlesque fable, Auden and Isherwood devote eight rollicking pages to an operation by a famous surgeon in a hospital. The occasion is pictured in a kind of parody of a church service. The musical voluntary is played upon a harmonium, while the students, nurses, anaesthetist, and surgeon come into the theater in solemn processional. The surgeon takes up his position by the operating table with his back to the audience, like the priest at the altar. They all in unison recite the creed. "I believe in *the physical causation of all phenomena* material or mental: and *in the germ theory of disease*. And in Hippocrates, the father of Medicine,

Galen, Ambrose Paré, Liston of the enormous hands, Syme, Lister who discovered the use of antiseptics, Hunter, and Sir Frederick Treves." These poets are evidently at the height of their faith in psychoanalysis, taking the side of Dr. Krokowski as against Dr. Behrens, and in the second article of their creed they proceed to make fun of the surgical treatment of diseases like duodenal ulcer and endocrine disturbance where, presumably, they would prefer a psychological approach. In the first article of the creed, the Hunter referred to was probably Sir William Hunter, the famous British surgeon. They do not perhaps remember that Hunter was on the side of the angels in the dispute between the British vitalists and the French mechanists and greatly admired on that account by no less angelic a philosopher than Coleridge. But for writers down on science for its materialism it was, I suppose, enough that he was a surgeon to make him a type of the materialist. Idealists and visionaries are so often on the side of quacks in any showdown with the recognized experts.

The parody of church liturgy continues with a responsive chant of students in celebration of the supreme greatness of the surgeon.

> DEC. The surgeon is great: let his name appear in
> the birthday honours.
> CAN. I was in danger of death: And he delivered me.

The occasion is carried through on a hilarious note. The electric lights go out through a blunder of the medical students. Nurses bring flashlights, but the surgeon cuts "the mesenteric" and the nurses inject hydrochloric acid instead of adrenalin, and the patient dies. The surgeon scolds the nurses, and the scene ends with "general dismay, screams, laughter, pursuit."

It is all great fun. The figure of the surgeon as tyrant, high priest, and prima donna, with his band of admiring acolytes, is made as ridiculous as it deserves to be when it is found in life. But some of the greatest and soundest achievements of medical science are denigrated and rendered dubious by association and innuendo; there is an apparent preference for speculative and tentative over established and verifiable methods of treatment. The general attitude toward medical science is that of an ill-informed faddist — the sort of person who would go to a chiropractor for the treatment of kidney trouble, or, suffering from astigmatism, would prefer yogi to an oculist. The animus of it all is clearly the poet's revulsion from the supposed metaphysical credo of medical science, *the physical causation of all phenomena.* There is a real philosophical problem worthy of consideration; but the general irresponsibility of these poets here is shown in the nonsensical bracketing of this belief with that of the germ theory of disease.

Whatever of seriousness there may be in the Auden-Isherwood farrago is found, with no touch of jeering parody, obscurantism, or philosophical pretentiousness, in Warren's "Pursuit" (*Selected Poems*) where the patient is in consultation with his doctor, presumably, for some nervous and run-down state that might be helped by medical treatment. The point of this poem and of several others in the same series is that this man's ailment is spiritual and not physical, and the doctor he consults is wise enough to recognize this fact, and modest enough not to undertake to treat it.

> The doctor will take you now. He is burly and clean;
> Listening, like a lover or worshipper, bends at your heart;
> But cannot make out just what it tries to impart;
> So smiles; says you simply need a change of scene.

There is nothing discreditable to medical science here. This doctor does not pretend to be a priest; he finds nothing the matter with the man physically; and he has the professional decency not to propose methods of cure for a mere indefinable state of mind. It is left to the patient to reflect on the doctor's suggestion of a change of scene.

> Of scene, of solace: therefore Florida,
> Where Ponce de Leon clanked among the lilies,
> Where white sails skit on blue and cavort like fillies,
> And the shoulder gleams in the moonlit corridor.

The patient has some acquaintance with philosophy, some disposition to halfhearted rationalizing of his impulses. Maybe what he needs is the solace of a love affair.

> A change of love; if love is a groping Godward,
>   though blind,

> No matter what crevice, cranny, chink, bright in
> the dark, the pale tentacle find.

This is not a satirical poem, let alone a burlesque, but a highly imaginative picturing of a man suffering from a psychological, or "spiritual," ailment or malaise. It is, to be sure, permeated with a subtle irony. But it is not the doctor that is the object of this irony so much as the man who is helpless to deal with his trouble because he has not the resolution to take serious measures and get to the root of it. There is, to be sure, a touch of humor in the treatment of the doctor, burly and clean, and with an unexceptionable bedside manner, as "listening, like lover, or worshipper, [he] bends at your heart." The only way that he casts doubt on science is his inability to "make out just what it tries to impart." He does not pretend to spiritual insight; but, approaching the situation on a purely physical plane, recommending simply a change of scene, he might be suspected of materialism and so of the scientific fallacy.

The case is the same with Warren's humorous picture of himself confronting the surgeon in his "Ode to Fear."

> When the surgeon whets his scalpel
> And regards me like an apple,
> And the tumor or the wart
> Sings, "The best of friends must part,"
> *Timor mortis conturbat me.*

The serious symptom here is the patient's morbid fear of death.

Still, there are touches in both of these poems of those aspects of the doctoring business that everybody dislikes. We transfer to the doctor some of the fearsomeness and general odiousness that attaches to our being sick. The doctor is professionally affectionate and even worshipful toward the illness that is his subject of interest and his excuse for being. His apparent tenderness and consideration for the patient is a specious mask for his professional coldness and objectivity. And all medical science comes under the imputation of indifference toward the individual human being.

This bending at your heart, this way of regarding the patient with the zest of one about to cut up an apple, have their echoes or counterparts in later poetry. And every appliance and precaution of doctor or surgeon, every paraphernalia of hospital care, becomes simply odious by association with your suffering, discomfort, and fear, and with the sense of the general illness that has infected our spirits. In Kees ("The Doctor Will Return," *The Fall of the Magicians*):

> The surgical mask, the rubber teat
> Are singed, give off an evil smell.
> You seem to weep more now that heat
> Spreads everywhere we look.
> It says here none of us is well.

In Nemerov ("Fragment from Correspondence," *Guide to the Ruins*):

> I know these men, with their white coats, their smiles;
> Their rubber and moist fingers sometimes in dreams
> Press tentatively against my naked heart,
> Over their masks the eyes are pitiless. . . .

In "Fables of the Moscow Subway," a poem reminiscent of Dostoevski, Nemerov has a doctor who is philosophical enough to be acquainted with Svidigailov's spider-infested bath house and with Plato's *Timaeus*, and is capable of going about his duties among the dead. He is a combination of Krokowski and Behrens.

> But the doctor, with smoldering cigar,
> Waked, and went patiently among the dead;
> Inquired how their parents were, and when
> They last had wet the bed or dreamed of God.

I will not undertake to explicate the doctor's dream that follows, in which Martin Luther is made to defy the Pope, migrate to England, and found the Boy Scouts. But I will venture to say that it is not intended to put the doctor in a more sympathetic light.

Brinnin, for his part, in "A Salient of War" (*No Arch, No Triumph*), has a list of notable persons who have returned to remind us of "the fine equation" between life and death, including Plato "in his universal jail," "glum Napoleon, Emperor of Snow," the Marquis de Sade, and Saint Francis, "the Saint / With sparrows on his fingers." And then "Even the *physicians with mechanical third eyes.*" They have all come back, and "In such rich agony / Our skeletons and embryos embrace." Since they appear in such mixed company, it is hard to say whether or not the physicians are meant to be disparaged — whether they are classed with Plato and Saint Francis or with "glum Napoleon" and "the excellent corrupt Marquis." But the mechanical third eyes are very suspicious. If these mechanical third eyes refer to the microscope, enabling the doctor to bring to light corrupt tissues and micro-organisms, these are probably evidences of a materialist philosophy and "the germ theory of disease."

In Thomas Merton ("Ode to the Present Century," *A Man in the Divided Sea*) his reference to doctors is certainly such as to be disparaging. Taking advantage of the boy's game of "cops and robbers," he refers to "cops and doctors," and it is their materialist and rationalist philosophy that makes them both poisonous.

> They chart the reeling of your clockwise reason
> Flying in spirals to escape philosophy.

Mona Van Duyn, in her "Death by Aesthetics" (*Poetry*, January 1954) has the full quota of ironic associations with the doctor in his consultation room. He is "love the healer," and, as in Warren, "an abstracted lover." He has his instruments, his "machinery of definition."

> The doctor approaches
> and *bends to her heart*. But she sees him sprout
>   like a tree
> with metallic twigs on his fingers and blooms of chrome
> at his eye and ear for the sterile ceremony.

Miss Van Duyn develops her theme at some length with great ingenuity and real imaginative power. It does it something of a disservice to call it baldly a psychosomatic interpretation of disease. In all the tissues and functions of her body we are enabled to

> see self. Self in the secret stones I chafed
> to shape in my bladder. Out of a dream I fished
> the ache that feeds in my stomach's weedy slough;
> this tender swelling's the bud of my frosted wish.

The doctor is merely an incident to a structure of thought and feeling that is subtle, complicated, and impressive. The irony is all-inclusive. The doctor is a mere incident to her general theme. But it will serve to illustrate the inevitableness with which the doctor's role, in our time, has been that of an unsympathetic impersonation of materialist and inhuman science.

My last example is something of a different order. It is a poem that moves on a lower level of intellectual seriousness and imaginative power. Peter Viereck, in "A Hospital Named 'Hotel Universe'" (*Strike through the Mask!*), typifies the earthy or materialist-realistic life by a hospital where the Keeper's aim is to keep the patients forever in their sickbeds. Sometimes they elude him and take flight to the moon; but when they get there, they find their Keeper the Man in the Moon. He gives them shock treatment (snips off half of a frontal lobe), and back they go to earth and their cots. They have lost their freedom and become subject again to what determinists call "necessity."

> But freedom, freedom waits to resurrect
> Whole galaxies IF ONLY WE RECALL
> The moon we dreamed.

They make the effort to get free, to recover the lost insight. But —

> To interrupt us — lest we recollect —
> A nurse brings breakfast, chirping "Cherrio."

This poet betrays, in baldest form, the animus that leads so many poets to their sour view of the scientist and the doctor as a representative of science. What this poet holds against science is that it deprives us of "the moon we dreamed." But his poem is a labored allegory in which fancy rather than imagination holds sway. And he simply produces a *reductio ad absurdum* of what, in more thoughtful writers, is a philosophical position that holds a considerable measure of truth. We cannot suppose that the more serious of our poets are ready to acknowledge that their grudge against doctors and scientists is grounded in a reluctance to give up the man in the moon.

35. GADGETS

Theoretical and applied science are equally objectionable to our poets, for in the ambiguity of abstract words, all the meanings of materialism are rolled together. People who never heard of determinism and have never doubted that they were free to choose among alternative lines of action, come under condemnation because they are fond of the comforts and conveniences that scientific research has made possible; and both the scientist and the lover of convenience are guilty by association with the usurer, the sensualist, the exploiter of labor, and him who grinds the faces of the poor, with all who put material goods and satisfaction before the humane and spiritual values of religion, art, and morality. And since the United States is the nation that has the highest living standard and has profited most from the conveniences provided by mechanical invention, there is considerable disposition among our poets to look upon America as the special home and church of materialism in every sense. While every middle-class citizen in France is going in debt for a refrigerator, a bathroom, or an American car, the odium for these inventions falls on us.

It is true that mere worship of material goods is abhorrent to moralists of all stripes, and that Auden, when his ideals were those of the social revolution, was full of prophetic warnings against the luxury and the dependence on mechanical appliances which were undermining the morale of British society, as in that brilliant little satire (poem XII in *Look, Stranger!*) beginning

> As it is, plenty;
> As it's admitted
> The children happy
> And the car, the car
> That goes so far
> And the wife devoted . . .

It is in the name of the spiritual life that Auden deprecates this satisfaction in material success, with his ironical conclusion:

> Let him see in this
> The profits larger
> And the sins venal,
> Lest he see as it is
> The loss as major
> And final, final.

The form *venal* is presumably a misprint for *venial*, and his contrast

Joseph Warren Beach

between venial and mortal sins, between high profits and final loss, would suit just as well the sentiments of his later religious phase. In all periods he was impatient with the spirit of self-indulgence, but it was not till he had come to America and found religion that he really let himself go in a large way on the

> vile civilities vouched for by
> *Statisticians*, this stupid world where
> *Gadgets are gods*,

thus conjuring in a single breath the devils of statistical science and mechanical invention.

The ingredients of this formula are indeed considerably more numerous and seductive than I have yet suggested; and the psychological appeal is to a widespread and populous, if not popular, audience. When Auden characterizes ours as a tawdry age, he is likely to capture all readers of taste and culture, who have been exposed to the charms of country life or of Old World cities that retain some of the features of Renaissance or medieval architecture. We may find New York handsome and exciting, but when we come to the sprawling ugliness of our other cities from Buffalo and Detroit to Chicago, Kansas City, and Los Angeles, we are made vividly conscious of what a price uncontrolled industrialism has made us pay for our cars, our heating systems, and our water closets. And this is equally true of almost every industrial city in the Anglo-Saxon world. Our churches are drearier than our warehouses and railroad stations. Our houses are sordid cottages and bastard chateaux, soon converted to mortuaries and rest homes. We cannot bear to wake in the morning or close our eyes at night upon these sights of desolation. We buy a lot in the country, and in five years we find ourselves living in suburbia, and spending an hour and a half a day getting to our offices and markets and back.

Thoughtful persons may realize that we are living in an age of transition, in which our architecture is only beginning to learn how to adjust itself to new building materials and living conditions; and sanguine temperaments may be able to envisage the time, a century hence, when our rapidly improvised cities may be all made over to suit the requirements of population and transportation. But elderly persons — who cannot hope to see that day — outraged aesthetes, and those inclined to interpret all accidents of history in religious terms may conclude that we are being punished for our sins. When we find that the convenience of the automobile and the freedom it gives to get into the country is turned into a nuisance by the resulting congestion in town and the menace of the highway, we fall into Auden's view of "Man captured by his liberty," with

> useful facts
> Become the user of his acts,
> And Chance the choices of his soul.

And we are inclined, like the philosopher-kings in *Erewhon*, to forbid all machines in the commonwealth and relegate them to museums as a warning to all future ages not to become the slaves of their machines. It does not occur to us that the proper alternative to being their slaves is to make ourselves their masters. The besetting sin of our age is not its materialism but its lack of organization.

One aspect of our rage for gadgets is wittily hit off by Berryman when he speaks of "the chromium luxury of the age." All people who have a taste for simplicity and modesty in the appurtenances of living will share the poet's dislike for vulgarity in display. They will be reminded of Veblen's *Theory of the Leisure Class* and his searching analysis of the motivation of that "conspicuous waste" which exhibited the vanity of the newly rich. Berryman's phrase occurs in a poem of 1940 ("A Point of Age," in *Poems*) in which he represents his start upon the spiritual pilgrimage and his sojourn in a town (Detroit) where he discovered

> Strike and corruption: cars reared on * the bench
> To horn their justice at the citizen's head
> And hallow the citizen deaf, half-dead.†

In the midst of the holocaust of war, he is in need of spiritual support from an earlier day, and he calls upon a rebel great-grandfather

---

* "Sat on" in *Poems*, p. 18; "reared on" as reprinted in *Dispossessed*, p. 9.
† "And deafen the citizen alive or dead" in *Poems*.

to witness his simple need "among the chromium luxury of the age," and help him search the annals of the past for the moral truth that will enable him to endure. His phrase for the age suggests its essential vulgarity; but vulgarity is in itself, of course, one symptom of the spiritual sin of pride.

There is a further associational hookup between vulgarity and commercialism, with its taint of exploitation. Here we are reminded of the socialist's grudge against capitalism as such. In a poem of 1939, "The Dangerous Year," Berryman reminds himself of the road that leads from commercialism to war. And he warns that it is time to forget the Christmas Tree view of life, with summer friendships by the lake, "for you are come upon / The shifting of the scene." And along with the tinsel on the Christmas Tree, you must

> Forget the crass hope of a world restored
> To dignity and *unearned dividends.*

The war that is coming is the fruit of hatreds "loosed from the labyrinth of your desire."

This note recurs in Brinnin in his poem "In Season of Actual War" (*No Arch, No Triumph*) with a more distinct reflection of the collectivistic ideology. "In season of actual war," the poet says,

> it is good to declare
> Death of the false and individual,
> The visions of an old cosmology . . .

He speaks of the old aristocracy of wealth playing the role of stagey kings.

> Theirs were the mansions and wedding spectacles,
> And theirs the black corrals of industry
> And the operatic morals of a world
> Singing the epic of its privilege.

And they had their décor of luxury and conspicuous waste. But now

> Farewell the giantism of *baroque*
> *Upholsteries in sickened house and heart* . . .

Here indeed we recognize, with a start of recognition, that the up-

holsteries in the house are a direct reflection of upholsteries in the
heart, and that both of these are symptoms of that sickness known
as personal vanity. In this case the moral hookup is clear enough.
But the upholsteries are damask, and perhaps hand-woven. They
are not mechanical gadgets, and they have no direct association
with "science" and the assembly line.

Some of our poets, like those of us who have a sentimental at-
tachment to the past, have a divided heart as between the ages of
luxurious appointments for the privileged and our age of mechanical gadgets for all. Chisholm's yen for the old days is not wanting
in a critical irony ("Elegy for All," *The Prodigal Never Returns*):

> Seldom the old world galloped from the plush stalls
> and heirlooms of its fathers

The deeds of the nobles were "flights / Of peacock vanity" that
"soon petered out." Love in those days was

> feared in hovels for elementary reasons
> of food and loss of sleep, and in the castles
> sneaked up the back stairs and revoked at dawn.

But, on the whole, his irony is weighted against our mechanically
promoted pleasures — our rapid movement and long-distance communication —

> we, who scatter miles
> like fertilizer to enrich the view,
> who hear tenderness down a telephone . . .

In "You, Horse" (same volume), the balance has gone decidedly
against the artificiality of our present manner of life. We have rendered ourselves independent of the changes of season, "comfortable
in the bad lands" and "using winter / For complaint"; "invention
has been invented / To hack at the land with ingenious destruction," etc. And the associational hookup with philosophical materialism is managed by an ingenious passage from destructive mech-
anisms to "intellectual complications" and "scientific theories" that
invade love and death and deprive us even of "the original / And
final power for sorrow."

And then, coming to the final degradation of "science," we have the use made of it by commercial advertising. Here Auden (in *The Age of Anxiety*) is on the firmest ground, and has merely to take his words directly from the daily paper or the radio broadcast. It does not matter what the article is that is being advertised. It has "that democratic / Extra elegance." It "Lasts a lifetime. Leaves no odor." It is "American made." It is

> Patriotic to own. Is on its way
> In a patent package. Pays to investigate.
> *Serves through science.*

Thus, with diabolical ingenuity, and with fullest historical documentation, Auden brings together in one poisonous package every item of pious charlatanism practiced by the college-bred ad writer for palming off his product and realizing a tidy profit for his patron (even after the taxes and costs of advertising have been covered). It is a telling piece of satire; materialistic science has been given its *coup de grâce* by its association with commercial blackguardism; and all for the greater glory of God!

None of the poets mentioned in this section has gone the lengths of Cummings in his rage against gadgets. We have seen earlier how he relegates the mass of mankind to simple inexistence because of their worship of gadgets along with other forms of "having." For these other poets have not taken the naive line of altogether giving up knowledge and thinking as a most virulent form of "having," and with their hold on knowledge and thinking, they have not lost their hold on logic. It is Cummings who furnishes a *reductio ad absurdum* of attitudes which in the others retain a considerable semblance of reason. But surely I have said enough, and more than enough, of this modern defender of the poet and lover against the inroads of materialistic science.

◆§ *GUILT AND INNOCENCE*

36. THE SENSE OF GUILT

As we noted abundantly in the earlier sections 4 to 7, the most obsessive of all images in the poetry of the thirties and forties is the
image of fear in its many forms. If we were to judge by our poets,
this particular period is the one, among all recorded in literature,
in which men have been most hagridden with fear and anxiety.
And we have also seen how generally these states of mind have
been associated with a sense of guilt. The sense of guilt and the
longing for innocence are perhaps, along with fear and anxiety,
the dominant emotions of the period in which we live if we are
to take the word of the poets we are considering. This association
of fear and guilt is not confined to American poetry. It is explicitly
made, for example, by Day-Lewis in his "Ode to Fear," which may
be found in a volume (*Short Is the Time*) published in 1945, at the
very climax of this panic among our poets. He speaks here of the
many "symptoms" of fear — planes, rumors, "sleep's prophetic
phantoms," all

> Condemning what we have built,
> Heartburn anxiety for those we love —
> And all, yes all, are proof of *an endemic guilt*.

At almost the same time Auden was writing in *The Age of Anxiety*:

> Behold the infant, helpless in cradle, and
> *Righteous* still, yet already there is
> *Dread in his dreams* at the deed of which
> He knows nothing but knows he can do,
> The gulf before him with *guilt beyond* . . .

Or again, speaking of man's inability to explain what are the most important facts of his life,

> God nor good, *this guilt the insoluble*
> *Final fact*, infusing his private
> Nexus of needs, his noted aims with
> Incomprehensible, *comprehensive dread.*

The striking difference in tone between these passages from Day-Lewis and Auden reminds us that, in the treatment of guilt and innocence, there is a wide variation in the implied philosophy, as the emphasis is laid on religious, on ethical-social, or on what we may call "psychological" factors, on what we might call private offenses (or sins) and types of behavior which have a larger social bearing and effect. It is frequently hard to distinguish between these several approaches to the subject, which, in some cases, are found in close association. But they are at least theoretically distinguishable; the emphasis on one or another of the factors is often indicative of the philosophical tenor of the several poets; and the occasional passage from one to another in a given poet during the period of his writing has great light to throw on tendencies broadly operating in the general thought of the time.

This change of emphasis is peculiarly striking in the case of Auden, and particularly important considering the very great influence he has had on other poets. The sense of guilt and of lost innocence is perhaps the dominant feature of Auden's writing all through, and the state of mind indicated might be the guiding thread in any psychological interpretation of his poetry, any attempt to distinguish the psychological drive that motivated him in his career as a poet, and, so to speak, sparked his imagination. In all periods of his writing he has been concerned with the loss of innocence and with the phenomenon of a bad conscience. In the earliest phase, his interest is in what may be called a bad social conscience as well as a bad conscience in regard to private offenses against a code of morals. And these two types of bad conscience are closely associated in his concept of personal discipline and avoidance of self-indulgence as essential to the man dedicated to the cause of social revolution. He is a soldier in the great war; he must keep fit, and ever on the alert against the enemy; and it is often hard to know whether the enemy is the man in the opposed camp or weakening vices within oneself that make him a poor soldier. This would account for the cryptic references in the "Journal of an Airman" to offending hands and some terrible weakness which the airman is hiding from his friends, and which, "If the enemy ever got to hear of it," would nullify his whole work. In "Paysage Moralisé" it is the private business of love that is in question, and innocent country surroundings are set against the corruptions of the city.

> And all the green trees blossomed on the mountains,
> Where *love was innocent*, being far from cities.

In one of the poems of *Look, Stranger!* the "worm of guilt," of which the speaker was guilty, refers to this same private business of love. In a sonnet of 1938 ("Wandering lost upon the mountains of our choice," published in the *Listener* of November 3, 1938) it is harder to make out whether the "innocent mouth" is meant to suggest the innocence of love under more primitive and natural conditions:

> Wandering lost upon the mountains of our choice,
> Again and again we sigh for an ancient South,
> For the warm nude ages of instinctive poise,
> For the taste of joy in *the innocent mouth*.

Certainly, as the poem appears in the sonnet sequence "In Time of War" in *Collected Poetry* seven years later, it has taken on a much wider range of reference. There it must stand for the general spiritual disorientation brought about by the great wars, with the noble lies with which they were provoked by those in power, and the pitiful victimization of the soldiers. The social wrong and general ethical perversions incident to world commercialism play a large part in the poet's theme here. And there are even hints of a religious hookup almost certainly not present in the sonnet when it was first written and published.

Very early in Auden's poems, innocence and guilt begin to have the broader reference to the social conscience. Thus in number XVII of *Look, Stranger!* there is reference to the change from the old feeling of England as the right setting for happiness, to the England of luxury, privilege, and exploitation against which the man of social conscience must set himself. It was once "the perfect setting" for complacent meditations of lovers.

> But now it has *no innocence* at all;
> It is the isolation and the fear . . .

the isolation and the fear, one understands, which are so much in contrast to the collective security promised by a socialistic order. And still earlier, in Auden and Isherwood's *The Dog beneath the Skin* we have the "famous man of letters" confessing his guilty conscience in connection with the war for which he is (like other "assassins") to blame because of his false ideology. As he hears the guns firing across the channel and thinks of young men being blown to pieces, "Every time I hear that, I say to myself: You fired that shell . . . Yes, I and those like me. Invalid poets with a fountain pen." In Auden and Isherwood's pacifist play, *On the Frontier*, the social character of guilt and innocence is in the ascendant. As the causes of war are national hatreds and the capitalistic commercial interests that bring them into action, the guilt is shared by everyone in all societies and cannot be avoided by the most conscientious and high-minded. Eric, the hero, who is opposed to war, and goes to prison, seeing himself "as the sane and *innocent* student / Aloof among practical and violent madmen," comes to realize that he was wrong.

> We cannot choose our world,
> Our time, our class. *None are innocent*, none.
> Causes of violence lie so deep in all our lives
> It touches every act . . .

In "New Year Letter" this notion of universal guilt associated with the social and political crimes of the period is elaborated in the fanciful terms of a detective story. The poet refers to the political atrocities in Asia, in Abyssinia, Spain, Austria, Poland, and Germany ("The Jew wrecked in the German cell"). A baffling crime has been committed which involves the whole world, and efforts are being made by police inspectors to discover the criminal.

> Yet our equipment all the time
> Extends the area of the crime
> Until *the guilt is everywhere,*

and we realize what "vast spiritual disorders lie" throughout the
world under "one impoverishing sky."

What I call the psychological interpretation of guilt and innocence comes strongly to the fore in *The Dog beneath the Skin.*
This appears in the authors' disposition to account for people's fear
and guilt in terms of childhood conditioning. I have earlier quoted
from their vivid account of "man caught in the trap of his terror,
destroying himself," of the horrid "monster of his childhood" that
perpetually haunts him, of

> Man divided always and restless; afraid and
>   unable to forgive:
> *Unable to forgive his parents, or his first*
>   *voluptuous rectal sins.*

Then follows all the kinds of fear under which he suffers, and all
the vain ways in which he seeks to find relief from his fears — including sickness and crime, religion and art, asceticism, money-
making, and "even *less innocent forms of power.*" The psychological emphasis is equally strong in *The Ascent of F6.* There is a
strong suggestion that Ransom's motives for undertaking the climb
in which he does not believe are somehow explainable in terms of
the silver-chord complex; and those of others among the climbers,
while they may not be traced back to their origins in childhood, are
reducible to some psychological complex. Thus David's — what
shall we call it? — masochistic compulsion to undertake feats that
frighten him. "Being frightened is his chief pleasure in life. He's
frightened when he drives a racing-car or seduces somebody's wife.
At present he prefers mountaineering because it frightens him most
of all." It is, accordingly, in this psychological frame of reference
that we may take the author's reference to "the *web of guilt* that
prisons every upright person and all those thousands of thoughtless
jailers from whom Life pants to be delivered."

The psychological origins and accompaniments of a sense of
guilt continue to be strongly emphasized in "New Year Letter,"

"The Quest," the epilogue to *The Double Man*, and *The Age of Anxiety*. But they no longer operate in a purely secular frame of reference, and are no longer seen to be self-sufficient. Behind them now lie the supranatural concepts of transcendental metaphysics and religion. In "New Year Letter," under the influence of psychotherapists like Groddeck, Auden is still strongly conscious of the part played in our guilt-complex by the mother-image, and, with the help of symbolic terms from Wagner and Goethe, he describes the process by which the man or boy becomes conscious of a guilt which is now no longer a matter of eternal truth, but "Only a given mode of thought / Whence my imperatives were taught." From Wagner's Siegfried he has the concept of

> The deep *Urmutterfurcht* that drives
> Us into knowledge all our lives.

From Goethe's *Faust* he has the concept of the terrible Mothers, and then of *das Weibliche* that leads us "To civilize and to create," and "bids us come / To find what we're escaping from." He thinks of himself as a boy dropping pebbles into a deep dark well, and from this oracle he learns, in Goethe's words, his mother will never return to him. She is not a part of him, his duty and love. And she bids him destroy her picture — or, as the psychologist would say, sever the silver chord. And then, the poet says, "I was conscious of my guilt."

But it is perfectly clear that this guilt is not, in the last analysis, explainable, or the associated sickness curable, in terms of any naturalistic psychology; that one must first get free from "reason's depravity," must free oneself from the bondage to "necessity," must cease to turn one's back on divine Truth, before one can recover one's lost innocence. The secret is transcendental. It lies in the opposition between Time and Eternity, known to Boethius and Spinoza; between Becoming and Being, known to the German existentialists as *Werden* and *Sein*, and in Auden's imagery it is promoted by his readings in Jung. The secret is to free oneself from the deceptive bondage of Becoming and Time (which is subject to necessity) and enter into the field of Being, in Eternity. It is a sort of conversion, which happens every day to lucky individuals, for whom some accidental happiness

> Catching man off his guard, will blow him
> Out of his life in time to show him
> The field of Being where he may,
> Unconscious of Becoming, play
> With *the Eternal Innocence*
> In unimpeded utterance.

In his explanatory notes, Auden cites definitions of eternity from the naturalistic Spinoza and the Christian Boethius, which sound very much alike: Spinoza: "Eternity, that is the infinite enjoyment of existence." Boethius: "Eternity is the complete and perfect possession of unlimited life all at once." These definitions both deal with transcendentals, and may have identical or disparate implications for theology. But it is clear enough that Auden, in his concluding apostrophe to the "unicorn among the cedars," is taking his transcendentals distinctly in the Christian sense of Boethius — and that it is God himself who must be relied on to lead us back into

> White childhood moving like a sigh
> Through the green woods unharmed in thy
> *Sophisticated innocence.*

In *The Age of Anxiety*, again, since the four characters in this modern mystery play are all victims of Time and Becoming, and the account of their malady comes out of their own mouths, the analysis is made almost altogether in terms of naturalistic psychology. Much attention is given in "The Seven Ages" to their conditioning in early childhood by the sense of shame and alienation inspired by parental disapproval of childish offenses. One might suppose that, in such passages, the pervading sense of guilt is being referred, in simple naturalistic terms, as its sufficient cause, to the effect on an infant's mind of the process of "housebreaking," with its stern admonitions and restraints upon natural processes, or, in general, to the moral prohibitions laid on a child in the effort to keep him free from private or social vices and make him a good character, together with the severe punishments by which these

rules are enforced and dark hints as to the sinfuln :ss or destructiveness of habits to which the child is prone. But that is by no means
the whole story. For while these characters in the drama are ailing,
unconverted souls, incapable of taking hold of the supernal means
of salvation, always taking refuge in spiritual "lies," they are at the
same time sophisticated intellectuals, with a glimmering of the truth
which their lives deny. And, especially in the end — with perhaps
some violation of dramatic propriety — the most thoughtful of
them, Malin, is allowed in his soliloquy to state the case in purely
religious (and philosophically transcendental) terms, plainly expressing the author's views. Indeed, the passages quoted at the beginning of this section, which occur early in the poem, are put in
the mouth of this same unregenerate Malin, who is capable, specu-
latively, of grasping the religious truth, the means of salvation,
which, in the advanced stage of his malady, he is incapable of em-
bracing effectually for the cure of his soul. In Auden's representation of guilt and innocence, we might say, then, that the psychological explanations remain true enough on the level of "scientific"
explanation, but are not thought of as going at all to the root of
the matter, or reaching the higher or deeper level of metaphysical
or religious truth, which underlies the appearances or data of the
phenomenal world. One might perhaps say that the child's relation
to the father — his admonitions and punishments and love — is an
"objective correlative" for the deity or what Auden calls elsewhere
in scholastic terms "one immortal one infinite Substance."

One might also suggest that *The Age of Anxiety* represents in
Auden's poetic progress very much what *The Waste Land* does
in Eliot's. In both poems the emphasis is on the spiritual lostness and
futility of a world without faith, but there are plentiful reminders
of the positive aspects of faith to be celebrated, or, in Auden, already celebrated, in other poems. When that is said, one might
feel bound to add that, considered simply as poetry, there is nothing in Auden remotely comparable to *Ash Wednesday* or the *Four
Quartets*.

When it comes to Warren's poems dealing with innocence and
guilt, we have the best examples in the period of the ideal use of

intellectual controls for giving shape and significance to the subjects as imaginatively conceived. Or we might better say — in order to avoid the dread dichotomy of meaning and effect — that the complexities of thought are most nearly identified in his poems with the complexities of feeling to which they correspond, and most strictly rendered in terms of situation and imagery. Warren is as much concerned as other poets of the period with the sense of guilt and the craving for innocence which, it is generally acknowledged by psychologists of all stripes, are primary facts of most human experience, however they are to be explained or justified. But there is in his poetry a vanishing minimum of the sort of abstract generalized statement about these mental states that is everywhere present in the passages cited from Auden.

For one thing, all but one of the poems in question present us with a particular situation or story which by itself serves to integrate the imaginative effect, and, imaginatively, to "control" and keep down any disposition to abstract commentary. In perhaps the earliest of the poems I shall mention, "Monologue at Midnight" (published in *Virginia Quarterly Review*, July 1936; and in *Eleven Poems on the Same Theme*, 1942) the situation involves two lovers running among the pines "in *joy and innocence*," whose "simplicity" is "doubled in the high green groining." But this "simplicity" is immediately followed by the reminder of disturbing complexities.

> And we have heard the windward hound
> Bell in the frosty vault of dark.
> (Then *what pursuit?*)

Then we learn that, in every season, these lovers are now followed by their shadows, "*like guilt.*" But are they sure it *was* guilt? (That is something about which philosophers might hold divergent views.)

> Or was it guilt? Philosophers
> Loll in their disputations ease.

We have now had introduced, without commentary, the symbolic images of the hound, with its echo in the night, the image of pursuit, and the states of mind indicated by the words *innocence* and

315

guilt. In the following stanza is added the image of a match flame "lensed within each watching eye," and associated somehow with the reflection in each of the lovers' eyes of the other's heart. In the following stanza is brought in the concept of time, associated with the image of flight, and so with that of pursuit already started, and the image of stone (perhaps suggestive of the concept of eternity). All these are now assembled in a single stanza bewilderingly evocative of the anxious want of security which has followed on the lovers' original simple feeling of innocence.

> The hound, the echo, flame, or shadow . . .
> And which am I and which are you?
> And are we Time who flee so fast,
> Or stone who stand, and thus endure?

To each of the lovers is now presented the question whether his state of being is best represented by the image of the hound in pursuit or the mere echo of his belling, by the image of the flame or that of the shadow, and whether they are best characterized in terms of time in its flight or of stone in its enduring stability. It is a set of alternatives sufficient to reduce anyone to a state of desperate anxiety. These lovers have need of something they do not have sure possession of; and what that is is suggested in the concluding stanza, along with a final sour note of skepticism or denial.

> Our mathematic yet has use
> For the integers of blessedness:
> Listen! the poor deluded cock
> Salutes the coldness of the dawn.

Like so many poems of our day, the full intellectual impact of the poem is accessible only to readers who have a considerable familiarity with the speculations of philosophers, and perhaps only to those who have a fairly wide reading in earlier literature and theology. It is an advantage to have some notion of the mathematical distinction between integers, or whole numbers, and irrational and fractional numbers. Whole numbers are certainly less distracting to the simple mind.

In Prokosch's poems and novels the sense of guilt and the nostalgic longing for innocence are pervasive notes in the richly textured music, but they seem much less radical or essential to the general theme than in a number of other poets. There is almost no attempt at analysis of their origins in either psychological or theological terms. They are rather felt as symptomatic of an endemic malady of the modern world, of which there are many other more prominent and threatening symptoms. As you leaf through either the novels or the poems, what most impresses you, along with the ever-present fear, the ever-present motive of flight, of escape from living and craving for death, is the general sense of futility and weakness, of loneliness, lovelessness, of desires unsatisfied, of introversion and perversion, of the vague searching for meaning that cannot be found, of lowered vitality accompanied by the feverishness that is manifested by decaying bodies and spirits. The general theme is the decay of civilization, and the longing for innocence and the sense of guilt are hardly more than incidents in a cosmic process. The protagonist of *The Seven Who Fled* meets a philosophic drunkard in Shanghai, who tells him: " 'My friend . . . I once had a vision. Life was changed for me after that. Is it possible, I began to wonder, that in this life man is after all not the hunter but the game? That he must *give up his innocence*, and then his youth, and his eagerness, and his love, and his faith in his fellow men, and his power, all for nothing? Without any real reward, except a final willingness to leave this world . . .' " In "Eclogue" (*The Carnival*) innocence and gaiety are associated with the days, now past, when we believed in guardian angels.

> No one dies cleanly now,
> All, all of us rot away:
> No longer down the wood
> Angelic shapes delight
> *The innocent and gay.*

In *The Seven Who Fled*, the mad lama explains to the protagonist about an old religion according to which wretched and degraded souls have the mission after death "to punish the crimes committed in utter darkness. To punish . . . those who have brought suffering without knowing it, those who have never purified with *the terror that results from wicked deeds* the wickedness that hides in

317

every heart." This is indeed a religious interpretation of the guilt complex. But it is not to be taken as a reflection of the author's views. It is a superstitious mythical construction of an ancient Black Faith "profoundly feared by the Buddhist lamas of Tibet" — a faith in which the emphasis is all on the fearsome punishment of unconscious guilt rather than on the prevention of evil or its correction.

When the poet speaks in his own voice, he makes no effort to explain the sense of guilt in psychological terms or refer it to any scheme of theological sanctions. In "The Boulevard" (*Death at Sea*) we have an impressive panorama of fear-ridden people on the sidewalks, in their attic rooms, in bars and concert halls; all

> Is a ceaseless flight: flight
> *From identity, from guilt, from the fear of death*
> *Into death . . .*

The guilt here referred to is not their private vices or their public crimes. It is a general endemic disease, a state of mind accompanying the decay of vitality. One of the most impressive of all his poems is an "Elegy" (also in *Death at Sea*) in which, again in panoramic procession, he reviews the frenzied hopes and despairs and self-contradictions of people in the mass, along with the breaking down of English material culture in the destructions of war.

> And now the scenery, the archaic scenery:
> The hills corroded, the negress fleeing the storm,
> *The small guilt-stricken whine of humanity*
> *As the old walls collapse.*

In this poem, there are many features suggestive of contemporary England — the barricades of tea, the hungry swarm silently leaving the city, the aerodrome settling into the night, the musicians playing down at the inn; there are names proper to England, and others suggestive of other European and American settings — the powdered bullfighter, the dancer from Idaho. The archaic scenery, the Negress fleeing the storm take us farther afield geographically and historically. The present collapse of England is a minor incident in a cosmic process which involves the recurrent destruction of decadent cultures since the beginning of recorded history. The old walls collapsing, under bombing raids, are both literal and symbolic; and the grief-stricken whine of humanity is hardly more than a reminder that the catastrophes of time are accompanied by the moral feelings of human animals capable of giving mythical form to their experience.

It will be seen that Prokosch's vision of the world process as it affects man is extremely broad and bold. And if he is a greatly neglected poet so far as both readers and critics are concerned, this might be attributed to the fact that few among either critics or ordinary readers are tough-minded enough to endure the hopeless bleakness of his outlook. Those who are willing, or eager, to acknowledge that men are incorrigibly sinful, fallen from grace, and worthy of the destruction that fell upon Sodom and Gomorrah, would still be outraged by a pessimism that so ignores the power of a divine grace always available in the world beyond time, and actually operative strongly in the souls of those whose desperate conviction of sin is in itself the guarantee that spiritual life is still active in the world and capable of making some resistance to the dry rot of "materialism." And as for the vastly larger body of readers who, whatever their religious professions, hold a more indulgent and hopeful view of human nature, who are impressed with the constructive ethical forces operative in individuals and in society, even though countered by natural passions and selfish interests that obscure their views of right and wrong, such readers — while they may fear the destruction of humanity by physical forces let loose by crazy or panicky political leaders — are not convinced that the whole social body of the world is more decadent at the present moment than at any previous period of recorded history. Such readers, if they fully understand what Prokosch is saying, are likely to think that his pessimistic view of human destiny is exaggerated and sensational and, as Eliot might say, that the emotion registered is in excess of the facts under consideration.

But as Eliot finds this to be true of such an acknowledged artistic masterpiece as Shakespeare's *Hamlet*, the critic of poetry as poetry must have more material reasons for ignoring a gifted poet. And I suppose that the main reasons acknowledged by our critics would be a certain romantic looseness of thematic structure in Prokosch's poetry. They might say that, while he is selective, in the way Poe is selective, in choosing just those images and items that will tend to reinforce the emotional effect intended, he has not "earned" his effect by an intellectual recognition of the inherent complexities of his theme (Warren); that he has made no employment of irony or tension (Tate) or paradox (Brooks), or any of the other means of giving intellectual structure to a poem if it is not to be swamped by mere imaginative self-indulgence. And they would probably add that, even in the indulgence of the imagination, he has let himself go in too uncontrolled a manner, so that the poems do not often have the tightness and economy which give to the classical poem its bright hardness and inner glow.

37. TIME AND ETERNITY

Still more, it would be of advantage to have some notion of the distinction between time and eternity as it appears in neo-Platonic philosophers, in theological speculation, and more or less in our poets from Spenser on down through Eliot. Our existence in time lays us open to many disabilities, humiliations, errors, and vices. It is not possible to conceive of complete innocence in anyone in the flesh, subject to its appetites and to the determination of so much of his action by the mere indifferent forces of nature. Even the un-Christian Shelley vividly felt the unsatisfactoriness of life in time, and congratulated the dead poet Adonais on his being freed from this by death.

> He has outsoared the shadow of our night;
> Envy and calumny and hate and pain,
> And that unrest which men miscall delight,
> Can touch him not and torture not again;
> From the contagion of the world's slow stain
> He is secure, and now can never mourn
> A heart grown cold, a head grown gray in vain . . .

Our philosophers, theologians, and poets have long been busy trying to build up and conceive of a state of being "out of time." In the strictest Platonic sense this would mean living in terms of ideal values, which are universal and not subject to the changeful-

ness and the perversions of time. Christian theology has provided
heaven and continued life without physical bodies to take care of
this need. Some of our most ingenious ethical philosophers have
argued that man is capable in his lifetime of cultivating ideal values
to such a degree as to free himself from "human bondage" – that
is, from the appetites and passions which alone give time a purchase
on us. Thus Spinoza; but his is a rigorously ethical and metaphysical
doctrine, and not acceptable to orthodox Christians. Among our
poets it is Eliot who has best done justice to the emotional values
of this time-and-eternity opposition in strict accordance with orthodox Christian theology.

This time-and-eternity opposition is certainly present explicitly
or implicitly in many of Warren's poems, especially in the set of
poems "on the same theme." And a number of Christian writers
with a theological bent have made their interpretations of Warren
as a "religious poet." They have done this in great detail and with
considerable plausibility.* Just how reliable they are in their interpretations – how faithful to Warren's intention in general and in
specific detail – we have no means of knowing without consulting
the poet personally. But it so happens that he has given us a big
lead in the interpretation of his philosophy in an explanatory note
to "Terror" in Friar and Brinnin's *Modern Poetry American and
British* (1951).

Following is Warren's gloss on the phrase *adequate definition of
terror*: "the *adequate definition of terror* (lacking to the *you* of the
poem, the modern man) is that proper sense of the human lot, the
sense of limitation and the sense of the necessity for responsible
action within that limitation. I should call that sense, when it is applied inclusively, *the religious sense* [my italics] – though I don't
insist on this. The pageants, the pleasures, the lust for power, the
appetite for violence, the devotion to isolated ideas or ideals (iso-

* Among religious interpreters of Warren are W. P. Southard, "The Religious Poetry of Robert Penn Warren," *Kenyon Review*, VII (Autumn
1945), 653–676; John L. Stewart, "The Achievement of Robert Penn Warren," *South Atlantic Quarterly*, XLVII (October 1948), 562–579; Howard
Nemerov, "The Phoenix in the World," *Furioso*, III (Spring 1948), 36–46.

lated because not related to some over-all conception of the human situation) do not suffice."

This over-all conception of the human situation, as he defines it, is, then, what Warren calls the religious sense. But he does not insist that we should call it that. So far as his specification goes, this conception would admit of a purely moral interpretation under various ethical systems that have been propounded by men who have no pretensions whatever to religious belief, and still less to particular theological beliefs in regard to the human situation. And that is, I think, the peculiar merit of Warren's "religious" poetry — that it does not insist on being taken in a theological sense — and is indeed conceived in imaginative terms capable of being appreciated and "understood" (in Eliot's sense) without reference to the technical formulations, or even the substantial supernatural assumptions, of any theology, Christian or otherwise. That makes it purer poetry to begin with, and it has an added advantage for the many readers who would be distracted and repelled by specifically theological references, while theological-minded readers are still able to make the references which for them are essential to the fullness of their satisfaction.

Everyone who lives at all above the instinctual level must at times be saddened by the indignities to which his spirit is subject by reason of the limitations and treacheries of life in a changeful temporal order. He will of necessity long for a state of being in which he may feel at one with the unchanging ideas-of-value to which he is devoted but from which he is perpetually distracted by his personal failures, by the sorry disillusionments of history, by his appetites and the welter of sense impressions. He longs, with Plato, with Aristotle, with the Xia mystics, with Edmund Spenser, with Spinoza, and with the poets of all time, to be taken up into the imaginative apprehension of things *sub specie aeternitatis*. Those who, in the English tongue, have done best justice to this universal longing of modern culture and sensibility are the English Romantics, Shelley, Keats, and Wordsworth. The classical English account of the process is in "Tintern Abbey," where Wordsworth describes

that blessed mood,
In which the burthen of the mystery,
In which the heavy and the weary weight
Of all this unintelligible world,
Is lightened: — that serene and blessed mood,
In which the affections gently lead us on, —
Until, the breath of this corporeal frame
And even the motion of our human blood
Almost suspended, we are laid asleep
In body, and become a living soul:
While with an eye made quiet by the power
Of harmony, and the deep power of joy,
We see into the life of things.

It so happens that the Romantic poets are out of favor with our contemporary poets and critics. Because they are imaginatively devoted to the cult of the good as the human ideal, because they do not have that fixation upon evil that is so paralyzing to the practical cultivation of good in living, because they were relatively free from the theological dogmas and the mythological framework of European religion, they are considered "sentimental," as if it were not sentimental to take for objective facts dogmas and myths which we have no natural means of establishing as true. (There are, to be sure, other theoretically more relevant objections to be brought to the Romantics — such as their wordiness, their effusiveness, their excess of imagery and decoration, objectionable to modern taste, which is in this sense "classical." And our modern theorists have been quick to take advantage of these objections to reinforce their objections to the "sentimentalism" of the Romantic philosophy. But that would take us too far afield, in our present undertaking.)

Now, for the poet, those things are true which are the subject of direct human experience. One of these is the want of satisfaction we have in our "temporal" experience and the craving we have for that way of envisaging things in terms of values not subject to time because they are ideal, and the essence of human aspiration. And for the poet, the word *eternity* — *faute de mieux* — stands for this way of envisaging things. It is of course a pity that the poet must have recourse to terms so loaded with abstract metaphysical, or anything but abstract theological, associations. And some of the greatest triumphs of poetry consist in the studied avoidance of such abstractions.

> Heard melodies are sweet, but those unheard
> Are sweeter; therefore, ye soft pipes, play on;
> Not to the sensual ear, but, more endear'd,
> Pipe to the spirit ditties of no tone . . .

I should certainly not wish to pin on Warren the label of Romanticism. But he has this in common with the Romantic poets: he has rendered most in imaginative terms the universal experience of modern civilized man suggested by the time-and-eternity opposition and by the terms *guilt* and *innocence* or the terms *innocence* and *experience*. One of the most beautiful of all Warren's lyrics, in tone, rhythm, evocative power, and harmony, is "Bearded Oaks." And above all the physical situation of the lovers, both literally and figuratively, is so happily used to establish the mood and incorporate the theme that the most carping critic would forgive, or fail to note, the abstraction with which the poem comes to its conclusion. The position of the lovers under the bearded oaks in the failing languorous underseas light, waiting the coming of "positive night," passes over insensibly into that of persons resting actually underseas like "twin atolls on a shelf of shade." This leads to a relatively long development of the theme of how coral grows beneath the water and, like the lovers themselves, is the result of long ages of storm and furious light, of violence and pressure and movement and noise. The history of the coral formations is imaginatively identical with that of the lovers. Their present stillness and rocklike firmness is the end product of endless movement, trouble and debate.

> Passion and slaughter, ruth, decay
> Descend, minutely whispering down,
> Silted down swaying streams, to lay
> Foundation for our voicelessness.
>
> All our debate is voiceless here,
> As all our rage, the rage of stone;
> If hope is hopeless, then fearless fear,
> And history is thus undone.

Guilt and Innocence

History is the record of change in time; and it is "eternity" that undoes history. The rage of stone is a paradox for the energies of an eternity whose force is not expressed in physical movement. There now follows a stanza referring back to the restless activities of the lovers, and then one referring to the change that has come over the quality of their love as darkness closes in. And the poem ends with relative abstraction:

> We live in time so little time
> And we learn all so painfully,
> That we may spare this hour's term
> To practice for eternity.

Perhaps it is mere perversity on my part to take *eternity* here for an abstraction. Perhaps it stands for that very concrete image of heaven, our living-after-death, as the darkness stands for that concrete image of dying. Perhaps the force of the whole passage, for Christian readers, is found in the familiar notion of our present life as a moral gymnasium, or elementary school, in which we learn the art of living after death. Perhaps all I can here claim for Warren as a poet appealing even to humanists and agnostics is that the poem as a whole is capable of being taken by them in terms of their own demythologized conception of the "human situation." Even disciples of Epicurus and Spinoza are aware of the practice called for in freeing oneself from "human bondage." And in any case, the whole conception (religious or ethical) is so well objectified in the particular situation and imagery that only an extremely rigorous critic would condemn it for its poetical impurity.

The time-and-eternity opposition is very closely linked with the innocence-and-experience or the innocence-and-guilt opposition. Readers of neo-Platonic literature are familiar with the notion that, in our innocent state, our identity is completely lost in the one, of whom nothing can be predicated. In order to have individual identity, it is necessary for us to descend into being in time, and in temporal conditions we necessarily lose our innocence. This concept is vividly dramatized in Warren's "Revelation." The child has spoken harshly to his mother, and in that he has certainly lost his innocence, and his act is followed by a frightening enlargement of awareness and a voluptuous exaltation of all his being. His world is filled with awe-inspiring prodigies, as the ancient world "when Sulla smote and Rome was rent" or Scotland when Duncan was murdered. But, in the face of his naughtiness, his mother was kind, and it was so that he "learned / Something important about love, and about love's grace." For it is necessary to live in time, to be separated from the eternal one, in order for us to become moral beings; such is the paradox of personality. The essence of the moral life is love, but "in separateness only does love learn definition."

The type-situation in human love is that between "lovers"; and it is inevitable that this should be the type-image in the concept of guilt and innocence — as in "Monologue at Midnight" and "Picnic Remembered." In the latter poem, as in the former, we begin with lovers on a day when leaf and hill and sky appeared so innocent,

> Their structures so harmonious
> And pure, that all we had endured
> Seemed quaint disaster of a child.

This situation is imaginatively presented in a beautiful stanza in which the lovers are now, not twin atolls, but twin flies, as in amber,

> With our perfections stilled and framed
> To mock Time's marvelling after-spies.

And so wrapped in "the bright deception of that day" (in the illusion of eternal perfections) they had no knowledge

> How darkness darker staired below;
> Or knowing, but half understood.

There are clearer intimations here than in "Monologue at Midnight" of what it is that troubles these lovers, staining their innocence and darkening their joy, making them "sweet bells jangled out of tune and harsh." The darkness that staired below they have now come to know:

> The jaguar breath, the secret wrong,
> The curse that curls the sudden tongue.

They are now like dead souls thinking back over the time of purity and harmony from their present place, "love's limbo, this lost under-land," but still mirroring from afar the light from "uncharted Truth's high heliograph."

38. PURSUIT

There is still one further motive suggested in "Monologue at Midnight" that continued to occupy a large place in many poems of this series of *Eleven Poems* and in the longer narrative poems that have followed. It is the image of pursuit, first evoked by the hound the lovers hear belling "in the frosty vault of dark." The image of the questing hound is immediately followed by the question "Then what pursuit?" Readers of my generation will inevitably be reminded here of "The Hound of Heaven," by Francis Thompson, a Catholic poet of the nineties whom even a poet of Warren's generation, if he be well read, cannot fail to have taken note of, however "dated" he must have seemed. And even a poet who may have closed his conscious mind to so ultra-romantic and flamboyant a writer as Thompson and for whom "The Hound of Heaven" may have been buried deep under the more approved tides of Marvell, Donne, Shakespeare, and what-have-you, might, without knowing it, have caught up at the critical moment Thompson's archetypal image of the hound of heaven relentlessly pursuing the writer's soul "down the arches of the years."

In Thompson it is the man who is pursued. Warren is much occupied throughout his writing with the double image of man as both hunter and hunted. In "Original Sin" a diffused sense of guilt pursues the man from childhood on through all his restless changes of habitat. Though having nothing to do with his "public experience or private reformation," it plagues him with a deep and unappeased unease. For he feels himself to be not a criminal but *l'homme moyen sensuel* or a Laodicean, neither hot nor cold. He has not faced the crucial question, first posed in the Garden and dramatized in the Last Judgment. He has not taken his definitive stand in the great debate between the powers of evil and the powers of holiness, by which alone he can recover his lost innocence.

The other side of the image of pursuit is developed in "Pursuit" and "End of Season." In the first, man is shown in pursuit of the answer, the secret, that *will* restore his innocence and peace. The hunchback on the corner, in his "imperious innocence," will not deign to enlighten him, nor the "feverish old Jew" in the waiting room at the clinic. The doctor can only advise a change of scene. In Florida he studies in vain the gorgeous flamingo, the girl whom the other guests shun, the child playing by the sea, and the old widow in black.

> She blinks and croaks, like a toad or a Norn, in the
> horrible light,
> And rattles her crutch, which may put forth a small
> blossom, perhaps white.

For Tannhäuser the Pope's rod blossomed like Aaron's, and one never can tell what unlikely creature may be the agent of the desiderated miracle. In "End of Season," we are again upon the beach and swimming in the "waters [that] wash [away] our guilt and dance in the sun." The hope has been that purification and release may be found in the "annual sacrament of sea and sun." But the ineffectual man knows that he is going back to the old mailbox, the old greetings, to "Summer's wishes, winter's wisdom," and his only hope is to "think / On the true nature of Hope, whose eye is round and does not wink."

The eye that is round and does not wink is, I presume, a symbol for eternity (for time winks) or for deity, often represented by the perfect circle, and the lost innocence can only be recovered in terms of truth untouched by the stain of time.

The recovery of innocence might be regarded as the central motif of Warren's poetry, both in the series of *Eleven Poems* and in the later narratives. We have it in "Original Sin" where, in the betrayal of hopes in the great adventures of life, the protagonist exclaims, "There must be a new innocence for us to be stayed by." We have it in "The Ballad of Billy Potts," where in the concluding chorus it is declared, "Our innocence needs, perhaps, new definition." And we have it in *Brother to Dragons* (1953), where, in this Hardyesque or Frostian masque beyond time, the voice named "R. P. W." draws the specific moral of the tragic tale. He speaks of our human yearning "for some identification / With the glory of the human effort"; and he declares that to make "an adequate definition of that glory," would be, "in itself, of the nature of glory." But, he goes on to say, "we must argue the necessity of virtue," and he makes the most illuminating statement of the case for virtue that you will find in years of reading.

> In so far as man has the simplest vanity of self,
> There is no escape from the movement toward fulfilment.
> And since all kind but fulfils its own kind,
> Fulfilment is only in the degree of recognition
> Of the common lot of mankind. And that is the death
>   of vanity,
> And that is the beginning of virtue.

> The recognition of complicity is the *beginning of*
>   innocence.
> The recognition of necessity is the beginning of freedom.
> The recognition of the direction of fulfilment is the
>   death of the self,
> And the death of the self is the beginning of selfhood.

What we have here is Christian ethics pure and simple but reconciled with the humanistic demand for self-fulfillment. There is no trace of theological assumptions. This very absence of theology, while it makes the position more acceptable to non-theological readers, may be a main reason why this poem has not received the imprimatur of the very critics with whom Warren has been most closely associated in the past. There are, of course, other reasons which the critic may prefer to give for his coolness to this great poem. He may object to the loose, free movement of the narrative and descriptive portions, somewhat like the ballad manner which gives so much dash and go to "Billy Potts," but which is so much in contrast with the compact, tight-wristed, "metaphysical" structure of the earlier lyrics.

And the same critic may particularly object to the portions that serve as chorus or commentary on the action, especially where the speaker is R. P. W. Personally, I consider that this new style is appropriate and well handled, and I am not prepossessed against it because it reminds me of more specious days before poetry in our language had gone so consciously metaphysical. The passage just quoted, in which the moral is explicitly drawn, is indeed open to the objection that it consists altogether of abstract statements related to one another somewhat in the manner of propositions in a syllogism, and that in this it comes too close to what we call prose writing. But this jealous guarding over the confines of prose and verse, this insistence that every idea in poetry must be rendered by symbolic indirection, would deprive us of many of our valued classics. *Brother to Dragons* is imaginatively strong enough to carry a considerable measure of this sort of philosophical commentary; and the final effect is enhanced by the sense we have that we are dealing with a spirit so wise and gravely speculative as Warren's.

At any rate it is interesting to note the evolution that has taken place in Warren's poetry since the beginning of his published writing. The same evolution may be noted in his novels. In *Brother to Dragons*, as in his later novels, while his dominant bias is ethical, there is plentiful provision of matter in character and incident to make possible a purely psychological account of how the actors were drawn into their tragic errors. But his own account is never confined to the limits of psychological explanation. His final concern *is* uncompromisingly ethical or "religious." But one notes the fading away of the particularities of theology. He has always been too much of a poet to let these particularities of theology destroy the imaginative effect of his poetic creation, as they sometimes do in the later poems of Auden. Insofar as they are latently present, they are taken in so broadly human a way that they are acceptable to the non-theological mentality. But the broadening has proceeded with the passage of the years. And in the passage quoted from *Brother to Dragons* — while he has lost somewhat in imaginative beauty in comparison with the *Eleven Poems* — the work as a whole has a far greater strength than the earlier lyrics, and the conception of "innocence" appears at length in its pure ethical effulgence.

All along, in Warren's dealings with guilt and innocence, we cannot fail to be reminded of Blake's opposition of the childish and the mature states of being represented by his *Songs of Innocence* and

330

Songs of Experience. While Warren does not yield the same political implications as Blake nor the same revolt against the puritan code of morals, as these have been elucidated by David Erdman in his recent study of Blake, he does share with Blake the realization that mature living and personal identity are to be had only at the cost of "complicity" in the temporal experience. We are also brought back to the first section of the present volume, and the innocence that Yeats desiderated for his daughter, the innocence whose "ceremony" was drowned in the blood-dimmed tide of his times. While Warren does not employ the mythological machinery of the Second Coming and the man-headed lion slouching toward Bethlehem, and while he never risks diluting the intense inwardness of his innocence with any association with ritual stateliness, one feels that his innocence is, like Yeats's, the comprehensive symbol for all that we have lost in our alienation from the Garden, all that must be regained if we are to have inner peace.

39. SEARCH FOR INNOCENCE

In Brinnin's references to innocence there seems to be no involvement with the theological doctrine of original sin — at least not in the earlier volumes. In *The Lincoln Lyrics*, innocence appears as the condition of the helpless Negro slave as opposed to the villainy of the slaveholder, in dark allusions to fables of sheep and wolf or fox (nos. xvi and xx). In *The Garden Is Political*, Brinnin has a poem, "New Year's Eve," in which he reflects on the brawling celebrations of New Year's Eve, 1939, and refers to the Munich agreement, "Since Prague is two months gone." The political events of this year, as "debased and cancerous" it "unwinds," brought shocking disillusionment to ardent liberals, as represented in this poem by two young lovers saying their farewells to one another. Theirs was "such reach of love" as, translated into political action, would have commanded

> Treaties of strict peace,
> Would have converted hangmen from their plans,
> Deployed the raiding planes,
> Put Christ in capitals and in the churches Marx.

But as it is, they cannot express themselves in hopeful terms.

> Who names the untranslatable and good,
> *Drowned innocence in blood?*

In another poem of this volume, "Heroes," Brinnin records the age's disillusionment with "time's pictured heroes." It is elsewhere, he says, that the schoolchild must look for inspiration. He has had enough

> Of learning tales of giants and their ways,
> Since *mortal families of the innocent*
> Deserve his imitation and his praise.

But it is in the following volume, *No Arch, No Triumph*, that one finds the half-dozen poems that best represent Brinnin as a responsible moral philosopher facing the plain public facts of the time, but determined not to relinquish the social values he cherishes or, in his discouragement, to lose the power of action. In "Observatory Hill" he first warns against the sort of innocence without realism that inspired our earlier poets and statesmen.

> Let Whitman go, and all the rest
> Who turned their broad glad faces on the West;
> Since all *deliberate innocence* must fail.

For "those of single vision are brought down." Somewhat less lucidly he invokes the names of Beethoven, Van Gogh, and Joyce, who "fixed the impartial lens and telescopic eye / Dead center down," and suggests how one, accepting the tragedy of the age, may still "move among your ruins conquering." In "Second Sight" he shows up the futility and essential defeat of those men of letters who run away from the challenge of the age into an egotistical and exhibitionist romanticism. It is the childishness of an age of disillusion that he deprecates.

> Lost, and unable to be lost, we turn again;
> Like *angry children looking for their innocence*
> Address the air with boisterous inconsequence,
> Brawling among ourselves while the picnic ends in rain.

The figure of angry children looking for their innocence appears in another poem of this volume specially intended "For My

Pupils in the War Years." This seems to be meant as a mild reproof
to his bookish students for their aloofness from the world of action.
Action may involve us in a "guilty" or impure world, and confinement of oneself to theoretical thought may guarantee one's
"innocence," but in a world where "truth is a result" of "making
faith," the scholar in his ivory tower had better avoid complacency.

> When rebels ride to action, you remain.
> For all *the anger of your innocence*,
> Accomplished and free, they will ride back again.

They at least have taken the risks of action.

> Their *guilt is brave*, and when you can believe it,
> With a cold grace you will take their adult hands
> For there is nothing to learn about death but how
>   to achieve it.

In all this we find that Brinnin has taken, on the subject of guilt
and innocence, a resolutely ethical stand, and that his ethical system is primarily concerned with social relations and values and very
little with men's "souls" in the private sense. There is here, so far
as I can make out, no confusion of ethical idealism with theological
dogma.

In Brinnin's volume from 1951, *The Sorrows of Cold Stone*, the
dominant note is that of a poet beaten down by the withering tem-
poralities of an age of wars (hot and cold), his social faith grown
thin or driven underground, turning backward into the twilight
realm of a traditional but discouraged mythology, celebrating love
and death in a resolutely metaphysical play of symbolism and paradox ("The Double Crucifixion"), showing time and nature against
a saddening perspective of doomsday ("Song for Doomsday Minus
One"), and complimenting his friends with acrostic poems that
associate their names with a disillusioned philosophy. Considered
purely as creations of the imagination, these are perhaps his best
poems, for his symbolism, for all its obscurity, flashes brilliant and
original images upon the eye. Considered as poetic "vision," they
are like a garden of wilted flowers. It is inevitable that *innocence*
should share in this general scorching under the sun of pessimistic
realism. Thus in "Could We but Lift a White Hand on This Day,"

innocence and love appear as the undiscriminating sentiments that welcome and confound all experience of nature and life, and undertake impossible feats of salvation.

> *Evil is that largesse of innocence*
> Life into life its moats and castles twines;
> Love squanders love, it cuts a royal wound.
> In spite of all we know, in stealth we're found
> Starting a suture for what will not mend.

In "Pretense Employs Us, Innocence Must Lie," innocence is represented as a "life lie," mendacious but necessary to keep us going at all. "The lightnings of mischance / Light all we live with, we must have pretense." This is, of course, the "deliberate innocence" which, as the poet earlier warned, is doomed to failure. But now he recommends it halfheartedly as a state of mind necessary to defend us from the utter blankness that is left to us in an age of values shipwrecked.

We have early seen that 1947 was a climactic year for volumes of poetry bristling with obsessive images. And in this year innocence appears in all its variant implications. Jean Garrigue, in *The Ego and the Centaur*, tries in the park to figure out the meaning of Yeats's "elusive and prehensile datum" — "The ceremony of innocence is drowned." Innocence is still everywhere evident in the lower animal and vegetable life. But men and women cannot look each other candidly in the face.

> The centre of that fury in which we live
> Is confessed by no one but the dead.
> Like strangers forced by hate, we greet
> Who find no saving faith before the brink
> And have plunged down into its boiling dark.

William Meredith, again, in his "Reconversion Sonnet" (*Ships and Other Figures*, 1948) refers back to Yeats's "ceremony of innocence." On Christmas he thinks of an earlier Christmas when "we" soldiers watched all night "From choice on Yeats and freedom or from need on war." Some of us are now dead, and war has altered from what it was and become simply "a neurosis men and nations have." The freedom they pursue moves ever far ahead of them, "and Yeats, as we have moved, means more or less."

> Across these changes *knowledge does not yearn*
> *To innocence*, and we cannot return.

Here the innocence to which knowledge does not yearn would appear to be something like that Whitmanesque "deliberate innocence" which Brinnin says must fail, and which Meredith identifies with Yeats's "ceremony of innocence" drowned in blood.

And another soldier-poet, John Ciardi ("The Park," *Other Skies*), viewing the world through his cross-haired bombsight while he burns cities and jungles, shares the feeling of so many of our poets that the guilt is not in the present destruction but in the "innocence" of those who earlier "dreamed by all the windows while time burned." His memory (in "Poem for My Twenty-Ninth Birthday," *Other Skies*) is "Our simplest day was *guiltier* than this."

> *Our innocence* shall haunt our murderous end
> Longer than statues or the tabled walls
> Alphabetized to death.

Weldon Kees, in *The Fall of the Magicians*, has a Kafka-and-Auden-inspired nightmare which seems to reflect and react against the general guilt complex of the times. (The Auden influence, shown in the form, is from "Paysage Moralisé," the Kafka influence, in the thought, is from *The Castle* and *The Trial*.)

> Hearing the judges' well-considered sentence,
> The prisoner saw *long plateaus of guilt*,
> And thought of all the dismal furnished rooms
> The past assembled, the eyes of parents
> Staring through walls as though forever
> To condemn and *wound his innocence*.

The condemnatory "eyes of parents" suggests, perhaps, the psychological way of explaining the sense of guilt in mature men by reference to the means by which elders instilled in the infant the elementary rules of decent behavior.

But still more the whole poem, "After the Trial," appears to be a protest against the Calvinist obsession with guilt, on the part of our parents, that condemns us to imprisonment in the same obsession. Our parents, while trying to preserve our innocence, also accuse us of a guilt which we would not naturally have, since we are "capable of innocence." We raise our voices to protest our innocence; but

> How can I deny my guilt
> When I am guilty in the sight of parents?

The deadly moral of the poem is summed up in the concluding tercet.

> We walk forever to the doors of guilt,
> Pursued by our own sentences and eyes of parents,
> Never to enter innocent and quiet rooms.

It was Alfred Hayes who, in the forties, spelled out in most realistic detail the moral degradation, the abandonment of all ethical ideals, that, as he found, characterized life during the war and postwar years in the United States and Europe. His poems are really naturalistic short stories cast in verse form. He has the factuality of Kenneth Fearing without Fearing's art of suggestive arrangement, his wit, his reduction to essence, or his mysterious evocation of the shivers. At any other period he might have been denied the title of poet. But he often adopts the dramatic monologue from Browning ("Arion to Epimachos His Father," "Dinner with Livia," "Welcome to the Castle"); he draws lavishly on the early Eliot ("The Big Time," "The Imitation of Faust," "The Loggia"); he was naturalistically documenting what everyone felt; and his magazine publications — in *Esquire, New Masses, New Republic, New Yorker, Partisan Review, Poetry* — eloquently proclaim the wideness of his vogue among those looking for something new and challenging. What he has to say, fortunately, needs no explication. The soldier's life is characterized in the plainest terms ("Arion to Elimachos His Father," *Welcome to the Castle*) — his drunkenness and sexual promiscuity — and then, more in terms of mental states:

> Separation, boredom, danger, humiliation, loss of purpose,
> the uncertain future, the vanished past, etc.

Hayes is not one haunted by some undefined "original" sin or by the guilt shared by "innocent" people who "dreamed by all the windows while time burned." He is confronted with actual cases of soiled lives. In "Union Square" (*The Big Time*), after a night of cheap dissipation in the Babylonish city, the speaker bids himself dream that "the pimp has acquired an honest man's reputation," and "the tart has become an *innocent girl* again." In "The Hotel Room," waiting for a girl in a hired room, he is destroyed by the acid of thought and crushed by the weight of restless ambition

> Until the simplest smile became suspect
> The *innocent eyes* appeared no longer *innocent*
> *nor true.*

In *Welcome to the Castle* there are a dozen poems on postwar Italy of which the burden is, in the midst of universal betrayals, "One trusted no one . . . For they were all enemies: the loveliest women, the friendliest men" ("The Fall of Rome"). This poet *is* haunted, in several poems, by what has become of him since he was a man in his twenties, and how far he has fallen off from the moral stature of his father.

> I thought: Oh what a slow affectionate fire they
>   cooked me with
> who've left me littler than I was
> but kept so well my father's features and my
>   natural hair.

In some, he imagines himself like a child shut up in the dark for punishment, with a child's scream in his throat ("The Child in the Dark"). In others he imagines himself the child in terror and joy while his fathers chants the ancestral hymns ("The Angel"). Perhaps the most effective dramatization of the lost innocence is the title poem to his volume, "Welcome to the Castle," where in a Browning monologue an aging sophisticate invites his young friends to "this grim and comic castle of my middle age," corrupting them in body and spirit with his sentimental honesty.

> For it's an honest age; our infamies disclosed,
>   all printed, up for sale —
> self x-rayed and self exposed . . .

What he wants is *men*, something that is not myself; and he will show them all the pleasures of the town.

> my friends, my friends, who understand me,
> whom I can trust and show what's in my heart —
> dear Guildenstern, dear Rosencranz.

Eliot, we see, is still in the wings ("Prufrock"):

> No! I am not Prince Hamlet, nor was meant to be;
> Am an attendant lord, one that will do
> To swell a progress, start a scene or two
>
> . . . .
>
> Full of high sentence, but a bit obtuse;
> At times, indeed, almost ridiculous —
> Almost, at times, the Fool.

When Wallace Stevens, in "The Auroras of Autumn" (title poem of a volume published in 1950), plays with the words *innocence* and *guilt*, he is dealing with these concepts in his own very special way. Innocence and guilt have here no ethical, still less any religious, reference; they have nothing to do with our political structures or social well-being, nor with freedom from sin or private offenses against a moral code. Innocence is here a purely metaphysical concept, the comforting concept of form as against formlessness, of timeless idea, secure against the changes and destructions of time. Stevens is grappling here, though in his own airy, fanciful way, with his constant problem of distinguishing between the world of empirical facts and that of ideal essences. He has his own fanciful mythology, some of it derived from religious tradition but quite innocent of theology. Thus his serpent is a symbol of sheer movement or formlessness. He has also a sort of demiurge, "an imagination that sits enthroned / As grim as it is benevolent." It is perpetually engaged in making and destroying; it is no friend to our stability on this planet, or even to itself, for its destiny is to find "What must unmake it and, at last, what can." It is, indeed, not easy to see how this creator differs from the serpent, or for that matter from the father image. The father is the one who lives in space and in time moving among the clouds; he "fetches pageants out of the air," summons musicians and dancing Negresses to a tumultuous festival, and stages plays in which there are no lines to speak. He is too much the illusionist and mere manipulator of stage sets to be a reliable favorer of "innocence." The mother is better. In her presence, that fills the room at evening,

> They are together, here, and it is warm,
> With none of the prescience of oncoming dreams.

But even the mother will be dissolved and pass away. And it is "farewell to an idea." But then the poet meditates on an innocence that is "not a thing of time, nor of place, / Existing in the idea of it, alone." This, like a Santayana with his realm of essences, he declares to be no less real.

> It is like a thing of ether that exists
> Almost as predicate. But it exists,
> It exists, it is visible, it is, it is.

It is "an *innocence of the earth* and no false sign / Or symbol of malice." It is "As if the *innocent mother* sang in the dark." She sang "in the idiom of the *innocent earth*, / Not of *the enigma of the guilty dream*."

This is the only reference to guilt in the poem, and the only allusion, if that is what it is, to the old myth of the Garden. For this sender-up of colored balloons into the cloud regions of metaphysics, the guilty dream served for the opposite pole to his special notion of innocence. It symbolized whatever is unstable and humanly unsatisfying in the realm of phenomena as opposed to comfortably secure in the timeless idea of innocence.

And this debonair pagan has a further turn to give to his concept in the closing poem of the set. His final term for the desiderated innocence is simply *happiness*, and his problem is to determine whether what we know is "unhappy people in a happy world," "happy people in an unhappy world," or "happy people in a happy world." The latter alternative, he finds, is simply *opéra bouffe*; the second is unrealistic; the first is the most plausible. And he directs his "rabbi" to convey this doctrine to his congregation. Stevens realizes that he must find some mythological figure to designate the occult power that underlies all thought and all phenomena; no congregation can do without it. And his flippant fancy hits upon "the spectre of the spheres." The world as it is is his contrivance, and it is a contrivance to satisfy his need for balance in the whole and so, fulfilling his meditations (his act of creation),

> In these unhappy he meditates a whole,
> The full of fortune and the full of fate,
> As if he lived all lives, that he might know,
> In hall harridan, not hushful paradise.

Stevens is one poet whom the reader must not take too solemnly. He is a ballet master forever designing new figures for his toe dancers on a Raoul Dufy backdrop. But the fundamental nature of the universe is a serious matter, often a fighting matter. Many readers will find Stevens's seeming aestheticism a frivolous and irreverent way of resolving the august problem of good and evil. Others will welcome this refreshing note of coolness in an atmosphere so hot and muggy as that of the 1940's. Stevens is, to be sure, not properly a poet of this decade. He is a holdover from the twenties. He was out of college and law school by 1904. His mind and style were well formed before the end of World War I. He could hardly be expected, even in the forties, to take on the tone of those who were very young men during the Great Depression and still youthful poets during the second war.

Another veteran of the early days, still living and writing, is Archibald MacLeish; and he is another who has not fallen under the spell of the sin complex. MacLeish has indeed passed through many phases and has played the Hamlet in his time. But in his latest published volume of lyrics, *Collected Poems, 1917–1952*, there is a poem in which he has stigmatized the modern introspective sense of guilt as something in our time that prevents men from steering a favorable course in the seas of life. It is a gnomic poem in four slight stanzas, and worth quoting entire. The German words in the title, "The Dichter as Doktor," may suggest an ironic attitude toward a morbid introspection that is sometimes fostered by the psychoanalytic school; and they certainly suggest that he is thinking of our poets.

The mal of the mirror,
The guilt of the glass,
Is our time's marrer.

Who can be steerer
Who stares for his star
At the eye of the starer?

Who can be finder
Who sails for the ship
That sails? He will founder

To wend not to wander
Helm must hold up
Toward the world, toward the wonder.

40. UNFAITH

Our poets of the thirties and forties were pretty generally inclined to attribute the decadent state of modern society to the loss of faith. Prokosch's philosophical Dutchman in *The Asiatics* associates this want of faith with the fact that in our age we have not really been alive: "Take away our clothes, our food, our liquor, our quaint sexual pleasures, our fatiguing little conversations and our loathesome excitements about this and that: what's left? A hollow thing, like one of those silver Christmas-tree ornaments, with no more blood or warmth . . . Nothing's left because *we never really believed anything*, we never rose above the world of objects, we never deep down within us were alive. It's the age of inversion, the negative age." De Hahn does not talk exactly like a religious man; he is one of "us" who are not alive enough to believe anything. But the fact that our state is the result of our never rising above the world of objects gives some hint that the missing faith may be religious in character. This is the European malady; the Asiatic malady is the very reverse of this. The Asiatic does try hard to rise above the world of objects and he has over long centuries been "searching for something." His state is that of never finding this precisely; never being quite sure; growing absent-minded; beginning to forget that he was looking for anything. A true Asiatic, says Prince Pursguzlu, "is never very happy. Because he desires nothing that he can see or touch. He looks forward to nothing in this life, be he a Mohammedan or a Buddhist or a Hindu or a Confucian. Or a Christian. He has given up hope in life." And the young American to whom he is speaking, and who is not any too happy, replies anxiously, "But I haven't given up hope." The Prince gazes at him. "Yes you have. Soon you will believe in a God." The eager young American is fed up on the world of objects, and soon he will be giving up hope in life and putting his faith in God — which, it is implied, will be his form of unbelief and decadence.

In "The Carnival" (*The Carnival*) Prokosch looks back nostalgically to the days when men had at least a religious faith with a supernatural sanction, and so, if not happiness, at least peace.

> Yes, holy were bread and wine for some, and the peace
> Of evening, fallen from the hand of One
> Who whispered, Love, and gave to the word a
> Whole new world of tunes and meaning!

But this has been irrecoverably lost, and what we are left with is

> The senility of the Tuscan castle,
> And the sobbing, fitful pulse of *the faithless*.

Auden in all periods of his writing was impressed with unfaith as a basic cause of national or international decadence. Only, the articles of faith were not the same for the young social revolutionary and the mature Christian. It was a strenuously moral world to which he summoned recruits in the 1930 and 1936 volumes of lyrics, a world based on faith in the good life as it may be realized in the ideal society. It was not that which he associated with theology and the church — not with the kind of spiritual mysticism that smoothly tells (no. xiv, 1930 *Poems*)

> The starving that their one salvation
> Is personal regeneration
> By fasting, prayer and contemplation . . .

One such he bluntly tells

> Your dream of Heaven is the same
> As any bounder's
> You hope to corner as reward
> All that the rich can here afford

Love and music and bed and board
While the world flounders.

Even what the young generation had been taught by their fathers
was vitiated by their want of a social conscience, and had not prevented England from running down industrially and spiritually.
In number XXII (1936)

When we asked the way to Heaven, these directed
us ahead
To the padded room, the clinic and the hangman's
little shed.

It was the selfishness, the luxury, the indifference toward the poor,
the exclusive concern for success and wealth that was stigmatized
in poems XVI ("It was Easter as I walked in the public gardens"),
XXII ("Get there if you can and see the land"), XXIX ("Consider
this and in our time"), and others in the first volume; poems
XII ("As it is, plenty"), XIV ("Brothers, who when the sirens roar"),
XVII ("Here on the cropped grass of the narrow ridge I stand"),
XXIV ("O for doors to open and invite with gilded edges"), XXX
("August for the people and their favourite islands"), and others
in the 1936 volume.

It was, in short, *materialism* in the ethical sense that constituted
unfaith for the earlier Auden. And it was presumably this ethical
unbelief, this want of moral and social idealism, that is referred to
by Ransom in *The Ascent of F6*, when he speaks of the thousand
in his day, "all swept and driven by the *possessive incompetent fury
and the disbelief.*" Happy he cries, are the dead. "They cannot be
made a party to the general fiasco. For of that growth which in
maturity had seemed eternal it is now no tint of thought or feeling
that has tarnished, but the great ordered flower itself is withering;
its life-blood dwindled to an unimportant trickle, stands under
heaven now a fright and ruin, only to crows and larvae a gracious
refuge. . . ."

This was 1937. But the three years that followed witnessed the
great conversion, and in "New Year Letter" faith and unfaith have
taken on a distinctly religious meaning. We have earlier seen how
Auden confuses the several meanings of the word *materialism* —

this exclusive devotion to material values with the philosophical materialism that strives after a monistic system in phenomena. Already in *The Dog beneath the Skin* (1935) Auden and Isherwood had taken advantage of this identification of meanings to lampoon science and medicine, with the burlesque recital of the surgeon's creed: "I believe in the physical causation of all phenomena, material or mental," etc. Auden has already accepted the dualism of body and spirit that will make it so natural for him to espouse the long-rejected theology. And in the meantime still another materialism has been discredited; and with the economic materialism of Marx, the whole reformist ideal of secular brotherhood seems to have given way under his feet. The progress of Nazi power and the outbreak of war give the *coup de grâce* to his form of idealistic faith, and, in "New Year Letter," with the general "war and wastefulness and woe,"

> Ashamed civilians come to grief
> In *brotherhoods without belief*,
> Whose good intentions cannot cure
> The actual evils they endure.

What he sees now in secular humanism is "the *Spirit-that-denies*." His benighted pilgrim in "The Quest" vainly calls on "Uncreated Nothing" to set him free. On God himself the pilgrim will not call. For

> The Nameless is what no free people mention;
> Successful men know better than to try
> To see the face of their absconded God.

And so, throughout *The Age of Anxiety* his misguided neurotics ineffectually mourn for "Our lost dad, / Our colossal father." The special ideal that sustained his faith during the thirties has now become "a Confucian faith in the Functional society." What their passions pray to is not the Cross or Clarté or Common Sense, but primitive totems. They ask the wrong questions and espouse mistaken theories. But

> His Question disqualifies our quick senses,
> His Truth makes our theories historical sins.

When we are wounded, he speaks as a man and savior,

Guilt and Innocence

concluding His children
In *their mad unbelief* to have mercy on them all
As they wait unawares for His World to come.

Seldom has any poet more explicitly and contritely abjured the heresies of his youth. And this poet has even had the resoluteness to suppress the many fresh and challenging poems of his early years in which these heresies were most clearly expressed.

Many of the poets who followed Auden have equally lamented the religious unfaith of the age; but they have been more half-hearted in their abjuration. For they seem to imply that, as creatures of this moment, they are themselves involved in the general loss of faith. Thus Chisholm ("Elegy for All," in *The Prodigal Never Returns*) can only look back with nostalgia to the time when men enjoyed the diminutive,

> the window-view of life, with the mauve and green
> unquestionable hills beyond life . . .

And one does not know whether the irony strikes most at the present or the past when he declares in "You, Horse":

> But we've rubbed out the Devil with wisecracks
> and healthy ribaldry,
>   And God and His angels
> Litter the parlors of spinsters, the holes of priests,
>   and the old curiosity shops
> With velvet debris . . .

And no clear faith in the old verities is expressed in "The Park at Evening," when he asks what remains to hold society together.

> The old component parts will stick together
> a decade or so, but O where are the few
>
> rapt intrepid molecules of faith
> that moved the Himalayas of our past,
> that wired the winds for sound and sowed the stars
> with apes and angels?

With the men of this generation it would appear, in the very words of the poet's title, the prodigal never returns to the faith of his fathers.

In Alfred Hayes there is at most uncertainty as to the lost faith.

345

Joseph Warren Beach

It is true that his Faust screams at the sight of hell; but that is because he is "uncertain of the world where" he belongs ("The Imitation of Faust," *The Big Time*). With his man in the hotel room ("The Hotel Room")

> The uncertainty of love was replaced by the certainty
> of hate
> knowing always the consequences of *the murder of
> belief*
> That who lies dead at last is always and only you . . .

In his poem on Heine ("Heine: A Biography of a Night," *Welcome to the Castle*), he has the German poet ask himself why he should not have stuck profitably to the law and practiced perjury and blackmail — "Why should a man sacrifice that for what a man is not even certain he believes?"

In the poems of Nemerov, the lash of sarcasm falls constantly on the points of view of the statistician ("The Place of Value . . ." *The Image and the Law*), upon those who would teach children that there is no Santa Claus, no God, no Life after Death ("The Triumph of Education"), and upon the cynical teachings of newspaper and radio ("For W——, Who Commanded Well"). But the very bracketing of God with Santa Claus introduces a note of skeptical ambiguity. We hear in *Guide to the Ruins* of "the gods with their noses knocked off" ("Guide to the Ruins"), of "the baffled involved brain / Of the old god over the vacant waters" ("Elegy of Last Resort"). And the general tone of the whole is to imply that, willy-nilly, and much as we dislike it, we are living in a world without religious faith.

This is naturally not the case with definitely congenitally Catholic poets like James Agee, Thomas Merton, and Robert Fitzgerald. Such writers naturally deprecate the widespread want of religious faith; but theirs is the serenity of those possessed of the faith, and they do not have the posture of men vainly tossing their arms as they see themselves going down with a sinking ship.

Brinnin is notable in the forties for his emphasis not on unfaith but on faith. And his faith would seem to be — at any rate in his three earlier volumes — very like the ethical-social faith of Auden

346

in the thirties. Thus in "Second Sight" (*No Arch, No Triumph*) what he is recommending is the social ideal of "life in its plurality." He is urging his readers to be active in their pursuit of this ideal, for "with the *making faith* we have to look toward its reality." And again, in "Meditation on Tombs," he is urging resolute action toward the realization of our ideal world as the means of confirming our faith. Even when we are not successful in our efforts, we can persist in them.

> The *faith survives the failure*, and we love,
> The pride is in the process, and we live.

There is here no appeal to theological sanctions. The tombs that inspire this meditation are Lenin's and Lincoln's. It is in our secular living that our faith is manifest. And our pride – our faith – is in the *process*. The discouragement that marks Brinnin's later volumes has not yet made itself felt. Here is a positive and hopeful note that is refreshing in the midst of so much that is negative and crestfallen. And this leads straight into our following sections, in which we shall take up the two final images to be discussed in this volume.

41. THE CROCUS

The symbolism of flowers has occupied poets from the beginning, and we are all familiar with the symbolic meanings of asphodel, rose, pansy, rue, and daisy. This brief section will serve to call attention to the hopeful symbolism of the crocus in a handful of recent English and American poets. In many climes the crocus (wild or tame) is the first flower of spring, and the wild blue crocus in the United States is sometimes called the pasqueflower, as a symbol of Easter and renewed life. It is presumably the wild crocus to which Spender refers in a touching passage in his *Vienna*. He has just been citing the cynical, the lying and unfeeling propaganda of the Viennese authorities in regard to the workers' tenements. And he turns for comfort to the thought of the crocus, as a symbol of something in nature that will resist the treacheries and inhumanities of politics.

> If only one can silence every voice,
> *Assertion of the primitive crocus,*
> Flooded with snow, but melting not to water,
> Melting into summer.

The putting down of the workers' revolt in Vienna made a deep impression on liberals everywhere, and Spender's poem was widely read and left a deep mark on the poetic mind. If the crocus was not a "natural" for hope in the recuperative forces of nature, Spender's reference would have been enough to give it currency. Five years later George Barker wrote a "Requiem Anthem for the Austrian Constitution" (*Selected Poems*) in which he laments "the Austrian strong man pinioned among the pillars," but sees him pulling down

348

around him "the column of subjugation." And that reminds him of the crocus.

> *The crocus breaks the rock*, the eagle from its errors
> Arises and inscribes liberty on the skies.

It may seem peculiar to speak of an eagle's errors; but Spender had a lot to say about the mistakes and failures of the leaders in the workers' revolt.

In Hugh Chisholm we have a poet so "sicklied o'er with the pale cast of thought" that he can resist the blandishments of spring and the crocus. In "Spring Is a Long Time" (*The Prodigal Never Returns*) we read:

> and spring is a long time coming.
> And when it comes with the warmth of death
> and love, with one touch of the sun
>
> and *one quick look at crocuses*,
> it comes with everybody's ghost
> everlastingly his own.

Yes, crocuses are symbols of renewed life, and (April is the cruelest month!) there are so many who go to their death as to the womb, and so many "who never will uncurl / out of their artificial dark / into the sunlight." Yes,

> Beginning is under every era
> ending or begun again,
> continuing eternity
>
> across the continent infinite.

Our "deaths and loves are difficult." And the more we consider how our lives and loves are involved with ending, "the less we shall despise our lives." It is, I think, a serious poem and not without its melancholy beauty. And it is distinctly a poem of the 1940's.

But there does sound in the 1940's another more exhilarating note, under the inspiration of the crocus. Chisholm has been greatly impressed with the early crocus as the symbol of prophetic hope. Thus in number II of the Lincoln lyrics, the winter landscape makes him think of the dismal auspices under which Lincoln was born. Neither the snow nor the stars promise that he was to be

> Prophetic as
> *First crocuses* beneath the teeth of snow,
> A man is born who is unpencilled there . . .

Brinnin, in "Mardi Gras," needing some relief from the depression of a world at war, bids himself

> Allow no corpse for obstacle,
> But *crocus-rude*, in errorless array,
> Seek some proud *alibi for guilt*
> Whose acrimonious result
> Identifies the race and stains its day.

Philosophy will not do it, nor the preachings of some "emblazoned charlatan."

> Yet if *the records of the crocus hold*,
> And if in that example we may build
> For straight successions of our tenure here,

then we may accept the auguries and quieting rhythm of summer. The records of the crocus are presumably the chronicle of seasonal rebirth and continuance of life, applicable to us men. And they may be made effective, as he goes on to say, if

> among the relics of defeat,
> We find some smoky hero breathing yet,
> And tend his wound, and teach him *second faith*.

The thought of this poem is expressed in a rather elaborately indirect, roundabout way. But so far as I can make it out, he is here recommending the same "making faith" as in poems already discussed in earlier sections. *Second faith* is a phrase modeled perhaps on *second wind*. And second wind is what the runner gets when he goes on running. Our faith in ideal ends is something that can only be recovered in action. It is a faith reborn like the crocus wherever winter yields to spring.

And thus we are brought to our final image, the image of the phoenix.

42. THE PHOENIX AND THE UNICORN

A number of our recent poets have gone back to the ancient mythical beasts, the phoenix and the unicorn, and, for the most part, have taken advantage of the hopeful or edifying symbolism long associated with them to mitigate the general despair of the times. The bird that rises once every millennium from his own funeral ashes makes his appearance three times in volumes of poetry published in 1935. In Gregory's *Chorus for Survival*, the phoenix image is applied (in section 14) both to the poet Emerson and to the entity that Emerson hails as "my America." He is made to say that in his heart he is

> That angry ancient legend of a bird
> Who walked alive
>> eating the ashes of his funeral urn

And then the marginal rubric "Phoenix" is set over against "my America," who is further characterized in mythical terms suggestive of Hart Crane:

> Thou art Atlantis risen from the seas,
> Bride of the Indian Summer and the corn . . .

In the third section of the same poem, the bird "that lives in fire" appears as a symbol of whatever it is in the soul of the poet himself and in the spirit "that walked with ancestors, / and gave us blood, spirit and god for which men die." It is this deathless thing

> that wakes men as they drown
> or perish in the sun

and again

> wakes the electric clock to ring in darkness . . .

Muriel Rukeyser in "The Lynchings of Jesus" (*Theory of Flight*) even more daringly and somewhat more effectively combines her figurative images, and in the full flush of her socialistic and revolutionary faith, she telescopes the phoenix image with those of Jesus and Icarus to indicate how the high-flying rebel is perpetually defeated, but in the end triumphant over the forces opposed to idealism.

> *Icarus' phoenix-flight* fulfils itself,
> desire's symbol swings full circle here,
> eternal defeat by power, eternal death
> of the soul and body in murder or despair

351

> to be followed by eternal return, until
> the thoughtful rebel may triumph everywhere.

Thus the youthful poet of the thirties gives a new twist to the death-and-resurrection myth embodied in the phoenix legend. As examples of the thoughtful rebel she summons Bruno, Copernicus, Shelley, and Karl Marx. And it is indicative of the temper of the times that her book was published as one of the Yale Series of Younger Poets, with an enthusiastic foreword by Stephen Vincent Benét.

The temper of the times was somewhat changed by 1942. But the phoenix image could still be invoked, now in honor of the "common man," the individual, burning on the funeral pyre of his chosen cause. John Berryman, in "Boston Common: A Meditation upon the Hero" (*The Dispossessed*), is saddened by the thought of "misled blood-red statistical men" ("your official heroes in a magazine") being mass-fed into the holocaust of world war. But he thinks of the real chivalry of our times in Spain, China, Leningrad, Syria, Corregidor (Beethoven variations "on a primitive theme"), and will not forget "the death of heroes."

> Who chides our clamour and who would forget
> The death of heroes: never know the shore
> Where, heir to the West, Starkatterus was burnt;
> And undergo no more that spectacle —
> Perpetually verdant *the last pyre*,
> Fir, cypress, yew, *the phoenix bay*
> And voluntary music — which to him
> Threw never meat or truth. He looks another way.

(One wonders whether perhaps the "voluntary music" is an echo of, or allusion to, the "defunctive music" of the priest in Shakespeare's "The Phoenix and the Turtle.")

Berryman in another poem of *The Dispossessed* ("Fare Well") sets the phoenix image in a less heroic key, and with greater ambiguity.

> O easy *the phoenix in the tree of the heart*,
> Each in his time, his twigs and spices fixes
> To make a last nest, and marvellously relaxes, —
> Out of the fire, weak peep! . . .

Father I fought for Mother, sleep where you sleep!
I slip into a snowbed with no hurt
Where warm will warm be warm enough to part
Us, as I sink I weep.

A few years earlier had appeared a rather long poem by Theodore Spencer entitled "The Phoenix" (Oscar Williams, ed., *New Poems 1944: An Anthology of American and British Verse*). The phoenix legend is here elaborately developed; and the poem ends on a wistful note of questioning. The sphinx from the North, the unicorn from the jeweled East, behemoth from the South, and roc from the West all come together, after a thousand years, to Heliopolis, to watch the pyre that will "redeem / Dead life through flame." The phoenix sinks down on his aromatic nest, and the sun kindles "the myrrh and frankincense / As cradle for *new innocence*." Then the four heraldic creatures return to their several homes. And the poet inquires

> Why is man so wrought
> That he must make his creatures
> Wistful to outlast Nature's
> Marriage of flesh and bone?

The "impossible miracle" occurs, he thinks, "because man hopes and fears." Each one, like the phoenix, goes back alone. And they leave the poet wondering whether his mind

> That has created you,
> And hence created Him,
> Was in creation blind,
> Or flowering from dead stem,
> Built better than it knew

In this same year 1944 was published a volume of poems by Kenneth Rexroth, *The Phoenix and the Tortoise*, including a long philosophic poem with the same title. At the beginning he states his general theme.

> Webs of misery spread in the brain . . .
> And I
> Walking by the viscid, menacing
> Water, turn with my heavy heart
> In my baffled brain, Plutarch's page —

353

> The falling light of the Spartan
> Heroes in the late Hellenic dusk —
> Agis, Cleomenes — this poem
> Of the phoenix and the tortoise —
> Of what survives and what perishes,
> And how, of the fall of history
> And waste of fact — on the crumbling
> Edge of a ruined polity
> That washes away in an ocean
> Whose shores are all washing into death.

One is at first tempted to associate this title with Shakespeare's "The Phoenix and the Turtle," for the simple reason that tortoise and turtle are synonymous terms for the same crustacean animal. But in Shakespeare's poem turtle means dove. And in any case the symbolic meanings attributed to the two birds (Rarity and Constancy, or Beauty and Truth) are totally unrelated to the probable symbolism of the phoenix and the tortoise in Rexroth's poem. There is, indeed, no precise indication of the symbolic significance of either of those mythical creatures. They probably both are emblematic of "what survives." The tortoise is notoriously long-lived. It is a sacred animal in many religions, sometimes associated with the creation, and in some mythologies it is conceived as that creature on whose back the world rests. The phoenix is, of course, an emblem of immortality, which in Rexroth is interpreted as the persistence of the patterns through the death of individual objects.

> The problem of immortality
> As a basic category —
> That passed away, so will this.
> The moraine creeps on the meadow;
> The temple dissolves in the jungle;
> The patterns abide and reassert themselves;
> The texture wears through the nap.

At any rate, it is not immortality in the conventional sense with which Rexroth is concerned; he is writing about the point in human action and choice at which one attains "value" and so escapes the net of "history" and determinism. This is presumably where the phoenix operates. Rexroth sometimes reminds one of Sartre's brand of existentialism. Only Sartre, in *L'Etre et le Néant*, thinks he proves the freedom of the will by strict logical process; whereas Rexroth evocatively suggests what we mean by phrases like "the self-determining person," "the individual discriminate," "myself as act." In a later volume, *The Dragon and the Unicorn*, he is equally provocative in his definitions of love as the open-sesame, but there the symbol is the unicorn.

Meantime we have to note the saucy, satirical use of the phoenix image in Nemerov's poem "The Phoenix" in *Guide to the Ruins*:

> In the City of the Sun
> He dies and rises all divine
> There is never more than one
> Genuine
>
> By incest, murder, suicide
> Survives the sacred purple bird
> Himself his father, son and bride
> And his own Word

It is Auden in our time who is most drawn to the image of the unicorn. A consideration of Eliot's "jewelled unicorns" that in *Ash Wednesday* "draw by the gilded hearse" is of little help in determining the role of the unicorn in Auden. We learn from the commentators that in Petrarch's *Triumph of Chastity* appears a car drawn by unicorns; but that in *Ash Wednesday* what is referred to is the apparent triumph of time. Perhaps in Auden's "Unicorn among the cedars," a suggestion was taken from the yews between which the silent sister was walking in Eliot's poem. The unicorn was often emblematic of chastity, and we have seen how, in Auden's "New Year Letter," in its "sophisticated innocence," it is associated with the dove (of science and of light) and with the deity himself.

The image of the unicorn recurs in *The Collected Poetry* and in *The Age of Anxiety* in connections that suggest a somewhat similar meaning. In "Kairos and Logos" we have an elaborately allegorical and philosophical poem, consisting of four sestinas setting forth the willful confusion of man in the temporal order, and especially in face of the new science, with its macrocosmic spaces and "the subatomic gulfs" that "confront our lives / With the cold stare of their eternal silence." But it begins with an earlier period of imperial pleasures and triumphs, disturbed only by the fear of death. In this pagan period there was an order (Christian) whose members "only feared another kind of Death / To which the time-obsessed are all condemned." These rare souls, concerned only with eternal Death, "came to life within a dying order." They were "sown in little clumps about the world" and set

> Against the random facts of death
> A ground a possibility of order,
> Against defeat the certainty of love.

In the second sestina we find a female character seeming to represent love, or possibly Mother Eve in the Garden. She is confronted by the unicorn, declaring "Child." She forgets she is not at home (in the eternal order), takes "the earth for granted as her garden," until the elements begin to treat her as a grown woman, frown upon her untidy home, laugh at her when she misspells a word. She turns "frightened and cruel like a guilty child," abuses the roses and the winds; until, without a word

> *The unicorn slipped off into the forest*
> Like an offended doll, and one by one
> The sparrows flew back to her mother's home.

In the third sestina, we have a male figure, who represents perhaps Adam (who named all objects in the garden), or possibly the world (in its temporal sense). His experience is parallel to that of the girl. He too is a victim of time; he becomes aware of "the shadow cast by language upon truth." And in the end, he

> saw himself there with an exile's eyes,
> Missing his Father, a thing of earth
> On whose decision hung the fate of truth.

And so we are brought to the conclusion, in the final lyric, that "we are not lost but only run away." For it is our willfulness that makes us subject to the confusions of time, preventing us from seeing things, through the Father's eyes, in the mystical light of eternity.

In *The Age of Anxiety*, the unicorn appears first (for Rosetta) as one of those delightful mythological creatures everywhere seen by man in his happy "Primal Age," when

> *unicorn herds*
> Galumphed through lilies; little mice played
> With great cock-a-hoop cats, courteous griffins
> Waltzed with wyverns . . .

But the Primal Age is long since past, and the age of spiritual enlightenment not yet attained. And as Malin has it:

> We're quite in the dark: we do not
> Know the connection between
> The clock we are bound to obey
> And the miracle we must not despair of;
> We simply cannot conceive
> With any feelings we have
> How *the raging lion is to lime*
> *With the yearning unicorn* . . .

Auden has telescoped together here the Biblical figure of the lion lying down with the lamb and the armorial figure of the lion and the unicorn supporting the British royal coat of arms. The raging lion here seems to stand for the unregenerate and time-obsessed heart of man and the yearning unicorn for the supernal Love which alone can save him from his rage.

And so, with the unicorn, Auden recommends to us the sole hope of a world in confusion, which is to be found in a nonsecular, a religious mysticism.

The mysticism of Rexroth, and the love he recommends, is of quite a different order, more suggestive of Muriel Rukeyser's, but without the latter's social-revolutionary involvements. His conception of love is mainly developed in *The Dragon and the Unicorn*. And in that poem he cites the symbolic titles of his two main philosophic volumes together with other traditional symbols.

> Love, like all the sacraments, is a
> Miniature of being itself.
> All things have an apparent
> Meaning and an opposite
> Hidden meaning brought forth by fire.

357

> *The phoenix and the tortoise,*
> *The dragon and the unicorn,*
> Man, eagle, bull and lion.

Rexroth, I think, nowhere explicitly identifies his several symbols, to show how each represents either the apparent meaning or the opposite hidden meaning. But we may assume that the unicorn is meant to symbolize the superior type of love "brought forth by fire." In an earlier section I have already cited one of many passages in which he describes this love which gives meaning to existence. It is clear that he associates it with his doctrine of value attained through free choice, in the teeth of deterministic necessity, as that doctrine is developed in *The Phoenix and the Tortoise*. And now in *The Dragon and the Unicorn*, he reiterates the idea that it is not under the "forms of serial time" that the world presents itself "in any important aspects."

> important experience
> Comes to us in freedom and
> Is realized in value,
> And the intellect alone
> Can know nothing of freedom
> And value because it is
> Concerned with the necessary
> And they are by definition
> Unnecessitated. *Love*
> Of course *is the ultimate*
> *Mode of free evaluation.*
> Perfect love casts out knowledge.

Rexroth's mysticism is distinguished from Auden's by the absence of any distinctively Christian cast and by the frankness with which he recognizes that our philosophy, like our religion, is "mythological" in character.

> The heavens and hells of man,
> The gods and demons, the ghosts of
> Superstition, are crude attempts;
> The systems of philosophers,
> The visions of religion,
> Are more or less successful
> Mythological descriptions

Of knowing, acting, loving —
You are Shiva, but you dream.

Still, Rexroth's mysticism is so high-flying, his perspective so cosmical and metaphysical, that it leaves him relatively immune to the special new disturbances and discouragements of our time. It is not that he has, like Auden, given up the fight for any secular meeting of our problems. He seems to occupy a citadel in which these local problems are but distant echoes of a world going on as usual on its lower plane.

And now, in fairness to men who do not enjoy these immunities of metaphysics and religion, we ought to mention the presence of a positive note in writers who have been most preoccupied with the negative aspects of the human scene. Even Weldon Kees, among his many pictures of a mad and dying world, can offer us in "Praise to the Mind" (*The Fall of the Magicians*) a program for the thoughtful individual worthy of the great stoic philosophers:

> Praise to the mind
> That slowly grows
> In solid breadth, that knows
> Its varied errors, shows
> And will admit
> Its witlessness.
>
> Praise to the single mind
> That sees no street
> Run through this world, complete,
> That does not meet,
> Bending at end,
> Remorselessly, its source.
>
> Praise to the mind
> That moves toward meaning,
> Kindness; mixes keenness
> With routine of
> Grace, has space,
> And finds its place.

Even Nemerov, in "Unscientific Postscript" (*The Image and the Law*), can offer us an aesthetic program in the spirit of Epicurus:

> It is not to believe, the love or fear
>
> Or their profoundest definition, death;
> But fully as orchestra to accept
>
> Making an answer, even if lament,
> In measured dance, with the whole instrument.

Even Chisholm can take time off, in the midst of elegies, to write in "For a Dead Lady" (*The Prodigal Never Returns*):

> These nights of never behind days of no
> would mince us into less than men, than mice
> were there not you, the few
> of you who come and go,
> doing the living loving that you do.

MacLeish, who had the hardihood in *Actfive* to envision our civilization as destroyed by violence and man reduced to mere flesh and bone (but even as flesh and bone, still capable of endurance and love), has never given way to the notion that our world is dying of its own debility. The final piece in his "New Poems (1951–1952)," in *Collected Poems, 1917–1952*, is "Hypocrite Auteur," in which he characterizes the spirit of the age as exhibited by the poets:

> Our epoch takes a voluptuous satisfaction
> In that perspective of the action
> Which pictures us inhabiting the end
> Of everything with death for only friend.

After developing this theme he declares that "A world ends when its metaphor has died." And he ends by declaring that what we require from our poets is the new metaphor.

> The journey of our history has not ceased:
> Earth turns us still toward the rising east,
> The metaphor still struggles in the stone.

And to our poets he says: "Invent the age! Invent the metaphor!"

And Brinnin, as we have seen, resolutely declined, at any rate during the early forties, to give up his "making faith" in the power of men in action to continue their fight for the good life. This note was eloquently sounded in "Death of this Death" (*The Garden Is Political*), where he praises those who died in battle for

> The possible dominion of the free,
> A calm community
> That, flowering in the culture of decay,
> Turns death to seed within our living day.

This figure of turning death to seed will serve appropriately to close the section dealing with the unicorn and the phoenix.

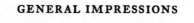

GENERAL IMPRESSIONS

This study, in spite of its length, is decidedly limited in its scope and pretensions. It is mainly factual and explicatory. My intention has been to illustrate, in American poets of two decades, the use of certain words frequently occurring in senses, or with a slant, somewhat peculiar to the period. I begin with certain words used in a way not quite usual in ordinary writing of the time, or given an extension of meaning beyond what would be natural, at any rate in prose (*ceremony*, *definition*) and with certain figures of speech taken from earlier writers and given special application to the moral and psychological obsessions of the time (the "tiger's spring," the lurking beast). There follows a long series of sections which illustrate the special symbolical use of words taken from landscape, geography, and travel (*islands*, *exiles*, etc.), in senses, again, betraying moral and psychological intentions characteristic of the period. There follow sections on the hero, showing the shift that has come over our poets' notions of what heroism implies in an age of world wars. Then, with verbal characterizations of the present age, we come to such abstractions as progress and science, revealing the poets' attitude toward what they find to be the false ideals of the age. A special set of sections deals with the moral problem of guilt and innocence and the radical problem of unfaith as seen by our poets. And finally we turn to certain images used figuratively (crocus, phoenix) to suggest the scant gleam of hope for the world which remains among a disillusioned and crestfallen group of writers.

My project, having to do with such recurring images and themes, limits my survey to those poets in whom they make a notable ap-

365

pearance. Many poets of distinction are left out of view because they have largely dispensed with these favorite images and themes. And general conclusions must necessarily be drawn in a cautious and tentative manner. However, a sufficient number of the more influential poets of the time do fall within our view to justify some approach to general conclusions. When I say influential I do not necessarily mean poets widely read by what we call "the reading public" or even those featured by Messrs. Untermeyer, Williams, Ciardi, and Elliott in their excellent anthologies. Influential, I mean, among "highbrow" readers of poetry (mostly themselves poets), eagerly sought after by editors of the more selective journals and of publishing houses of high rank, and certainly considered as of importance at the time of publication.

My primary intention has been to review the facts, and this involves a large amount of "explication" of passages in which the particular words and images are used. And this is particularly true in the earlier sections where we have to do with concrete images used symbolically rather than with abstractions whose denotation is commonly agreed upon. It is only secondarily that I allow myself critical estimates, and that mostly in regard to the relative effectiveness of the image for the imagination as it is used in a particular context.

But this, of course, involves crucial principles of poetic art; for it involves the association of ideas as it operates in the poet's imagination, and as (with "tact") it may be made to operate in the reader. Still more, it involves what we may call the association of images, and how this may be made to operate for the reader. I have had frequent occasion, in particular cases, to complain, not merely of willful obscurity, but of what seems like the poet's failure to realize imaginatively the very images he invokes. The most besetting fault of many recent poets is the ill-considered mixture of abstract intellectual language with the indirections of symbolic language, in which, too frequently, the symbol actually evokes no image, being, as it is, no real image but a mere intellectual counter or conventional hieroglyph. This misfire is most likely to occur where the word used is one of those modish words caught up and cher-

366

ished because it is *à la mode* rather than because it has been *seen* by the poet. It is like so many configurations in "modern" painting which are not drawn from the painter's own observation, or even do not stand for something in his own psychic underground, but are more or less automatically echoed from some other painter who is all the rage.

One is interested, again, in the degree of intellectual subtlety, the pregnancy, of a given favorite word or image where it is taken up by one poet from another. How much does the individual poet *do* with a given word in his exploration of a moral problem or a twist of human nature? And here we find cases, I think, of poets (like Malcolm Brinnin) whom we go on reading for the suggestiveness of their thought even where we are disappointed with them for their failure to deal imaginatively with their subject. Naturally, however, we do not like to think of a poet's intellectual faculties as distinguished from his imagination. Our ideal requires the harmonious working together, the inseparability, of a poet's faculties, and we are bound to take special note of cases, such as those of Warren and Jarrell, in which we so often find them in perfect fusion.

Above all, the question of originality is raised by our discussion, and would be explicitly raised in every instance if I were more confident of my own discrimination and of the reader's patience. For originality — freshness of vision — is not merely a matter of innate force, of what we call "genius" where it is notably present. It is often a matter of something very like *sincerity*. A writer of secondary power may indeed be perfectly sincere and at the same time conventional and dull, providing that he is modest enough in his undertakings, and contents himself with the limitations of his own natural or inherited thought and sentiment. It is where he strains himself to follow a new mode, with its daring innovations and its modish vocabulary, that he is most likely to make us feel that he is affected, and to that degree insincere. I am very well aware how hard it is for any poet, or any man, to be himself. I am keenly aware of the prodigious difficulties overcome (and the great good luck involved) in the making of a moderately good poem.

(I realize how very much any poet, however original, derives from his predecessors and from the tradition.) I do not like taking the high critical tone toward some poet of real though minor endowment because I feel him to be somewhat weakly imitative of some more original writer. And I have refrained so far as possible from solemn adverse or critical pronouncements. But I have necessarily suggested, or implied, in several cases, that a given writer owes more to imitation than to original insight or invention. And that is why I have so often called attention to the "source" of certain phrases or stylistic tricks. We all know that, in any given exhibit of contemporary paintings, the few really original canvases are lost in a sea of imitators, more or less well skilled in composition and the putting on of paint, but drearily suggestive of great models whose essence they have missed because it is not their own.

And that is the case with poetry of our moment, poured upon us in torrents, before time has had the benign effect of eliminating all but the most original. I have the feeling that, taken as a whole, the thirties and forties have been, for reasons that might be discovered, a period of great earnestness, ingenuity, and sophistication in the writing of poetry, but that they have brought to light very few poets of the originality and the stature of Robinson, Pound, Eliot, Frost, Sandburg, Masters, Jeffers, Stevens, Crane.

To begin with, the climate of the period seems to have been less favorable to the free and natural movement of the creative imagination. The Great Depression, the second war, and the cold war weighed too heavily on the spirits of our poets to allow that geniality (in both the German and the English sense) of feeling that most favors the flowering of the imagination. The low ebb of religious faith, which in Robinson, Masters, Eliot, and Jeffers still served as a stimulating challenge to the writers, who could react to it strongly in their several ways, now, in its long continuance, operated as chronic depressant. Poets could no longer either exult in their emancipation from the old faith or make their protest against unfaith in more than a weak manner. In view of the world's agony, after the first flush of socialist enthusiasm, they were left so confused and disconcerted that the utmost earnestness in grappling with the problem could not save them from the frost. They had lived too long with a world not guaranteed by supernatural grace, and there were none of them strong enough in sheer humanism to derive any genuine enthusiasm from that.

There were also literary reasons that tended to hamper the free and genial movement of the poetic faculties. In the mere historical rhythm they had reached a moment of reaction against the free-handed procedures of their predecessors, themselves carried triumphantly forward by their own revolutionary reaction against the Victorians and Georgians. And even when they model themselves upon the earlier men and largely share their poetic theories, their work is tighter and drier, with less movement, less color, and much less comprehensiveness in its coverage of man's emotional being. Their concern is too much limited to man's soul, and they write too much off the top of their minds. For one thing, they tend to neglect the individual, and they neglect the techniques of dramatizing of which so much advantage was taken by Robinson, Frost, Eliot, and Masters. They have quite abjured the element of truth there is in the old saying *Ut pictura poesis*. They call up isolated images, but they do not revel in picture and atmosphere like Pound and Aiken, the Imagists and Sandburg, Williams, Jeffers, and Stevens — most of whom took so many cues from the plastic arts and named so many poems portraits and landscapes and episodes in gray. Nor do they realize the affinities of painting and music as did Pound and Aiken and Fletcher and Sandburg, with their nocturnes and tone poems and color symphonies and jazz fantasias.

Their greatest technical revolution was in clearing off the brittle shining lacquer of poetic diction as it had established itself in Tennyson and Swinburne and Rossetti, and opening up for poetry the infinite varieties of colloquial and even reflective prose, so that all our voices may be heard; and at the same time freeing it from the metronomic monotony of the iamb and anapest and from the precisionism of the perfect rhyme. In the first of these they were faithful followers of Frost and Robinson and the Imagists and others among the early giants and in the second, followers of Pound and Masters and Jeffers; and in both, of their own most prestigious contemporary, Auden. Any of us who savor poetry in our day can relish the special prose tonalities that distinguish the "modern" poet. And where this is done with taste and judgment, and with some conception of what it is, along with this, that makes a poem still a poem, there is doubtless something gained. But this control is not always present; and many a poem makes its way in its little world because it is not possible to distinguish in it any principle of form whatever. (It is certainly not prose; for the distinguishing feature of prose is that it cultivates the clarifying conventions of grammar and rhetoric and always has its eye on the reader and his comfort.)

The earlier generation of poets were all more or less innovators in form and style. And this applies to the Imagists, to Lindsay, to Aiken, Millay, Wylie, to Kreymborg's *Others*, and to many more poets of merit who do not bulk so large from our point of view as those whom I have called the Founding Fathers. They were fashioning new vessels to hold the heady wine of new creativeness that poured from them. They were and felt themselves to be innovators. But they did not in large measure depend for their effect on being "different," though an exception may be noted in Pound. Even in the prefaces to Amy Lowell's anthologies of "Imagist Poets," the freedoms she sought were aimed at restoring to poetry its ancient bill of rights. There was no doubt some healthy pride felt in their originality — in what distinguished them from the tame conformism of their immediate predecessors in England and America. Some breath of the French Cénacles has reached them. But there was no conscious air of their being of different stuff than other men. They were different from other poets and thereby more likely to win a hearing from the nonliterary, as indeed they did.

With the later generation we have more the impression that they had given up hopes of reaching beyond the clientele of the *New Republic*, the *Sewanee*, the *Kenyon*, and the little reviews; and that they took what pride they could in being different from the vulgar. They had been to Paris and were exiles in Philistia. They had been admitted to the mysteries of the Muse. They were the sole keepers of the world's conscience. But the world was a mess, and they had little hope of saving it save by prayer and fasting. And so they retreated to the deserts of the Thebaid and the fastnesses of Greek mountains and carried on their rituals in monastic seclusion. And the world went on its way, built its own churches, and carried on its profane worship without benefit of clergy.

Thus we come to a point that involves both the intellectual climate of the time and the special situation of the poet; we note how much more, in the decades considered, the poet had withdrawn from the world, given up hopes of a hearing by the world, and shut himself up in his stockade of sneering isolation. This had begun long since in the Old World, in France as early as the 1840's with the artists' sense that philistinism had taken over in politics and science and in the world of the triumphant bourgeois, and that they were left stranded in their ivory towers. Their only recourse was to *épater le bourgeois*, or simply to give up any effort to communicate with the mass of men too gross in their sensibilities to take in, or care for, what the artist had to offer. The case was more acute with the poets than with painters, composers, and playwrights. For there were subsidized galleries where at length the painters could be seen and come to be appreciated, and opera and concert halls and theaters where innovators in music and drama could have a hearing. In England the cold breath of isolation came much later; not till the aesthetic nineties did the poets consciously make their retreat from the world, and there were no poets of the caliber of Baudelaire and Mallarmé to give this movement much importance. In America, still later did this social phenomenon manifest itself. Robinson and Frost, Eliot and Sandburg, Jeffers and Aiken did not think of themselves as a race apart. They wrote as men to men; and even when they introduced startling innovations in technique, they wrote in the common language of literate men, and within the framework of long-established cultural traditions. It was only Pound in those days who deliberately set himself apart from the mass of *homo vulgaris* and took for granted that good poetry is by its nature caviar to the general. (O Molière! O Shakespeare! O Milton! Pope! Keats!) Stevens certainly wore a garb "expressed in fancy," and he never found a large audience; but throughout his life he continued to use impeccable English and to shape his thought

371

fastidiously in recognizable forms. And what he had to convey in his fluid symbolism was sharply distinct and of the utmost importance to men who care to set their thoughts in a philosophical pattern in the tradition of Plato and Kant and Santayana. Stevens certainly goes far afield in his exoticism, but he makes no show of being an alien in Hartford. His main free occupation was establishing the validity of our subjective values, but he never does this at the expense of the objective world of common sense. I do not remember his indulging in petulant slurs on science. Science he takes for granted, and he makes his start from that ground.

It is in our sections on progress and science that we find many of our poets so obstinately entrenched in their antirationalism and so utterly cut off from the intellectual world in which they were born. (For in this latter part of our study we turn almost altogether from their pet words and symbols to their pet ideas and prejudices.) And here we find another clue to their isolation in the modern world, and realize how much they are cause as well as victim of this chilly state of things. Often one feels that our poets, with all their intellectual complexity, have actually fallen behind the march of mind in the modern world, and that their sophisticated distrust of the empirical method in science is actually more benighted than the simplicities and crudities of the popular trust in it.

On one point, indeed, our poets seem to be in line with popular thinking — at least as this is officially represented in all our organs of publicity. For many of them, their bulwark against corrosive science is constructive religion. But I do not think our reading public would recognize what they call religion in the puzzling shape given it by our poets. Perhaps the largest number of religious believers are fundamentalists, for whom religion is a theological system as precise and factual as science itself, and indeed a sort of supplementary science, except that it has its bases outside the world of empirical knowledge and furnishes a formula for saving their souls and securing immortality; and our poets are educated men, out of a cultural level too critical to accept this view in its integrity. Another great segment of believers, especially numerous in Europe and the American North, is made up of those for whom the Church is an instrumentality for preserving conventional morality, and the general structure of our mores, and keeping family and society in a healthy condition, based on some loosely conceived notion of deity, and often accompanied by some vague hope of a life after death. These people are for the most part better educated and culturally more congenial; but, from our poets' point of view, they are decidedly tainted with utilitarian and humanitarian assumptions. They are inclined to think that sin is preventable by right conditioning and that vice may be reduced with the help of social agencies and the elimination of poverty and injustice. With them the mythological element in religion approaches the vanishing point as the "scientific" spirit gains ground. They are, of course, "against sin"; but their emphasis is on the cultivation of the good life. The poets are uncomfortably hung up between the theological scientism of the fundamentalists and the sociological scientism of the more liberal churches. The fundamentalists at least retain their naive faith in the devil; and while that is a little too crude for the poets, it does serve with the vulgar the same function as the poets' myth of metaphysical evil. And any myth is for the poets better than no myth. For they labor under the notion that mythology is the life-breath of poetry.

It may be true that mythology is the life-breath of poetry, in the sense that symbolism has more appeal to the imagination than verbal abstractions. But no mythology can long be very effective with the reader of poetry unless the symbols used connote something valid for the feelings, and for the mind too if the mind is involved; and the mind must be somehow involved if the feelings are to take it seriously. At the present moment most potential readers of poetry are scientific-minded. And our poets necessarily cut themselves off from their most promising audience if they do nothing but sneer at the current processes of thinking.

There is a large and growing body of thoughtful persons who, in the United States, often call themselves humanists. They are distinguished from religious believers by their shift of emphasis from speculative opinions on the origin and ultimate nature of the universe to the cultivation and pursuit of so much of good living as is ideally conceivable for human beings in the world as we find it. They agree with science that, in the absence of empirical evidence, nothing can be predicated as to the ultimate moral nature of the universe. They agree with religion that man's salvation is to be found in ideal values; but they have given up the notion of religious believers that no good is possible for man except in terms of a supernatural will and sanction.

One might expect that the humanists' devotion to the ideal would commend them to poets; but in the present state of the poetic mentality this is rarely the case. Our poets for the most part are not tough-minded enough to bear the thought of an idealism not guaranteed by powers outside of humanity itself. This is, I suppose, a symptom of that strain of the childlike which has so often been pointed out as the peculiar merit and charm of the poetic temperament. But it is also associated with the realism, often amounting to cynicism, which characterizes American poetry of our day. They have lived through a period of catastrophic wars and economic distress unparalleled since the time of Napoleon, perhaps even since the religious wars of the sixteenth century. Not too well read in history, they are apt to think that our times are peculiarly agonizing, and that diabolism is now more active in human society than in the good old days. With some of them the troubles of the public world have been doubled by psychological conflicts and disturbances in their private life; normal family life has been denied them; and suicide, alcoholism, and other forms of alienation have testified to their loss of nerve. These things may be as common in other social groups; but they are peculiarly noticeable and of public concern when they are found in those who are known by their verbal utterance.

I do not wish for a moment, in these critical animadversions, to urge any touch of censorship on the free expression of opinions and feelings about the world — whether it be Aiken's reduction of the human experience to an amoral process of atomic combination and decomposition, or Tate's desperate clinging to evil as the sole guarantee of spiritual salvation, or Jeffers' aristocratic preference of nonhuman to human phenomena, or Cummings' relegation to inexistence of "mostpeople" because they are incapable of the poet's special brand of "love." What I mean to suggest is simply that our poets are not in a position to complain of the philistine insensitiveness of the public so long as they represent so meagerly the concerns, the attitudes, the joys and exultances, the agonies and aspirations, the disenchantments and the braveries of the great mass of the population — including most of those who read books, trust to scientific method for the solution of scientific problems, enjoy driving cars and planes and monkeying with machines, prefer comfort to discomfort, see many evidences of progress in the material world and in the world of human relations, accept their responsibilities in family life and take some pleasure in them, try to keep their vicious propensities under control, but think more of the good life they aim at than of the devil they dodge, and maintain some measure of what used to be called "faith in humanity."

As for the moral terrors, the mental anguish or "anxiety," which seemed to so many poets the dominant feature of the modern world, these are seemingly confirmed by statistical evidence from our mental hospitals. And it is not unnatural to assume that this widespread state of mind has been intensified by political and economic conditions in the twentieth century and by the widespread loss of faith in the supernatural. But even here it is doubtful whether the common run of men, intellectuals and nonintellectuals, would find themselves at home in the macabre moral scenery and atmosphere to which our poets have invited them. All men are conscious of the material dangers that beset them in the modern world. The fear of economic collapse and poverty has been all-pervasive, even in America, since the end of World War I. The imminence of war presents all persons of military age with the fear of death or disablement and their dependents with the fear of penury and widowhood. Since the development of atomic weapons, everyone is aware that whole populations are in constant peril of annihilation, and that we may actually be on the verge of Armageddon. But these are not, for the average citizen, moral fears. They are in the same category with automobile accidents, the sinking of ships at sea, the threat of cancer, cerebral hemorrhage, or heart failure. There are special anxieties peculiar to women in our day with their entrance into occupations outside the home, the uncertainty as to the natural functions of women and their proper relations with men, the sense so many of them have that personal dignity requires them to distinguish themselves in public life. And here certainly we have the fears and frustrations and conflicts that come from a divided mind and an uncertain conscience. But even these are not readily associated with the religious sense of guilt that our poets so much feature.

As for the religious sense of guilt, that is certainly largely present with us, but one does not see why it should be regarded as a peculiar feature of our times; it has been a leading feature of Christian civilization from the time of St. Paul down through Calvin and Billy Graham.

BIBLIOGRAPHY AND INDEX

◄§ *VOLUMES CITED IN THE TEXT*

Agee, James. *Permit Me Voyage*. New Haven, Conn.: Yale University Press, 1934.

Aiken, Conrad. *Preludes for Memnon*. New York: Scribner, 1931.

Auden, W. H. *Poems*. London: Faber and Faber, 1930, 1933.

———. *The Orators: An English Study*. London: Faber and Faber, 1932.

———. *Look, Stranger!* London: Faber and Faber, 1936.

———. "The Traveller," *New Statesman and Nation*, 16:314 (August 27, 1938).

———. *Another Time*. New York: Random House, 1940.

———. *The Double Man*. New York: Random House, 1941.

———. *The Collected Poetry of W. H. Auden*. New York: Random House, 1945.

———. *The Age of Anxiety*. New York: Random House, 1947.

———. "Sonnet," *Listener*, 20:943 (November 3, 1938).

———. *Nones*. New York: Random House, 1951.

Auden, W. H., and Christopher Isherwood. *The Dog beneath the Skin, or Where Is Francis?* New York: Random House, 1935.

———. *The Ascent of F6. A Tragedy in Two Acts*. New York: Random House, 1937.

———. *On the Frontier. A Melodrama in Three Acts*. New York: Random House, 1938.

———. *Journey to a War*. New York: Random House, 1939.

Auden, W. H., and Louis MacNeice. *Letters from Iceland*. London: Faber and Faber, 1937.

Baker, Howard. *A Letter from the Country and Other Poems*. Norfolk, Conn.: New Directions, 1941.

Barker, George. *Selected Poems*. New York: Macmillan, 1941.

Benét, Stephen Vincent. *Nightmare at Noon*. New York: Farrar and Rinehart, 1940.

Berryman, John. *Poems*. Norfolk, Conn.: New Directions, 1942.

———. *The Dispossessed*. New York: William Sloane Associates, 1948.

Bishop, John Peale. *Now with His Love*. New York and London: Scribner, 1933.

Bottrall, Ronald. *Farewell and Welcome*. London: Editions Poetry, 1945.

Brinnin, John Malcolm. *The Lincoln Lyrics*. Norfolk, Conn.: New Directions, 1942.

———. *The Garden Is Political*. New York: Macmillan, 1942.

———. *No Arch, No Triumph*. New York: Knopf, 1945.

————. *The Sorrows of Cold Stone. Poems 1940–1950.* New York: Dodd, 1951.

Chisholm, Hugh. *The Prodigal Never Returns.* New York: Farrar, Straus, 1947.

Ciardi, John. *Other Skies.* Boston: Little, Brown, 1947.

————, ed. *Mid-Century American Poets.* New York: Twayne, 1950.

Conrad, Joseph. "Heart of Darkness," *Youth and Two Other Stories.* Garden City, N.Y.: Doubleday, 1903.

Cowley, Malcolm. *Exile's Return. A Narrative of Ideas.* New York: Norton, 1934.

Crane, Hart. *White Buildings: Poems by Hart Crane.* New York: Liveright, 1926.

Cummings, E. E. *No Thanks.* New York: Golden Eagle Press, 1935.

————. *Fifty Poems.* New York: Duell, Sloan, 1940.

————. *One Times One.* New York: Holt, 1944.

————. *Poems 1923–1954.* New York: Harcourt, 1954.

Day-Lewis, C. *Short Is the Time. Poems 1936–1943.* New York: Oxford, 1945.

Eberhart, Richard. *Song and Idea.* London: Chatto, 1940.

Eliot, T. S. *Poems.* New York: Knopf, 1920.

————. *The Waste Land.* New York: Boni and Liveright, 1922.

————. *Murder in the Cathedral.* London: Faber and Faber, 1935.

————. *Collected Poems 1909–1935.* New York: Harcourt, 1936.

————. *East Coker.* London: Faber and Faber, 1940.

————. *Dry Salvages.* London: Faber and Faber, 1941.

————. *Four Quartets.* New York: Harcourt, 1943.

Engle, Paul. *American Song.* Garden City, N.Y.: Doubleday, 1934.

Fearing, Kenneth. *Collected Poems of Kenneth Fearing.* New York, Random House, 1940.

————. *Afternoon of a Pawnbroker and Other Poems.* New York: Harcourt, 1943.

————. *Stranger at Coney Island and Other Poems.* New York: Harcourt, 1948.

Fitzgerald, Robert. *A Wreath for the Sea.* Norfolk, Conn.: New Directions, 1943.

Five Young American Poets. 1st series, Norfolk, Conn.: New Directions, 1940. 2nd series, 1941. 3rd series, 1944.

Friar, Kimon, and John Malcolm Brinnin, eds. *Modern Poetry: American and British.* New York: Appleton-Century-Crofts, 1951.

Garrigue, Jean. In *Five Young American Poets.* 3rd series, Norfolk, Conn.: New Directions, 1944.

————. *The Ego and the Centaur.* Norfolk, Conn.: New Directions, 1947.

Gregory, Horace. *No Retreat.* New York: Harcourt, 1933.

————. *Chorus for Survival.* New York: Covici, 1935.

————. *Poems 1930–1940.* New York: Harcourt, 1941.

————. *Selected Poems of Horace Gregory.* New York: Viking, 1951.

Hayes, Alfred. *The Big Time.* New York: Howell, Soskin, 1944.

————. *Welcome to the Castle.* New York: Harper, 1950.

James, Henry. "The Beast in the Jungle," *The Better Sort.* New York: Scribner, 1914 ed.

Jarrell, Randall. *Blood for a Stranger.* New York: Harcourt, 1942.

Joyce, James. *Exiles.* New York: Viking, 1951.

Kees, Weldon. *The Fall of the Magicians.* New York: Reynal, 1947.

MacLeish, Archibald. *The Hamlet of A. MacLeish*. Boston and New York: Houghton Mifflin, 1928.

———. *Poems 1924–1933*. Boston: Houghton Mifflin, 1933.

———. *Actfive and Other Poems*. New York: Random House, 1948.

———. *Collected Poems, 1917–1952*. Boston, Houghton Mifflin, 1952.

MacNeice, Louis. *Poems*. New York: Random House, 1937.

———. *The Dark Tower and Other Radio Scripts*. London: Faber and Faber, 1947.

Meredith, William. *Love Letter from an Impossible Land*. New Haven, Conn.: Yale University Press, 1944.

———. *Ships and Other Figures*. Princeton, N.J.: Princeton University Press, 1948.

Merton, Thomas. *A Man in the Divided Sea*. Norfolk, Conn.: New Directions, 1946.

Merwin, W. S. *The Dancing Bears*. New Haven, Conn.: Yale University Press, 1954.

Moore, Marianne. *Selected Poems*. London: Faber and Faber, 1935.

———. *Nevertheless*. New York: Macmillan, 1944.

Moss, Howard. *A Swimmer in the Air*. New York: Scribner, 1957.

Nemerov, Howard. *The Image and the Law*. New York: Holt, 1947.

———. *Guide to the Ruins*. New York: Random House, 1950.

Owen, Wilfred. *Poems by Wilfred Owen*. London: Chatto, 1921.

———. *The Poems of Wilfred Owen*, ed. Edmund Blunden. London: Chatto, 1952.

Patchen, Kenneth. *Before the Brave*. New York: Random House, 1936.

———. *First Will & Testament*. Norfolk, Conn.: New Directions, 1939.

———. *The Selected Poems of Kenneth Patchen*. New York: New Directions, 1946.

Perse, St.-J. *Anabasis*, with a translation into English by T. S. Eliot. London: Faber and Faber, 1930.

———. *Exile and Other Poems*, trans. Denis Devlin. New York: Pantheon, 1949.

Prokosch, Frederic. *The Asiatics*. New York: Harper, 1935. Reissued, New York: The Press of the Readers Club, 1941.

———. *The Assassins*. London: Chatto, 1936.

———. *The Seven Who Fled*. New York and London: Harper, 1937.

———. *The Carnival*. London: Chatto, 1938.

———. *Death at Sea*. New York and London: Harper, 1940.

Rexroth, Kenneth. *In What Hour*. New York: Macmillan, 1940.

———. *The Phoenix and the Tortoise*. Norfolk, Conn.: New Directions, 1944.

———. *The Dragon and the Unicorn*. Norfolk, Conn.: New Directions, 1952.

———, ed. *The New British Poets*. Norfolk, Conn.: New Directions, 1949.

Rukeyser, Muriel. *Theory of Flight*. New Haven, Conn.: Yale University Press, 1935.

———. *The Green Wave*. Garden City, N.Y.: Doubleday, 1948.

Shapiro, Karl. *Trial of a Poet*. New York: Reynal, 1947.

Spender, Stephen. *Vienna*. New York: Random House, 1935.

———. *The Still Centre*. London: Faber and Faber, 1939.

———. *Ruins and Visions. Poems 1934–1942*. New York: Random House, 1942.

Stevens, Wallace. *Parts of a World*. New York: Knopf, 1942.

———. *Transport to Summer*. New York: Knopf, 1947.

———. *The Auroras of Autumn.* New York: Knopf, 1950.

Tate, Allen. *Poems 1928–1931.* New York: Scribner, 1932.

Untermeyer, Louis, ed. *Modern American Poetry. Modern British Poetry* (combined edition). New York: Harcourt, 1942.

Van Duyn, Mona. "Death by Aesthetics," *Poetry*, 83:207–209 (January 1954). Reprinted in *Valentines to the Wide World.* The Cummington Press, 1959.

Viereck, Peter. *Strike through the Mask!* New York: Scribner, 1950.

Warren, Robert Penn. *Thirty-Six Poems.* New York: Alcestis Press, 1935.

———. *Eleven Poems on the Same Theme.* Norfolk, Conn.: New Directions, 1942.

———. *Selected Poems 1923–1943.* New York: Harcourt, 1944.

Wilbur, Richard. *Ceremony and Other Poems.* New York: Harcourt, 1950.

Williams, Oscar. ed. *New Poems: 1944. An Anthology of American and British Verse.* New York: Howell, Soskin, 1944.

Yeats, W. B. *The Collected Poems of W. B. Yeats.* New York: Macmillan, 1934.

INDEX

"Spain 1937," 114, 226
"Speaking of Poetry," 5, 9
Spears, Monroe K., 106, 107, 116, 117
Spencer, Theodore, use of phoenix image, 353
Spender, Stephen, 51, 54, 83, 86, 120, 156, 181, 251: use of tiger symbol, 28–32; style, 31, 148–150; theme of fear, 78–79, 124; use of island symbol, 123–125, 126; concept of exile, 143, 150–151; concept of hero, 227; use of crocus symbol, 348, 349
Spenser, Edmund, 320, 322
"Spinning Heart, The," 102
Spinoza, Baruch, 293, 312, 313, 321, 322, 325
"Spring Is a Long Time," 349
Stein, Gertrude, 242
Stevens, Wallace, 102, 212, 368, 369: use of *definition*, 95–96; concept of hero, 96, 209–213; use of island symbol, 132–133; style, 210, 211, 213, 340, 371; and innocence, 338–340
Stevenson, Robert Louis, 293
Still Centre, The, 124, 148
"Still Life," 262
"Strange Meeting," 29
Stranger, use of image: by Auden, 145; by Jarrell, 177, 178–180; by Garrigue, 192, 193; by Fearing, 247. *See also* Exile
"Stranger, The," 193
Stranger at Coney Island and Other Poems, 247
Strike through the Mask!, 275, 301
"Strings' excitement, The," 4, 26
"Structure of the Plane, The," 255
Style, and poetic art, 12–18, 143, 366–372: Berryman, 8, 86–87, 135, 178; Auden, 14, 27–28, 35, 47, 55, 145, 189, 200, 220, 221–222, 269, 272; Yeats, 17; Spender, 31, 148–150; Aiken, 62, 68; Gregory, 71–72, 76; Pound, 72; Eliot, 76, 268; Chisholm, 81–82, 272–273; Warren, 90–91, 93, 95, 217–218, 315, 316, 320, 324, 329–330; Brinnin, 100, 101, 102, 134, 135, 138, 166, 333; Mac-Leish, 100, 186, 206–207, 231–232, 238; Nemerov, 102; Perse, 175; Jarrell, 178, 179, 181–182; Crane, 190, 256; Shapiro, 192; Garrigue, 193; Mac-Neice, 193–194; Stevens, 210, 211,

213, 340, 371; Cummings, 242; Fearing, 243, 248–249, 336; Benét, 250; Patchen, 250–253; Fitzgerald, 252; Rukeyser, 256–257; Rexroth, 259; Kees, 262; Van Duyn, 299; Prokosch, 319–320; Tate, 320; Hayes, 336
Sun Also Rises, The, 12
Swimmer in the Air, A, 10
Swinburne, Algernon, 369
Synesthesia, 17

Tate, Allen, 51, 69, 374: and fear, 45–46; style, 320
Tennyson, Alfred, 240, 289, 369
Terror, use of theme, 375–376: in Eliot, 25–26, 44–45, 94; in Auden, 46–47, 49, 58–59, 79; in Prokosch, 58–59, 77–78; in Aiken, 62–69; in Spender, 79, 124; in Day-Lewis, 79, in Chisholm, 80–82, 142; in Warren, 95, 97. *See also* Fear
"Terror," 93, 96, 97, 216, 321
"Testamentary," 252
Thackeray, William Makepeace, 273
Theory of Flight, 254, 257, 351
Theory of the Leisure Class, 303
"Third Temptation, The," 163
Thirty-Six Poems, 96
"This Place in the Ways," 255
"This Voyaging," 139, 192
Thomas, Dylan, 222
Thompson, Francis, 269, 327
Tiger, use of symbol, 19, 20, 365; by Eliot, 20, 23, 24, 32; by James, 25, 32; by De Quincey, 25, 42; by Wilbur, 25–26; by Auden, 26–28, 33–36; by Spender, 28–32; by Owen, 29; by Blake, 32; by Prokosch, 32–33; by Hayes, 36–41
Tillyard, E. M. W., 7, 14–15, 150
Time and eternity, concept of, 282: in Warren, 89, 316, 321–322, 324–327; in Jarrell, 180; in Cummings, 290. *See also* Eternity
"Tintern Abbey," 276, 322
"To a Friend Gone to Fight for the Kuomintang," 230, 286
"To Carthage then I came," 13
"To My Pupils," 27, 47, 140, 196
"Toccata of Gallupi's, A," 75
"Tragedians, The," 54, 58, 129
transition (magazine), 156, 170

394

Waste Land, The, 13, 24, 32, 38, 39, 40, 44, 49, 72, 73, 110, 172, 185, 195, 247, 268, 314

Water, use of symbol: by Auden, 105, 113, 145, 163; by MacLeish, 113, 185, 186, 187; by Eliot, 113

"Way, The," 189

Welcome to the Castle, 36, 40, 60, 164, 241, 260, 263, 336, 337, 346

"When You and I Were All," 182

White Buildings, 119, 190

"White Collar Ballad," 230

Whitman, Walt, 69, 70, 71, 249, 254, 257, 287, 332, 335

Wilbur, Richard: use of *ceremony,* 9–10; use of tiger symbol, 19, 25, 26

Williams, Oscar, 353, 366

Williams, William Carlos, 369

Wings of the Dove, The, 43

"Winner Take All," 244

Wordsworth, William, 28, 147, 253, 269, 293, 322: poetic diction, 15–16; attitude toward science, 275–276

"World Is a Wedding, The," 5, 82

World War I, 69, 147, 172, 183, 208, 218, 232, 375

World War II, 17, 83, 114, 131, 147, 172, 228, 232, 284, 368

World War III, 250

Wreath for the Sea, A, 252

Wylie, Elinor, 370

"Xantha Street," 262

Xenophon, 182, 210

Yeats, W. B., 331: use of *ceremony,* 3–12 *passim,* 334, 335; style, 17

"You, Horse," 285, 305, 345

Zaharoff, Sir Basil, 32